THE GREAT COLD WAR

THE GREAT COLD WAR

A Journey Through the Hall of Mirrors

GORDON S. BARRASS

STANFORD SECURITY STUDIES

An Imprint of Stanford University Press

Stanford, California 2009

Stanford University Press
Stanford, California

Library of Congress Cataloging-in-Publication Data

Barrass, Gordon S.
The great Cold War : a journey through the hall of mirrors / Gordon S. Barrass.
p. cm.
Includes bibliographical references and index.
ISBN 978-0-8047-6064-5 (cloth : alk. paper)
1. Cold War. 2. United States—Foreign relations—Soviet Union. 3. Soviet Union—Foreign relations—United States. I. Title.
D843.B257 2009
909.82'5—dc22

2008032384

Printed in the United States of America on acid-free, archival-quality paper. Typeset at Stanford University Press in 10/14 Minion.

This book is dedicated to two of my friends who contributed to a peaceful ending of the Cold War,
ANDREW MARSHALL *and* ANATOLY CHERNYAEV

Contents

Acknowledgments

I am particularly grateful to a number of friends who have given me wise counsel and much help as I have developed this book—Rodric Braithwaite, Percy Cradock, Fritz Ermarth, Benjamin B. Fischer, James Hershberg, Maureen Lippincott, Douglas MacEachin, Bridget Smith and Arne Westad.

Besides the people I interviewed at length for this book, who are mentioned in the Sources on pages 451–57, there are several others whose help I have greatly appreciated: David Armstrong, Mie Augier, Simon Blundell, Bryan Cartledge, Taylor Downing, David Dunn, Lawrence Freedman, Rosemary Hale, Beatrice Heuser, Curtis Keeble, Mark Kramer, Robert Legvold, David Manning, Vojtech Mastny, Ernest May, Stephen Mayer, Michael McCGwire, Timothy Naftali, Uwe Nerlich, Robert Norris, Christian Ostermann, Clare Parkinson, Richard Pipes, Michael Ploetz, Stephen Rearden, Svetlana Savranskaya, Bernd Schaefer, Mary Soames, William Taubman, Natalia Yegorova and Tatiana Zhukhova.

The staff at Stanford University Press deserve my special thanks. Since our first contact, Geoffrey Burn, the director, has been immensely enthusiastic, supportive and considerate, as have his assistant Jessica Walsh and my editor John Feneron. They are a team I have really enjoyed working with.

There is no one, however, to whom I am more indebted than to Kristen Lippincott, my wife, who over several years has with affectionate persistence encouraged me to write this book, and shown boundless tact and good humor while doing so.

THE GREAT COLD WAR

Prologue

Cold Sweat

Just past midnight on September 26, 1983, Lieutenant-Colonel Stanislav Petrov settled into a chair in a secret bunker hidden deep beneath the woods some fifty kilometers outside of Moscow. Petrov was the duty commander in charge of monitoring the Soviet early-warning satellites positioned to detect an American missile attack.

The one hundred and twenty people working with Petrov that night were on tenterhooks as military tensions between the Soviets and the Americans had not run so high since the peak of the Cuban Missile Crisis, twenty-one years earlier. After Reagan became president in 1981, the Americans had been attempting to systematically undermine Soviet confidence in their own defenses. Moscow had raised tensions even higher in early September 1983 by shooting down a Korean passenger aircraft that had inadvertently entered Soviet airspace. And in just two months' time, the Americans would begin deploying in Germany their new Pershing-II missiles, which many Soviet experts believed could reach targets in Moscow in around ten minutes, thus denying the Soviet leadership any chance of retaliating.

At 00.40, the alarms roared into action. "For 15 seconds," Petrov later recalled, "we were all in a state of shock." On the panel in front of him, the word "Launch" pulsed in red letters. For the next few minutes, one of the satellites reported the launch of one missile after another—five missiles in total, all heading towards the Soviet Union. Suddenly, the warning flashing in front of Petrov's eyes read "Missile Attack."

Automatically, this information had been flashed to the top military commanders, the chiefs of the Soviet General Staff. Petrov now had seven minutes to verify whether the attack was real, as that would leave just enough time for Yuri Andropov, the Soviet leader who was on a dialysis machine in a Moscow sanatorium, to order Soviet missiles to be launched against America. Under enormous strain, Petrov and his staff raced to complete the technical cross-checks in hopes of finding that it was a false alarm. To their horror, everything they checked confirmed that an attack had begun.

Petrov should now have pressed the button in front of him to confirm to Andropov that an attack was underway. But he did not do so. "I had a funny feeling in my gut," Petrov recalled years later. "I didn't want to make a mistake." He was certain that the Americans would never attack with just five missiles and suspicious that the Soviet ground-based radars had not detected them ten minutes later as they should have done. "I declared that it was a false alarm, but I did not know for sure."

Months later, Soviet investigators determined that bursts of sunlight reflecting off clouds above Montana had caused a faulty satellite computer to report the missile launches. This incident remained secret for another fifteen years.[1]

We can't know for certain what the Soviet response would have been had Petrov not declared the false alarm. Andropov was dead within six months of this event, and other high-ranking people who would have been involved in a decision to launch a retaliatory strike died not long thereafter. How close the world was to an accidental nuclear war, then and in the weeks that followed, remains a hotly debated issue. What is clear, however, is that this was just one of several incidents during the Cold War that might have triggered a nuclear conflict.

Despite the fact that the United States and the Soviet Union never engaged in direct military conflict, the Cold War was much more serious than most people imagine. It was a toxic mix of history, ideology, geography and strategy. There was, however, no real equivalence between the two systems. The Soviet Union had soon overwhelmed the idealism of communism with violence, oppression and lies. The Cold War was a struggle, not a game of chess, though certain episodes might give that impression.

Both the Soviets and the Americans were extraordinarily innovative in developing weapons and designing strategies meant to "deter" the other side—spurring the most intense and costly arms race in history. In Europe, the casualties of the Cold War were relatively low, and number in the thousands—but millions of people died in related conflicts elsewhere: Korea, Vietnam, Afghanistan, Africa and Central America. It was not just a war of military confrontation, but one fought on many fronts—ideology, economics, culture and espionage. In many respects it was "The Great Cold War."

One reason the true gravity of this period is not more widely appreciated is that few people on either side had the full picture. In 1994, Zbigniew Brzezinski, President Carter's national security adviser, explained: "From the Cuban Missile Crisis of 1962 through until the confrontation over Euro-missiles began in the late seventies, most people did not expect war to break out between the Soviet Union and the United States. It was those who knew most about the rivalry who were the most concerned." [2]

A New Look

Yet even those "who knew most" had a less than perfect understanding of what was happening.

During the last years of the Cold War, I was Chief of the Assessments Staff in the Cabinet Office in London and, as such, a member of the Joint Intelligence Committee of the Cabinet (the JIC). Every week, the JIC brought together the most senior people responsible for the collection and assessment of intelligence, along with those dealing with policy on foreign affairs, defense and security etc. Using the intelligence we had, the Assessments Staff drafted the papers that, after discussion at the JIC, were then sent to the prime minister, members of the government and senior officials.[3] We often had reliable information about what the Russians had done, but at times we were not sure of their motivation.

When I joined the Diplomatic Service in the mid-sixties, the Cold War dominated international affairs. In trying to figure out what was going on, I sometimes felt as though I were in a hall of mirrors, where nothing was quite what it seemed to be. The revelations that have emerged over the past two decades—from the opening of previously locked archives, the declassification of documents and the publication of memoirs—have shown that this was, in fact, often the case. That is why the subtitle of this book is *A Journey Through the Hall of Mirrors.*

The details now available about key meetings at both the Kremlin and the White House, for example, have made it possible for us to have a more complete and balanced picture of how the two sides viewed each other, and of the complex mix of factors that led them into the Cold War and eventually out of it. The new material has also made it easier to address the three big questions that need to be considered in examining any long confrontation: "Why did it start?" "Why did it last as long as it did?" and "Why did it end the way it did?"

I also wanted to explore several strategic issues. For example, why, by the mid-eighties, had the two sides amassed between them over 60,000 nuclear warheads and in Europe more powerful conventional forces than at any time since the end of the Second World War? What determined how far each side was willing to go to try to win the Cold War? Why did it take so long for the Soviet Union to realize how fundamentally weak it was and, on the other side, for the far richer and far more technologically advanced United States to grasp how strong it was? And, finally, what impact did secret intelligence have on the development and ending of the Cold War?

To begin to answer these questions, I traveled to Washington, Paris, Brussels, Berlin, Warsaw and Moscow to interview nearly a hundred people who were involved in the events that transpired between the forties and the end of 1991. They included top policy makers, strategists, military commanders and key figures in the world of intelligence. Together these interviews provided some eye-opening accounts of what was going on behind the scenes, as well as many valuable insights into the mixture of insecurity, ignorance and ambition that drove the rivalry between the two opposing forces.

The interviews I conducted with those on the "Eastern side" of the conflict made clear the extent to which the harrowing experiences of many Easterners during the Second World War and its aftermath shaped their outlook on the world, and defined the roles they would play within their own countries. It was a reminder to those of us who have grown up in open societies not to be too hasty in judging those who have not. Within the communist regimes, there were sane and moral people who wisely kept their true thoughts to themselves, until an opportunity for greater honesty presented itself.

Entering the Hall

As I embarked on this project, I discussed it at some length with my friend Ernst Gombrich, a renowned art historian. During the Second World War, Ernst had shown a flair for "getting inside the mind" of the Germans through their radio broadcasts, which he and others were helping the British government monitor from a manor house in the English countryside.

In later years, Ernst would often remind his students: "When you look at a painting, the question you should be asking is not whether you like it or not, but 'What was the artist trying to do and why did he do it that way?'" Because of his fascination with perception, he liked the idea of a book that tries to envision how both sides saw things.

"When did the Cold War begin?" Ernst asked. "Do you think it started in '47 or with the Bolshevik Revolution of 1917?"

"Nineteen seventeen," I replied, "but if you really want to understand what happened, I think, you need to look back much further. But should it be to 1847, the year before Karl Marx launched his *Communist Manifesto*; or 1747, as events began to unfold towards the first clash of arms for centuries between Russians and the Germans; or even a century earlier, to 1647—when the views of the Puritans were beginning to shape America and Russian explorers of the new Romanov dynasty had reached as far as the Pacific?"

"Go for 1647!" Ernst said. "Over a period of three hundred years the main trends can be seen more clearly; so too can the influence of geography." His response was not unexpected. Over sixty years earlier he had written *A Little History of the World*, a fine children's book that is still educating many adults—and not only when they are reading it to their children at bed-time.

Although it is widely believed that the Cold War can be understood by starting the story after the Second World War, I think Gombrich was right—and so this book begins by looking briefly at those earlier years. It is here that we see some of the prominent features of the Cold War begin to emerge.

As we track the evolution of the Cold War through to its end, I believe we should bear in mind President Kennedy's warning to graduates of Yale in 1962:

> For the great enemy of truth is very often not the lie—deliberate, contrived and dishonest—but the myth—persistent, persuasive, and unrealistic. Too often we hold fast to the clichés of our forebears. We subject all facts to a prefabricated set of interpretations. We enjoy the comfort of opinion without the discomfort of thought. Mythology distracts us everywhere—in government as in business, in politics as in economics, in foreign affairs as in domestic affairs.[4]

I mention this because a number of myths now surround the history of the Great Cold War: the assumption that the Soviet Union posed no real threat to the West; the belief that détente could have worked; the idea that the West prevailed because America was strong, its people united and its allies supportive; that the Soviet collapse had nothing to do with outside pressure; and that the real lesson of the Cold War is that victory was achieved by Reagan's toughness, with Gorbachev's contribution being of far less significance.

These myths need to be looked at carefully because they are dangerous. They not only distort history; they also distort the lessons to be learned from it. And while the Cold War was in many respects unique, those lessons have tremendous relevance to the issues we face in the 21st century.

Why Did It Start?

FROM RUSSIAN RIVER TO THE ELBE

Tsar Alexander I leads his troops though Paris, accompanied by King Frederick William of Prussia, March 31, 1814. (By Jean Zipper. Musée Carnavalet, Paris)

1 Soaring Eagles

Worlds Apart

Because the rivalry between Russia and America became clear long before the Bolshevik Revolution of 1917, it is useful to look back a little further into each country's history in order to see the origins of the tension.

Russia had been built up by autocratic tsars, who ruled through a highly centralized regime backed by the Orthodox Church. Since the collapse of Byzantium in 1453, Moscow believed it had become the "Third Rome," with a God-given destiny to gather the peoples of the world to the Orthodox faith.

The national symbol was the double-headed eagle of Byzantium, with one head supposedly looking back to ancient Rome and the other looking forward from the new one. At the end of the 15th century, Italian engineers were to strengthen the fortifications of the Kremlin and to build the Faceted Hall, which was modeled on one of the most admired Italian palaces of the day—the Palazzo Diamante in Ferrara.

At the end of the 17th century, Peter the Great set about modernizing Russia with extraordinary determination. He created St. Petersburg, his splendid new capital on the shores of the Baltic, to symbolize Russia's growing involvement in Europe. By 1758, there had been the first clash of arms in centuries between the Russians and the Germans, with Russian troops advancing close to Berlin; twelve years later, Catherine the Great ordered the most dramatic military move Russia had yet made—sending its navy into the Mediterranean to destroy the Turkish fleet.

At the turn of the century, the Russians moved much farther westwards, battling against the armies of revolutionary France in Italy and Switzerland. The biggest battle began in 1812, when Napoleon invaded Russia, and within a year he had lost most of his massive army of half a million men. In 1814, Tsar Alexander I led his victorious troops through Paris, along with those of his Prussian and

Austrian allies. While Alexander went on to London, where he was treated as the hero who had liberated Europe, his troops made their way home.

After Napoleon's final defeat at Waterloo in 1815, Tsar Alexander had a major voice at the Congress of Vienna, which shaped the political geography of Europe for the next hundred years. After the trauma of the Napoleonic wars, Alexander hoped it would be possible to create a new Russian identity that would enable the country to have a greater say in European affairs through the establishment of a European confederation, without undermining the stability of Russia itself. Alexander failed to achieve that goal, but he did gain control over much more of Poland, which he believed would provide a forward line of defense in central Europe.

As the 19th century progressed, Russia's former allies began to fear its imperial ambitions. To the south, the Russians were pushing the Ottoman Turks back through the Balkans in the hope of gaining control of the Turkish Straits, which linked the Black Sea with the Mediterranean. At the same time, their advances into Central Asia alarmed the British, who believed that the Russians were intent on gaining a warm-water port on the Indian Ocean. They jostled with the British for influence in Afghanistan, whose king was given a truly imperial welcome to St. Petersburg in 1905.

All the while America, too, was developing its own distinctive identity. The Puritans who arrived in Massachusetts Bay in the early 17th century brought with them a revolutionary mix of ardent beliefs, not simply about religion, but about politics, economics and society as well. They believed their task was to create a New Jerusalem and then take their "shining example" to the rest of the world.

By the end of the next century, through the War of Independence with Britain and much heated debate over the drafting of the Constitution, the Americans had accomplished the first great political revolution of the modern age. They had paved the way for the establishment of a new political system based on the aspirations of freedom and liberty.

The new republic expanded westwards with remarkable speed and under its emblem of the bald eagle, whose great strength was seen as symbolizing the American ideal of freedom. Unfortunately, the Founding Fathers and many other members of the political elite owned cotton and sugar plantations, which were the major source of their wealth. Although slavery was legally abolished in 1865, after a bloody Civil War, problems over racial equality would continue to blight America's reputation for well over another century.

Getting Closer

A century after Russia's intrepid explorers reached the Pacific in 1647, they laid claim to Alaska. Then, in the 18th century, the Russians began establishing a few trading posts along the Pacific coast. The post furthest to the south was opened in 1812, at the mouth of a river, still known as the Russian River, in what is now northern California.[1]

Even though the United States only stretched as far west as the Mississippi, there was already a growing sentiment that the nation's "manifest destiny" was to extend its territory to the Pacific. With it grew the belief that the Americans were entitled to have all of North and South America within their sphere of influence. In 1823, President Monroe proclaimed that the Americas were "henceforth not to be considered as subjects for future colonization by any European powers . . . ," and this new policy immediately became known as the Monroe Doctrine.

The first country to be formally warned-off was Russia, which two years earlier had banned foreigners from Alaska, where it was preparing to commercially exploit the land it claimed. Despite this problem, Russia and the United States remained fairly friendly, reflecting their shared wish to keep Britain and France in check. The high point of this period came in 1867, when Russia decided that it was too difficult to sustain the development of Alaska and amicably sold it to the United States.

As the United States consolidated its hold across the continent, immigrants poured in, and its population grew larger than that of any European state other than Russia, in addition to which it had developed a strong and stable republican government. It had also just become the world's largest industrial nation. Trade and investment were booming in Latin America, and the annexation of Hawaii in 1898 had provided a stepping-stone across the Pacific that would make it easier to promote American business interests in Asia.

The United States embarked on its first overseas war in 1898, putting an end to Spain's savage efforts to retain control over Cuba, Puerto Rico, the Philippines and Guam—Spain's remaining colonial possessions in the Caribbean and the Pacific. The success of this venture reaffirmed the widely held American belief that the United States had the moral authority to be the advanced-guard of a new civilization. The following year, Rudyard Kipling wrote his memorable poem "The White Man's Burden," explaining to Americans that building empires was a long and costly process.

As the 19th century came to a close, American and Russian commercial

Europe in 1914

interests were coming into conflict in China, where the government was weakening year by year. The Americans wanted free trade, whereas the Russians were more interested in gaining control over the northeastern province of Manchuria, with its rich resources and warm-water ports on the edge of the Pacific. As the United States hoped, Russia's expansion into China was checked by Japan, a rapidly rising power in Asia. In 1904–5, the Japanese trounced Russia's army in Manchuria and sank most of its main battle fleet at the Tsushima Strait, which separates Korea from Japan (see map on p. 28).

Relations between Washington and St. Petersburg had also soured as a growing number of Americans became aware of the brutality of the Russian government. Indeed, some American bankers were so angered by Russia's treatment of its Jews that they provided much of the finance that had enabled Japan to defeat Russia in 1905. By 1911, the United States government bowed to pressure from American Jewish groups and abrogated the 70-year-old Russian-American commercial treaty. This was the first time that Americans had felt that they could interfere in Russia on human rights; it would not be the last.

The setbacks Russia suffered in Asia led to modest political reforms at home, but they resulted in the emergence of weak political parties and their involvement in a parliament that had little power. An even bigger change was already underway as Russia's economy began to take off, growing faster than that of any other major state as grain exports boomed.

As a result of the growth of trade, more Western Europeans were living in Russia and ever greater numbers of Russians were visiting Western Europe. While Russia's extraordinary cultural creativity—in music, ballet, literature and art—was all widely admired in Europe, open-minded Russians were collecting some of the finest modern French art. During the *belle époque* that preceded the First World War, the Russians had a greater presence in Europe than the Americans.

The Americans, meanwhile, wanted the world to know that they were a rising military power. Having restructured the army so that it could act as an expeditionary force overseas, the American government set out to show the flag by sending its new "Great White Fleet" to circle the globe in 1908. It was the largest naval force ever to have made that voyage. And during the two decades before the First World War, the Marines were sent into Latin American and Caribbean countries some twenty times, usually in response to demands from Wall Street to ensure that governments would not default on American loans or to protect American investments.

Fear of Revolution

Long before the Bolsheviks seized power in Russia in 1917, there was a pervasive fear of revolution not just among Europeans, but also among Americans.

The harshness and misery that accompanied industrialization built up pressures for radical change. According to Karl Marx, revolution would be the locomotive of history that would lead the exploited into a more just and prosperous world. In 1848, he issued his *Communist Manifesto* in which he backed this idea with his famous rallying call—"Workers of the World Unite!" The Franco-Prussian War of 1870 sparked a revolution in a part of Paris—the so-called Paris Commune—which brought into the open the intense anger that lurked within the proletariat.

As the authorities across Europe tightened their control, some people turned in desperation to anarchism. In the twenty years before the First World War, five European heads of state and dozens of other prominent figures were assassinated by anarchists and many other leaders narrowly escaped. In 1901, President McKinley became the most prominent of their victims in America.

Anarchism was much more widespread in autocratic Russia. Between 1881, when anarchists assassinated Tsar Alexander II, and the outbreak of the First World War, some two and half thousand people died as a result of anarchist attacks and roughly the same number were executed by the tsarist government for having being involved in them.

In Western Europe, over the course of the three decades leading up to the First World War, most Marxists became social democrats, a process helped by timely social legislation and by the fact that workers had gained a political voice through the formation of trade unions. Nonetheless, fear of revolution persisted in America, where businesses continued to oppose unions, social security and injury compensation, and where social democracy was generally considered little more than communism in disguise.

In Russia, revolution did not progress according to Marx's predictions. After three exhausting years of war against Germany, widespread unrest among the relatively small working class and fear the army would mutiny, Tsar Nicholas II abdicated in February 1917. That November, Vladimir Lenin led the Bolsheviks, Russia's small hard-line communist party, to power—not by a popular revolution, but through a *coup d'etat* that enabled them to seize control of the politically weak provisional government and win popular support by proclaiming utopian aspirations and promising land to the peasantry.

In a world plagued by poverty and injustice, the new creed of Marxism-Leninism, which promised prosperity and justice for all, had enormous attraction. But in Russia it swiftly adopted the authoritarian character of tsarism, along with faith in the ability of violence to secure political ends. Lenin assured the Russian people that their revolution would be defended with "merciless measures," and it was.[2]

Arthur Koestler, the former communist who had written *Darkness at Noon*, published in 1940, described how he and so many others who did not wish to engage in violence coped with the horrors of a revolution whose ideals they supported. He wrote, "I learned to classify automatically everything that shocked me as 'the heritage of the past' and everything I liked as 'seeds of the future.'"[3]

Whereas "Holy Russia" believed that God had given it a divine mission, Soviet Russia believed that "history" had tasked it with promoting proletarian revolution across the world—a far more messianic venture that would bring it into conflict with the capitalist powers of the world. But even if Russia had not become a communist nation, there would almost certainly have been growing friction between Russia and America. They were, after all, two rapidly expanding and fundamentally different powers.

The Clash of Ideologies

Had they ever met, perhaps the only thing that Ronald Reagan and Vladimir Lenin would have agreed upon was that the struggle between socialism and capitalism would end only when one of them gave up. In many respects, the start of the Cold War can be traced back to 1917, when Lenin called for a world revolution that would eliminate capitalism because, as he saw it, "we cannot live in peace; in the end, one or the other will triumph."[4]

The Bolsheviks were not the only ones promoting a major new ideology on the world stage in 1917. That same year, the entry of the United States into the First World War gave the Americans their first chance to do just that. But the Americans did not champion their cause with either the ardor or the constancy of the Bolsheviks.

In bringing the American people into the war against Imperial Germany and the Austro-Hungarian Empire, President Woodrow Wilson appealed to their idealism. Americans disliked the thought of being part of a "balance of power," but they responded positively to Wilson's call to fight "the war to end all wars." The public accepted his claim that the right to national "self-determi-

nation" and prosperity through free trade would help make the world safe for democracy.

Following the defeat of Germany, the Bolsheviks lost control of three territories that Russia had long regarded as important to its security—the so-called Congress Kingdom of Poland, the Grand Duchy of Finland and the Baltic provinces that soon became Lithuania, Latvia and Estonia. They hoped to regain the advantage through world revolution. Communists made violent attempts to seize power in Germany, Hungary, Slovakia and Finland.

In Russia, beginning in 1918, the Allies began trying to unseat the "Red" Bolsheviks by backing the "Whites," the group of tsarist supporters and others who opposed the communist coup. In 1919, efforts to break a strike by longshoremen in Seattle who refused to load arms to support the "Whites" led to a five-day general strike that paralyzed the city. Many Americans reacted hysterically to what was being portrayed, with the help of the Department of Justice, as the creeping menace of communism.

The "Whites" might well have won had they received more help from the Allies, but the Allies soon tired of their involvement in the civil war. In 1921, they pulled out their forces, hoping they would eventually be able to tame the Bolsheviks in other ways. A year earlier, Lloyd George, the British prime minister, reflected this hope when he argued: "We have failed to restore Russia to sanity by force. I believe we can do it and save her by trade . . . The simple sums of addition and subtraction which it inculcates soon disposes of wild theories."[5]

This was not the way the Bolsheviks viewed the world. For them the Soviet Union was not just a great power pursuing expansion in search of security, but the capital of an international revolutionary movement. Its leaders adhered to a closed system of thought that distorted their vision of the outside world and ruled out much of the normal give-and-take of international dealings.

Although the Bolsheviks saw themselves engaged in a long and ultimately victorious struggle with the forces of capitalism, they recognized that at times they would need to reduce the intensity of the struggle, by advocating the creation of united fronts against a common enemy or the pursuit of such policies as peaceful coexistence and détente. These, however, were temporary devices, pauses on the way to the predestined goal.

By 1919, having fought and won the "war to end all wars," the American people partied, abandoning Wilson's internationalism and quickly returning to the isolationism that many had long favored. In 1920, the Senate refused to ratify the Treaty of Versailles that had established the League of Nations, with

the result that there was now little hope of maintaining peace through "collective security." In the years to come, the disconcerting vacuum of power that this created became increasingly dangerous.

Soviet-American Relations Begin

To build up Soviet strength, Lenin needed credits and technology from the very capitalists he soon hoped to overthrow. In 1922, he began calling for "peaceful co-existence" and "correct" relations with other countries. Many foreign leaders and businessmen accepted that this really was what he wanted—even though Moscow was, at the same time, helping to develop revolutionary communist parties in countries and colonies all over the world.

Despite the absence of diplomatic relations between Washington and Moscow, the United States was providing a quarter of all Soviet imports. In late 1933, Washington finally established diplomatic relations with Moscow, making the United States the last major power to do so. This was the beginning of the complicated relationship between Josef Stalin and Franklin D. Roosevelt.

Stalin was a revolutionary whose successful bank robberies provided the money that kept Lenin going while he plotted revolution in Russia from the safety of Western Europe. Stalin was a pseudonym that meant "man of steel," and it resonated well with the name "Lenin" (also a pseudonym, but one whose meaning is still debated). In 1922, Lenin made Stalin general-secretary of the party.

By the time of his death, two years later, Lenin had become deeply troubled by certain defects in Stalin's personality. He was right to be so, as Stalin was skillfully and murderously manipulating Lenin's aready ruthless system, perhaps with a little additional guidance from Machiavelli's *The Prince,* which was specially translated for him. But unlike several of the other leading Bolsheviks, Stalin had little firsthand knowledge of the outside world, having made only two brief trips into Western Europe, both before the First World War.

As far as Stalin was concerned, there was no hope of a communist world revolution in the foreseeable future. He believed that first the Soviet Union needed to develop "socialism in one country" so that it would be strong enough to deter any would-be attacker. In the meantime, he would exploit whatever opportunities might arise to spread communism in other countries. For Stalin, the goal of "socialism in one country" could be achieved only through the elimination of all domestic opposition and by industrializing the Soviet Union at breakneck speed.

The human cost of these twin policies was appalling. By the time war broke out in 1941, perhaps as many as 20 million people had been executed, died in slave-labor camps or perished in the famines that followed the forced collectivization of agriculture.[6] On the night of December 12, 1938, alone, Stalin personally signed death warrants bearing the names of 5,000 people, after which he went to his private movie theater to enjoy two films, one of them a comedy called *Merry Fellows*.[7]

Few Americans know what an important part their country played in building up Soviet industry. In the twenties and thirties, Americans designed over 600 major factories, oversaw the construction of the biggest hydroelectric dam and established the truck and automobile industry. At the peak there were probably some fifteen thousand Americans working in the Soviet Union.

While Stalin was trying to build socialism in one country, Roosevelt was hoping to revive capitalism in another—and through far more humane means. A landslide victory brought him to the White House in 1933, as the first Democratic president in twelve years. During the campaign he had promised the American people a "New Deal" to banish the horrors of the Great Depression, which had halved America's national income and dragged millions of Americans into poverty and despair.

As Roosevelt began his presidency, the hopes of continued peace were beginning to fade. Japan was expanding into China, Hitler had taken control of Germany and both powers had withdrawn from the League of Nations. Roosevelt understood that the United States would not be able to stand on the sidelines much longer. Within nine months of entering the White House, he proposed that the United States and the Soviet Union should establish diplomatic relations.

When the first American ambassador to the Soviet Union arrived in December 1933, he received not only unprecedented courtesy, but also a big wet kiss on his cheek from Stalin. But the fundamental differences between the two countries soon made such an amicable relationship unsustainable.

Forced Cooperation

Even as war became increasingly likely, uncertainties over Hitler's intentions fueled the suspicions of all concerned. Whereas the British and the French hated communism more than Nazism, Stalin's aim was to see Germany wear itself out in a war with Britain and France.

In August 1939, the Soviet Union and Germany concluded the infamous Molotov-Ribbentrop Pact, named after their respective foreign ministers. There was far more to this so-called non-aggression pact than was known at the time. Just eight days later, on September 1, Hitler invaded western Poland, and Britain and France swiftly declared war on Germany.

In accordance with the secret clauses of the pact, Soviet troops soon moved into eastern Poland. Stalin then demanded that the Finns agree to an exchange of territory so that Leningrad could be better defended. When the Finns refused, he seized much of what he wanted during the "Winter War"—though at a cost of 125,000 Soviet troops. Three months later, in June 1940, Stalin took control of the three Baltic Republics—Lithuania, Latvia and Estonia. Within less than a year, he had recovered much of the Tsarist Russian territory that had been lost as a result of the First World War.

Stalin's hopes of seeing Germany weakened soon evaporated. In a series of stunning victories, Hitler had conquered Norway, Denmark, the Low Countries and France, while British forces had been ignominiously evicted from the Continent. Although the intelligence of an imminent German attack became stronger with each passing day, Stalin still suspected this was part of a cunning plot to draw him into the war before Hitler had really decided to attack. When Richard Sorge, a German correspondent and an outstanding Soviet spy, provided accurate reports on Hitler's intention to invade Russia, Stalin dismissed him as a lying "shit."[8]

Stalin continued to play for time, with strategic raw materials still being exported to Germany. When the German invasion began on June 22, 1941, Stalin was so shaken that he left Viacheslav Molotov, his foreign minister, to inform the Soviet people what was happening. Further humiliated by the rapid advance of Hitler's armies towards Moscow, Stalin retreated briefly to his dacha outside of Moscow. Whatever his colleagues thought about his misjudgments, they were agreed that Stalin was the only person who had any chance of rallying the people to defeat Hitler. But it was not until July 3 that Stalin made a radio broadcast from the Kremlin, calling on the public ("brothers and sisters . . . my friends") to band together to defeat the Nazi invaders.[9]

Only when Stalin and Winston Churchill, Britain's wartime leader, faced the prospect of defeat could they finally join in a common cause. Churchill had a deep hatred of both communism and Nazism, but the threat of Nazism was far more immediate. He justified his willingness to join with Stalin by saying, "If Hitler invaded Hell, I would make at least a favorable reference to the Devil

"The Spirit of Union" caught the public mood, but the big question was whether one could be confident that, like Dewar's, "It never varies." (Courtesy of John Dewar & Sons)

in the House of Commons."[10] Stalin would no doubt have concurred with the sentiment.

"Mother Russia" Goes to War

Faced with the prospect of defeat, Stalin rightly judged that the cheapest and quickest way to inspire his troops was to make their military commanders more closely resemble the victors of Russia's past. Through his newfound British ally, Stalin obtained large amounts of gold braid that soon began to appear on the uniforms of Soviet officers.

In December 1941, the Japanese attacked the US Pacific Fleet at Pearl Harbor and expanded their war of conquest from China into southeast Asia. Hitler's simultaneous declaration of war on the United States brought the Americans into alliance with both Britain and the Soviet Union. After almost a quarter of a century, America was once again going to be a major player in European affairs.

Japan, however, remained neutral in the Nazi-Soviet war, a decision that was crucial for Stalin's regime. Reliable intelligence about Japanese intentions enabled Stalin to transfer troops from Siberia in time to defend Moscow.[11] Similarly, the Japanese did not interfere with the rapidly growing volume of American military aid that was being sent across the Pacific in American ships flying the Soviet flag.

At home, Stalin played on Russian nationalism. Many conscripts and volunteers fought with fervor, feeling that after the years of Stalin's terror they were again "free to be Russian" and to defend "Mother Russia." Before long, the portraits of Marx and Engels hanging in the Kremlin were replaced by those of the Russian heroes of the Napoleonic Wars and after the Red Army's great victory at Stalingrad, in February 1943, Stalin took to wearing a marshal's uniform.

We now know that intelligence from Britain—based on the deciphering of Germany military communications (code-named *Ultra*)—contributed to the victories of the Red Army. Its importance increased greatly after Stalin obtained unsanitized versions of the decriptions from his own agents in Britain and so took them more seriously.[12]

So, too, did military aid from Britain, and above all from America, which provided roughly $150 billion worth of supplies and equipment at 2007 prices. In the summer of 1944, Marshal Rokossovsky, one of the most talented Soviet commanders of the Second World War, destroyed the same number of German divisions on the Eastern Front that were confronting the Allied forces in France on D-Day.

As the Germans were pushed on to the defensive, a new prospect was emerging. Either Soviet troops would come face-to-face with the Americans and British in a defeated Germany or one side might cut a deal with the Germans at the other's expense. Given what had happened in 1941, Stalin was taking no chances. There was a dramatic upsurge in Soviet espionage against these two countries.

Soviet Intelligence had the benefit of some promising sources in Britain (who came to be known as the "magnificent five"), one of whom had already reported on British plans to develop an atomic bomb. The primary intelligence effort, however, took place in America, with high priority being given to America's war aims, military technology and the atom bomb. Moscow's efforts were greatly aided by the presence of many intelligence officers among the some 5,000 Soviet officials in New York and Washington, who were arranging for American supplies to be shipped to the Soviet Union.

2 Face-to-Face

Towards an Accord

When Roosevelt, Churchill and Stalin (the Big Three) met together for the first time in Tehran at the end of November 1943, they had real incentives to try to come to terms. They were, after all, close to exhaustion, in midst of the second world war in one generation and with no wish to face a third. They feared that unless they found a way to cooperate with each other, Germany and Japan would be strong enough to threaten them again within twenty years.

Both Churchill and Roosevelt felt that they detected a distinctly tsarist streak in Stalin's foreign policy. Roosevelt, more so than Churchill, was prone to think that he could get through to "Uncle Joe" as one politician to another, even recording that at the Tehran Conference "we talked like men and brothers."[1]

For Stalin, however, it was not a question of choosing between great power interests and the pursuit of revolution, it was a matter of how best to achieve both. Although Stalin retained an ideological conviction that the Soviet Union would eventually find itself at war with the United States and Britain, his recent dealings with them seemed to have made him think that such a war could be delayed for many years. During this period he would seek to strengthen Soviet power and gradually spread communism abroad.

One of the reasons Stalin and Roosevelt got along was that neither liked to take up firm stances until they knew whose army occupied the territory. When Churchill asked Stalin about his post-war territorial ambitions, over dinner during the Tehran conference, Stalin replied "when the time comes we will speak."[2]

The discussion soon moved on to how the peace would be kept once the war was over. The president took the lead and proposed that, after the war, the United States, Britain, the Soviet Union and China should act as the world's "four policemen," cooperating through a new international body called the United Nations. By getting all four to sign up to this during the war, not afterwards,

The Occupation of Germany and Austria, 1945

Roosevelt hoped to prevent the United States from retreating into the disastrous isolation that had followed the Treaty of Versailles. Stalin understood that Roosevelt's proposals offered the Soviet Union a status greater than anything ever achieved by Imperial Russia, a yardstick he frequently used.

With surprisingly little difficulty, the Big Three approved a preliminary agreement on Germany in September 1944, just as British and American troops were approaching the Rhine, while, in the east, the Red Army was preparing to cross the Vistula in Poland. Under this accord Soviet forces would occupy the eastern half of Germany, while the western part would be shared by the Americans and the British (and later the French). Berlin would be similarly divided. This was a deal that gave Stalin every incentive to continue the war. In Austria, which had been incorporated into Germany in 1938, a similar pattern was followed, but with Soviet forces occupying only about a third of the country.

Under the pressure of events, the Big Three failed to carefully consider the question of Berlin. Instead of proposing that the capital should be at the meeting point of the three zones, they adopted a simpler solution that left it deep within the Soviet one. Access to the city was to be sorted out once the fighting was over. That issue was to aggravate relations for years to come.[3]

As the war with Germany moved towards its close, three of Stalin's top diplomats were separately tasked with considering how relations were likely to develop with Britain and America. All three argued that cooperation among the Big Three was the only effective basis for a stable post-war world. The key to success, the three Soviet diplomats predicted, would be agreement on each power having its own "spheres of influence," though this would not necessarily be easy to achieve.[4]

There were signs, nonetheless, that agreement would be possible on spheres of influence. Late one night at the Kremlin in October 1944, Churchill put before Stalin a page from a notebook setting out the percentage of influence he thought the two sides should have in each of the countries in Eastern Europe and the Balkans (though not Poland). Stalin did not argue about the percentages; he simply leaned forward and with a pencil placed a large tick of approval on the paper.

Stalin must have thought that Churchill's cynical approach augured well, especially as Anthony Eden, Churchill's foreign minister, pressed Molotov on how the agreement could be implemented. A month later, he declared publicly that the Alliance was not accidental; it arose from "vitally important and long-lasting interests," above all "preventing new aggression or a new war, if not forever, then at least for an extended period of time."[5]

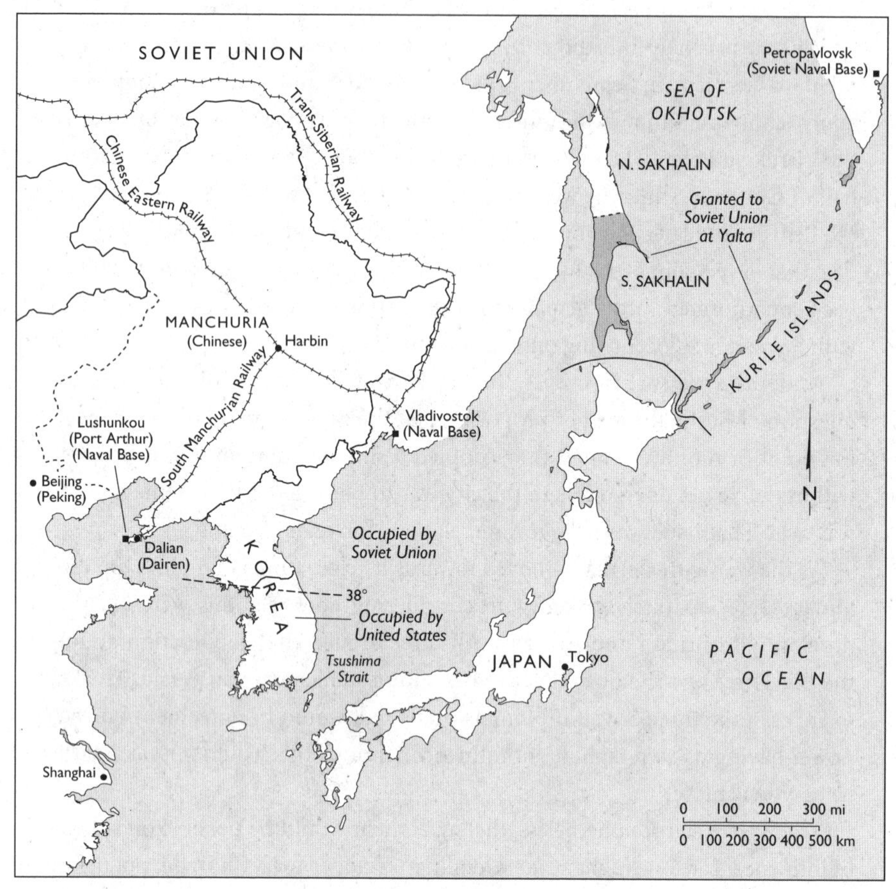

Soviet Gains in the Far East at the End of World War II

The Big Three next met at Yalta in February 1945, at the Livadia Palace, the last tsar's summer home that looks out over the Black Sea. They felt they were moving towards a settlement. They agreed in principle that there should be two spheres of influence in Europe, a Soviet one in the east and an Anglo-American one in the west.

Roosevelt and Churchill accepted that the Soviet Union would regain most of the territory of Tsarist Russia that had been lost in 1917 (see map on p. 38); in addition, Stalin was particularly pleased that Roosevelt had also agreed to the restoration of what he regarded as the "former rights of Russia violated by the treacherous attack of Japan in 1904."[6]

Stalin took careful note that Roosevelt had said that "two years would be the limit" that Congress was likely to accept for American troops remaining in Europe after the war.[7] The prospect of an American withdrawal from Europe was of enormous significance for Stalin. If that were to happen, the Soviet Union would become the preponderant power on the continent which, in turn, would greatly enhance the chances of Germany and other European countries eventually becoming communist.

Although Stalin agreed with Roosevelt (and Churchill) that the governments in their respective zones of Europe should be elected "democratically," they had markedly different understandings of what that meant in practice. The most contentious issue would be the future of Poland, a nation that had plagued and obsessed Russia centuries before the creation of the Soviet Union. Poland would become a litmus test of just how workable the relationship among the Big Three would be after the war.

The Polish Question

As the Puritans set about creating their "New Jerusalem" in America, Poland was already one of the great powers of Europe. Hitler's army reached the outskirts of Moscow, Napoleon's captured the Kremlin, but only the Polish army ever occupied it for any length of time. The national day of modern Russia is November 4, which commemorates the uprising that ejected the Poles from Moscow in 1612.

From the early 18th century, Poland became the victim of various partitions between Austria, Germany and Russia, which until the First World War controlled the lion's share. It re-emerged as an independent state in 1919, not by grace of the Treaty of Versailles, but because the Poles had fought to create an independent Poland.

As the menace of Nazi Germany grew, the Poles adamantly refused to ally themselves with the Soviet Union and Stalin became determined there would never again be a Polish state that could undermine Soviet security. Immediately after Stalin's troops gained control of eastern Poland in 1939, one and a half million Poles, including many of the elite, were deported to the Soviet Union, where half of them soon died and some 30,000–40,000 were killed on Stalin's orders.

After Hitler attacked the Soviet Union, Stalin reversed course and wanted to enlist the Poles against the Germans. General Wladyslaw Anders was permitted to lead some 120,000 Poles out of the Soviet Union to join up with the hard-pressed British fighting the Germans in North Africa. Stalin then set about creating a second Polish army, under Soviet control, to retake Poland from the Germans and form the core of a new Polish army in a new Poland.

A clash between the Big Three over Poland was inevitable. Roosevelt was strongly committed to helping the Poles, especially as the bulk of the five million Americans of Polish descent voted for the Democrats. For Churchill, Poland was the country for whom Britain had gone to war against Hitler in 1939 and whose government-in-exile in London had over 200,000 troops valiantly fighting alongside the British. On the intelligence front, the Poles had made an extraordinary contribution to the Allied war effort, especially by helping the British to read much of Germany's secret military communications.[8]

The Polish government-in-exile in London, however, was deeply suspicious of Stalin's intentions, especially after it was discovered, in 1943, that 4,500 Polish officers had been massacred on his orders at Katyn three years earlier. For his part, Stalin was adamant that the new Polish government had to be friendly to Moscow and under communist control.

Allied complaints about Soviet conduct in Poland infuriated Molotov, Stalin's foreign minister. Three days after the Yalta Conference ended on February 11, 1945, he angrily wrote on a document, "Poland—Big deal!" At no time, Molotov noted, had the Soviet Union been asked whether it liked the governments being set up in Western Europe. "We have not interfered," he added, "because it is an Anglo-American zone of military action."[9]

When the government-in-exile launched the Warsaw Uprising in the summer of 1944, the Soviet armies who had reached the other bank of the Vistula River watched for two months as the Germans savagely suppressed it. Stalin was pleased to have the Germans weaken the largest and most effective resistance movement in occupied Europe.

Foreboding

"The war shall soon be over," Stalin remarked to a guest at a Kremlin banquet. "We shall recover in fifteen or twenty years, and then we'll have another go at it," with a view to spreading communism to more countries.[10] The guest was Josip Broz Tito, whose communist partisans had just liberated Yugoslavia from the Germans; the date was April 1945, barely two months after Yalta.

At almost the same time, Roosevelt, whose life was ebbing away, was losing hope that he and Stalin would come to terms on Poland. In May 1945, with Germany close to defeat, Churchill even went so far as to ask his chiefs of staff whether the West could take some military action that would compel Stalin to make concessions over Poland. The conclusion of this most sensitive assessment (known as *Operation Unthinkable*) was a resounding "No!"[11]

Although it seems that Stalin knew nothing of this operation, his suspicions would certainly have been aroused by other allied actions. The British and the Americans had already bombed Germany's uranium mine and taken away its stockpile of uranium before it fell into Soviet hands; now Soviet Military Intelligence had intercepted Churchill's instructions to Field Marshal Montgomery to collect and store captured weapons for a possible rearming of German troops.[12]

On April 12, as these suspicions festered, Roosevelt died, leaving Harry S. Truman, his vice president of just five months' standing, to take over. Truman was a decent, straightforward mid-westerner with good political judgment, but he was woefully unprepared for his new role as he had not been privy to Roosevelt's thinking on Stalin and the post-war world. At his swearing-in ceremony, he told a group of reporters, "If you ever pray, pray for me now."[13]

Meanwhile, in the middle of Germany the multimillion-strong Soviet and Allied armies were rapidly moving towards each other. On April 25, Russian and American soldiers came face-to-face for the first time on the River Elbe, just south of Berlin. Within a week, Hitler had committed suicide and on May 7 a shattered Germany had no option but to surrender unconditionally, with the Allies taking control of the country as they had agreed at Yalta.

The View from the White House

In the wars against Germany and Japan some 350,000 Americans had lost their lives, nearly all of them troops, which was a mere fraction of the Soviet losses. The Americans were now twice as rich as they had been when the war started and had never had it so good.

The Americans had geared up for war at extraordinary speed, mobilizing almost 12 million men within three years. In the last year of the war alone their unprecedented industrial power had enabled them to produce a phenomenal 100,000 aircraft and 30,000 tanks, along with the huge naval forces that enabled them to fight wars on two fronts simultaneously at vast distances from home. And America's leaders expected that they would soon have an atomic bomb.

With the United States unquestionably the world's pre-eminent economic and financial power, many influential citizens wanted their country to act as a superpower. The Great Depression, many Americans argued, did not stem from the failure of America's economic policies, but from the trade restrictions imposed by the major imperial powers—Britain, France, the Netherlands and Portugal. America should therefore use its financial muscle to open these markets to American exports and investment. This would help the nation to end colonialism, resist communism and champion democracy.

Before the end of the war, the Joint Chiefs of Staff had drawn up lists of overseas locations where America would require bases to promote America's interests in its new global role. As early as 1944, an Australian diplomat in Washington noted that there were "signs in this country of the development of a somewhat ruthless Imperial attitude."[14]

The View from the Kremlin

The Soviet experience of war could hardly have been more different. Stalin had no doubt that, among the Allies, the Soviet Union had made by far the largest contribution to the defeat of Hitler as close to 80% of total German losses were on the Eastern Front. The price of victory had been horrendously steep, costing in all over 25 million Soviet lives[15] and most of the country to the west of Moscow had been laid to waste.

At war's end Stalin seemed to have felt like Tsar Alexander I preparing to take part in the Congress of Vienna in 1814 that would settle the future of Europe. He wanted his rewards.

The Soviet people wanted theirs, too. They had been led to believe that their victory would bring greater freedom and prosperity. There was talk not only of private businesses being allowed once more, but of American department stores opening in Soviet cities. Leading scientists were asking to be allowed to

After the Victory parade in Red Square, Moscow, crowds mill up Gorky Street; the Kremlin can be seen in the background, June 24, 1945. (Yakov Khalip, courtesy of his son Nikolai)

travel abroad freely, and troops were returning from Germany with dangerous thoughts about wanting better standards of living and greater liberty, much like those who had returned from Paris after the defeat of Napoleon.

On May 10, crowds of elated Russians thronged into Red Square for the first of the victory celebrations. Some uniformed servicemen from the American and British embassies were cheered and carried on the shoulders of the exultant Muscovites; one Red Army major cried out, "Now it is time to live!"[16] The climax of the celebrations came on June 24, when Stalin took the salute at a huge and magnificently choreographed victory parade. As Marshal Zhukhov, the conqueror of Berlin, led the parade on a white charger, spectators cheered "That's our St. George!," referring to the patron saint of Moscow.

All of this was totally unacceptable to Stalin. The days of "Mother Russia" were over. He wanted control and needed discipline. His way of keeping the people in line was to raise the specter of a foreign threat. In 1944, workers in Moscow were already being warned that problems with the Allies lay ahead. By April 1945, some party activists were being told that the British and the Americans were the enemies of the Soviet people.

Although the Soviet Union had emerged as one of the two great powers in the world, it was not the equal of the United States. Its national income was probably a mere 15% of America's. At the same time, Stalin was acutely aware that his country had become vulnerable in a way it had never been before—to strategic air power, which had enabled the Americans to inflict appalling damage on Japan from bases 2,500 km (1,500 miles) away.

As if that were not bad enough, Soviet Intelligence was reporting that the Americans were close to producing an atomic bomb. Catching up with America militarily would be far harder than Stalin had once thought. On June 27, less than three weeks before he set off for Potsdam, Stalin assumed the title of "Generalissimo."

Still, Stalin had to proceed with caution. He had much to gain from a workable relationship with the West, including billions of dollars of reparations from Germany and loans from the United States. Another major benefit, he saw, was that it could help communists increase their influence in Western Europe. As the war in Europe came to an end, Stalin observed, "Today socialism is possible even under the English monarchy; revolution is no longer necessary everywhere."[17] The prospects looked particularly good in France and Italy, where the communist parties had played major roles in the resistance movements.

SIZING EACH OTHER UP

Ruined Berlin, the Brandenburg Gate, 1945. (Courtesy of the German Information Service)

3 A World Transformed

By the Lake at Potsdam

On July 17, 1945, the Big Three convened at Potsdam, in the relatively undamaged outskirts of Berlin, to try to agree on a post-war settlement. The most pressing issue was Germany, which, strategically speaking, was now the most sensitive place on earth. Both sides believed that if the other gained control of all of Germany, or had all of Germany on its side, they would be the dominant power on the continent.

Basically, their agreements on the occupation of Germany were going according to plan. Once the fighting was over, the armies of the Big Three fairly quickly pulled back to the zones of occupation they had earlier agreed upon. A little while later, the American and British contingents were allowed to cross the Soviet zone in order to occupy their respective sectors of Berlin.

The problems they faced, however, were daunting. The Germans had fought hard to avoid defeat, with the result that virtually all of their cities had been bombed and shelled into ruins. Millions of Germans were expected to die of hunger or cold during the forthcoming winter. The Big Three urgently needed to agree on how they would run the country.

Their task was made all the more difficult because on the Western side there were new players. This was Truman's first meeting with Stalin and during the conference, as a result of an ill-timed British election, Churchill was replaced by Clement Attlee, the prime minister of the new Labour Party government. Although Atlee was more experienced than Truman in foreign affairs, he, too, had no previous experience of dealing with Stalin.

At Tehran and Yalta, when asked whether Germany should be dismembered at the end of the war, Stalin's answer had been "This is what we prefer."[1] On June 4, he had reflected this view when he privately told the German communists, who were returning from Moscow to the new Soviet zone, that there would be "two Germanys."[2]

Europe's New Frontiers at the End of World War II

The day after Germany surrendered, however, Moscow announced it wished Germany to remain one country. Not only would this give Stalin some leverage over what happened in all of Germany, but in the short term he could make a stronger case for taking reparations from the western zones as well as his own. The reality on the ground, however, was rather different.

Towards a Divided Germany

Before the Potsdam Conference began there was, in effect, already a complete "wall" between the Soviet zone and those of the Western Allies. Truman and James Byrnes, his secretary of state, soon concluded that the Western Allies should accept this split. Not only would that keep Germany weak, but it would also reduce friction with the Soviet Union at a time when many other issues still needed to be addressed.

Byrnes quickly brokered a package deal under which there would be a *de facto* division of Germany. It also included a tacit agreement that the Soviet Union would have control of East Germany and Eastern Europe, while that of the Americans and the British would extend across West Germany and the western part of the continent (including Italy, which until recently had been Hitler's ally).

To reduce the threat that Germany might pose in the years to come, Stalin expelled some 15 million Germans from East Prussia, West Prussia and Silesia—people whose families had lived in these territories since the Middle Ages. It was the largest forced migration, over such a short period, in history. At least a tenth of the expellees died. About a quarter of the remainder settled in the Soviet zone of Germany, while the remainder traveled on into the western ones. Stalin kept the Konigsburg region of East Prussia. This was "a small piece of German territory" that he felt the Russian people were entitled to given the terrible losses they had suffered.[3]

Equally importantly, Stalin moved the Polish state westwards. He had already absorbed back into the Soviet Union the Western Ukraine, which had been part of Tsarist Russia before the Poles took control of it once again in 1921. Poland was compensated for that loss with parts of eastern Germany, plus the remaining part of East Prussia, and the lands stretching along the Baltic coast as far as Danzig from which the Germans could be expelled (see map on p. 38). Ethnically, Poland would be more Polish than it had been for centuries.

These changes satisfied a deep historical urge. The new frontiers were virtually those proposed by the last tsarist foreign minister.[4] And there were other major benefits. The possession of so much former German territory would ensure that the Poles remained Soviet allies. And with the Polish frontier now just 70 km (44 miles) from Berlin, Moscow would be well placed to intervene in German affairs.

Stalin also took back from Romania, Hitler's wartime ally, the province of Bessarabia that had earlier been part of Tsarist Russia. This meant that Stalin had reestablished controlled over all the territory that the Bolsheviks had lost after 1917, with the exception of most of Finland.

At Stalin's insistence, Truman and Attlee accepted these frontier changes, pending an agreement on the terms of a final peace treaty with Germany. Stalin attached such importance to them that he tacitly accepted the fact that the Soviet Union would in future control less than a third of the German population. The implication of this, not fully appreciated by the West at the time, was that Moscow would have virtually no hope of ever gaining a majority in any all-German election.

"Stalin was not unduly concerned about having much less than half of Germany," General Viacheslav Kevorkov, who had been the KGB's leading authority on German affairs, explained. "Given the problems he already had with America and Britain, the existence of a united Germany could create dangerous tensions. It was, therefore, better to have part than to risk all. Keeping alive the idea of German unity was another matter. That could be used to put pressure on the West."

For this reason, Stalin clearly liked Byrnes's "spheres of influence" approach. He also was pleased that the Allies had accepted that he would get $10 billion of reparations from Germany. At the end of the conference, he praised Byrnes for having "worked harder perhaps than any of us to make this conference a success." He added, "those sentiments, Secretary Byrnes, come from my heart."[5]

This division of Europe into two spheres of influence would, nevertheless, generate tension. Stalin had made it abundantly clear during the conference that all governments in Eastern Europe must be friendly to Moscow. "A freely elected government in any of the countries," Stalin had earlier acknowledged during the conference, "would be anti-Soviet, and that we cannot allow."[6] In Romania and Bulgaria Stalin had already ruthlessly asserted his authority and seemed set to do the same in Poland.

While Stalin's determination to control the "levers of state power" in each of these countries made both the Americans and the British fear the worst, their refusal to give him *carte blanche* reinforced his suspicion that they wanted to undermine his influence in his zone. Had Stalin played his cards better over Poland during the past two years, the Americans might have soon withdrawn from Europe; instead, that prospect began to fade rapidly.

The last hopes of compromise were vaporized by the atomic flash over Hiroshima—this, Stalin believed, had stripped him of much of the power he had acquired through the costly victories of the Red Army.

Atomic Shockwaves

"We have perfected a new weapon of unusual destructive force," Truman casually told Stalin after a dinner at Potsdam.[7] In uttering these words, Truman hoped he was sending Stalin a strong warning; little did he know that he had just fired the starter's gun for the most dramatic arms race the world has ever seen.

On the first day of the Potsdam conference, July 17, Stalin informed Truman that he would declare war on Japan on August 15, with attacks beginning in Manchuria and Korea. He said that he had promised Roosevelt at Yalta that, three months after the defeat of Germany, he would join in the war against Japan. By "keeping his word" Stalin hoped he would "help ensure the continuation of the good cooperation he had earlier enjoyed with Roosevelt."[8]

Stalin also hoped that such "good cooperation" would add to his share of the spoils in Japan and restore Russian influence in northeastern China and Korea. In Moscow, before and after the Potsdam Conference, Stalin relentlessly pressed T. V. Soong, Chiang Kai-shek's foreign minister, to accept Moscow as China's protector against a resurgent Japan.

The same day that Stalin made his commitment to Truman, Truman received a top secret message that the first atomic test, at Alamogordo in the New Mexican desert, had been successful. Atomic bombs would soon be ready to force the Japanese to surrender quickly and without further American casualties. Henry Stimson, Truman's secretary of war, noted that this would enable the United States "to get the homeland (of Japan) into our hands before the Russians could put in a substantial claim to occupy and help rule it."[9]

When Truman mentioned his "new weapon" to Stalin on July 24, he thought Stalin had not understood the import of his remarks. Stalin did, but only in part it seems. Since 1941 he had been receiving first-rate intelligence on Anglo-American efforts to develop an atomic bomb. What he appears not to have taken in is the speed with which Truman would use it.

Exactly two weeks later, on August 6, the first American atomic bomb was believed to have killed over 70,000 people instantly in Hiroshima. Sensing the Americans were trying to cut him out of a settlement, Stalin immediately declared war on Japan. The next day, the Americans dropped another atomic bomb on Nagasaki. When Stalin received Averell Harriman, the American ambassador, in the Kremlin the next day, he made it clear that he thought there had been no need to use the atom bomb: "Japan was about to surrender anyway."[10]

Catching Up

Stalin's calculations about what would determine influence in the post-war world had been thrown into disarray. At a secret gathering in the Kremlin in mid-August, Stalin told his top atomic scientists: "Hiroshima has shaken the whole world. The balance (of power) has been destroyed! Provide the bomb—it will remove a great danger from us."[11]

Stalin had initiated an atomic bomb program two years earlier, but had not given it high priority because he did not believe it would produce results in time to influence the outcome of the war. Now breaking the American monopoly would be a mega-undertaking. It would impose tremendous strains on the war-ravaged Soviet economy, even though Stalin had some of the most brilliant scientists in the world and, thanks to Soviet Intelligence, the details of the American bomb dropped on Nagasaki.

Horrified by what had happened at Hiroshima and Nagasaki, many influential Americans were advocating that both atomic bombs and atomic energy should be controlled by the United Nations. While this view commanded much popular support in America, Stalin simply could not believe that the United States, which had invested so heavily in developing atomic weapons, would really abandon the advantage they bestowed on them. He suspected that the American aim was to block the development of his nuclear program while at the same time secreting away some of these devastating weapons for their own future use.

After his initially heated reaction, Stalin developed a more measured view of the amount of damage that atomic bombs could cause. At the same time, Klaus Fuchs, a British nuclear physicist working at Los Alamos, was reporting to Moscow that the Americans had very few bombs.[12] He was right—the Americans had only nine bombs in July 1946. Such a small number would not be able to bring to its knees a country almost two and a half times the size of the continental United States.

Nevertheless, from the moment Truman first alluded to the atomic bomb, Stalin was determined not to be intimidated. Stalin publicly downplayed its significance. A year after Hiroshima he let the world know, through an interview with a British journalist, that as far as he was concerned, "The atomic bomb is meant to frighten those with weak nerves."[13] He had already set out to show the Americans that his were not.

Seeking a Settlement

After the defeat of Japan, although many issues remained contentious, both sides demobilized quickly. To facilitate negotiations, each side had made gestures to the other. The British excluded the Poles from the victory parade in London in June and along with the Americans had begun turning over to Stalin's secret police—and almost certain death—those Soviet prisoners of war and others who had sided with the Germans. For his part, Stalin cut off support to the communists in Greece and pulled his troops out of northern Norway, despite Soviet territorial claims in the region.

The discussions got underway at the Council of Foreign Ministers meeting in London in September and continued in various forums through December 1946. Stalin was willing to horse-trade, but determined the West should never feel that they had forced him to make concessions. But even Molotov, his foreign minister, was shocked by the tough orders Stalin sent him. One of them, sparked by a hint of flexibility on Molotov's part, said: "The Allies are pressing on you to break your will and force you into making concessions. It is obvious that you must be completely adamant."[14]

Stalin believed that by making maximum demands at the outset, he would be able to secure his lesser goals in the end. This approach, however, misfired. It was one thing for Molotov to call for Soviet trusteeship over Tripolitania (the Italian colony that became Libya), which for the first time would give the Soviet Union a presence in the Mediterranean, but when this was combined with mounting pressure on the Turks for territorial concessions, including a base on the Turkish Straits (see p. 46), the Americans and the British became very concerned about Stalin's expansionist aims.

The Americans managed to unsettle the Russians just as successfully. When Secretary of State Byrnes proposed a treaty to demilitarize Germany for twenty to twenty-five years, with the allied occupation being gradually dismantled as disarmament proceeded, Stalin regarded it as a Trojan Horse. This seemingly reasonable proposal, he said, would in practice provide "a formal sanction for the United States to play the same role in European affairs as the Soviet Union," and, along with the British, to "take the future of Europe into their hands."[15] This was anathema for Stalin.

In some respects, the situation in Japan was even worse. In August 1945, Truman had firmly rejected Stalin's proposal that Soviet troops should occupy part of Japan and continued to block any Soviet involvement in the running of Japan. Stalin vented his anger in another message to Molotov: "I consider it the height of impudence that the British and the Americans, who call themselves our allies, did not even want to hear us on the Control Council in Japan."[16]

Although in late 1945 Stalin quietly called off Marshal Zhukov's visit to America, he did accept Truman's proposal that Soviet and American troops should both withdraw from Czechoslovakia. Meanwhile, the communists were defeated in Hungarian municipal elections—even though those elections had been supervised by the Russians.

A few weeks later, in November, Stalin had a most revealing conversation in Moscow with Wladyslaw Gomulka, the head of the Polish Communist Party. "I am completely certain that there will be no war," Stalin said. The Allies' aims, he insisted, were first to "force us to yield on contentious issues concerning Japan, the Balkans and reparations," and second, "to push us away from our allies—Poland, Romania, Yugoslavia and Bulgaria." But he still thought that "it is possible" that there would be an agreement with the Americans.[17]

Darkening Clouds

Despite what Stalin had said to Gomulka, the previous hope, even expectation, of continuing good relations among the Big Three was coming under increasing strain.

Western observers were quick to spot that in a major speech in Moscow on February 9, Stalin had repeated, for the first time since he had allied himself with the British and Americans, the standard Marxist-Leninist line that capitalism made war inevitable. In what became known as the "Long Telegram"—and it certainly was—George Kennan, the American charge d'affaires in Moscow, asserted that "Stalin's speech marked the renewal of the lengthy, life-and-death struggle between communism and capitalism." Stalin was "no longer interested in 'socialism in one country'"; he wanted to "destroy America."[18]

The shockwaves this assessment sent through Washington in February 1946 were amplified a few days later when the news broke that twenty-two members of a Soviet spy ring had been arrested following the defection in Ottawa a few months earlier of Igor Gouzenko, a Soviet code clerk. His devastating revelations of Moscow's success in acquiring American atomic, military and political secrets, were not made fully public at the time. In March, however, news leaked out that Elizabeth Bentley, an American communist, had given the FBI the names of 150 people working for Moscow, including forty employees of the government, some in very high places. These first breakthroughs on the intelligence front were a real wake-up call—Americans now realized just how successful Moscow had been at penetrating their affairs.[19]

Kennan understood well Stalin's general outlook and aims, but that was not the subject of Stalin's speech. Although Stalin did refer, briefly, to the idea that capitalism made war inevitable, he also spoke positively about the wartime cooperation with Britain and the United States. Although he said that the Soviet Union needed to build its strength over the next fifteen years, so that it would never be attacked again, his immediate aim was to end rationing, improve the supply of consumer goods, cut prices and work more closely with noncommunists who shared the general aims of the party. In other words, Stalin hoped for a tactical pause in his longer-term struggle with the West.

On March 5, Winston Churchill, now the Leader of the Opposition in the British Parliament, rode with Truman through Fulton, in the president's home state of Missouri. Their destination was Westminster College, a most appropriately named venue for a speech by Churchill. The occasion is best remembered for Churchill's stark observation that "From Stettin in the Baltic to Trieste in the Adriatic, an iron curtain has descended across the continent." His theme, however, was "The Sinews of Peace."

Churchill rejected the idea that war was inevitable, let alone imminent, and made complimentary remarks about the Russians. Peace could best be assured, he said, "by reaching now, in 1946, a good understanding on all points with Russia." Stalin would not have objected to that, but he would have been put on his guard by Churchill's proposal that this could be achieved by "strengthening the unity and military capabilities of the West," especially the English-speaking nations.[20]

Tensions with Moscow eased somewhat when shortly after the Fulton speech Moscow indicated its willingness to include some non-communists in the Romanian and Bulgarian governments and Soviet troops were quietly withdrawn from the Danish island of Bornholm in the Baltic Sea. Meanwhile, Stalin continued to seek gains in Iran and Turkey.

Probing

In 1941, Britain and the Soviet Union occupied Iran to prevent it from siding with Germany. At the end of the war, the British troops withdrew from southern Iran, but even after the agreed date of withdrawal, Moscow let it be known that Soviet forces would remain in the north "pending examination of the situation." The British and the Americans rightly judged that Stalin wanted to annex this oil-rich region. At the newly established United Nations, in early 1946, they began pressing for Soviet troops to leave Iran.

The atmosphere improved a little in May 1946, when Soviet troops belatedly did so. The Americans and British thought that this was in response to their increasing pressure in the United Nations. In fact, we now have documents showing that Stalin had already decided to pull them out in exchange for an agreement with the Iranian government to establish a joint oil company (which Tehran never ratified) and in the light of other important considerations (see below).[21]

Stalin was also pressing for major concessions from Turkey, about which he thought in decidedly tsarist terms. He wanted free passage for his ships into the Mediterranean while controlling the entry of those of others into the Black Sea, which led to the southern shore of the Soviet Union. During the war, the Americans and British had been sympathetic to his request for a base on the Turkish Straits. When, at the end of the war, it was clear that they no longer were, Stalin began taking unilateral action.

In June 1945, even before Potsdam, Molotov demanded that the Turks return the part of eastern Turkey that the Soviet Union had ceded to them in 1921 (territory that Tsarist Russia had captured from the Ottoman Empire in 1877–78). When the Turks did not yield, Moscow abrogated what was, in effect, a friendship treaty between the two counties and called on the Turks to accept joint control of the Straits. In August 1946, Stalin started massing troops along the Turkish frontier with Soviet Armenia.

These moves against Turkey produced a war scare in Washington—the first of the Cold War. According to a top secret plan, code-named *Operation Pincher*, America would retaliate against a Soviet attack on Turkey with a massive strategic bombing campaign like those it had mounted against Germany and Japan, though this time there would be nine atomic bombs at their disposal. The Americans began flying along the periphery of the Soviet Union and Soviet-controlled Eastern Europe to collect intelligence, especially about gaps in Soviet air defenses.[22]

In December, Truman dispatched to the eastern Mediterranean one of America's two largest aircraft carriers. It was named after the man who had worked hardest to reach an understanding with Stalin—Franklin D. Roosevelt. As far as the world at large was concerned, Stalin took the hint and pulled back his troops from the Turkish frontier. It also seems that Soviet Intelligence had provided him with details of *Operation Pincher.* Molotov later recalled: "It is good that we retreated in time or [the situation] would have led to joint aggression against us."[23]

While Truman and his senior colleagues believed America's possession of the atomic bomb deterred Stalin from taking military action, they were increasingly frustrated by his unwillingness to do what they wanted. Truman instructed two of his top staff, Clark Clifford and George Elsey, to prepare an assessment of Soviet conduct since the end of the war.

Their report, which reached him in September, was explosive. Because the Soviet Union was expansionist, they argued, the United States had to be "prepared to wage atomic and biological war."[24] Truman was shocked, because he still believed that the power of the atomic bomb made it a terror weapon, a "weapon of last resort." "If that report were leaked," he said, "it would blow the roof off the White House and the Kremlin."[25] He immediately recalled the few copies that had been circulated and locked them in his safe.

That same month Nikolai Novikov, the Soviet ambassador in Washington, sent a similarly gloomy telegram to Molotov—but one focusing solely on American actions since the war, not what the Soviet response should be. Novikov's conclusion was that the United States was preparing for "the prospect of war against the Soviet Union . . ."[26]

A Partial Deal

Even at this stage, however, both Truman and Stalin were keen to avoid confrontation. When Truman addressed the opening session of the UN General Assembly in New York on October 23 he declared that "Conflict is not predestined."[27] As he stepped from the podium, Molotov rushed to shake his hand. No wonder, as earlier that day in Moscow, Stalin had publicly announced the acceleration of demobilization.

By the end of 1946, Stalin had accepted that Italy and Japan were both in the Western zone of influence. A deal was struck on Trieste, with Stalin persuading Tito to accept far less than he had hoped for. These concessions, Stalin told

Molotov, had been necessary because they made it possible to consolidate the gains he most needed—the formal Western acceptance of his security zone in Eastern Europe. At Yalta, the Allies had already accepted Soviet control over Poland; now they had accepted it over Romania, Bulgaria and Hungary, and recognized Moscow's special relationship with Finland. The West had not realized just how much importance Stalin attached to this matter.

Controlling Eastern Europe, however, would not be easy. It was comprised of seven countries, plus the Soviet zone of Germany, and with over 80 million people, its combined population was more than half that of the Soviet Union itself. Armed resistance was continuing in Poland, and in none of these countries could the communists hope to win in a free election. Initially, Stalin instructed them to enter coalition governments with "bourgeois" parties. Each communist party would have to have its own road to socialism—approved, of course, by Stalin.

Not only from a Western perspective, but also from Molotov's, Stalin's negotiating strategy was counter-productive because he could have got the same result without creating such antagonism. But from Stalin's point of view, the great gain was that the United States would continue to treat him with caution. And he could still expect there would be many opportunities for him to exploit—especially in the Third World.

Pushing Forward in the Third World

Immediately after the war, Stalin had done nothing to arouse fears about the expansion of communist influence in the Third World. He had recognized Chiang Kai-shek's regime as the sole government of China and as one of the five permanent members of the Security Council of the newly established United Nations. He also agreed that Britain, France and the Netherlands should reassert their control over those of their colonies occupied by Japan.

Stalin's efforts to spread communism abroad before the Second World War were well known. The big question that remained unanswered was how much effort Stalin would now put into promoting revolution in the Third World, where colonies were beginning to demand independence and independent countries, such as Egypt and Iran, wanted less Western interference in their affairs. Here, Stalin's secret archives have provided some fascinating insights.

Western and Soviet interests in the countries of the Third World were very different. Broadly speaking, the West wanted to protect its stake across the board, in large part because it was heavily dependent on the import of raw materials from the Third World and exports to them; the Soviet Union, on the other hand, wanted to deprive the West of those resources, less because it needed them itself, but because by doing so it would weaken "the capitalist system." Moscow had the considerable advantage of only having to invest effort where circumstances encouraged it to think gains could be made.

Initially, Stalin focused his attention on Asia. In 1946, while he was still seeking an accord with the West on European issues and Japan, Stalin wrote to the leader of the communists that he had abandoned in northern Iran. In his letter he explained that "We decided to withdraw troops from Iran and China in order . . . to unleash the liberation movement in the colonies . . ." Less than four years later Stalin would use the same ploy in Korea.[28]

Meanwhile, Mao Zedong's communist armies, literally, continued to gain ground in China, helped by Stalin's decision to hand over to them the massive stocks of arms that Soviet forces had taken from Japanese troops that had surrendered to them in Manchuria in August 1945. In late 1946, Truman was reluctantly coming to accept the view that Chiang Kai-shek's Nationalists were corrupt and no amount of American backing would turn them into a credible government. The implication was that the United States might have to accept a communist victory in China, an outcome that many Americans would find abhorrent. For the immediate future, however, Europe remained at the heart of Stalin's concerns.

4 Getting Colder

Germany—Divisions Deepen

Markus Wolf, who later became head of the East German Foreign Intelligence Service, was in the first group of German communists who, in May 1945, flew into Berlin from Moscow, where they had sought sanctuary in the thirties.

"Our task," he explained to me when I interviewed him in 2005, "was to establish a broad anti-Nazi coalition that would attract voters across the whole country. We were told that the German road to socialism would be long, but it was much rougher than we expected. Few people felt guilt for what had happened under Hitler and nearly all of them hated the Russians." Given this mood, Moscow agreed with Walter Ulbricht, the leader of the German communist party, that the communists had to consolidate their power quickly.

The bad example set by the Russians worked to the advantage of the Allies as they began rebuilding democracy in their zones from the grass roots upwards. This process opened the way for a heated debate over unification that was won by Konrad Adenauer, the leader of the Christian Democrats. His priority was to create a new West Germany that could become strong and responsible through being a democratic and free-market state tightly bound to the West. Only when West Germany had become a strong power, Adenauer argued, would Moscow accept unification.

Three months before the war ended, Stalin was telling a visiting Czechoslovak delegation that "our allies will try to save the Germans and conspire with them (against us)."[1] In September 1946, Secretary of State Byrnes declared that Germany's future lay with the West. Contrary to what Roosevelt had told Stalin, Byrnes said that American troops would stay in Germany so long as any other occupying force remained there. For Stalin this meant that within a few years a revived and powerful West German economy could be adding its weight to an Anglo-American crusade against the Soviet Union.

Stalin's concerns only grew more intense as the political tide in Germany turned against the Soviet Union. The first post-war elections in Germany took place in the Soviet zone in September 1946. "The result of these municipal elections was quite a shock for Moscow," Wolf recalled. "Even with Soviet backing, the SED only won 50% of the vote; the Communists alone would probably have won less than 20%."

The deepening split over Germany reflected the fact that there was no mutually acceptable solution to the German problem. The main western interest was, in the words of one British official, to make "the Russians appear to the German public as the saboteurs of German unity";[2] the main Soviet interest was to hold out the prospect of unification in order to prevent the establishment of a new West German state.

Economic Vulnerabilities

"General Winter" played a major role in ending two of Europe's greatest military adventures—Napoleon's incursions into Russia in 1812 and Hitler's in 1941. In 1946/47, the "General" inflicted the worst winter in living memory across the whole of Europe. The developments this extreme weather set in motion chilled a frosty relationship into a very Cold War.

The first challenge stemmed from the fact that America's main ally, Britain, was on the verge of bankruptcy. In February 1947, the British government informed Washington that it could no longer support Greece (which was under threat from communist insurgents) or Turkey (which had only recently staved off Soviet pressure for a base on the Turkish Straits). There were no longer three superpowers, just two.

In front of a joint session of Congress on March 12, the president declared that the United States had "to support free peoples who are resisting subjugation by armed minorities or by outside pressures."[3] Winning support for what became known as the Truman Doctrine was not easy—as since 1946, isolationist Republicans had controlled Congress. Truman acknowledged privately that he had to hype the threat in order to get the $400 million he needed to shore up Greece and Turkey.

Although the word was not mentioned, this was the beginning of "containment." At this juncture, however, "containment" took on a wholly unexpected dimension, as the president was forced to face the specter of all of Western Europe collapsing into chaos. Fortunately, his new secretary of state was General

George Marshall, a man of commanding presence and one highly respected for his vision and drive.

After six weeks of fruitless discussions in Moscow on the German problem, Marshall had a private meeting with Stalin in the Kremlin. As a rule, Stalin told him, "when people had exhausted themselves in dispute, they recognized the necessity for compromise."[4] Marshall sensed Stalin was stringing out the negotiations in the hope that the Western zones would soon plunge into chaos.

Nothing has emerged from the Soviet archives to suggest that this was Stalin's aim; he may have simply been holding out for the reparations he wanted. Be that as it may, the terrible economic hardship Marshall saw in West Germany reinforced his conviction that urgent action was needed to prevent the country from becoming uncontrollable. Shortly after his return to Washington, he launched the idea of an economic recovery program, for all of Europe—which was also open to the Soviet Union. It soon became known as the Marshall Plan.

Initially, Stalin thought the Plan might be advantageous for the Soviet Union and the countries of Eastern Europe. Soon, however, he came to the conclusion that it was aimed at drawing Eastern Europe into the Western orbit. When he received reliable intelligence in June that the West wanted to exclude the Soviet Union from the program, Molotov was ordered to pull out of the conference in Paris where the Europeans were trying to coordinate their position.[5] Stalin not only barred his East European satellites from taking part, but also the still independent Czechoslovakia. As Jan Masaryk, the Czech foreign minister at the time described it, "I went to Moscow as the foreign minister of an independent sovereign state and I returned as a Soviet slave."[6]

Stalin's concerns about American intentions were reinforced by an article in the July issue of *Foreign Affairs* on "The Sources of Soviet Conduct," published under the pseudonym of "X." It was soon revealed that the article had been written by George Kennan, the author of the "Long Telegram," who was now in charge of policy planning in the State Department.

Kennan argued that, because communism contained within it "the seeds of its own decay," the United States did not need to defeat the Soviet Union, only to outlast it. America's policy towards the Soviet Union should therefore be "a long-term, patient but firm and vigilant containment of Russian expansive tendencies."[7] He called for the defense and support of key regions in the world, such as Western Europe. Although he intended that this should be done politically and economically, not militarily, he did not say so explicitly.

In September, Walter Lippmann, the most distinguished columnist of his day, responded with a sharp critique on containment in an article entitled "The Cold War," which did much to popularize that term. He argued that American foreign policy should be guided by realism, with decisions being based on a case-by-case analysis of American national interests, not the application of general principles presumed to be universal. If that distinction was ignored, Lippmann said, America would find itself drawn into wars on behalf of ambiguous causes that produced inconclusive outcomes.

Although Truman remained opposed to the militarization of the Cold War, the United States was beginning to give more attention to the military aspects of containment. In July, the month Kennan's article was published, Congress approved the National Security Act. For the first time, the United States would have a Department of Defense, a Joint Chiefs of Staff, a National Security Council and a Central Intelligence Agency.

Militarily, however, the United States was not as powerful as Truman had imagined. In April 1947 he was profoundly shocked to learn from the newly formed Atomic Energy Commission that the number of atomic bombs in the American stockpile was "zero." In terms of usable atomic bombs, the number was correct. The United States did have the components for constructing about ten bombs, but in order for these to work they would literally have to be glued together.[8]

The number was so small because America's extremely expensive uranium enrichment plants had been closed down soon after the war. Truman could take comfort from the fact that the plutonium plants had already resumed full production and the atomic stockpile would soon grow. Nevertheless, by July 1947, there were still only enough components for thirteen bombs.

But there were no indications that Stalin was preparing for war.

Two Hostile Camps

Within six months—from the autumn of 1947 to the following spring—the erstwhile allies had split into two hostile camps. The confrontation would no longer be between two superpowers, but between two alliances—and the members of each would be the source of endless headaches and occasional nightmares for their respective patrons.

The Truman Administration took the lead and began shaping what would later become the Western Alliance. It firmly believed that if containment was to work it would not be enough for the Western Europeans to recover economically. Their lack of unity, which was largely responsible for the failure to check the rise of Nazi Germany, must not be allowed to continue. As a precondition for Marshall Aid, Washington insisted on the sixteen Western European recipients establishing an Organization of European Economic Cooperation, to develop long-term economic cooperation and reduce trade barriers—not only between the Europeans themselves, but also with the United States.

On September 22, 1947, the day on which the West Europeans finalized their request for aid, Stalin set about tightening control over his own camp, where his "united front" policies had not brought the communists the gains he had hoped. Andrei Zhdanov, a leading member of his Politburo, summoned the main European communist parties (six from Eastern Europe, plus the French and Italians) to a meeting at Szklarska Poreba, a small spa in southwestern Poland, not far from the Czechoslovak border.

Zhdanov began the meeting by asking each of the parties to describe the situation they faced. There was a lot of uncertainty about how quickly the communists could consolidate their grip in Eastern Europe. The Hungarian delegate, for instance, explained it was still an open question whether his country would become a people's democracy or a bourgeois democracy. Having heard the speakers out, Zhdanov then told them that there was no longer any uncertainty as the world was now split into "two major camps."[9]

Stalin had decided that the time had come to consolidate communist power across the whole of Eastern Europe. The communist parties in France and Italy (along with that of Czechoslovakia) were also ordered to free themselves from coalition government and to seek more power. Towards the end of 1947, waves of violent, communist-led strikes disrupted industry in Italy and almost brought the French Fourth Republic to its knees.

Despite the worsening atmosphere, Truman was still confident that long-term containment, mainly economic and political, could work. "As long as we can out-produce the world, can control the sea and can strike inland with the atomic bomb," Secretary of Defense Forrestal observed in December 1947, "we can assume certain risks otherwise unacceptable."[10]

Lining Up

When Soviet-backed communists staged a coup in Prague on February 25, 1948, there was consternation in the West, as this was the seizure of a democratic state that was not occupied by Soviet troops. For Stalin, however, the existence of an independent Czechoslovakia, posed a serious threat because it created an enormous kink in his Iron Curtain—stretching from the American zone of Germany right through to the frontier of the Soviet Union itself, thus splitting his security zone in two. Czechoslovakia was also one of the main sources of uranium for his atomic bomb program.

Stalin nevertheless understood that the Prague coup had given a great impetus to the development of an Atlantic alliance. He knew from the first-rate intelligence reaching him from Soviet spies within the British Foreign Office that the Brussels Treaty—which would be signed on March 17—would be directed against the Soviet Union, not Germany.

This treaty was the brain-child of Ernest Bevin, the visionary British foreign secretary, who for years had struggled to prevent the communists from gaining power within British trade unions. The treaty brought together Britain, France and the Benelux in an organization to coordinate the defense of Western Europe. With that in place, as Bevin knew, it would be easier for the Americans to discuss with them the creation of "an Atlantic security system."

On that same day, Truman told Congress that events in Czechoslovakia showed that the Soviet Union had a clear design to take the rest of Europe. This was "one of those moments in world history," he said, when "it is far wiser to act than to hesitate."[11] His speech impelled Congress to approve selective military conscription and the Marshall Plan.

From April 1948 to June 1952, the United States provided economic aid at a rate that has not been seen before or since—on average 1.1% of America's gross national product each year, which would be roughly equal to the expenditure of $550 billion between 2003 and 2007.[12] Although this was less than the Europeans had asked for, it successfully sped economic recovery and gave an impetus to European thinking about the need for economic integration—an initial step on the long road toward the creation of the European Union.

Despite the fact that Stalin was now saying that there were two hostile camps, he was still not keen on confrontation on all fronts at all times. On February 10, Stalin once more changed tack on Greece. He told Tito that the time had come to abandon the communist guerrillas as they could not win. Continued support for them would only complicate Moscow's already difficult relations with the Americans and British, who "will spare no effort" to keep Greece in their sphere.[13]

Stalin also moved quickly to dissuade Sweden from abandoning its neutrality and aligning itself militarily with the West. He did this through a treaty signed on April 6 with his recent enemies the Finns. It was the terms of this treaty that gave birth to the pejorative term "Finlandization," implying that a country was not neutral, but merely a "protectorate. "Over the years, however, the Finns cleverly exploited their new closer ties with the Soviet Union to their economic and political advantage.

A key test of wills was already underway in Italy where there was a real possibility that the two million-strong Italian Communist Party would win the general election in April. The Papacy directed an unprecedented campaign against the communists; at the same time, the CIA embarked on its first "political influence" operation, channeling $2–3 million, a considerable sum in those days, to non-communist parties.

Years earlier, Stalin had doubted the influence of the Catholic Church and jokingly asked, "How many divisions has the Pope?" The answer, in 1948, was "more than the Italian Communist Party." The Christian Democrats won an overall majority, for the first and only time after the war.

5 Becoming More Military

The Berlin Blockade

Stalin was deeply concerned that the Allies were getting closer to creating a Federal Republic of Germany that would be aligned with the West. He also knew they would soon introduce a new currency, the Deutschmark, into their zones. The new currency was intended to stamp out inflation and revitalize the economy of the Western zones, but it would also undermine that of the Soviet zone.

From Stalin's archives nothing has come to light to suggest that he really expected to be able to stop this process. All indications are that his real aim was to find a suitable moment to force the allies to withdraw from Berlin, so that he could consolidate his control over eastern Germany.[1]

The Americans feared that if Stalin did try to eject them from Berlin, they were ill prepared to stop him. "We are playing with fire while we have nothing with which to put it out," Secretary of State Marshall told the National Security Council in February 1948. Nearly all of the 135,000 American troops in Germany were tied up with occupation duties and the sole division capable of fighting had just twelve tanks.[2] Indeed, following the rapid demobilization in 1945–46 the Americans had no significant force anywhere in the world that was ready to go to war.

In March, Marshal Vassily Sokolovsky, the commander of Soviet forces in Germany, pulled out of the Allied Control Council, and the Soviet authorities began interfering with the flow of supplies into West Berlin. On June 7, tensions rose further, following the Western powers' decision to allow "their" Germans to begin drafting a constitution for a federal German state, one that would be economically integrated into Western Europe and soon become a major beneficiary of Marshall Aid.

When the Allies introduced their new Deutschmark on June 18, Stalin began to implement his contingency plans. While closing the borders between the Soviet and Western zones and further tightening the flow of supplies to West Berlin, Sokolovsky moved most of his troops, which in the past year had increased to around 250,000, from the central and eastern parts of the Soviet zone, up to the Inner-German border and around Berlin—and he did so with a speed that surprised the Americans.

Although divided into four Allied zones, Berlin still functioned as a single entity, run by the Berlin city assembly that was headed by a mayor who was a non-communist from West Berlin. Despite much Soviet pressure, the assembly approved the use of the new Deutschmark in the Western sectors of the city, and the even newer Soviet Ostmark in East Berlin.

Shocked by this turn of events, Sokolovsky rang Molotov in Moscow for instructions. He was told to do nothing to provoke military confrontation. Instead, the Soviets decided from the morning of June 24 to impose a blockade on West Berlin by cutting it off from East Berlin and the surrounding Soviet zone. All road, rail and canal routes into West Berlin were severed—but air travel was left alone. After all, Stalin wanted concessions from the West, not another war. The CIA's reporting from Berlin confirmed that this was the case.

Stalin judged that the Allies had little hope of airlifting essential supplies to the two million West Berliners. Although the Western press leapt to the conclusion that the B-29 bombers Truman had immediately dispatched to Europe could be used to launch an atomic attack, they could not. We do not know whether Stalin knew this was a bluff, but he stuck to his course, believing time was on his side.[3]

But the airlift surprised everyone—it soon came to be seen as one of the wonders of the modern world. American and British air forces broke all records when, in a single day in April 1949, some 1,400 planes brought supplies into the city. Also, despite the best Soviet efforts, East Berliners succeeded in smuggling substantial amounts of food to their relatives and friends in the Western sector. The West Berliners themselves made it clear through their stoic efforts and mass rallies that they wished to remain part of the Western world.

Stalin had confidently told Western ambassadors in August 1948 that he would lift the blockade if the West withdrew the new currency and stopped all progress towards the creation of a new West German state. Just nine months later, Stalin wanted the West to lift its counter-blockade, which was now seriously affecting the whole Soviet zone. As is so often the case in diplomatic crises, a face-saving solution was devised. The two blockades were lifted simul-

The Berlin Blockade—A British view of Stalin master-minding the negotiations, September 1948. (British Cartoon Archive, courtesy of the *Daily Express*)

taneously on May 12, and arrangements were made for the foreign ministers of the Four Powers to discuss the German problem. Neither side cherished any hope of an agreement.

The Federal Republic was established just eleven days after the end of the blockade; the German Democratic Republic (still widely known as East Germany) followed five months later. Allied forces remained in the west and Soviet forces in the east. There were now two Germanys.

General Clay, the America commander in Germany, wrote in his last dispatch to Washington on May 27, 1949, that throughout Europe Berlin had become "the symbol of our determination to resist communist expansion."[4] It was also more than that. The military presence of the Western Allies in Berlin reflected their refusal to accept the permanent division of Germany and Europe as a whole—this was a political challenge to Moscow that would resonate through the rest of the Cold War.

Communist Triumphs

When Liu Shaoqi, Mao's deputy, met with Stalin in Moscow in July 1949, Stalin made it very clear that he was unwilling to take any action that could give the United States a pretext for attacking the Soviet Union. If another war were to start, he said, "the Russian people would not understand us. Moreover, they would chase us away."[5]

In August 1949, after the Soviet Union had broken America's atomic monopoly, a full year before most American experts had predicted, Stalin began to feel more confident. Although this first bomb was an exact copy of the one the Americans dropped on Nagasaki (the details had been provided by Klaus Fuchs), the success of the test was an extraordinary testament to the brilliance of Soviet scientists and the ruthless ability of the Soviet system to mobilize resources. Stalin was so certain it would be successful that even before it took place he showed Liu's delegation a film of what purported to be the test.

A month before the Soviet test, Truman had a major change of heart about nuclear strategy. Having failed to secure international control over nuclear technology, he decided that America "must be strongest in atomic weapons."[6] By this he did not simply mean that America should have more atomic bombs than the Russians, but that it should have the ability to fight a prolonged atomic war on the lines that Clifford and Elsey had outlined in September 1946. This decision injected enormous momentum into the arms race.

Less than two months after losing their atomic monopoly the Americans were faced with another spectacular communist success, this time in China. On October 1, 1949, Mao Zedong, having ousted General Chiang Kai-shek and his Nationalists from the mainland, proclaimed the People's Republic of China and began extending its control into Tibet. The Americans were shaken by the arrival of the inevitable and fearful of what else it might portend.

Mao was not just a highly successful communist revolutionary, he was a leader with a profound understanding of China's history. As the Nationalists were heading for defeat, Mao did what earlier emperors had done. He read and re-read the massive dynastic histories of China that so trenchantly analyzed how power had been won and lost. While recognizing Stalin as a great leader and the head of the world communist movement, Mao regarded himself as someone who had paved the way for communism in the Third World.

Behind the scenes, there was friction. Mao deeply resented the fact that the Bolsheviks had not kept their promise to return the 800,000 square kilometers (half a million square miles) of Siberian territory that China had been forced to cede to Russia in the 18th and 19th centuries. During the more recent past, advice from Stalin's representatives in China had led the Chinese communists into some costly disasters. In addition, Mao was deeply embittered by Stalin's decision in 1945 to recognize the Nationalists as the legitimate government of all of China.

In late 1949, Mao was finally invited to Moscow, where his discussions with Stalin were prolonged and difficult. Stalin had compelled the Nationalists to "restore" the "Russian rights" in northeastern China (see map on p. 28), ostensibly to help the Soviet Union defend China against Japan; recognize Mongolia as an independent country; and grant extra-territorial rights in the far western province of Xinjiang, where there were deposits of valuable minerals, including uranium. Now that the communists were victorious, Mao argued, a new and more balanced treaty would be appropriate.

Though infuriated by Mao's early demonstration of his "independence," Stalin realized he would have to make concessions so that the world at large would see unity in an expanding communist world. In the end, Mao did get a defense pact with the Soviet Union and some much needed economic aid, though not on generous terms. Even more demeaning from Mao's point of view was that Stalin insisted on retaining Soviet extraterritorial rights in China. These included keeping the railway and the naval base in Manchuria for the next decade and the establishment of joint Soviet-Chinese companies to mine minerals in Xinjiang province.

The Sino-Soviet Treaty, signed in the Kremlin on February 14, 1950, marked one of the biggest shifts in the international balance of power since the end of the Second World War. In a trice, the world political map had changed—the communist alliance now occupied 50% more of the globe's surface.

But these were early days, and Stalin did not grasp the full significance of Mao's victory. Before long, Mao would become a force to be reckoned with in the international communist movement.

Preparing for Trouble

As the band played "I've got plenty of nothing," the representatives of the United States, Canada and ten Western European states settled down in Washington on April 4, 1949, to sign the multiple copies of the North Atlantic Treaty. The music was highly appropriate. Although the Americans were for the first time committing themselves to the defense of Western Europe, Secretary of

State Dean Acheson had assured Congress that the treaty did not commit the United States to deploying a substantial number of troops in Europe.

The original purpose of the treaty Lord Ismay, the first Secretary-General of Nato, later observed was "To keep the Americans in, the Germans down and the Russians out."[7] The night before the treaty was signed the British and French foreign ministers, reflecting Ismay's sentiment, voiced opposition to Germany's future membership of the Atlantic Alliance. Secretary of State Acheson told them that they would have to accept it. Five years later, they did so.

Having come to the conclusion that the world was divided into two hostile camps, Stalin had set about strengthening his armed forces. He poured yet more money into costly air defense. Radar networks were extended right around the country and work began on a first-rate interceptor (the Mig-15), powered by the latest jet engines, which Stalin thought the British had been mad to sell to him. Tens of thousands of anti-aircraft batteries were installed around cities and military facilities.

The Soviet long-range bomber force was also rapidly expanded so that it could attack the forward bases from which the Americans would launch their atomic attacks. Its new aircraft were exact copies of an American B-29 bomber that had been forced to land in Siberia during the war and Stalin had refused to return it. Large numbers of long-range bombers were needed, because for several years ahead they would have to use conventional, not atomic, bombs.

In strengthening his political grip over Eastern Europe Stalin faced a serious problem with the leader of the strongest military country within Eastern Europe—Marshal Tito of Yugoslavia. Tito, who was the only Eastern European leader to have liberated his country, felt entitled to make his own decisions, an attitude that outraged Stalin. When he failed to cut Tito down to size, Stalin tried to get rid of him.

Four days after the beginning of the Berlin Blockade, Stalin severed relations with Yugoslavia, believing that just by "wagging his finger" he would be able to unseat Tito.[8] He failed, and Tito further humiliated Stalin by moving closer to the West. In 1950, the United States began to supply economic aid to Yugoslavia. Over the next five years, the aid would total $1.2 billion (which was almost as much as West Germany received in Marshall Aid). American assistance even included arms.

To deter anyone else from stepping out of line, Stalin set about terrorizing the East European communist parties through a series of show trials that were a sickening replay of the "Great Purge" he had orchestrated in the late thirties.

The sacrificial victims were portrayed as having committed the Tito-like offenses of insubordination and "ideological deviationism," even when they had not done so.

Ironically, the purges were the least terrible in Poland where nationalism was strongest and the Poles were known to be fearsome fighters. By the end of the forties, the communists controlled Poland, but Poland was far from being communist.

Stalin was similarly cautious with the East Germans, mainly because he did not wish to antagonize their fellow countrymen in West Germany. In 1944, he is purported to have said that "communism fitted Germany as a saddle fitted a cow."[9] Although Stalin withdrew his support for the "German road to socialism" and the communist party was told to tighten its grip on the country, he sanctioned no purges of the party or show trials of its members.

No Rush to Arms

In January 1950, Truman announced that the United States would continue to develop the hydrogen bomb (or H-bomb as it was generally known), which would be massively more powerful than the atomic bomb. This was being done, the president said, because it could not allow its menacing adversary to gain a lead in this field. Truman did not know that in June 1948 Soviet scientists had told Stalin that they could build a bomb that would be far more powerful than anything the Americans had. A delighted Stalin immediately gave them the go-ahead.[10]

Truman's top scientific advisers had strenuously opposed opening up competition in this field. To assuage them, he instructed the National Security Council to prepare a paper outlining the role these new weapons could play in American policy. This paper, "U.S. Objectives and Programs for National Security" (widely known as NSC-68), reached him in April.

The communists, the paper noted, were already contesting American and Western interests around the world. They had just gained control of China and serious communist insurgencies were underway in Indochina and Malaya. Within a few years, the Soviet Union would have developed a substantial stockpile of atomic bombs. "The year of maximum danger" was said to be 1954, as by then the Soviet Union would be strong enough to attack Western Europe.

The Soviet Union could only be contained, the paper argued, if America had a "preponderance of power"—both conventional and nuclear. Without that, "containment—which is in effect a policy of calculated and gradual coercion—is no more than a policy of bluff." As the United States was at least four times richer than the Soviet Union, it could easily afford to pursue a confrontational policy.[11]

Truman adamantly rejected the paper's recommendations because he disliked the idea of provoking confrontation and hoped that his possession of the H-bomb would itself ensure that the communists remained cautious. Instead, he tried to curb military expenditure. He did accept, however, that intelligence was of the utmost importance—it was urgent that the American government be watching closely for any signs that the Russians were preparing to invade Western Europe.

To this end, in September 1949, the CIA and SIS, the British Secret Intelligence Service, began trying to infiltrate groups of émigrés into Eastern Europe and the Soviet Union. Nearly all them were caught and quickly executed for being foreign spies—they had been betrayed by Kim Philby, a senior SIS officer who was working for Moscow.

As it became increasingly clear that the Soviet Union was not a *status quo* power, but a global competitor, it was difficult for Truman to sustain his restrained approach. Nonetheless, that left open the question of how he would respond. It was soon clear that the American people found it easier to agree on the general crusading principles they wished to guide their foreign policy than on the cold specifics of what was and what was not in America's interests.

In May 1950, Truman put his foot on the beginning of a long and slippery slope into the quagmire of Vietnam. The Soviet Union and China had just recognized the communist insurgents as the legitimate government of the country, and China was now supplying them with arms across their common border. Truman responded by financing French efforts to regain control of Indochina.

Truman also provided financial assistance to the British to suppress the insurgency led by the Malayan Communist Party, which was basically a Chinese ethnic movement, rather than a nationalist one. The British argued that if Indochina fell to the communists, so too would Malay, which produced half the world's natural rubber and a third of its tin. The spread of communism had to be checked in Indochina.

One month later, war broke out in Korea. From then on, the Cold War would be a much more military confrontation.

6 Korean Blunders

Stalin's New Interest

"America's primary weapons," Stalin jokingly told Zhou Enlai, China's foreign minister, after the Korean War had been raging for two years, "... are stockings, cigarettes, and other merchandise. They want to subjugate the world, yet they cannot subdue little Korea."[1] There is no doubt that Stalin relished seeing the Americans and their allies failing to win that war, but he had no idea of what a heavy price the Soviet Union would pay for his brief satisfaction.

The Russians had been eyeing Korea since the 1860s, when China ceded southern Siberia to Russia and Korea became a new neighbor, with the two counties sharing a small frontier strip on the Sea of Japan. As agreed with Truman at Potsdam, Stalin declared war on Japan in August 1945. Soviet forces moved against the Japanese in both Manchuria and Korea. Since there was no natural dividing line on the Korean peninsula, Soviet and American forces were to meet at the 38th parallel. Soviet troops did not move south of this line, even though the Americans arrived a month late.

The division of Korea provided the Soviet Union with a buffer zone in the Far East. As in Europe, the two zones soon developed differently. To head their regime in the north, Moscow brought in Kim Il Sung, a refugee who had for several years commanded a Korean unit in the Soviet army and was a KGB agent. In the south, the Americans installed Syngman Rhee, an equally authoritarian figure, who had lived in the United States for the past thirty-five years.

After Stalin rejected nationwide elections in 1948, Rhee was inaugurated as president of the Republic of Korea. A month later, Stalin made Kim president of the new Democratic People's Republic of Korea, and named the southern city of Seoul, not Pyongyang, as its capital.[2] In both states clashes between left- and right-wing factions were exacerbated by economic hardship and political repression. With the death toll from this factional violence moving towards

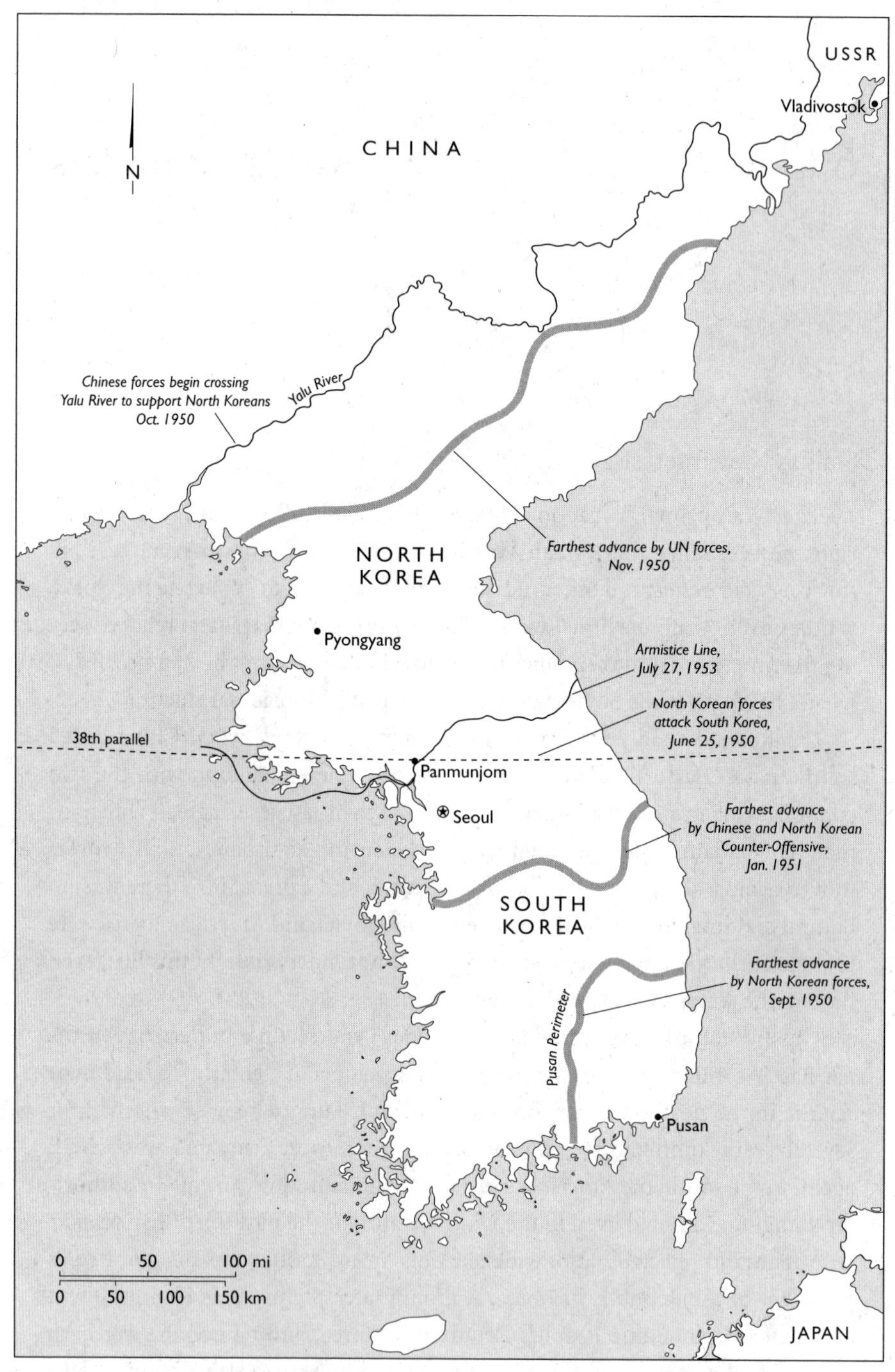

The Korean War, 1950–53. (Tokyo and all southern Japanese cities are less than 1,000 km [600 miles] from South Korea)

100,000, Kim and Rhee each hoped they could gain control of the other half of the country. There were sizeable military incursions across the 38th parallel in each direction.

As Stalin expected the Americans to help Japan re-emerge as a military power, he began strengthening his forces in Vladivostok and the island of Sakhalin that faced northern Japan. In 1949, during the Berlin Crisis, Stalin rather craftily withdrew Soviet troops from North Korea. And, just as he hoped, the Americans followed suit. This could open up an opportunity for the communists in North Korea to seize control of all of Korea. This would not only remove the Americans from the mainland of Asia, but in the event of war, Japan would be caught in a Soviet pincer, vulnerable to Soviet air offensives from both the north and the south of Korea.

The Pentagon was not oblivious to this threat. On May 10, 1949, two days before an agreement was reached on lifting the Berlin Blockade, the first American reconnaissance flight was made into Soviet territory. The aim was to find out whether the latest Soviet bombers had been based in the Kurile Islands, which were close to northern Japan. A second flight was made over Vladivostok, the major Soviet city in the Far East, on March 10, 1950, some three and a half months before the outbreak of the Korean War.[3]

The balance of power in the Far East changed dramatically in October 1949 when Mao led the communists to victory in China. Even so, in mid-December 1949, Stalin rejected Mao's request for an alliance on the grounds that it would give the Americans an excuse to abrogate the Yalta agreement, to which Moscow still attached such importance.

On January 6, 1950, Stalin changed his mind. He informed Mao, who was still in Moscow, that he was ready to conclude a treaty. Less than a week later, on January 12, Secretary of State Acheson made America's first public statement about its defense perimeter in Asia. It ran, he said, from the Aleutian Islands, through Japan and the Ryuku Islands to the Philippines. He made no mention of Korea or the island of Taiwan (to which Chiang Kai-shek and his Chinese Nationalist government had just fled). That proved to be a fatal error.

Just eighteen days later, Stalin gave Kim a tentative green light to invade the South. In a telegram he warned Kim that "such a large matter . . . needs large preparation . . . so that there would not be too great a risk."[4] Soon a team of Soviet generals were working with Kim and his military commanders to develop the plans for seizing the South. On February 14, the Soviet Union and China signed the mutual defense pact mentioned above.

The Korean War

Kim secretly visited Moscow in April 1950 to plead for the final go-ahead. This time, Stalin was more positive. The new Soviet alliance with China, he said, had made the Americans even more hesitant to challenge the communists in Asia. "Information" (i.e. intelligence) from the United States confirmed that "the prevailing mood is not to interfere."[5]

This information was probably more important for Stalin than the fact that he had just tested an atomic bomb. He had no atomic weapons with which he could attack Western Europe, whereas Truman had plenty with which to attack the Soviet Union. At the outbreak of the Korean War, however, the United States had a total of only seven active divisions, the nearest of which was in Japan.

Stalin informed Kim that the Soviet Union could not get involved in the war because it faced "serious challenges elsewhere . . . especially in the West,"[6] (where the previous year Nato had come into being). If necessary, Kim would have to rely on the Chinese, who shared his wish to dislodge the Americans from the Asian mainland. He agreed, however, to provide arms for the attack and more advisers to help plan it.

For almost a year Mao had also been helping Kim by sending back some 60,000 ethnic Korean troops (and their weapons) who had been fighting in Mao's own army. In May 1950, Mao promised Chinese support to Kim if things went wrong.[7]

Kim launched his offensive on June 25 and quickly pushed the South Koreans back from the 38th parallel down to an enclave around Pusan at the southeastern tip of the Korean peninsula. Coming after the Prague coup, the Berlin Blockade and the communist takeover of China, this development stunned Truman's administration. It was yet another move in a global communist offensive.

With Moscow having withdrawn from the Security Council (because the communists had not been given China's seat), the Americans had no difficulty getting full UN backing for their intervention. The commander Truman appointed was General Douglas MacArthur, the hero of the war in the Pacific and currently the "viceroy" of Japan. American reinforcements began to arrive in Korea, while bombers capable of carrying atomic bombs were flown into bases in Japan.

By late August, Stalin felt all was going according to plan. "The United States was set to squander its military prestige and moral authority," he told Klement Gottwald, the president of communist Czechoslovakia. "If events forced China to come to North Korea's aid the United States would be embroiled in a protracted war. That would not only postpone a third world war indefinitely, but it would give the time necessary to consolidate socialism in Europe."[8]

By late September, MacArthur's forces were rapidly advancing towards the 38th parallel. Meanwhile, at America's instigation, the UN had established a commission on the re-unification of Korea. Moscow and Beijing were in no doubt about what the Americans had in mind—a reunified Korea under American control.

Just two weeks later, as MacArthur's forces were pushing the North Koreans up towards the Chinese frontier, Stalin called on Mao to honor his pledge. This sparked a heated debate among the Chinese leaders. On October 12, Stalin told Kim that the situation was "hopeless" and that he should evacuate all the troops and equipment he could to China and the Soviet Union.

The following day, the Chinese leaders did what Stalin had hoped they would—they agreed that they could not accept American forces along their frontier. They let it be known that if the Americans advanced farther, China would intervene. The Americans paid no heed. Two days later, on October 15, the first Chinese "volunteers" began crossing the Yalu River into North Korea, followed on November 26 by "waves" of troops from the main Chinese force. The American government was horrified by the implications of its catastrophic misjudgment.

The Chinese were soon forcing the Americans and their allies into a traumatic and bloody retreat back down the peninsula. They pushed on despite a vague threat by Truman to use the atomic bomb and by January 1951 were far to the south of the 38th parallel. Angered by his own miscalculation, General MacArthur publicly called for American attacks on China.

Truman feared any such attack could drag the United States into war with the Soviet Union. In April 1951, he in effect fired MacArthur, relieving him of all his duties as commander in both Korea and Japan. We now know that Truman was also fearful that Soviet actions would compel him to attack the Soviet Union. American intercepts had revealed that many of the Mig-15 fighters with Chinese markings that were attacking their aircraft were flown by Soviet pilots. Great efforts were made to prevent this intelligence leaking out. That would have been almost impossible had senior members of the Truman Administration known the full extent of Moscow's involvement in the war. By 1953, there were a total of 70,000 Soviet pilots, gunners and technicians in the North.[9]

Although the UN forces under the command of General Matthew Ridgeway were now facing not only the North Korean army, but a Chinese force of around a million men, they gradually regained the initiative. While the North Korean and Chinese armies still held a small amount of territory to the south of the 38th parallel on the western side of the peninsula, the UN forces made considerably greater gains to the north on the eastern side. But there a bloody stalemate ensued. Allied losses had been heavy—over 36,000 American and over 400,000 South Korean troops had been killed, and the war was not yet over.

Rehabilitating Japan

As Washington came to accept that it would "lose" China in the late forties, it hoped that Japan would once again become a bulwark against the Soviet Union in East Asia, as it had been against Russia in the early part of the century. The Emperor was rehabilitated and aid poured in to restart the country's ruined industries, which helped stem the rising tide of discontent that the Japanese communist party was exploiting.

Japan was still occupied by American troops, though few were fighting units. Once the Korean War started, however, Japan became a major base and an "unsinkable aircraft carrier" within easy striking distance of the Korean peninsula. The task of supplying allied forces fighting in Korea was eased because Japanese industry was quickly able to meet their needs, doubling its total output in just three years.

The Americans speeded up the negotiations between Japan and its former enemies on a peace treaty, which was concluded in 1951 on terms favorable to Japan. No reparations, for example, were paid to any of the countries Japan had fought against or occupied since it began expanding into Asia in the early 1930s. Unlike the West Germans, however, there were few Japanese who wished to see their country rearm, even for their own self-defense; the government did, however, accept that the Americans should continue to have bases in Japan and Okinawa.

At the end of the Korean War, America feared that the Japanese economy, which was highly dependent on trade, would slump into a deep recession that would inflame anti-Americanism. As other Asian countries still hated the Japanese for their earlier atrocities, the United States had to ease the restrictions it had imposed on Japanese trade with China. Gradually, the Japanese economic recovery got underway once more, aided by the fact that Japan, protected as they were by the Americans, was spending virtually nothing on defense.

Less Quiet on the Western Front

With the Americans tied up in Korea, the Allies were genuinely worried that the Russians might seize the opportunity to invade Western Europe, which was not well defended. Had Western Europe been invaded during Nato's first year the United States had the ability to destroy Soviet industry with the two to three hundred atomic bombs it had, while mobilizing a massive force to retake Europe. The Americans and their Allies would then probably have gone on to invade the Soviet Union and install a new regime, just as they had done in Germany a few years earlier.

Within three months of the outbreak of the Korean War Truman dispatched four American combat divisions to West Germany. By 1951, the buildup of American forces in Europe was in full swing. At the invitation of the French government, Nato based itself in Paris, with General Eisenhower, the first Supreme Allied Commander Europe (SACEUR), having his military headquarters not far from the capital. Within just three years the alliance was becoming a military force.

Truman began working on integrating West Germany into the alliance and preparing the way for German rearmament, a notion that truly disturbed Stalin. In March 1952, he responded with a diplomatic bombshell. In formal diplomatic notes he proposed to the Allies the creation of a united Germany—one that would be neutral, but would have its own forces. A month later, he sent another note that recognized the need for free German elections as the preconditions for establishing an all-German government.

Stalin was so confident that the West would reject his proposals that even before the Allies had replied he told Ulbricht, the East German communist leader, to press ahead with "building socialism."[10] This would help to consolidate his grip over this key part of his western flank. Stalin then set out to do the same in Czechoslovakia, the other country facing Nato forces in central Europe. There, he staged his biggest show trial in Eastern Europe. Its chief victim was Rudolf Slansky, the general secretary of the communist party itself. Slanky was ridiculously accused of being part of a Zionist conspiracy to destroy communism.

The Approaching Danger

With the outbreak of war, the creation of a "preponderance of power" swiftly became national policy in the United States. The defense budget soon tripled to nearly $50 billion a year, with America's armed forces rapidly expanded from 1.5 million to 3.6 million men. Uranium and plutonium production rose sharply and the output of atomic bombs surged. American war planners now pushed for the creation of a full war-fighting force by 1954, the date that NSC-68 had identified as the "year of maximum danger." In 1952, Nato countries undertook to build up a force of 100 divisions.

In addition, new technology enabled the Americans to make atomic bombs seven times more powerful than the one dropped on Hiroshima—even though they used the same amount of plutonium. At that time, the Americans already had some 800 atomic bombs, and probably a quarter of those were the new higher-powered ones. This was more than twice the number that, one year earlier, the Soviet General Staff had assumed were needed to destroy the Soviet Union.[11] The Strategic Air Command believed that it could deliver a coordinated attack that would leave "virtually all of Russia . . . a smoking, radiating ruin at the end of two hours."[12]

The continued public assertion by the Americans and Nato that 1954 would be "the year of maximum danger" kept Stalin on tenterhooks. As he had no intention of starting a war, he seems to have assumed that 1954 was the year when the West thought that it would be strong enough to attack and defeat the Soviet Union.

Stalin had also taken several steps to strengthen his defenses. At the end of 1950, Moscow alerted its East European allies to be prepared for war by the end of 1952, not 1954, which left some leeway for them to get ready in time.[13] While he encouraged the North Koreans and the Chinese to continue fighting in Korea, he had further expanded his army, which now totaled some 5 million men, with ground and air forces being strengthened in both Europe and the Far East. By late 1952, he had amassed about seventy atomic bombs and a small number of slow-moving planes that had the range to reach targets around the Soviet periphery.

At the same time, Stalin's colleagues felt he was becoming increasingly paranoid and unpredictable. At the beginning of 1953, Moscow announced the arrest of a group of "Kremlin doctors" on the trumped-up charge of planning to assassinate the Soviet leadership. Those who were Jewish were alleged to be agents of a Zionist organization based in New York. Stalin intended to implicate the American embassy in Moscow in the conspiracy, thus linking anti-Semitism with anti-Americanism. This would enable him to tighten his grip on the country as it approached the critical year of 1954. Had Stalin not died in

March 1953, heaven knows how many more people would have been killed in the purges he would have unleashed.[14]

As the Korean War dragged on, American and British reconnaissance flights began probing deep into Soviet territory. Altogether the international situation had become so tense, one senior Soviet official later wrote, that "Another turn of the screw might have led to disaster."[15]

Was the Cold War Unavoidable?

The answer is, unquestionably, "Yes."

The Big Three had fought Germany together not as allies championing a common cause, but as ideological rivals forced into partnership by extraordinarily rapacious adversaries. Through that war the Soviet Union and the United States had become superpowers who faced each other at several points around the globe. Sooner or later, they were likely to confront each other at one of them. Nevertheless, after all the suffering of the war both sides had a wish for peace.

The Americans generally, along with many West Europeans, felt that the Russians had fought splendidly and it should be possible to reach a real understanding with them as sensible fellow human beings. The Americans wanted to deal with the Soviet Union as just another great power—but one that was far more interested in a long-term accommodation with the United States, than in expansion and revolution.

Many Russians hoped that this is what would happen, but their country was controlled not just by a communist party, but one headed by Stalin. Stalin, certainly wanted peace, but in order to consolidate his gains, strengthen the Soviet Union and expand its influence abroad before another war between capitalism and communism became inevitable.

Maxim Litvinov, the former Soviet foreign minister, understood Stalin's thinking well. He had remained on good terms with him for some forty years, since helping him escape from some members of the working class in London who had taken exception to Stalin propositioning a local girl.[16] In June 1946, Litvinov once again took an extraordinary risk and warned the West of trouble ahead.

Litvinov told Richard Hottelet, the CBS correspondent in Moscow, that the "root cause" of the trouble "was the ideological conception prevailing here of the inevitability of conflict between the communist and capitalist worlds." The

Soviet leadership, he said, was aiming to build a post-war peace on "the outmoded concept of . . . the more [territory] you've got the safer you are." No Western concession would satisfy the Soviet leadership. As Litvinov had put it three weeks earlier to Walter Beddell Smith, the American ambassador, "I now feel the best that can be hoped for is a prolonged armed truce."[17]

Even though a Cold War was inevitable, it was still unclear how "armed" the "armed truce" would be. Russians often argue that had the West shown greater understanding of Stalin's legitimate security concerns, the Cold War would not have become so confrontational—and the Russian people would not have suffered so much. After all, they point out, Tsar Alexander I had been able to reach a settlement at the Congress of Vienna in 1815 that lasted for a century, with Russia having influence in Europe, while avoiding too much European meddling in Russian affairs.

It is true that Tsarist Russia had had some success in managing this difficult relationship. But its rulers were royal, its economy capitalist and it needed to be part of the European balance of power. Stalin, however, was not Alexander I and the Soviet Union no longer viewed the world as Russia had.

The steps that Stalin and Truman had taken to protect their respective positions had ratcheted up their suspicions of each other. Although the two sides were prone to misunderstand each other, usually it was their absolutely correct understanding of the other's intentions that generated such friction.

Nothing did more to intensify the confrontation, however, than Stalin's ill-judged Korean war. Containment now assumed a more military character, with the rapid increase in the number and power of atomic bombs leading to a change in strategy. Truman came to believe that American deterrence should henceforth be based on its ability to destroy not only Soviet industrial targets, but also a whole range of military ones, especially their nuclear forces, the airfields they used, their storage facilities and production plants.

Strategically, this judgment was like crossing the nuclear Rubicon. By 1952, the Chief of the Air Force was telling Truman that there were now five to six thousand targets that would have to be destroyed. Overwhelming nuclear superiority had become the goal of American deterrence.

Even with "a preponderance of power" it would never be easy for the Americans to decide what was in America's best interest and what was not. The choices would be painful because American military power was ill suited to fighting dedicated guerrilla forces on their home territory. And given the scale of political and social upheaval in the Third World, the United States was unlikely to be able to prevent further communist victories. To make matters worse, the United States was in no doubt that before long the Soviets would have fast aircraft able to attack targets in America with atomic weapons. This could bring to an end America's "splendid isolation" in a way that the Japanese attack on Pearl Harbor never had.

Many Americans have lamented their country's failure to exploit its atomic monopoly to secure a "satisfactory solution" to the problems that arose with the Soviet Union over Germany and Eastern Europe. But no one has been able to cogently explain how this was to be done—or to predict what the Soviet reaction to any such attempt would have been. The Soviet leadership would themselves soon face the question of what leverage could be gained with nuclear weapons, and similarly fail to find a satisfactory answer.

Following Stalin's death the big question in both Moscow and Washington was "Will it now be easier to reduce tension and the risk of war and, if so, on what terms?" This subject had just gained a new urgency because, in November 1952, the United States successfully tested its first thermonuclear device, which meant that before long it would have the H-bomb—a weapon that could be more than a thousand times more powerful than the atom bomb dropped on Hiroshima just seven years earlier.

Why Did It Last So Long?

“Bravo”—H-bomb test, Bikini Atoll in the Pacific, March 1, 1954. (U.S. Department of Defense)

7 Easing Tensions

New Leaders

By 1953, the Cold War had been transformed—not only by the death of Stalin and the advent of the H-bomb, but by the election of Dwight D. Eisenhower as America's new president.

Eisenhower had a rare combination of talent and authority. He was the only man ever invited by both parties to stand as their candidate. He chose the Republicans because he feared that they would otherwise lead the country back into isolationism. Eisenhower won with 55% of the popular vote and the Republicans managed to gain control of both houses of Congress for the first time in a quarter of a century.

During the war, Eisenhower had commanded the largest seaborne invasion force in history and had done well in handling the complex politics of the Alliance. He was widely known for his ability to spot an exaggeration a mile away. More recently, he had been highly successful as Nato's first Supreme Commander, doing much to boost morale in Western Europe. Thanks to his self-confidence, his belief in consensus and a measured pursuit of long-term policies, Eisenhower was able to bring an Olympian calm to the White House.

The mood in the Kremlin could hardly have been more different. The new leaders felt extremely vulnerable as Stalin had left them in a tense confrontation at a time when America's nuclear superiority was accelerating. Well aware of that, prime minister Georgi Malenkov turned a new page in Soviet diplomacy when he spoke at Stalin's funeral, declaring that "there is no dispute . . . which could not be settled by peaceful means with any country, including the United States."[1]

The new Soviet leaders faced acute problems at home as they began jostling for power in the vacuum left by Stalin's death. Two and a half million people were still in slave-labor camps, and the rest faced terrible shortages of food, housing and consumer goods. Most of the leaders judged that they could only retain control by creating a somewhat more humane form of socialism. Even Beria, the ruthless head of Stalin's secret police, soon began churning out proposals for far-reaching economic reforms, along with some political ones, too.[2]

Within two years, the Kremlin was in the hands of Nikita Khrushchev—a man whose character was distinctly different from that of Stalin and of Eisenhower. Although he had little formal education, he was a highly original, if at times undisciplined, thinker. He had risen to the top levels of the party under Stalin, but this meant that he had been, as he later confessed, "up to my elbows in blood."[3] He never forgave Stalin for making him an accomplice in his terrible crimes. His craving for redemption played no small part in his later denunciation of Stalin and his determination to realize the aspirations of communism not only in the Soviet Union, but in the Third World as well.

Khrushchev had come face-to-face with the harsh "capitalist exploitation" of the workers when, in the decade before the Bolshevik Revolution of 1917, he worked in Yuzovka, a Russian mining town founded by a Welshman called Hughes in the 19th century. But there he had also tasted a better life, as a relatively well-paid engineering fitter; he had a photographer take a picture of him and his wife for which he wore a black tie and evening jacket.[4] He wanted the Soviet people to prosper—not through the re-introduction of private enterprise, which was an anathema to him, but instead by exploiting planning and science.

Having virtually no experience of foreign affairs, he was haunted by Stalin's withering remark to his political heirs: "You'll see, when I'm gone the imperialistic powers will wring your necks like chickens."[5] To mask his deep sense of insecurity—and that of his country—Khrushchev bragged and threatened. His unpredictable ways of handling issues kept both his adversaries and his allies in doubt about his real aims.

In diplomacy, Khrushchev relished the idea of engaging in battle and then seeing what happens, as that could play to his often astute political instincts and visceral talent for intimidation. But like Eisenhower, he had endured too many of the horrors of one war to have an appetite for another. He never watched war films because he felt that "even the best war film is a lie."[6]

Eisenhower's "New Look"

Eisenhower inherited a country that felt beleaguered. The Americans were bogged down in Korea, and with signs that communist insurgency was spreading in Southeast Asia they feared they would be dragged into Korean-type imbroglios elsewhere in Asia or beyond. In Europe, relations with Nato countries were becoming more difficult. Although economic recovery was well underway, the Europeans were not willing to build up the large conventional forces needed to defend Europe; at the same time, the French bitterly opposed Germany's entry into Nato and the related issue of its rearmament.

In his first State of the Union message on February 2, Eisenhower proclaimed that "there is but one sure way to avoid total war, and that is to win the Cold War"—a statement he believed would "scare the Russians to hell."[7] The chances of his remarks having that effect were greatly enhanced by the fact that Soviet Intelligence knew that Washington was seriously considering using nuclear weapons to force the Korean War to a close.[8]

While America was unquestionably the predominant nuclear power, it would not be long before the Russians could pose a nuclear threat—not merely around its periphery, but also to the continental United States itself. Within just two or three years Soviet bombers were expected to have the necessary range and would probably carry H-bombs.

The Americans had already started preparing for such an eventuality. In 1951, the Federal Civil Defense Administration began establishing community bomb shelters and instructing people how to protect themselves, which it did with the help of such films as *You Can Beat the A-Bomb* and the famous *Duck and Cover*—which, with a cheery soundtrack, told children to do just that as soon as they saw the flash of a nuclear blast.[9]

America, Eisenhower firmly believed, could never win the Cold War by becoming a "garrison state," but only by being the beacon of the "free world," sustained by a flourishing economy and the creation of a more just society. Government revenue, therefore, should be invested in education, health-care and welfare, not wasted on weapons. This would require urgent cuts in America's defense expenditure—which by 1953 was consuming over 17% of America's GNP, compared with less than 5% in 1946.

On April 16, in response to various statements from Moscow suggesting changes in Soviet foreign policy, Eisenhower gave his speech on the "Chance for Peace," in which he asked what the Soviet Union was willing to do. Was it willing to use its influence to bring about a truce in Korea and peace in Indochina, would it allow self-determination in Eastern Europe and agree to arms control under stringent inspection?

Several days later the new Soviet leadership responded by printing the president's speech in full in *Pravda.* The accompanying editorial asked the United States to explain what it would do to achieve the peace it sought. For its part, the Kremlin said it was ready for serious discussions and negotiations.

The Solarium Project

Shortly thereafter, Eisenhower called for a review of his options in dealing with the Soviet Union. This was the Solarium Project, so called because the first meetings of the leading participants were held in the solarium at the White House. It produced the most wide-ranging study on American policy towards the Soviet Union undertaken by any administration. In the early summer of 1953, three teams of experts (civilian and military) spent over a month working up the best possible arguments to support three different options.[10]

The first option was for America to be able to contain communism and outlast it; the second was how to deter any Soviet or Soviet-sponsored aggression across "lines" that the United States would specify; while the third option was what would be involved in going on the offensive and "rolling back" communist control where it had already been established.

Eisenhower's summary of the reports by these three teams in July was as trenchant as it was lucid. He would not, he said, pursue any strategy for which he could not win the support of America's allies; nor would he accept one that increased the risk of general war, because soon the Soviet Union would be able to drop atomic and thermonuclear weapons on the United States. In such circumstances, America could no longer contemplate preventive wars or the "rollback" of existing communist regimes. And it would not always be able to push back new communist advances in the Third World.

As major conventional wars had to be avoided, there was no point in maintaining costly large armies. American strategy, Eisenhower declared, would have to be based on a "manifest determination" to "use its atomic capability and massive retaliatory striking power" to deter a Soviet attack.[11] If America's vital interests were at stake the stark choice would lie between thermonuclear war and compromise. While the other side had to be made aware that America would "press the button" to defend its vital interests, America would also have to try to find a compromise.[12] This was indeed brinkmanship, but conducted with prudence.

Meanwhile, in both countries "the wizards of Armageddon" were hard at work. America's success in testing a thermonuclear device in November 1952 had made Stalin's heirs even more cautious. Their own successful test of a thermonuclear device in August 1953 had a similar effect in the Eisenhower Administration because it showed the Soviets were not simply copying technology, they were making innovations. Within a month even the deeply anti-communist Secretary of State Dulles felt the need for "a spectacular effort to relax world tensions on a global basis."[13]

Dulles, however, soon recovered his *sangfroid.* When he proclaimed the Administration's "New Look" foreign policy to the Council on Foreign Relations in New York on January 12, 1954, he went beyond Eisenhower's threat of "massive retaliation" and declared that the United States would deliberately escalate a crisis so as to force the communists to confront a choice between backing down and incineration. In essence, he hoped that relentless pressure would rupture Soviet control over Eastern Europe. This took brinkmanship to a new level.

Under Eisenhower "containment" became more assertive, with America's security being based on an imbalance of nuclear terror. When Eisenhower first took office, the United States had only about 1,000 nuclear weapons. For his policy of deterrence to work, he needed far more nuclear weapons and orders were placed for them. "The cost of this program was enormous," James Schlesinger, who was later chairman of the Atomic Energy Commission, explained. "By the time it reached its peak during the Eisenhower era, the commission was consuming some 10% of the total federal budget." Nonetheless, building up such a huge nuclear deterrent cost only a fraction of what it would have to maintain large conventional forces.

The Kremlin's "New Look"

Given the scale of the problems at home, the Soviet leadership was keen to have stability abroad. Khrushchev, for one, said that he "constantly feared that the United States would compel the Soviet Union and its allies to retreat in some region of the world."[14] The shift away from Stalin's foreign policy was swift.

First and foremost, the Soviet leaders wanted to end the Korean War before the new Republican Administration decided to escalate it. They took the decision even before they buried Stalin on March 9, which was two months before Eisenhower threatened to attack China with nuclear weapons if the fighting did not stop. Not knowing that the decision had already been made, Eisenhower and his colleagues took the Soviet acquiescence as a sign that such threats could force their adversary to back down.

Elsewhere, efforts were made to mend fences. Diplomatic relations were restored with Yugoslavia, Greece and Israel, and territorial claims against Turkey were dropped. Then, in May, the new Soviet leadership began to be overwhelmed by events in Eastern Europe, where discontent with Stalin's economic exploitation, brutal policies, and widespread purges was already festering into protest. Large numbers of refugees were continuing to flee from East Germany, while Soviet diplomatic and intelligence sources reported a state of "near total chaos" in the Czechoslovak economy, "severe deficiencies" in Hungary and "extremely detrimental conditions and disruption" in Romania.[15]

The German Uprising

In April 1952, Stalin had told the leaders of East Germany to press ahead with "building socialism." He should have known better. Back in September 1948, he allegedly complained about the East German communists being overzealous, telling them that "you German communists, like your ancestors, are Teutons!"[16]

Within months, the steps that Ulbricht, the hard-line leader of the communist party, was taking to build socialism were seriously antagonizing much of the population. In the half-year before Stalin's death in 1953, Soviet Intelligence officials in East Germany were sending reports back to Moscow that openly acknowledged that East Germany no longer had "even the slightest attraction for citizens of West Germany."[17] By May 1953, just after Stalin's death, it was clear to Moscow that "the presence of Soviet troops is the only thing enabling the current regime . . . to survive."[18]

Ulbricht and his colleagues were summoned to Moscow. When they asked to close the inter-Berlin border to stem the exodus, they were told that such a step was "politically unacceptable" and "grossly simplistic."[19] After a severe dressing down they were told in no uncertain terms that they had to pursue more moderate policies. On his return home, Ulbricht mishandled the shift to moderation, among other things by ordering longer working hours. For the first time since 1945, East Germans began venting their long-standing grievances in public, blaming the communists for "turning us into slaves" and "keeping Germany divided" under Soviet domination.

By mid-June a rebellion was underway that was not only anti-communist, but anti-Soviet, with over a million people taking to the streets in East Berlin and hundreds of other cities and towns. Soviet tanks and troops were ordered to crush the uprising and did so swiftly, killing over one hundred people, with another hundred people being executed subsequently, and well over a thousand sent to labor camps.

Moscow's only consolation was that the Allies had done nothing to help the uprising, nor did they do anything to stop its suppression.

Mending Fences

In July 1953, just a month after the Berlin Uprising, an armistice was signed in Korea, though the forces of the two sides were still dug in where they had become stalemated some two years earlier. Following months of diplomatic contact, all the main parties who had been involved in the Korean War and the fighting in Indochina met in Geneva in April 1954.

Although they reached no settlement on the future of Korea, they did agree to respect the armistice (which has remained in force ever since). Tensions were further eased when Moscow facilitated a face-saving settlement in Indochina, in part with the hope that France would continue to oppose German rearmament. Pending elections, Vietnam was divided, with the communists being left in control of the north and the non-communists in the south, while Laos and Cambodia were granted independence.

From Moscow's point of view, the really bad news in May 1954 was that the Federal Republic of Germany had just regained a considerable degree of sovereignty and become not only a member of the Western European Union, but also of Nato. To deal with the growing power of the West, a new three-pronged approach evolved in foreign policy, a veteran Soviet diplomat recalled. It was to prop up Eastern Europe and tie it closer to the Soviet Union; to create, wherever possible, buffer states between the two opposing blocs; and gradually open up more normal relations with Nato countries.[20]

That year, after Khrushchev had prevailed over Molotov in some fierce debates, Moscow finally agreed that the Four Powers should conclude a peace treaty with Austria and recognize its neutrality. Khrushchev felt that this widely acclaimed treaty, which was signed in Vienna in May 1955, demonstrated "we could orient ourselves in foreign affairs without Stalin's instructions . . . we had exchanged our kid's shorts for adult trousers . . . We could feel our own strength."[21]

Days later, Khrushchev flew to Yugoslavia to "beg forgiveness," as he put it, from Tito and the Yugoslav communist party for Stalin's hostility towards them from 1948 until his death. Tito accepted the apology, but did not rejoin the international communist movement. Khrushchev also returned to Finland the Soviet base at Porkalla, which was part of the settlement forced on the Finns at the end of the war.

Khrushchev made an even greater effort to win over Mao, who was still smarting from the way Stalin had treated him. Despite their differences, Mao had been willing to accept Stalin as the leader of the world communist movement; now that he was gone, Mao wanted to have a far greater say in what it should do.

Initially, Khrushchev had some success. Although he refused to write-off the $2 billion Korean War debt for the Soviet equipment the Chinese had used in the Korean War, he did agreed to return to China control of Dalian, Port Arthur and the branch of the Trans-Siberian railway that ran through the northeast of the country, as well as provide large-scale economic assistance.

Nonetheless, Khrushchev suspected that Mao's "sickly sweet politeness . . . was all insincere." In his memoirs, he said that on his return to Moscow he had told his colleagues that Mao would never agree to any communist party other than the Chinese leading the world communist movement. "A conflict between us and China is inevitable."[22] This was probably not how he felt during his visit, as it was during this visit that he agreed to help China develop an atomic bomb.

Roll-back in the Third World

If the communist advance was not checked in Indochina, Eisenhower feared that all the countries of Asia could fall one after the other. The assumptions underpinning the "domino theory" were not rigorously scrutinized within his administration. This was a serious error as there were major differences between the situations in Indochina and elsewhere in the region.

Eisenhower never intended that American troops should be directly involved in defending these countries. His aim was to build them up through a combination of economic and military aid, plus help from American military advisers. Reforming corrupt right-wing regimes to fight communist insurgents would prove difficult, however, especially when the insurgents were supported by a neighboring state. This problem was never fully debated within the Administration. As a result, America's interests in Asia remained vaguely defined, with the option for withdrawal becoming more and more politically difficult as the American presence increased.

One of Eisenhower's major worries was that communist takeovers could deprive the West of access to vital raw materials. Oil supplies were a growing concern to the Americans, who were beginning to import sizeable amounts of oil because they could no longer produce enough to meet their own needs.

The first problem arose in Iran, where in 1951 the increasingly left-wing government moved to nationalize the oil industry, Britain's most valuable overseas asset. The CIA and British Intelligence worked together to foment opposition in Tehran to Mossadeq's government, which was forced from office in August 1953, when the young Shah was restored to power. This operation was considered a major triumph. Britain was able to hang on to 40% of the Iranian oil industry; the Americans took over most of the rest, and the Shah became America's main ally in the region.

Success in Iran reinforced Eisenhower's faith in "special operations" to "roll back," as Dulles liked to say, communist advances in the Third World. Things did not work out so well, however, in Guatemala. In 1954, the recently elected left-wing government nationalized some of the assets of United Fruit, the American company that had long dominated the economy. The United States feared that other Latin American countries might follow suit.

Once again, the CIA played a major part in bringing down the government. Over the next decade, as more American aid was poured into Guatemala than any other Latin American country, the brutality of the Guatemalan army ensured growing support for guerrillas, which set in motion a spiral of violence and bloodshed. Despite this outcome, the Eisenhower Administration continued to believe in the necessity of such covert activity.

Monitoring the Threat

The success of containment, Eisenhower believed, required America to have a more measured assessment of the military aspects of the threat it faced. He was also insistent that in the nuclear age everything possible had to be done to guard against a surprise attack and war by miscalculation. "Without intelligence," Eisenhower said soon after becoming president, "you would only have your fears on which to plan your own defense arrangements . . . [and that would] . . . make us an armed camp."[23]

Despite the improvement in the atmospherics of East-West relations, the Americans and the British stepped up their spy-flights over Soviet territory to gather intelligence on the development of Soviet nuclear weapons, bombers and later missiles.[24] Before the end of the year Eisenhower had approved the development of the U-2—a spy-plane that could fly at around 21,000 meters (70,000 feet), beyond the reach of Soviet interceptors or air-defense missiles.

While that work was underway, other spy-flights were stepped up. In the spring of 1956, the Americans mounted an unprecedented spying operation against the Soviet Union. In just seven weeks, 156 surveillance flights were made into Soviet airspace—to take photos and to eavesdrop on Soviet communications, radars etc.[25] The planes used included the reconnaissance versions of the B-47s, the Strategic Air Command's new long-range nuclear bomber, flying over the North Pole and into Siberia to probe for gaps in Soviet radar defenses. The operation ended with a squadron of these reconnaissance aircraft flying in formation in broad daylight several hundred miles into Soviet territory as if they were going to launch a nuclear attack.[26]

The United States lost around 170 airmen on these sureveillance flights between the late forties and early sixties, mainly as a result of aircraft being shot down close to the territory of the Soviet Union, Eastern Europe, North Korea and China.[27]

8 Living with the Bomb

The Quantum Leap

To understand how relations developed between Washington and Moscow during the latter half of the fifties and into the sixties, it is worth pausing to look at the impact that nuclear weapons were having on Soviet and American leaders.

President Eisenhower summed up the anxiety of both sides when, in his inaugural address in January 1953, he pondered the future: "Are we nearing the light . . . Or are the shadows of another night closing in upon us? . . . Science seems ready to confer upon us, as its final gift, the power to erase human life from this planet."[1] Eisenhower was not indulging in rhetoric and Khrushchev shared this horror. Having seen a film of the first Soviet thermonuclear test in August 1953 he came home, according to his son Sergei, depressed and unable to sleep for days.[2]

Both Eisenhower and Stalin's successors had been shocked by the power of these devices. On March 1, 1954, the first American test of an H-bomb at Eniwetok Atoll produced a yield of 15 megatons, three times more than expected, which made it over *one thousand times* greater than the bomb dropped on Hiroshima. Just ten days later, Georgi Malenkov, then the Soviet premier, declared that the Soviet Union wanted a stable and durable peace, since "a new world war . . . with modern weapons means the end of world civilisation."[3] He proposed a minimum deterrent strategy based on nuclear retaliation in order to make more resources available for light industry and consumer goods.

There was much sense in Malenkov's view, but from the political perspective, deterrence has always been a complex and often controversial issue. In January 1955, as part of his plan to oust Malenkov from office, Khrushchev criticized his speech for being "politically harmful." Molotov's far sharper critique went right to the point. "A Communist," he said, "should speak not about the "destruction of the human race," but about the need to prepare and mobilize all forces for the destruction of the bourgeoisie."[4] But soon after Khrushchev gained pre-eminence within the leadership he adopted Molotov's position.

Trying to Deter

One of the common aspects in both sides' thinking about deterrence was that they wanted to make it clear that they would not be intimidated by the threat of nuclear war.

In the fifties and sixties, much of the Pentagon's thinking on Soviet military affairs was done by the RAND Corporation, a consultancy that did a large amount of work for the American military, particularly the air force. Some of RAND's staff had access to highly sensitive intelligence. One of its top analysts of Soviet military affairs at that time was Andy Marshall, a man of elfish charm and lively intelligence who, like Ernst Gombrich, was fascinated by why people and institutions did things the way they did.

"The nub of the matter," Marshall emphasized, "was that neither side knew for sure what would deter the other. This is a problem we would wrestle with until the end of the Cold War." He went on, "This was hardly surprising as deterrence is deeply rooted in the psychology of leaders, their cultural background, the assessments supplied by military staffs and nuclear experts, as well as their traditions of statecraft. At the beginning of the Cold War, there were few who were well-versed in the psychology of the other side, or for that matter the history and culture that had nurtured it."

One of the most important factors driving the arms race was the constant innovation in military technology, which could fundamentally change the strategic balance (see below). In essence this was, as Walt Slocombe, the deputy undersecretary for defense policy planning in the Carter Administration, explained, "a race between American technology and the Soviet ability to throw almost unlimited resources at a problem once they decided to do so." In the process, both became captives of forces that were practically independent of their own will and comprehension.

Another complication was that the two sides thought about security in fundamentally different ways. Generally speaking, as the stronger power, the Americans focused on the broad issue of the failure of the world to stand up to Hitler in the thirties; the Russians, being the weaker power, focused on how the assassination of a single man at Sarajevo in 1914 had rapidly led to a world war.

The "Sarajevo 1914 syndrome," Slocombe pointed out, affected the Americans, too. "The real problem was not to deter the Soviet Union from waking up one morning and launching an attack, but to deter the kind of Soviet action that had the potential to snowball into a nuclear crisis. We had to avoid being trapped in a situation where backing down was unacceptable. We needed something between surrender and Armageddon—and we had to convince the Soviets that we had those options and could execute them."

In assessing the danger their nations faced, neither side could separate the military calculations of the threat from their broader assessment of the other's intentions. As they believed those intentions were based on a long-standing ideological threat, the accent was always on the worst-case scenario. Assessing intentions was thought to be extremely difficult as judgments could rarely be proven. As former president George Bush told me in 2005, "I had learned when I was director of Central Intelligence, way back in 1976, that it is very hard to measure 'intent.' Thus there were many areas, many situations where I never felt absolutely certain as to what the Soviet Union might do."[5]

As leaders could change their minds, analysts focused on capabilities rather than intentions, often taking their adversary's contingency plans as a statement of their real intentions. Small forces were not viewed as a sign of benign intent, simply as weaknesses that would soon be made stronger. Planning was done not just on the basis of the present worst-case scenario, but also the worst future case. Each side consistently exaggerated its adversary's capabilities, while underplaying its own. The greater the reassurance sought, the greater the number of weapons required.

Although those people closely involved with nuclear weapons had a good idea of what damage individual weapons could do, no one really knew what a major nuclear war would be like, and no one could be sure how the other side would respond. In the sixties, an American air force general accused a civilian strategist of "not knowing a damn thing about nuclear war." "With respect General," the strategist rather tartly replied, "I've fought just as many nuclear wars as you have!"[6]

Getting the military to consider new options was never easy, especially when they involved showing restraint in a crisis. When one of McNamara's strategists tried to convince General Thomas Powers, the commander of the Strategic Air Command, of the benefits of doing so, he bellowed: "The whole idea is to kill

NUCLEAR WEAPONS

The "yield" of nuclear weapons is expressed in terms of tons of TNT. The damage caused not only results from the blast (which accounts for roughly half of the yield), but also from the fires that the heat of the explosion ignites and the lethal effects of radiation. Robust and fire-resistant buildings suffer less damage.

Nobody knows for sure what the yield was of the atomic bomb dropped on Hiroshima, but many experts say it was equal to 12,500 tons of TNT (12.5 kilotons). Some 70,000 people died immediately; roughly the same number died over the next few years from radiation sickness and injuries. Casualties were particularly high because most of the buildings in the city were wooden, and the attack was unexpected. By the early fifties, America had atomic bombs with yields ranging up to 500 kilotons.[7]

The thermonuclear weapons, which were first deployed in 1954, were far more powerful. By 1960, the Americans had a bomb in service with a yield of 25 megatons. In 1961, the Russians tested a prototype "super-bomb" with a yield of 50 megatons as a warning to the Americans, but Khrushchev refused to allow it to be mass produced, because he considered it to be an extremely costly and inefficient weapon.

A 10-megaton warhead exploded over the center of Washington would kill instantly some 1.4 million people (which is around 70% of the population within the Beltway); the death toll from the same-sized warhead exploded over Moscow would be far higher because the population density is so much greater—some 7 million people (or approximately 75% of the population within the Ring Road).[8]

those bastards! . . . At the end of the war, if there are two Americans and one Russian, we win!" The strategist retorted with the sage observation "Well, you had better make sure they're a man and a woman!"[9]

Neither side understood just how scared the other was of nuclear war. Nonetheless, once each side believed the other could kill tens of millions of its citizens, they came to doubt that their opponent would take risks that they would not. After all, especially after they had entered the missile age, they feared that even if they did launch a surprise attack the other side would still be able to retaliate with devastating and unacceptable consequences.

Although the Americans did much more planning than the Soviets about what options they would have in certain circumstances (as is explained in later chapters), they were always somewhat vague about what their response would be. "It is in fact a rule in the US," Slocombe pointed out, "that the president

MISSILES

The four characteristics that are important for missiles are range, payload (or throw-weight), accuracy and how quickly it can be fired.

Initially, the speed with which a missile could be launched was of critical importance. By the early sixties the Americans had solid-fueled missiles that could be fired quickly. At that time Soviet intercontinental ballistic missiles used highly corrosive liquid fuel and took some eighteen hours to ready for firing, which meant they could be destroyed on the ground by American bombers, and even more easily by American missiles. It was not until the late sixties that the majority of Soviet intercontinental missiles could be fired within minutes.

Payload refers to the weight of the warhead or warheads that a missile can carry, not to their explosive power. Over the years it has become possible to get the same explosive power out of smaller and smaller warheads. Because the Americans were skilled at miniaturizing warheads, they were able to fit three separate ones onto the same missile. The Russians were less quick to miniaturize their warheads and so needed to have larger missiles. Later, the fact that their large missiles could carry such big payloads meant that they could put up to ten warheads on one missile alone.

Greater accuracy not only increases the chance of hitting a target, but also to use smaller warheads for a specific task. Accuracy is particularly important when attacking bunkers deep underground or missile silos that are heavily protected by reinforced concrete and steel doors. The Americans always had the lead in this field for most of the Cold War.

American missiles have names that usually convey something about the character of the missile—Atlas (massive), Midgetman (small), Minuteman (always ready to fire). Soviet missiles have always been designated by letters and numbers, but for reasons of security these were never disclosed during the Cold War. Indeed, different designations were used in different circumstances.

The West got around the problem by giving each type of Soviet ballistic missile a designation beginning with "SS," meaning "surface-to-surface" missile. The first one they detected became SS-1, the second SS-2 and so on. When the Cold War closed, the latest Soviet missile was the SS-25.

never takes part in war games, and so far as I know, whenever someone plays that role the controller stops the exercise at the point where a decision to go nuclear will be taken. Thus the mystery is always preserved."

Both sides wanted reassurance that the nuclear forces they had amassed would deter any attack. But once intercontinental ballistic missiles that could travel at about 200 km (125 miles) a minute had been developed, such assurances were difficult to achieve. In the sixties, at the beginning of the missile age, "early warning" was provided by ground-based and airborne radars. The Americans, who had the good fortune of having forward-based radar stations in Greenland, could hope to know of a missile attack some twenty minutes before they arrived; the Kremlin had no more than ten minutes and, because the relatively short distance from the missile launch sites in the Western Soviet Union, let alone Eastern Europe, the Elysée and No. 10 had just four.

Even for those who had twenty minutes' warning, it would always be difficult to decide how to respond; for those with only four minutes it could well be too little time in which to order a retaliatory attack. This is why, into the seventies, the Soviet General Staff had to think in terms of "pre-empting" an American attack if they were confident that one was going to be launched against them.

I got a feeling of what it was like to be faced with the news of an imminent attack from a colleague who was one of the duty officers at the Foreign Office in London in the early sixties. He was summoned from his bath one Sunday morning by the special red telephone he never wanted to hear ring. When he picked up the receiver the clipped voice at the other end simply said: "Just testing the four-minute warning system, Sir" and the line went dead.

The young man pondered what he would have done had the message been "Soviet missiles here in four minutes, Sir!" The only thing he could think of was to pour himself a drink and enjoy a last, brief look over St. James's Park before the nuclear version of Armageddon began.

So Very Different

There was, of course, more to deterrence than just nuclear weapons; conventional forces also played a key part in the balance of power, especially in Europe.

Although any war that did break out in Europe could quickly spread from the Arctic to the Mediterranean, the most critical area was Central Europe—the region that lay between the Baltic and the Bavarian Alps, stretching from the Channel to the Western frontier of the Soviet Union. To the west of the front line between the two alliances lay Denmark, West Germany, the Benelux and France; to the east were East Germany, Czechoslovakia and Poland.

From the Inner-German border it was just 30 km (19 miles) to Hamburg,

80 km (50 miles) to the North Sea and about 450 km (280 miles) to Calais; in the other direction, it was almost 1,000 km (620 miles) to the Soviet frontier. It was far harder for the Americans to bring reinforcement into West Germany by sea than it was for the Soviets to move theirs overland into East Germany and neighboring western Poland.

"As we began comparing Soviet and American forces back in the fifties and early sixties, I was struck by just how great the asymmetries were—from the top to the bottom. That is why it took such a long time for them to understand what the other was doing and why," Marshall recalled. The Soviet forces were large, manned by conscripts and led by a relatively small core of officers and non-commissioned officers. Unlike American troops, most Soviet conscripts could not drive or use sophisticated equipment. Command was complicated by the fact that, increasingly, the Soviet forces were made up of ethnic groups that spoke little Russian.

The Soviets and the Americans had very different views about how long a war would last. Believing it would be long, the Soviets stockpiled vast and costly amounts of equipment and ammunition. The Americans, on the other hand, never planned to fight a long conventional war.

The Soviet strategy, in the event of war, was based on employing massive forces in carefully planned, large-scale offensive operations. The Soviet General Staff needed its commanders to obey orders from above, not take initiatives from below. Soviet pilots received the minimum training required to fulfill a specific function. Soviet interceptors, for example, followed a lead pilot, who was himself being told what to do by ground-control.

American forces, on the other hand, whose strategy was defensive, had to expect the unexpected, and so for them, initiative was essential. American pilots were trained to far higher standards than their Soviet counterparts, because their aircraft were capable of executing a much larger variety of tasks.

General Staff v. Joint Chiefs

The Soviet General Staff was an elite group that regarded itself as one of the pre-eminent institutions of the Soviet state. For them, the Soviet Union had been born in war and needed to survive in war, with the military having the first call on the nation's assets.

The General Staff took pride in the fact that its lineage dated back to the age of Peter the Great and their tsarist predecessor had been modeled on the Prussian General Staff. In St. Petersburg, the Imperial General Staff had been housed in one of the finest buildings in the city and that tradition was continued when the Soviet General Staff moved to Moscow after the revolution. Between them the Imperial General Staff and its Soviet successor had focused on the issues involved in fighting a war in Europe for some two and a half centuries.

After the terrible humiliation they had suffered in 1941, the General Staff were determined never again to be unprepared or wrong-footed. This line of thinking was vividly captured in an exchange in the mid-eighties between Anatoly Dobrynin, the long-time Soviet ambassador in Washington, and Marshal Akhromeyev, the chief of the General Staff.

Dobrynin asked the Marshal straight out, "Do you believe the United States and Nato could attack us some day?" "It is not my mission to believe or not believe," the Marshal retorted. "We proceed from the worst conceivable scenario of having to fight the United States, its West European allies, and probably Japan. We must be prepared for any kind of war with any kind of weapon. Soviet military doctrine can be summed up as follows: 1941 shall never be repeated."[10]

Stalin had not given the General Staff much chance to shape policy in the atomic age and Khrushchev had pushed through his own radical approach to deterrence that relied heavily on the use of nuclear weapons. Under Brezhnev, however, the General Staff would regain its status and support for a strategy of deterrence that combined both nuclear and conventional forces.

From then on, the General Staff brooked little interference from outside. Even within the Politburo, only a few members had any say in military matters. The defense minister was either a career officer or, as in the case of Dmitri Ustinov, a product of the party and the military-industrial complex. Policy was not debated publicly and within the Party only in restricted groups.

All Soviet military operations were planned and coordinated by the General Staff. The intellectual young officers who were selected for it—and made their career in it—thought profoundly about the nature of war, the strategies that were required and the impact of new technology. They were masters of the art of conceptualizing the ramifications of warfare. The deep-penetration operations they developed and tested in massive and realistic maneuvers in the mid-thirties helped Soviet forces first to defeat the Japanese on the Mongolian/Manchurian frontier in 1939 and later the Germans.

The General Staff had a well-earned reputation for devising operations that took account of the strengths and weakness of their adversaries, but also those of their own troops and equipment. They wanted to prepare thoroughly in order to win, not take gambles that could risk disaster. As Marxism-Leninism was considered a science, so, too, was war. The laws of war, the General Staff believed, could be determined through the careful study of why battles had been won and lost, from ancient times to the present.

They did this not just by examining the impact of the strategies and tactics that had been used, but also such very practical issues as the ratio between each side's troops, equipment, munitions, logistics etc. Complicated mathematical formulae would tell a commander what he needed to do in order to break through particular lines of defense, or what would determine his rate of advance in different circumstances.

Nato's forces were assessed in the same methodical way, with tables showing, for instance, how a Belgian division compared with an American one. Detailed calculations were made on what Soviet forces would require to defeat them.The General Staff always erred on the side of caution.[11]

The American Joint Chiefs of Staff were a very different creature. The Prussian model had always been thought to be too militaristic. As a result, the JCS was (and still is) a fairly small group that tried to coordinate the four independent services—the army, the navy, the marines and the air force, between whom the rivalry was intense. Each service had its own strong lobbies in Congress.

Officers were seconded to it for tours of duty, not for the whole of their career. The services were under civilian control through the president, who is the commander-in-chief, and his secretary of defense, always a civilian. Congress oversees defense policy and has budgetary control, which means that political and bureaucratic interests often trump military considerations. There is much informed public debate about defense.

The American armed forces have produced some fine intellectuals and great strategists. They have usually spent time teaching at the service academies/war colleges or in the staff of their own service, but they have never had a general staff career in the Soviet sense. They did, of course, study the history of war, but they were much more interested than their Soviet counterparts in the broad lessons and how they could be adapted to modern conditions. Their tradition was to identify the problem, think how to solve it and pour in resources needed to implement it.

At the highest levels, too, the differences were extreme. Most of the top Soviet leaders had substantial wartime experience, either as officers or as party watchdogs overseeing marshals and generals. It was not accidental that Brezhnev liked wearing a marshal's uniform, and, at the top, the party and the military leadership were practically fused. Gorbachev was the first exception. This was not the case on the American side, except for Eisenhower and the partial exception of Kennedy.

9 The Spirit of Geneva

Slowly Rising

In June 1955, smiling broadly, Eisenhower and Khrushchev clinked their glasses at the beginning of the cocktail hour. The venue was the Palais des Nations, the home of the ill-fated League of Nations, and a building that commands magnificent views across Lake Geneva to the snow-covered Alps.

The "Spirit of Geneva," which brought a more relaxed atmosphere to international relations, emerged from a six-day summit meeting between Eisenhower, Anthony Eden (the British premier), Edgar Faure (the French premier) and Nikolai Bulganin (the Soviet premier). Although in protocol terms Khrushchev was not the leader of the Soviet delegation, he was its most important member, as he headed the communist party.

The general thaw in East-West relations that the atmosphere at this meeting signified probably did owe something to the hi-balls that Eisenhower had laid on for the delegates at the end of their first day of discussions, and to Khrushchev's liking for "the magnetic, attractive quality about the way [Eisenhower] treated people."[1] But it is clear that the far more lethal fireballs generated by tests of the new H-bombs played every bit as important a role.

There had also been a major shift in Moscow's attitude towards West Germany, where the upsurge in industrial production had created an "economic miracle" within a decade of the war. On May 6, 1955, West Germany gained its independence, albeit with some caveats.

While the Western Allies retained the right to block any settlement of the German Question of which they disapproved, Chancellor Adenauer had wrung considerable concessions from them. The allies had not only recognized the Federal Republic as the legitimate representative of the German people in international affairs (to the exclusion of the German Democratic Republic), but had also accepted it as a full member of the Western European Union and Nato,

Summit dinner, hosted by the Swiss president, Geneva, July 23, 1954. *Left to right:* Khrushchev, Prime Minister Eden (white jacket), French Foreign Minister Pinay, Soviet Premier Bulganin, Swiss president Pettitpierre, President Eisenhower and the American ambassador, Frances Williams. (Corbis)

to which Adenauer announced that West Germany would contribute twelve combat divisions and an air force.

Four days after this announcement of German rearmament the United States, Britain and France invited the Soviet Union to Geneva for a summit. This would be the first such gathering since the Potsdam Conference at the end of the war. Despite having stridently opposed German rearmament, Moscow quickly accepted the invitation to Geneva.

The Summit

The Geneva Summit was Khrushchev's first real journey to the West and his initial encounter with the leaders of its three main powers. As he touched down in Geneva he was mortified to see the huge and modern aircraft on which

Eisenhower had flown in. "It made ours look like an insect," he lamented.[2] This was a humiliation for the Soviet Union which was, after all, hoping to portray itself as riding on the wave of the future.

One small piece of news cheered his spirits. Immediately after his arrival, Khrushchev sent the head of his bodyguards into town on a special mission: to find out how much it would cost to buy another gold-plated Swiss watch like the one that he had bought at Yuzovka forty years ago. That watch seemed to link the pleasures of his youth with his faith in technology and science. When he learned how cheap Swiss watches now were, he bought some for his family, too.[3]

At Geneva, the unavoidable German Question was once again center stage. After the East German uprising two years earlier, it was hardly surprising that Khrushchev's top priority was a non-aggression pact that would ensure that there would be no Western interference in Eastern Europe. Only then, he said, would Moscow be willing to discuss unification. The West, on the other hand, insisted there could be no reduction in military forces in Europe until the two Germanys had been unified—on terms acceptable to the West. Meanwhile, it refused to recognize East Germany as a legitimate state.

Despite the lack of real progress on the main issues, Eisenhower and Khrushchev did succeed in establishing good personal relations, with the general atmosphere being further improved by the presence of Marshal Zhukov, the Soviet minister of defense, with whom Eisenhower had got along well when they had first met in 1945.

Eisenhower told Zhukov that he believed that the growth of atomic and hydrogen weapons made war even more senseless than before. Zhukov agreed and noted that he personally had seen "how lethal this weapon is." He was not exaggerating. The previous September he had supervised a military exercise during which a 20-kiloton atomic bomb was dropped from a plane and 44,000 soldiers immediately thereafter staged a mock battle at the test site to simulate nuclear war under "realistic" conditions. Many died later as a result of their exposure to radiation.[4]

Both Eisenhower and Khrushchev left Geneva convinced that the other did not want war. As Khrushchev put it, "our enemies probably feared us as much as we feared them."[5] But there was a fundamental difference. At a speech to party activists in East Berlin on August 9, Erich Mielke, the head of East German security, reflected the conclusions that Khrushchev had drawn from the summit. Geneva had shown, Mielke said, that "there is fear of war" in some parts of the West and "we have to exploit that fear." The Americans, he continued, would not go to war over West Germany, let alone West Berlin, which he was confident that the East German secret police could seize in the foreseeable future.[6]

Khrushchev felt that he should be rewarded for the many steps he had taken to ease tensions. Above all, he hoped Eisenhower would invite him to America—an honor that no previous Soviet leader had enjoyed. But Eisenhower's advisers feared that by treating Khrushchev as an equal, they would encourage neutrality among some of their allies in Europe and in the Third World. The British did not feel so constrained. In 1956, Khrushchev was invited to Britain, where he was received by the Queen and gave British leaders their first real taste of his penchant for intimidation.[7]

The West German Phoenix

"Despite the crushing defeat we had inflicted on the Germans, we never doubted that West Germany would soon become a powerful force," General Kevorkov, the KGB's top expert on Germany, recalled as we talked about the evolution of Moscow's policy towards Bonn. "That is why, before Geneva, there was a major reversal of Soviet policy. We had to try to cultivate West Germany."

Ulbricht wanted Khrushchev to insist on the Allies treating East Germany as an equal of West Germany and to get them out of West Berlin, through which large numbers of East Germans continued to flee to the West. When Khrushchev invited Adenauer to come to Moscow in September, without any preconditions, Ulbricht was furious.

In Moscow in September, Khrushchev and Adenauer had some tough and heated discussions. Contrary to American wishes, Adenauer agreed to establish diplomatic relations in return for the repatriation of the some 10,000 German POWs and 20,000 "detained civilians" still in Soviet captivity. Much to Khrushchev's chagrin, the establishment of diplomatic relations with West Germany brought minimal benefits to the Soviet Union. Adenauer continued to strengthen his ties with the West (becoming a founding member of the European Economic Union in 1956), adamantly refused to deal with East Germany and pressed ahead with rearmament.

This did not diminish Khrushchev's dream of dismantling Nato and the Warsaw Pact, which was reflected in a discussion he had with Hans-Christian

Hansen, the Danish prime minister, in March 1956. The Soviet leadership, Khrushchev said, would "continue to reduce our armed forces unilaterally" so that "you will find it hard to justify Nato before public opinion."[8]

While Khrushchev did what he said he would do, cutting Soviet forces by over 2 million men between 1955 and 1958, the United States increased the number of its nuclear weapons in Europe ten-fold, from around 100 to 1,000, most of which were deployed in West Germany. Over the three years that followed Khrushchev's meeting with Adenauer, Moscow's concerns moved closer to becoming nightmares. West Germany's economy continued to boom and it seemed as if the Germans would break their earlier pledge and acquire nuclear weapons. Papers prepared for the Soviet leadership warned of the danger of a revived Germany eventually uniting with Poland and stripping the Soviet Union of its buffer zone.

The Soviet Union still needed to find a way to deal with Germany.

Brightening the Socialist Beacon

As much as Khrushchev wanted to ease tensions with the United States, he was keen to make gains in the Third World. He believed this could be done by working with the nationalist leaders of the new states who were resisting pressure from their former colonial rulers. These new leaders were attracted to socialist economic planning because it enabled them to strengthen the power of their recently established governments.

One of the press photos of Khrushchev and Bulganin in India in December 1955 looked like a scene from a fancy-dress party, with the two men in white tropical suits and smiling beneath elaborate ceremonial turbans. But it was the clearest indication that Moscow was now taking a new approach to the Third World. "B & K," as the press often called them, also visited Burma and Afghanistan, which like India would soon begin to develop closer ties with Moscow.

In April 1955, shortly before the Geneva Conference, Moscow backed the conference of almost thirty African and Asian nations, held at Bandung in Indonesia. It was there that Zhou Enlai, the Chinese foreign minister, promoted the idea of "peaceful coexistence." Most delegates thought this meant live-and-let-live, while in fact it meant promoting normal relations between countries while the communists sought to extend their influence abroad and prevent foreign influences from affecting their own societies.

The most decisive step in Khrushchev's new approach came when Gamal

Abdel Nasser, the president of Egypt and the leading Arab nationalist at this time, turned to Moscow after Washington refused to supply him with arms. This opened up an unprecedented opportunity for the Soviet Union to align itself with the leader of the pan-Arab nationalist movement. While discussions continued at the Geneva Summit, a Soviet ship was loading Czech arms for Egypt.

In 1956, over 3,000 shopping malls opened across America, where people were enjoying unprecedented gains in their standard of living. That same year, America reached a key point in economic development: a greater number of people were now employed in service industries than in manufacturing or agriculture. This is a kind of economic progress that the Soviet Union never achieved.

Though the standard of living in the Soviet Union lagged far behind that of the United States, it had improved in the three years since Stalin died. Prisoners were being released from the camps and the political atmosphere was more relaxed. The grounds of the Kremlin had been opened to the public, young Soviet poets had more freedom and some Western pop music was tolerated. The "spirit of Geneva" was being felt in Moscow.

In this atmosphere, in February 1956, Khrushchev opened the 20th Party Congress, the first since Stalin's death. It was a key event in the Cold War with manifold implications for Soviet domestic and foreign affairs. He told delegates that a war between communists and capitalists was no longer inevitable as the Soviet Union was now so strong. Different countries could take different roads to socialism. Because Soviet economic success would show people that socialism was superior to capitalism, Khrushchev said, countries would in future go socialist through the ballot box. When we spoke in 2004, Sergei Khrushchev told me, "My father genuinely believed this."

Khrushchev had a naïve faith that socialism, once purified of its Stalinist stain, would regain its vitality and enjoy the genuine support of the people and that its achievements would help wash away the blood that had been shed in its name. To this end, on the last day of the Party Congress, Khrushchev unexpectedly delivered his six-hour "secret speech" revealing and detailing Stalin's horrendous crimes against the Party (but not those against Soviet people as a whole).

Delegates were stunned to hear that in the purges between 1935 and 1940 alone nearly two million people had been arrested for anti-Soviet activities, 700,000 of whom had been shot. Khrushchev's harrowing denunciation of Stalin, as William Taubman, his biographer, astutely commented, "was the bravest and most reckless thing he ever did."[9]

Although Khrushchev's secret speech was not published in the Soviet Union, millions of Soviet party members were briefed on it. Khrushchev's hope of revitalizing socialism was widely shared, especially among the young, who regarded themselves as "the children of the 20th Party Congress." The failure of the Soviet Communist Party to live up to their expectations sparked the dissent and "new thinking" that later did so much to influence Gorbachev's varied reforms.

For those in the party who had believed in Stalin's greatness, Khrushchev's revelations were a traumatic shock and a most unwelcome public reminder of the extent to which they were implicated by Stalin's crimes.

Turmoil in Eastern Europe

The head of the Polish Communist Party, Boleslaw Beirut, died of a heart attack when he read Khrushchev's secret speech. Other East European communist leaders who were in much better health certainly had palpitations, which was hardly surprising because Khrushchev had dangerously undermined their authority.

The CIA soon acquired a copy, and the entire text of the speech was published in the *New York Times* on June 5, 1956. Before long, the main points were widely known throughout Eastern Europe. One of those who read it was Markus Wolf, the Moscow-educated 33-year-old head of East German Intelligence: "At one stroke, our worst fears about a system to which we had pledged our lives had come true."[10] "At home," he continued, "I ripped down the photo I had of Stalin looking benign as he smoked his pipe."

In Poland, workers rioted in Poznan in June under banners of "Bread and Freedom" and "Russians Go Home." Over seventy were killed. Then, in August, a million people gathered at Czestochowa to mark the 300th anniversary of this shrine's supposedly miraculous deliverance from the siege by a foreign army. Before there was any further violence, the Polish Communist Party decided to bring back Gomulka as its leader and give him the free hand in pursuing a "Polish road to socialism."

Khrushchev feared Gomulka's changes would lead to the collapse of communism in Poland and its withdrawal from the Warsaw Pact. In mid-October Khrushchev flew uninvited into Warsaw to demand that the Polish leadership reverse their recent decisions. The discussions were stormy. To show his determination, Khrushchev ordered Soviet troops to start moving from their barracks in Poland towards Warsaw, but his bluff was called when it became clear the Poles would fight.

Gomulka made it easier for Khrushchev to back down by insisting, in rather emotional terms, that Poland was a reliable ally and needed Soviet friendship "as without the Soviet Union Poland would not be able to exist as an independent state."[11] The Soviet Politburo unanimously decided, on October 21, 1956, to "display patience" for the time being. As Khrushchev told his colleagues three days later, "Finding a reason for an armed conflict [with Poland] now would be very easy, but finding a way to put an end to such a conflict would be very hard."[12]

Two days later, as Gomulka was telling 500,000 people in Warsaw that Soviet troops were returning to their bases, demonstrators in Budapest were demanding reforms. When the Hungarian government called in Soviet troops to restore order, the Hungarian Revolt began.[13]

In the Kremlin there was hope that a new relationship could be worked out with Hungary, just as it had been with Poland. To defuse the crisis, the Politburo quickly appointed Imre Nagy to head a new government. He promised to pursue a Hungarian road to socialism and Soviet troops were withdrawn from the capital. On October 27, Secretary of State Dulles said in a major speech: "We do not look upon these nations [Poland and Hungary] as potential military allies. We see them as part of a new and friendly and no longer divided Europe."[14] This was a moderate statement by Dulles's standards, but still worrying from Moscow's standpoint.

The following day, October 30, Hungarian radio broadcast a declaration by the Soviet leadership that offered a new relationship with all the countries of Eastern Europe and expressed its willingness to withdraw Soviet troops from Hungary. The implication was that Moscow would treat Hungary as a neutral country—like Austria, Finland or Yugoslavia. The offer came too late. In the Hungarian capital demonstrators were already calling for an end to communism and lynching officials in front of Party headquarters; Nagy was losing control.

Suez

While chaos was spreading in Budapest, a major crisis had begun involving Egypt, Moscow's main client in the Third World. On July 26, after having received a large shipment of Soviet arms, President Nasser seized control of the Suez Canal, which a century earlier had been built by the French and was still owned and run by them and the British. Britain and France, who saw Nasser as a threat to their interests throughout the Middle East, conspired with the Israelis to take it back. On October 29, after months of secret plotting, Israeli forces attacked across Sinai. Two days later, British and French forces arrived, according to plan, to occupy the Canal Zone and separate the two combatants.

On the night of October 30, as the Anglo-French forces were moving into Egypt, Khrushchev later recalled, "I could not sleep. Budapest was like a nail in my head." When the Politburo met in Moscow the next morning he was adamant that the Soviet Union could not afford to lose both Hungary and Egypt. "If we depart from Hungary," he said "the Americans, English and French ... will perceive it as a weakness on our part and will then go the offensive."[15]

The leadership's decision to intervene militarily was reinforced when the next day Nagy proclaimed Hungary's neutrality and withdrew from the Warsaw Pact.[16] There were also disturbing signs that unrest was brewing elsewhere in Eastern Europe, as well as in some of the non-Russian republics of the Soviet Union.

Soviet troops intervened in massive numbers on November 4, and crushed the uprising. The following day Moscow issued a statement vaguely threatening Britain and France with a nuclear missile attack if they did not withdraw from Egypt. "In what position would Britain have found herself," it asked rhetorically, "had it been attacked by more powerful states possessing all types of modern weapons of destruction?"[17]

Before this statement was issued, lack of support and financial pressure by the United States had already compelled Britain and France to abandon their intervention. But Khrushchev saw their withdrawal as a triumph for his technique of menace. He was all the more pleased because his missiles could not reach either country, indeed none of them were on "active duty" at the time.[18] This victory encouraged him to bluff, and to take greater risks.

Coming just three years after the Berlin Uprising, the confrontation with Poland and the bloody suppression of the Hungarian Revolution were painful reminders to the Soviet leadership of how unstable their supposed "security zone" was. In Hungary, a thousand Soviet troops had lost their lives and some four thousand Hungarians had been killed or would soon be executed. The majority of the Politburo felt the troubles in both countries stemmed from the failure to provide the people with adequate standards of living. To forestall political trouble at home more money was poured into improving Soviet living standards, especially for the industrial workers.

Soon Khrushchev was claiming that, before long, Soviet living standards would surpass the Americans. He began in May 1957 by claiming that the Soviet Union would overtake the United States in meat and dairy production; he went on to make bolder claims after the successful launches of two satellites in October and November. As Khrushchev and his colleagues were unwilling to radically reform the Soviet economy, serious progress would only be possible if some form of détente could be reached with the West.

Khrushchev's hopes had been raised by the fact that the West had not intervened in any of the three crises. But what Khrushchev really wanted was for the West to recognize that there were two systems in the world. He sought assurance that the West would not interfere in his system, while he continued to support what he termed "national liberation movements" in the Third World and "class struggles" in more developed countries.

10 Into the Missile Age

Nuclear Weapons—America Races Ahead

During the first five years of Eisenhower's presidency, the number of warheads in America's nuclear stockpile soared from about 1,000 to about 5,500; some two-thirds of these were bombs for Strategic Air Command, the long-range bomber force. Strategic Air Command, headed by General Curtis Le May, began to pursue a policy of what might be called "assertive deterrence."

By 1956, Le May had some 1,200 B-47 bombers that could strike at targets in the Soviet Union from bases in the United States. That January, Le May ordered almost all his bombers into the air for a simulated nuclear attack. In another exercise, called *Operation Powerhouse*, his planes flew nearly one thousand simultaneous sorties from more than thirty bases around the world to intimidate the Soviet Union.[1]

The surge in the size of America's nuclear stockpile was possible because the new plants commissioned by Truman were beginning to produce prodigious amounts of enriched uranium and plutonium. At the same time, scientists at the Livermore and Los Alamos Laboratories were extraordinarily inventive in using this plenitude of fissile material to create nuclear weapons for almost every conceivable military task.

By the late fifties, there were bombs of many different sizes; warheads for short-, medium- and long-range ballistic missiles; ground-launched, ship-launched and air-launched missiles to destroy aircraft above the battlefield or the target they were attacking; mortars that could be fired from the back of a jeep (with considerable risk to the crew) and artillery shells, the earliest of which was 280mm wide and fired from a cannon that could only be moved with great difficulty; mines to blow up bridges and create obstacles; and nuclear depth charges.

Each of the three armed services pressed for more nuclear weapons to enhance their capabilities at a time when conventional forces were being cut back.

Test of 280mm atomic cannon, 1953. (U.S. Department of Defense)

Given the backing that each had in Congress, they all got much of what they wanted. At the same time, Nato reached another major milestone—by deciding to rely primarily on "tactical" or battlefield nuclear weapons for its defense. A rapid buildup began in 1956 and, before long, Nato was looking like a nuclear porcupine, having by 1960 amassed some 3,000 nuclear weapons.

Advantage Khrushchev

Shortly after Stalin's death in 1953, Sergei Korolev, the director of the Soviet missile program, gave the Politburo their first briefing on ballistic missiles. As Khrushchev put it: "We gawked at what he showed us."[2] There was now the prospect of the Soviet Union being the first to have an intercontinental ballistic missile. Once again, technological innovation would ignite profound feelings of insecurity.

At last, Soviet leaders hoped they could achieve something that would make the United States respect them. Several years later, in January 1959, Khrushchev told the American ambassador that if he got down on his knees and prayed in a "Holy Orthodox Church" for peace, the West would not believe him. But if he walked towards the West with "two missiles under my arms, maybe I'd be believed."[3]

A British communications intelligence team had been the first to monitor Soviet missile tests. Posing as archaeologists they had traveled to the mountains of Iran near the Soviet border from where they could listen-in to the radio communications associated with the tests.[4] Before long, the Americans had established a large, permanent monitoring post in Turkey.[5] Then a high-level defector brought out firsthand details of the Soviet program, including indications that the Soviets were developing a massive missile.[6] In 1955, Eisenhower received intelligence that Soviet missiles would soon be able to strike America's strategic air bases in Western Europe and Japan and, within just a few years, the United States itself.

Fortunately, for Eisenhower, the U-2 spy-plane would soon be ready. Having seen photos of American cities taken from a U-2 flying at around 21,000 meters (70,000 feet), Eisenhower recalled in his memoirs how impressed he was by the quality of the photography: "we could easily count the automobiles on the streets and even the lines marking the parking areas for individual cars."[7]

Soviet leaders were incensed to learn that the initial flight in 1956 had passed over Spaso House, the American ambassador's residence in Moscow, while they themselves were there for the first time attending his July 4th reception. Later, Khrushchev recalled that the United States "never missed a chance to demonstrate its superiority."[8] For Eisenhower, however, the results were rewarding. By the summer of 1956, after the first five U-2 spy flights over the Soviet Union, the CIA was able to disprove the air force's assertion that there was a "bomber-gap" in Moscow's favor.[9]

Khrushchev soon got his revenge. On August 26, the Soviet news agency *Tass* announced the successful test of an intercontinental ballistic missile. To Khrushchev's considerable annoyance, the United States showed virtually no interest in this remarkable achievement. In September, Korolev alerted him another opportunity to gain the advantage—this time by launching an artificial earth satellite before the Americans did so during the International Geophysical Year, which ran from July 1, 1957, through to the end of 1958. Khrushchev leapt at the chance.[10]

On October 4, 1957, *Sputnik*, the world's first satellite, beeped its way over

Deterrence is difficult, November 13, 1957. (C. Cummings, British Cartoon Archive, courtesy of the *Daily Express*)

America. A month later, Moscow put another satellite in space, this time carrying a dog. America's self-confidence was shattered. "I had no idea," Eisenhower said, "that the American people were so psychologically vulnerable."[11]

The first American attempts to launch their own satellites failed and were quickly referred to as "Flopniks." The trauma would have been even greater had the American people known something that has only recently come to light: two American defectors, who had been providing American military secrets for many years before they fled to the Soviet Union in 1950, had been helping with the *Sputnik* project.[12]

The anguish of the Americans would have been tempered, on the other hand, had they known that all three of Moscow's claims were false. First, these satellites had not been launched by new mass-produced intercontinental ballistic missiles, but by huge unwieldy prototypes that weighed over 300 tons; the second satellite launched was not larger than the first; and, as we learned from a defector in 1971, the dog did not survive for nearly two weeks in space but was dead before it got there.[13]

On November 7, the Gaither Committee submitted to Eisenhower the report he had commissioned on *Deterrence and Survival in the Nuclear Age*. The report warned that the overall Soviet threat was set to increase, as its economy was already a third as big as America's and growing 50% faster. By 1959, the report said, the Soviet Union "may be able to launch an attack with intercontinental ballistic missiles carrying megaton warheads against which [the] Strategic Air Command will be almost completely vulnerable . . ." It called for massive increases in defense and civil defense.[14] The timing was wildly wrong, but the understanding of Khrushchev's strategy was not far off the mark.

Details of the Gaither report were soon leaked to the press, compounding the anxiety of the American people. But by 1957, research had begun in a valley in California that would transform the world to a far greater extent than the recent Soviet successes in space. Some young American engineers, backed by a rich entrepreneur, had started a company that within two years had produced semiconductors, one of the most revolutionary inventions of the 20th century. This was the beginning of Silicon Valley.

Advantage Eisenhower

"Eisenhower was very perceptive about the Soviet missile threat," Andy Marshall, then a strategist at RAND, pointed out. "His gut instinct was right. The first Soviet intercontinental ballistic missiles were so large that they were only transportable by rail, which limited the areas to be searched. By the late fifties the U-2 over-flights had found no bases or deployed missiles." In other words, there was nothing to support the claims by Khrushchev, US Air Force and the Democrats that there was a "missile gap" in Moscow's favor. It was also improbable that the Soviets could convert the prototype of a missile into a weapon more speedily than the Americans—and it had taken them 115 tests before they could produce six intercontinental missiles a month.

In public, the president voiced his skepticism, while remaining silent on the intelligence he had. Marshall noted that "As we were facing a gradual deterioration in our strategic advantage, not an immediate crisis, Eisenhower believed that we should re-establish America's strategic superiority in a calm and measured way."

America's vulnerability to surprise attack was already being reduced by dispersing its long-range bombers and placing them in revetments. Before long, one-third of its bomber and tanker fleet was kept on runway alert and a dozen fully armed B-52s were in the air at all times.

The Americans, who regarded the strategic bomber as an effective military instrument, had been slow to invest in missiles, but belatedly their missile program was coming to fruition. In January 1958, the American government used a military missile to launch its *Discovery* satellite into a far higher orbit in space than *Sputnik*. From then on, the Americans kept the lead in satellites.

Later that year, an American missile flew about 10,000 km (6,000 miles), twice as far as any Soviet one had ever done. By the end of the decade, the Americans had deployed a total of just over 100 medium-range missiles to Britain, Italy and Turkey—all of which could reach the western Soviet Union, and some of which could reach Moscow itself.

"No event since Pearl Harbor set off such repercussions in American life," the historian Walter McDougall later wrote of *Sputnik*. *Sputnik* transformed the Cold War from a limited "military and political struggle" into one that became total, "a competition for the loyalty and trust of peoples fought out in all arenas of social achievement, in which science textbooks and racial harmony were as much tools of foreign policy as missiles and spies."[15]

Shocks & Bad Lessons

After the bloody suppression of the Hungarian Revolution in November 1956, Khrushchev was desperately keen to burnish the image of socialism. His efforts to do so the following year led to two notable shocks in Moscow—one that came from the West and the other from the East.

One of the boldest steps Khrushchev took was to host the World Youth Festival in Moscow during the summer of 1957. The people of Moscow gave thirty thousand young foreign visitors an exuberant welcome, which made for some excellent propaganda. The spontaneity and massive scale of the welcome, however, made it impossible for the official organizers and the KGB to control the very free exchange of ideas that was taking place. And those discussions had a lasting impact on many Russians.

To show the world that the international communist movement was still unified and under Soviet leadership, Khrushchev convened a conference in Moscow in November 1957—the biggest such gathering since the Second World War. From Khrushchev's point of view the timing was excellent: *Sputnik II* had just been launched, and the reputation of the Soviet Union was riding high.

Khrushchev wanted agreement that the main task of the world communist movement should be to reduce the risk of another world war, and to strive to establish international relations based on "peaceful co-existence." Mao, on the other hand, shocked delegates by declaring that socialist countries should not fear war because, no matter how great the cost, the socialists would be victorious. If, he said, "we lose 300 million [people] what of it?"[16] Although the final communiqué of the conference papered over the cracks, beneath the surface the Sino-Soviet split was becoming wider and wider.

Meanwhile, both Moscow and Washington were closely monitoring developments in the Middle East. After Suez, Eisenhower had declared America's "resolve to block the Soviet march to the Mediterranean, to the Suez Canal, and the pipelines and to the underground lakes of oil which fuel the homes and factories of Western Europe."[17] In the summer of 1958, American and British concerns were thrown into sharp relief when a coup brought left-wing army officers to power in Iraq.

London and Washington viewed the change with deep foreboding as Iraq was a key member of the Baghdad Pact that linked Britain, Turkey, Iraq, Iran and Pakistan in a defensive alliance along the southern flank of the Soviet Union. There were also fears that Iraq could seize control of Kuwait and the other Gulf States, which were already major suppliers of oil to the West.

As much as Khrushchev wanted Iraq to align itself with Moscow, he privately urged the leaders of the coup not to provoke the West. At the same time, despite opposition from some of his colleagues, he threatened to go to war to defend the new regime in Baghdad.[18] Soviet forces began staging some large-scale maneuvers along the Turkish and Iran frontiers, apparently prompted by reliable intelligence about British and American plans to intervene against Iraq through these countries.[19]

Before Khrushchev had issued his threat, the United States and Britain had decided against intervening in Iraq. The military risks were too great, and the leaders of both countries rightly feared that intervention would inflame Arab nationalism throughout the region. They settled for sending a token British force into Jordan and an American one into Lebanon (two countries where

Egyptian and Syrian-backed radicals wished to overthrow regimes aligned with the West). When the American marines waded onto the beaches of Beirut they were not met with gunfire, but by a warm welcome, like a circus coming to town. Vendors offered them refreshingly chilled drinks—at premium prices, of course.

Recently, secret documents have emerged which demonstrate that Khrushchev interpreted America's failure to intervene in Iraq as a further triumph for his policy of threatening the West with war. Khrushchev was developing bad habits.[20] He loved to intimidate, but his nerves were not as steely as Stalin's. The biggest problem with his brinkmanship was that he was the strategic underdog, and he himself was frightened of war. The potential costs of any miscalculation were becoming incredibly grave.

CRISIS MANAGEMENT

"Of course, one does see why President Kennedy's just a little nervous—after all, Washington's not *all* that much further from Cuba than London is from Russia." 24.x.62

Cuban Missile Crisis—European and American Perspectives, October 24, 1962. (Osbert Lancaster, reprinted by courtesy of the *Daily Express*)

11 Khrushchev's Gauntlet

Back to the German Question

Khrushchev liked to say that he hoped to get the German settlement he wanted by "squeezing the testicles of the West" in Berlin.[1]

Khrushchev had no interest in trying to unify Germany. As he had told the French prime minister, Guy Mollet, in 1956: "We prefer 17 million Germans under our influence to 70 million Germans in a reunited Germany, even though they may be neutralized." But to make East Germany viable Khrushchev needed to end its pariah status and remove the threat posed by the Western presence in Berlin, which was "a dagger pointed at its heart."[2]

In the fifteen years since the end of the war, some 2.5 million East Germans—one-sixth of the population—had already fled to the West in search of a better life. Khrushchev was confident that the exodus could be stemmed by turning East Germany into a "showcase" for socialism on the front line of the Cold War. Both he and Ulbricht, the East German leader, asserted that by 1961 living standards in the East would be higher than those in the West. This was patent nonsense. In any event, Ulbricht's new policies so alienated the East Germans that they again began fleeing to the West in droves.

In December 1958, just a few months after saber-rattling over Iraq, Khrushchev had a new threat for the Western Allies: he stated that, if they did not leave Berlin, he would sign a separate treaty with East Germany and pass to it all Soviet rights concerning Berlin (including control over Allied access to the city). By the time the ultimatum was due to expire, in May 1959, Khrushchev had managed to put twelve missiles in place in East Germany that could hit London and Paris with 300-kiloton warheads. But he made no mention of their existence, nor did he issue any further threats.

From Khrushchev's point of view the big breakthrough came during the summer when he received an invitation to visit the United States that September—

the first Soviet leader to have the honor. Khrushchev was so thrilled that he postponed his deadline for settling the Berlin question. The day before Khrushchev set off, his confidence received a major boost when a Soviet missile placed the first man-made object on the moon.

To demonstrate Soviet technological prowess Khrushchev decided to fly to Washington in the latest Soviet turbo-prop airliner, a hazardous venture as it was still being flight-tested.[3] The aircraft did, however, reach its destination without mishap, except that it was so high off the ground that the red-carpeted American stairway could not reach the cabin door. Nevertheless, the fifteen-day visit, on which Khrushchev was accompanied by both his wife and his son, soon got off to a good start.

Khrushchev was keen to make a favorable impression. At the state dinner at the White House he did not follow the American tradition of wearing white tie or the black tie he had once worn in his youth, but appeared beaming in a smart lounge suit, escorted by his wife elegantly dressed in an evening gown. As Khrushchev traveled across the country, however, his temper soon became frayed by Americans who wanted to protest over various aspects of Soviet conduct. Fortunately, he was impressed by much of what he saw and some of the people he met. As his son, Sergei, told me, "Although my father would never say so publicly, he recognized that the United States was a very wealthy country. We may have just landed a space capsule on the moon, but catching up with America economically would be a very big challenge."

During their talks on Germany, Eisenhower acknowledged that the situation in Berlin was "abnormal." In the end, it was arranged that the leaders of the Four Powers would meet in Paris on May 14 to try to resolve the Berlin problem. Upon his return to Moscow, Khrushchev immediately addressed a large, specially assembled audience on the success of his visit. To the great surprise of his audience, he ended his speech by crying out, "Long Live Soviet-American Friendship!"

Such friendship, Khrushchev hoped, would settle the German problem to his satisfaction. But optimism had got the better of his sense of realism, in part because he could not grasp how great the political differences were over Germany and Eastern Europe. And these differences were one of the fundamental reasons why the Western alliance had come into being in the first place.

Khrushchev the Strategist

While Khrushchev misjudged Western attitudes towards Germany, he did have some very shrewd insights into the characteristics and dilemmas of the nuclear age. He rejected the views of his traditionally minded military establishment and wanted new problems to be thought about in new ways.

Like Eisenhower, Khrushchev considered military expenditure a waste of money. Unless the military were tightly restrained, "their inordinate demands could bring our country to ruin . . ."[4] He wanted deterrence to be effective at the lowest possible cost, as did Robert McNamara, the cost-cutting CEO of the Ford Corporation who would soon become Kennedy's secretary of defense.

Only nuclear missiles, Khrushchev firmly believed, could provide deterrence on the cheap. In December 1959, shortly after returning from America, Khrushchev embarked upon a military revolution by establishing the Strategic Rocket Forces, which would be pre-eminent in the new military hierarchy. He ordered the production of 200–300 intercontinental ballistic missiles with large warheads—these would be able to eliminate most of America's strategic bombers, as well as their new intercontinental missiles, which were expected to be based above ground. They would also inflict catastrophic damage on the country. This, he felt, would be enough to deter the Americans.[5]

While Khrushchev's new strategy remained top secret, he sought to deflect attention from his current weaknesses by continuing to boast. At the end of 1959, he delighted in telling journalists that, in just one year, 250 intercontinental missiles with H-bomb warheads had rolled off Soviet production lines like sausages. In fact, he had only four—they weighed 300 tons a piece and took many hours to ready for firing. What were being produced in large numbers were medium-range missiles, some 600 of which were "lined up along the Soviet border from Leningrad to Odessa like artillery pieces, each having a target in Western Europe."[6]

Khrushchev was also determined to use cheap missiles to replace his expensive conventional forces. "Inflated armies," Khrushchev insisted, "are only needed for attack; they are not needed for defense."[7] As Nato did not have large armies, he announced that the Soviet army would once again be slashed, this time by almost a third, which would bring the total down to approximately 2.5 million men. To compensate for its loss of firepower, most conventional artillery in the remaining divisions would be replaced by short-range nuclear missiles, which were regarded as a sort of super artillery.

Just over two weeks later, Khrushchev told his colleagues that these cuts had been made to prove to the West that he really was sincere about disarmament. This, he hoped, would make it possible to realize "our most sacred dream," which was the dismantling of all the Western military alliances.[8]

Even with the cuts in conventional forces, Soviet military expenditure leapt by more than 50% between 1960 and 1962 as Khrushchev poured more money into nuclear weapons. By 1962 nearly a third of the state budget was going to the military—and the real cost was far higher.[9] In the transcript of his tape-recorded memoirs, his remarks about troop reductions come directly after he expresses his belief that the United States was using the arms race to destroy the Soviet economy "and by that means to obtain its goals even without going to war."[10] This was not American policy at the time, but, two decades later, it would be.

No Deterrence on the Cheap

As was so often the case in the nuclear arms race, just as one side thought it was gaining the upper hand, it was in for a nasty surprise. Looking back on his days at the Livermore Laboratory, Harold Brown (the first scientist to become secretary of defense) recollected that "in the late fifties and early sixties only a few Americans knew what a huge lead the Americans had in two key areas of missile development—the miniaturization of warheads and solid rocket fuel."

"The new technology," Brown explained, "would soon make it possible to put a 1-megaton warhead on a small intercontinental ballistic missile that could be launched instantly from a silo (the Minuteman) or a submarine (the Polaris). Each of these would be fairly well protected against attack and relatively cheap."

The Navy leapt at this opportunity and argued for a radically new, low-cost form of deterrence that was minimalist by the standards of the day. It involved having at sea at all times enough Polaris missiles on submarines to hit 200 major Soviet targets. That, many analysts believed, would be "sufficient to destroy all of Russia." The main reason the Navy's case was not accepted was that the proposed fleet would take seven years to build and during that period the Soviet Union could acquire a massive lead over the United States in missiles.

In 1958, Eisenhower approved the development of both the Minuteman and the Polaris missiles. His decision reflected the emerging consensus that America's nuclear deterrent should be based on a "triad" of land-based missiles, submarine-based missiles and the already well-established bomber force. That would ensure that the United States would always be able to retaliate, even after a massive surprise attack. Two years later America had a stockpile of over 18,000 nuclear warheads with a total yield equal to 1.3 million detonations the size of the one exploded over Hiroshima.[11]

At a press conference on February 4, 1960, Eisenhower said, far too late, that there was no need for a deterrent to be more than "completely adequate" for compelling the respect of any potential opponent. This is what Khrushchev thought, too, though he hadn't said it publicly. If Eisenhower had had reliable intelligence on Khrushchev's thinking, the arms race might have been curbed.

As it was, the interest in low-cost deterrence quickly eroded on both sides. The more the Americans felt that their overall strength was ebbing, the more prone they were to favor massive nuclear reassurance. For his part, Khrushchev sought to compensate for Soviet weakness by exaggerating Soviet strength and indulging in threats.

In his farewell broadcast to the America people in January 1961, Eisenhower warned them that the potential for the "disastrous rise of misplaced power" by the military-industrial complex "exists and will persist." The powerful groups to which Eisenhower referred were already pressing for a large American missile force. In June 1958, for example, the Joint Chiefs of Staff "after careful study" recommended that within a decade the stockpile of warheads should be between 51,000 and 73,000![12]

The Joint Chiefs did not get anywhere near that many warheads. Nevertheless, America's missile force grew much larger than either Eisenhower or Kennedy wanted. This stemmed from the huge buildup of the Strategic Air Command and the American nuclear stockpile under Eisenhower, which had created a strategic culture that could not think in terms of smaller options, especially in the face of Khrushchev's bragging. The concept of deterrence was yielding to one of absolute security.

Khrushchev's Revenge

"We are getting to the point," Eisenhower told his close colleagues in early 1960, "where we must decide if we are trying to prepare to fight a war, or to prevent one."[13]

Eisenhower's remark was triggered by his concern over the highly provocative nature of America's spy flights. When, in 1958, the Soviet Union felt strong enough to protest about the U-2s flying over its territory, Eisenhower stopped them. However, with concern continuing to mount over Soviet progress in developing its missile force, Eisenhower, with great reluctance, approved further U-2 flights in February and April 1960.

With even greater reluctance, the president approved one last flight just before the summit meeting that was set for May 1960 in Paris. The plane would fly over the intercontinental ballistic missile sites in European Russia and hopefully scotch, once and for all, the air force's claim that there was a "missile-gap" in Moscow's favor. On May 1, 1960, a U-2 piloted by Captain Gary Powers took off from Peshawar in Pakistan and headed across the Soviet Union towards Norway in search of Soviet missile sites. Had Powers completed his flight, the photography would have shown that there was no missile gap.

Soviet air defense forces, however, not only tracked the plane, but shot it down—their first success against these offensive intruders. In some respects, this was a blow from beyond the grave by Julius Rosenberg, the Soviet atomic spy who had been executed in 1953. Recently it has come to light that the successful Soviet missile was equipped with a proximity-fuse, based on the one that Rosenberg had provided to the Russians back in 1944.[14]

Khrushchev tried to compel Eisenhower to apologize publicly for what had happened, hoping he would then make greater concessions on Germany at the forthcoming summit in Paris. When Eisenhower refused to bend to Khrushchev's attempt to humiliate him, the summit collapsed. That did not matter, as Eisenhower had nothing of substance to offer on Germany anyway.

Wanting Third World Gains

Both Eisenhower and Khrushchev thought that what happened in the Third World could tilt the global political balance. In his second Inaugural Address Eisenhower called on the American people to do more to help the third of mankind who were engaged in a "historic struggle" to free themselves from grinding poverty. This was the only way, he said, to prevent a huge part of the world from falling under Soviet control and assure America's prosperity. His efforts over the next four years to persuade the American people of the importance of the Third World proved to be one of the most frustrating experiences of his life.[15]

While the German problem continued to fester, Khrushchev could see that important new opportunities were opening up in Cuba and Africa, where several European colonies were gaining independence. In Africa, the Soviet Union had the great advantage of not being thought of as an imperial power or being tarnished by the racism and segregation that so afflicted America's reputation abroad, especially during the fifties and sixties.

At the beginning of 1959, Fidel Castro successfully overthrew the Cuban dictator Fulgencio Batista. Washington hoped that he might be a moderate reformer, but by the end of the year, however, his expropriation of property and execution of opponents showed he was a radical with communist inclinations. Khrushchev was ecstatic as he believed this could be the first of a series of left-wing revolutions in Latin America.

By the summer of 1960, Khrushchev had not only offered Castro financial aid, but was promising to defend the Cuban Revolution. "Should the aggressive forces in the Pentagon dare to start intervention against Cuba . . . [they] . . . would be well advised not to forget that, as has been shown by the latest tests, we have rockets that land accurately in a predetermined square target 13,000 km (8,000 miles) away."[16]

That same year, the Belgian Congo gained independence, with Patrice Lumumba, another left-winger, as prime minister. When the copper-rich province of Katanga seceded, backed by Belgian mining interests and Belgian troops, the Congolese government called on the United Nations for help. Although the UN did send troops, they were unwilling to enter Katanga. In response to a request from Lumumba, Khrushchev began sending him arms, as he had earlier done in Cuba. Alarm bells rang in Washington.

Following Lumumba's dismissal by his president, Khrushchev decided to go to the UN General Assembly in New York to rally support for him. By the time he reached New York, however, the Congolese army had taken control of the country, seized Lumumba (who was soon murdered) and ordered the closure of the Soviet and Czechoslovak embassies. Khrushchev was furious and sensed that the Americans were ultimately responsible for what had happened.

Khrushchev's anger and frustration over these issues and his dislike of the way the debates went may all have contributed to his outburst in the General Assembly on October 12, when he is widely believed to have banged his shoe on the table to the horror of his entourage (even though he may not have done so).[17] The one big benefit he got from his visit was that for the first time he was able to meet Castro. They hugged each other like long-separated lovers, which politically they were.

The issue that was coming to the boil, however, was not Cuba but East Germany. In November, Khrushchev assured Ulbricht that if, by the end of 1961, the new Kennedy Administration had not agreed to leave West Berlin under one guise or another, he would sign a peace treaty with East Germany. Khrushchev was quick to add, though, that while the final goal was gradually to push the Western powers out of West Berlin, Moscow could not be expected to risk war by sending troops into West Berlin.[18]

12 Showdown in Berlin

Passing the Torch

At the time John F. Kennedy became president in January 1961, Americans were becoming obsessed with the apparent dynamism of the Soviet Union—an obsession which did much to boost Khrushchev's ego.

After the success of *Sputnik,* Khrushchev had been even more bullish about socialism being the wave of the future, boasting that the Soviet economy would overtake that of the United States. The best Soviet independent estimate at the time was that the economy was around a fifth the size of America's, which was less than half what Khrushchev was claiming, with growth rates continuing to fall. Oleg Bogomolov, the director of the Institute of the World Socialist Economy, told me that when he mentioned this to Yuri Andropov, then in charge of relations with socialist countries, Andropov chided him: "Why do you give me such a hot potato? It's too hot to eat and too hot to handle!"

The Americans, still haunted by the Great Depression and their country's first balance-of-payments deficit in 1958, were prone to accept Khrushchev's ludicrous claims. Their fears had been kept alive by the three economic downturns in the fifties and were now being reinforced by the rapid inroads of European and Japanese manufacturers into their market.

Kennedy, America's youngest president, personified youthful vigor and determination. In his inaugural address, he told the American people, "the torch has been passed to a new generation." He would, he said, do whatever was necessary to re-establish America's superiority. He called on his fellow countrymen to "pay any price, bear any burden, meet any hardship, support any friend, oppose any foe."[1]

One of the main planks of Kennedy's election campaign was that he would reverse the "missile gap" that Eisenhower had allegedly allowed to develop in Khrushchev's favor. Following the launch of *Discovery*, America's first photo-reconnaissance satellite, in August 1960, Washington soon had a far more comprehensive picture of the development of Soviet missile forces. In February 1961, McNamara, Kennedy's secretary of defense, let slip to journalists that he "did not think the Soviet Union had more missiles than the United States."[2]

Whereas Kennedy was embarrassed by McNamara's disclosure, Khrushchev was mortified. The emperor's clothes no longer looked impressive. Faced with such a disadvantage, he decided that he would now have to be even tougher in his dealings with the West, especially with Kennedy. As Kennedy and Khrushchev approached their first summit meeting in Vienna in June, they began sizing each other up. They were not just thinking about the balance of power, but also about their respective powers of leadership.

Since becoming the Soviet leader in 1955, Khrushchev's confidence in his own judgment had grown. He believed that he had shown his mettle by moving swiftly in 1956 to prevent Hungary from withdrawing from the Warsaw Pact. Although America's nuclear forces were far stronger than his, Khrushchev comforted himself with the belief that Kennedy was young, inexperienced in foreign affairs and by temperament not a strong leader.

In his inaugural speech, Kennedy had declared that the United States would respond strongly to every challenge. He had, however, shown himself to be very weak on Cuba, an island that was just some 150 km (90 miles) off the American coast that the Americans had, in effect, controlled since the Spanish-American War of 1898 until Castro's revolution of 1959.

Kennedy backed the CIA's plan, prepared at Eisenhower's request, to cut out this revolutionary cancer before it spread to Latin America. Cuban émigrés had been recruited and trained, but Kennedy greatly reduced the air support in the hope of concealing America's hand in the invasion. In April 1961, the invasion turned into a fiasco at the Bay of Pigs, with 1,400 Cuban émigrés being killed or captured by Castro's forces. Khrushchev hoped that this setback would make Kennedy more malleable. On the contrary, Kennedy now felt that he had to show even firmer resolve.

Confrontation in Vienna

Meanwhile, in East Germany, Khrushchev faced a fiasco of a different sort. In the first six months of 1961, another 100,000 East Germans fled to West Berlin. In May, just a few weeks before the summit in Vienna, Khrushchev decided to step up the pressure for a settlement, even though he was concerned that

American hard-liners could push the young president toward war. Soviet plans for blocking Western access to Berlin were refined. In the end, however, the Politburo decided against closing the air corridors, along which Allied aircraft were allowed to fly to and from Berlin, for fear that it would provoke a sudden escalation of conflict.

Kennedy's determination to be resolute was strengthened by President De Gaulle shortly before the summit. De Gaulle, who had a profound understanding of the ways of the weak, insisted that Khrushchev was bluffing: "If he was really willing to fight over Berlin, the war would have started long ago." He told Kennedy that it was his job "to make sure Khrushchev believes you are a man who will fight."[3]

Shortly before leaving for Vienna, Khrushchev told the Politburo that the German question "is the key issue." He would have to be tough, he said, because Kennedy was "a son of a bitch."[4] With a crisis brewing over Berlin, the State Department advised the president that "in order that the possibilities of a disastrous miscalculation be reduced, it is absolutely vital for [the Soviet Union] to understand that Berlin is of paramount importance to the U.S."[5]

The omens for the summit were not good. They were not made better by Khrushchev arriving in Vienna with the conviction of a man who felt he was riding on the crest of history. His confidence had been bolstered by the fact that, just a few weeks earlier, Yuri Gagarin had become the first man to venture into space, making a ninety-minute orbit around the earth.

From the beginning the talks did not go well. Kennedy's general references to the dangers of miscalculation infuriated Khrushchev, because they touched on one of his most sensitive spots—the fact that he was the one who risked making the miscalculation. When they did get on to the subject of Berlin, Kennedy said he was not contesting East Germany's right to stop the exodus, but he would fight to protect America's rights in West Berlin. Khrushchev then went even further in his efforts to browbeat the young president into making concessions, dramatizing the issue by raising his voice and thumping the table.

Khrushchev declared that it was up to the United States "to decide whether there would be war or peace." If there was no agreement with the Allies on Berlin by December, Khrushchev told Kennedy he would sign a peace treaty with East Germany. Kennedy knew that this was simply a device to enable the East Germans, not the Russians, to squeeze the Allies out of Berlin. In that case, the president retorted, "there will be war."[6] This was, by far, the worst ending yet to a Soviet-American summit. Kennedy was thoroughly shaken by the experience.

But, judging now from what happened subsequently, it is clear that Kennedy had also shaken Khrushchev.

"I was very interested to see," Markus Wolf pointed out, "that shortly after Khrushchev returned to Moscow, he appeared in military uniform for the first time since he became general secretary."

Vital Interests

Khrushchev had good reason to be cautious. He understood full well that an Allied economic embargo against East Germany would be very costly for him; one against all of Eastern Europe could be disastrous, because it would greatly increase the risk of uprisings there.

On his return to Washington, Kennedy and his staff began thinking about what could be done to deter Khrushchev. Five weeks later, on July 13, the president received invaluable help when Allen Dulles, the director of Central Intelligence, personally briefed him about Colonel Oleg Penkovsky, a very well-connected Soviet Military Intelligence officer who had recently begun cooperating with the British and the Americans.

Dulles showed the president the recent report from Penkovsky on what Marshal Varentsov had told him about Khrushchev's plans to cut off access to Berlin and to compel the allies to negotiate with the East Germans. Penkovsky went on to make the important point that Khrushchev's nuclear forces were far weaker than he was claiming. "The firmness of Khrushchev," he said, "must be met with firmness."[7] By mid-July, satellite photography had confirmed Penkovsky's initial report, showing that Khrushchev had less than twenty launch sites for intercontinental missiles and even fewer operational missiles.

On July 25, Kennedy turned the tables and threw down his own gauntlet in front of Khrushchev. In an address to the American people, he declared that the United States would defend the "people of West Berlin, even in the face of force . . ." In other words *West Berlin* was a vital American interest that would be protected, he said, by "all means."[8] He called on his countrymen to know what to do and where to go in case of a nuclear attack. Kennedy reinforced his commitment by announcing a major increase in the defense budget and a call-up of reserves. To reduce the risk of war, he made it clear that he was willing to negotiate on reasonable proposals.

Intelligence reports reaching Khrushchev from the head of the KGB lent weight to what Kennedy was saying. They indicated that if the access routes to

Berlin were blocked the Allies intended to respond robustly, using economic and military measures "that could threaten the security of the Soviet Union."[9] A report from East German Intelligence was far more chilling. It revealed that if conventional forces failed to reopen the access routes to West Berlin, Nato would use tactical nuclear weapons.[10] This was in essence a reflection of discussions between the Americans, the British and the French that had not yet crystallized into a contingency plan, though it did reflect the way some senior officers were thinking.

Khrushchev was a bully and a gambler, but not a suicidal maniac. He had *already* got the message. In March, he had given Ulbricht the go-ahead to prepare a contingency plan for erecting the Berlin Wall. When Ulbricht told the Soviet ambassador in late June or early July that "if the present situation of open borders remains, collapse is inevitable," Khrushchev could see that he had a way out of the crisis.[11]

Avoiding War

Almost immediately, Khrushchev agreed that detailed preparations should begin for closing off East Berlin from the Western sectors. At the beginning of August, Khrushchev told Ulbricht and other East European party leaders that the Berlin Wall was an urgent necessity. The Wall would, of course, be followed by the long-promised peace treaty—though that would have to be approached "in a well-thought out way, without impulsiveness."[12] In essence, however, Khrushchev was fudging the aims of a peace treaty.

No indications of this important change in Khrushchev's plan filtered through to Penkovsky or the West. Work began on implementing *Operation Rose* on August 13. First the East Germans put up a barbed-wire barricade; when the Allies did not respond to that, they started building the Wall. It was soon finished, cutting off East Berlin from West Berlin completely, except for a few tightly controlled crossing points. "It's not a very nice solution," Kennedy said privately, "but . . . a hell of lot better than war."[13]

A new series of Soviet nuclear tests began on September 1. Over the next three months, thirty-one weapons were tested—the largest series of tests (in terms of explosive yield) in world history. On October 17, with those blasts continuing, Khrushchev announced he was lifting the Berlin ultimatum.

Four days later, in response to the renewed Soviet nuclear tests, Kennedy authorized Roswell Gilpatrick, his Deputy Secretary for Defense, to make a public statement that would leave the world in no doubt that the "missile gap" was now decisively in America's favor. Its retaliatory strike would be even more devastating than any pre-emptive Soviet strike.

On the very next day, October 22, before Khrushchev had time to decide how he would respond, Ulbricht set out to assert the right of East Germany to be accepted as an independent state equal to West Germany. Ulbricht made his first move by ordering the East German police to bar a senior American diplomat from entering East Berlin unless he showed his papers, which he refused to do.

The following day, the East Germans announced that all Allied civilians crossing the border would have to show their papers to the East German police. By the end of the month, a daisy-chain of minor incidents had led to a 16-hour standoff between American and Soviet tanks at Checkpoint Charlie, the main crossing-point between the American and Soviet zones of Berlin. Urgent messages between Washington and Moscow prevented this confrontation from escalating into a shooting match.

When Ulbricht complained that Khrushchev had let him down, Khrushchev retorted that a peace treaty with East Germany alone could have provoked an economic embargo that would have crippled the whole socialist bloc. "Even without such an embargo," he told Ulbricht, "we had to sell $450 million worth of gold on the London Exchange to keep East Germany afloat."[14]

Three days after the standoff at Checkpoint Charlie, on October 30, the Soviet Union tested a "super H-bomb," which it called the *Tsar Bomba*. Even though that was done at half-capacity, it produced a blast of 58 megatons and a "flash" that could be seen 1,000 km (620 miles) away. It was far greater than anything tested before or since. It was a warning to the Americans not to try to exploit their advantage.

The Meniscus

The same day, on Khrushchev's orders, Stalin's body was removed from the Lenin-Stalin mausoleum in Red Square, sending a further signal to the Soviet people of his wish to provide them with a less awful form of socialism.

At the same time, a dangerous new twist became apparent in Khrushchev's thinking on Berlin. At a meeting with some of his Politburo colleagues on January 8, 1962, he admitted that "the enemy is strong . . . that is why [Kennedy] could play the same trump card against us that we were trying to play against him—the position of strength card."[15] The simple fact was, Khrushchev said, that the West was not going to agree to a German peace treaty. It was "better to have Berlin for aggravating the West, than to make concessions."[16]

Khrushchev went on to use the metaphor of the liquid meniscus to explain the permanent tension he now believed was necessary both to preserve and advance Soviet interests in a world where the Americans had the strategic advantage. "We should increase the pressure . . . but don't pour the last drop to make the cup overflow." "If we don't have a meniscus," he went on, "we let the enemy sleep peacefully."[17]

While Khrushchev still hoped that some combination of coercion and a face-saving formula would result in the Allies leaving Berlin, he set out to build up a clear advantage in intercontinental missiles by 1963. In the meantime, Khrushchev tried to put pressure on the Allies by interfering with the three air corridors into West Berlin. The Allies then readied thirty-six fighters to escort transport aircraft along each of the corridors from West Germany into Berlin. "We let the Soviet air-controllers know that we were coming. Just before we all took off, the restrictions were lifted," one of the pilots recalled.[18]

The Berlin Crisis that had run through the summer and autumn of 1961 had been nerve-wracking not only for Khrushchev, but also for Kennedy and McNamara. They had shuddered at the thought that an incident at Checkpoint Charlie could have led to all of America's B-52s taking off to destroy the Soviet Union. Civilian control was quickly reasserted over the use of nuclear weapons held by the military. PALs (Permissive Action Links) were soon being fitted to all nuclear weapons to prevent them being used without proper authorization. For years to come, however, many senior American officers doubted how effective PALs would be in times of crisis or the opening phase of a war.

Counterforce

Shortly after the Berlin Crisis, Khrushchev faced his own fiasco, which was that the Soviet Union was completely caught off-guard by the rapid development of America's missile forces.

As the Americans became increasingly concerned about their vulnerability to a Soviet missile attack, the US Air Force began considering whether it could destroy all Soviet nuclear forces before they could be launched against the United States. Marshall recalled that in 1959/60 he and a colleague at RAND had worked with the air force on a top-secret study that concluded that it could be done.

Although it seems that Khrushchev did not know of this report, he was quick to realize that he now faced a completely unexpected situation. The American missile force was already expanding at disconcerting speed. According to official pronouncements, 200 Minuteman missiles would be operational before the end of the year (1961). The services were pressing for enormous increases in nuclear forces. General Thomas Powers, the commander of Strategic Air Command, called for 10,000 intercontinental ballistic missiles, while the Navy wanted to have 100 missile-carrying submarines.[19]

McNamara fought long and hard to put a cap on the buildup of America's strategic nuclear forces. In the end, he laid down some arbitrary figures—1,000 Minuteman missiles deployed in hardened silos, plus the 54 massive Titan missiles that already existed; 41 submarines carrying a total of 656 Polaris missiles and 600 B-52 bombers—a grand total of 1,710 launchers. This was a vastly larger force than McNamara initially had in mind, but it was the smallest force the American military and their allies in Congress would accept.

These numbers were massive, going far beyond the size of any force that Khrushchev had discussed with his colleagues or even bragged about building. They were intended as a signal to him of the technological prowess of the United States and its unwillingness to put up any longer with his outrageous claims. "This meant that in a crisis," Marshall commented, "Khrushchev no longer had any prospect of using pre-emptive strikes to destroy America's ability to inflict nuclear devastation on the Soviet Union."

More worrying still, in January 1962, Kennedy implied that another invasion might be launched against Cuba; then in March he said in an interview that, in certain circumstances, the United States might have to strike first against the Soviet Union with nuclear missiles.[20]

Khrushchev would have been less concerned had he known of Kennedy's discussion with General Le May, the chief of the air force, in May 1961. When the president asked him how many Americans would die if the Soviet Union attacked first, he calmly said 60 million. When the president asked how many would die if the Americans struck first, Harold Brown, the director of defense research at the Pentagon, replied "probably 20–30 million." Kennedy responded firmly, saying "I don't see there is very much difference. The answer is the same: There must never be a thermonuclear war."[21]

Even Worse News for Khrushchev

To make matters worse, all was not well with the Soviet missile program. At the Black Sea resort of Pitsunda in February 1962, Marshal Moskalenko complained bitterly to Khrushchev about the state of the Strategic Rocket Forces he commanded. Not only did he have few missiles, but the best of them took 20 hours to prepare. Before they could be fired, Moskalenko lamented, "nothing would be left of us."[22] Khrushchev promptly sacked the bearer of such disagreeable news.

The General Staff quickly formulated plans to respond to the American programs, this time with Soviet missiles not being made by the artillery industry, from which they had originated, but by the technologically more advanced aviation industry. Khrushchev accepted their recommendation that the Soviet Union should have a large number of light missiles to match Minuteman; around 50 heavy missiles that could destroy cities, plus a few super-heavy missiles to destroy command-and-control centers located deep underground.

These new plans were an important step forward in Khrushchev's thinking about deterrence. Many of the new missiles would be protected in silos. In addition, Khrushchev already had submarines that could fire cruise missiles with nuclear warheads—and work had begun on developing submarines that could fire ballistic missiles. For the first time, the Soviet Union would have a retaliatory capability. But one big problem remained. The new land-based missiles would not be ready for some five years. In the intervening period, the Soviet Union would become even more vulnerable to an American pre-emptive attack.

According to the memoirs that Khrushchev dictated after being ousted from power, the idea of deploying missiles in Cuba came from a flash of inspiration that he had while on holiday by the Black Sea in May 1962. The Americans had already deployed medium-range missiles in Turkey, Italy and Britain. Therefore, Khrushchev reasoned, he could redress his sense of vulnerability by secretly deploying comparable Soviet missiles to Cuba and so making Kennedy feel equally threatened.

The stage was being set for the Missile Crisis.

13 At the Cuban Precipice

Khrushchev's Big Idea

The Cuban Missile Crisis was the closest the world has ever come to nuclear war. For both Kennedy and Khrushchev it was a drama of Shakespearian intensity.

"This will be an offensive policy," Khrushchev told his colleagues on May 21, 1962, when he proposed to them that Soviet missiles be deployed to Cuba. It would, he said, redress the strategic imbalance, protect Cuba and, hopefully, make the United States more flexible on Berlin and other contentious issues.[1]

In July, the Soviet leadership authorized *Operation Anadyr*. This was a massive logistical undertaking that involved the clandestine dispatch of forty medium-range missiles with nuclear warheads, plus over 50,000 troops and airmen to protect both the missiles and Cuba itself. From Cuba these missiles could destroy most major American cities and the main bases of the Strategic Air Command. Their presence would make the Soviet deterrent considerably more credible.

Later, Khrushchev added eighty nuclear-tipped cruise missiles that could strike ships up to 150 km (90 miles) away, short-range missiles that could be used against an invasion force and the American base at Guantanamo Bay, plus six atomic bombs.

Only recently have documents been found that show that once the November mid-term congressional elections were over and American politicians were less likely to posture politically, Khrushchev planned to push once more for West Berlin to become a "Free City." If that failed he would probably create a crisis atmosphere and try to get his way by taking the matter to the United Nations.[2] One of Khrushchev's colleagues had warned him of the risks of being caught out trying to sneak missiles into Cuba. He should have listened.

Despite the success of Soviet efforts to conceal what was going on, John

McCone, the director of Central Intelligence, became suspicious. He began reviewing the secret intelligence reports that suggested something strange was happening in Cuba. Why, he asked himself, were the Russians installing surface-to-air missiles in parts of Cuba where there were no airfields for them to defend? The only possible explanation was that they would be used to protect new missile sites. On August 10, McCone dictated a memorandum for President Kennedy "expressing the belief that installations for the launching of offensive missiles were being constructed on the island."[3]

Kennedy made it clear, in two speeches in early September, that if Soviet offensive missiles were installed in Cuba "the gravest issues will arise." In case that happened, Kennedy obtained authority to call up 150,000 reservists. Khrushchev was undeterred. At the White House, on October 18, Andrei Gromyko, the Soviet foreign minister, personally assured the president that no offensive missiles or nuclear weapons would be introduced into Cuba. Kennedy knew he was lying because two days earlier he had been informed that a U-2 spy-plane had detected the construction of missile sites on the island.

Caught Out

Kennedy immediately brought together his advisers in a task force known as Ex-Com. They were told, thanks to intelligence from Penkovsky, that some medium-range missiles that could reach Washington would soon be operational, though preparing them for firing would take hours; the sites for the longer-range missiles (which could reach all major American cities except Seattle), would not be ready for another two months.

The CIA suspected that Soviet nuclear warheads, at least for the first type of missiles, had already reached Cuba, but it did not know how many there were or where they were stored. Nor did it know that Soviet forces also had anti-ship cruise missiles and tactical missiles, both with nuclear warheads.

Some members of Ex-Com pressed for immediate air strikes, and even for an invasion of Cuba. Although the president knew that Khrushchev's missile force was far weaker than his, he was alert to the risks of such action, saying they would be "one hell of a gamble."[4] There was no guarantee that once the fighting started one of the Soviet missiles would not explode above a sizeable American city or that Khrushchev would not respond by seizing West Berlin, thus creating an even greater risk of nuclear war.

On the afternoon of October 22, the White House announced that the presi-

U-2 photo of Soviet missile launch site in Cuba, October 25, 1962. (U.S. Department of Defense)

dent would address the American people at 7 pm EST on a "matter of national importance." The Soviet leaders were somewhat relieved when they heard that in his address the president had only gone so far as to declare that the "secret, swift and extraordinary buildup" of Soviet forces in Cuba was a "provocative and unnecessary change to the *status quo*." While urging Khrushchev to withdraw the missiles and "move the world back from the abyss of destruction," Kennedy announced that the United States would impose a "quarantine zone" around Cuba to prevent the inflow of further "offensive military" cargoes.[5]

While the president was speaking, American forces worldwide were put on a higher state of nuclear alert than at any other time during the Cold War. Every hour of the day and night, over sixty B-52 bombers were on airborne-alert and in easy striking distance of the Soviet Union. Within days the Strategic Air Command had over one thousand bombers ready to take off for the Soviet Union at fifteen minutes' notice. In addition, it had some 180 missiles that could reach the Soviet Union—from Turkey, Italy and the United States itself.

In the Soviet Union, the Strategic Rocket Forces were also put on high alert, but they still had only some forty missiles that could reach America. That same day in Moscow, Penkovsky was arrested. Concern about the secrets he might have divulged to the Americans and the British was so great that he was being interrogated by the general in charge of counter-espionage. It soon became clear that the West knew much about the weaknesses of the Soviet missile force.

General Danilevich, then a young officer with the Soviet forces in Poland, recalled the crisis many years later. "We were ordered to stop all exercises, return to our command posts and be ready for action. We were completely sure that war would begin within 24 hours. So the situation really was on the edge of a precipice. If there were a careless move on either side, it could have led to a nuclear war."[6]

As nearly two hundred American warships began moving into place to enforce the quarantine, Khrushchev condemned it as "an act of aggression." Nevertheless, as the quarantine came into force on October 24, no Soviet ships were still heading towards the exclusion zone. When Dean Rusk, the secretary of state, heard this news he sighed with relief. "We're eyeball to eyeball, and I think the other fellow has just blinked."[7] That is not quite what happened. Thirty hours earlier, Khrushchev had ordered the sixteen Soviet ships on their way to Cuba with the longer-range missiles and warheads to return home.[8]

Fearing that Khrushchev might not withdraw the missiles already in Cuba, Kennedy had earlier ordered preparations for an invasion. This would begin with an air attack of over 1,000 sorties, accompanied by a D-Day-scale invasion of 125,000 troops. They would take ten days to complete their task and were expected to suffer nearly 20,000 casualties.

Backing Down

The archives show that from as early as October 25 Khrushchev had accepted that he would have to back down. Although the intelligence Khrushchev was receiving exaggerated the willingness of the United States to invade Cuba, it was a reminder of the risks he faced once Kennedy had refused to accept the deployment. His meniscus had become extremely precarious. On October 26, Khrushchev told the Politburo that "We have been warned that war could start today . . . We have to concentrate on the main point: If the United States . . . pledges not to attack Cuba, we will withdraw our missiles."[9]

That day, Khrushchev sent Kennedy an emotionally charged message signaling that he wished to step back from "the abyss" to which the president had referred to in his declaration four days earlier. He hinted that if Kennedy agreed not to invade Cuba, then the Soviet Union would dismantle and remove its missiles from the island. That same night, Castro pleaded with Khrushchev to respond to any attack on Cuba with a full Soviet missile attack on the United States, an idea that horrified Khrushchev.

The following day, October 27, is rightly remembered as "Black Saturday." As Michael Dobbs writes in his recent book: "If the Cuban missile crisis was the defining moment of the Cold War, Black Saturday was the defining moment of the missile crisis. It was then that the hands of the metaphorical Doomsday Clock reached one minute to midnight."[10]

As the day began in Moscow, Khrushchev thought he might still "win" the duel. He had just seen an article written two days earlier by Walter Lippmann, the influential American columnist, proposing that the confrontation be settled by Moscow pulling its missiles out of Cuba and the Americans pulling theirs out of Turkey. Later that morning Moscow Radio broadcast such a demand from Khrushchev.[11] Kennedy did not reject the idea out of hand. "Let's not kid ourselves," he told his executive committee, it was a "very good proposal."[12]

But before the committee's discussions had progressed far, alarming news boosted tension to record levels in both Washington and Moscow.[13] Soviet fighters were chasing a U-2 spy plane that had strayed into Soviet airspace, another had been shot down over Cuba (without Moscow's approval) and low-level reconnaissance planes flying over the island were being fired on by the Cubans themselves. Had the U-2 made it back from Cuba with its photos showing that the American base at Guantanamo Bay was in range of Soviet tactical nuclear missiles there would have been consternation in the White House.[14]

At the Abyss

Even so, the Joint Chiefs of Staff recommended to the president that the invasion of the island start no later than Monday. The president commented to his top advisers that "time is running out," a judgment reinforced by a briefing showing that "the missiles are on the launchers" in Cuba. What they did not know was that at noon that day the nuclear warheads had reached the launch sites of the missiles that were targeted on Washington.[15]

Within five minutes of this briefing, Robert Kennedy, the president's brother, was meeting with Anatoly Dobrynin, the Soviet ambassador, to tell him "time is of the essence and we shouldn't miss the chance." He reiterated the president's pledge not to invade Cuba and assured Dobrynin the American missiles would come out of Turkey in 4–5 months as long as nothing was said publicly about it.

The president was taking a considerable risk. In disregard of America's Nato obligations, and in contradiction of his public statements, the president had shown himself ready to bargain away installations of great importance to an ally in pursuit of security for the American mainland. Had this become known at the time, Kennedy would have come under sharp criticism.

As McNamara left the White House on the night of Saturday, September 27, he wondered whether he and millions of other Americans would live to see another day. Khrushchev was even more shaken by the turn of events, especially by the fact that a U-2 had been shot down over Cuba without authorization from Moscow. Khrushchev "shit his pants," Vasily Kuznetsov, the deputy foreign minister, later graphically recalled.[16]

In Moscow late on the evening of Black Saturday, believing reports that Kennedy would announce an invasion the following day, Khrushchev prepared to back down publicly. Dobrynin's account of his meeting with Robert Kennedy, which reached the Politburo the following morning, reinforced the sense of urgency. To ensure that Khrushchev's response reached Washington before any fateful decision was taken, it was broadcast by Moscow Radio at 5 pm on Sunday, when it was only 9 am in Washington. Khrushchev said that, as the president had given assurances that the United States would not invade Cuba, he was willing to withdraw those weapons "which you describe as offensive" from the island and allow UN representatives to verify that this had been done.[17]

While neither Khrushchev nor Kennedy had wanted war, events could easily have spun out of control. On Black Saturday, for instance, Moscow had sent an urgent telegram to General Isa Pliev, the Soviet commander in Cuba, that not only banned him from launching the medium-range missiles without explicit instructions from Moscow, but "categorically . . . prohibited" the use of tactical nuclear weapons as well.[18] Nonetheless, had the Americans launched an invasion, Soviet troops may well have resorted to using their tactical missiles armed with nuclear warheads, whether Moscow gave them the go-ahead or not.

The same day another catastrophe was averted at sea. When an American warship had begun dropping depth charges to force a Soviet submarine to surface, the Soviet officers inside the submarine thought that war had already broken out. They debated whether they should use their nuclear torpedo against an American warship in the vicinity. The three key officers took a vote—one voted for, and two against. This was a good day for democracy.[19]

Although Khrushchev was still embittered by having been forced to climb down, he and his colleagues had been traumatized by this drama. Ten days later a Soviet air marshal told the wife of the American ambassador in Moscow that he was now willing to believe in God.[20] Kennedy, his advisers and the American people had also been horrified by the crisis, as had their allies. Both sides wanted to avoid a repetition. "Perhaps now," Kennedy wrote to Khrushchev, "as we step back from danger, we can together make progress" in the vital field of disarmament.[21]

Fresh Hopes

"We may not love each other," Khrushchev told the American ambassador as they stood beneath the gilded chandeliers at a reception in the Kremlin, "but we have to live together and may even have to embrace each other, if the world is to survive."[22] The occasion was a reception on November 7, 1962, to mark the 45th anniversary of the Bolshevik Revolution.

At the Politburo meeting on December 3, 1962, Khrushchev gave his colleagues his post-mortem on the Cuban Crisis. Not only had the Americans agreed to withdraw their missiles from Turkey and Italy, he said, but they had also pledged not to invade Cuba. "Cuba has been maintained," he rightly asserted, "as a center of the revolutionary movement." At long last, the United States had been forced to respect the Soviet Union and to recognize that it had its own interests in the Western Hemisphere. Above all, he said, "We are members of the World Club. They themselves got scared."[23]

Kennedy took the first big step towards easing tensions by keeping his word—in March 1963, the Jupiter missiles were withdrawn from Turkey (and from Italy, too). In June, Kennedy made a conciliatory speech in which he called for a "fresh start" in Soviet-American relations. "We must conduct our affairs in such a way that it becomes in the Communists' interest to agree on a genuine peace . . . to . . . let each nation choose its own future, so long as that choice does not interfere with the choice of others."[24]

This was, Khrushchev said, the best speech by any American president since Roosevelt. It was a step towards détente. In the improved atmosphere, agreement was soon reached on establishing a "hot line" for communication during crises, as well as on a treaty banning nuclear tests above ground, underwater and in space. There was now, Khrushchev felt, a real prospect of building a better, calmer relationship with Kennedy.

New possibilities had also opened up with West Germany. Shortly before Kennedy's speech, Adenauer, now 88 years old and nearing retirement, privately let Khrushchev know that he favored a broad normalization of relations. He could, he said, accept two Germanys, a divided Berlin and no change to the Polish-German frontier for 30 years. Almost immediately, Khrushchev was telling his colleagues "Let's change the tactics. We will not get an agreement with the Americans." In other words, if progress was going to be made on the German issue, Moscow would have to concentrate on Bonn, not Washington—but that major shift in Soviet policy would only get underway at the end of the sixties.

At the same time, however, neither side wanted the other to be able to intimidate them with nuclear weapons. The withdrawal of Soviet missiles was negotiated between John McCloy, Kennedy's adviser on arms control, and Kuznetsov, the deputy foreign minister. After the details had been finalized, Kuznetsov said, "Well, Mr. McCloy, we will honor this agreement. But I want to tell you something. You'll never do this to us again."[25] For their part, the Americans pressed ahead with the massive planned expansion of their nuclear forces.

An Assassination & an Ousting

Khrushchev was delighted when in mid-November 1963 he received word that Kennedy was interested in a two- or three-day summit during which they could "calmly talk everything over." Such a meeting could do much to improve his standing at home and abroad.

A week later, Kennedy was assassinated in Dallas. In keeping with the constitution, Lyndon Johnson, his vice president, became president for the rest of Kennedy's term. Whereas Kennedy had been a charismatic leader, Johnson was an effective one, who persuaded Congress to pass social legislation that was way beyond Kennedy's reach. Khrushchev, however, never had a chance to establish a working relationship with Johnson as on October 24, 1964, he himself was ousted from office.

At the Politburo that day his erstwhile supporters attacked the recklessness of both his foreign and domestic policies. Alexander Shelepin, the head of the KGB, first taunted Khrushchev on the economy by asking the rhetorical question "When did you get the idea that things are going well?" before blaming him for the slump in economic growth over the past decade from 11% to 4%. In foreign policy, he accused Khrushchev both of putting too much faith in peaceful coexistence with the United States and for risking war over Suez, Berlin and Cuba. Other members of the Politburo added the charge that he had taken the country down the wrong path because of his "morbid competition with America."[26]

In his defense, Khrushchev said that his contribution had been to put an end to Stalinism—"The fear is gone and we can talk as equals."[27] But the leadership still feared the Soviet people. They were shocked by the speed at which the people had taken advantage of the "thaw," the easing of restrictions which allowed people somewhat more freedom of speech and expression. "We in the leadership," Khrushchev later said, "were consciously in favor of 'the thaw' ... But we were all scared, really scared. We were afraid that 'the thaw' might unleash a flood which we wouldn't be able to control, and which would drown us."[28]

The pressures that a thaw could create were evident at the Kiev opera house on the day in 1961 when Yuri Gagarin became the first man to venture into space. On stage was Gerry Scott, a British jazz singer, a million of whose records had already been sold in the Soviet Union. In a figure-hugging dress she sang "as if drinking a Martini in the bath." When she honored Gagarin by singing "How High the Moon," the audience went wild.[29] It was Ms. Scott's last performance in the Soviet Union.

Salutary Lessons

The decade between Stalin's death and Kennedy's assassination began with both sides hoping to ease tensions but ended with them becoming increasingly competitive, and coming closer to nuclear war than they ever would again.

At the end of the war, Stalin had said that if the Big Three did not work together, Germany could again pose a threat to them in fifteen years. By the end of the fifties there was a threat, but different from the one Stalin had imagined—it came from the specter of the collapse of East Germany, followed by that of the other socialist regimes in Eastern Europe.

When Khrushchev tried to prevent this happening during the Berlin Crisis of 1961, he came face-to-face with the agonizing dilemma of the nuclear age, one that Eisenhower had earlier identified—recognize your adversary's vital interests or accept the risk of thermonuclear war. He opted for the Wall not the War, a solution that Kennedy found acceptable. But Khrushchev realized that he would still have to come to terms with West Germany.

The arms race was spurred by the sharply contrasting American and Soviet views of deterrence and the difficulty each side had in understanding the other's approach. Both Eisenhower and Khrushchev did come to see advantage in stripping nuclear deterrence down to the minimal levels of "mutually assured destruction." But new weapons were constantly generating new insecurities and yet more competition. This led Denis Healey, the former British defense minister, to wryly observe that "It only takes five percent credibility of American retaliation to deter the Russians, but nine-five percent credibility to reassure the Europeans."[30] And in both Moscow and Washington much reassurance was needed.

The Berlin and Cuban crises surely caused many sleepless nights both in Moscow and in Washington. A feeling would soon emerge that it was not enough to survive such crises as they occurred—every possible effort had to be made to avoid them all together.

Despite having accused Khrushchev of following the path of "morbid competition," his successors soon followed in his footsteps, encouraged by signs of American weakness and still buoyed by the belief that history was going their way. But given how weak the Soviet Union was economically, this was a high-risk strategy.

THE RISE OF DÉTENTE

Top: Saigon: American troops under fire during the Vietcong's Tet Offensive in February 1968. (U.S Department of Defense) *Bottom:* Prague: A Czech girl shouts "Ivan GO Home!" to Soviet soldiers, August 26, 1968. (Corbis)

14 One Bed, Two Dreams

Old Roots, New Shoots

"One bed, two dreams" is an ancient Chinese saying about marriage that aptly describes Soviet and American efforts to establish an era of détente. By the mid-sixties strong urges certainly impelled each side to try to get along with the other, but reaching an accommodation would be difficult; sustaining it would be harder still.

The concept of détente, a relaxation of tension between adversaries, emerged when French was the language of international diplomacy—and most of that was conducted between the European powers themselves. It grew out of the search for a balance of power—and that balance could only be maintained on the basis of the cold calculations of *realpolitik*. In exploring their possibilities, however, both Moscow and Washington were caught up in problems that were far more complex than those faced by the earlier European practitioners of this policy.

Fear of nuclear war had made both countries think more carefully about the risks they were willing to take. During the Arab-Israeli Six Day War of 1967, misunderstandings were averted by using the "hot line" that had been set up between the White House and the Kremlin in the wake of the Cuban Missile Crisis.

Both sides also showed an increased interest in negotiating arms control agreements, though each side had rather different reasons. Towards the end of the decade the Americans wanted to curb the rapid expansion of Soviet strategic nuclear missile forces that were on the point of overtaking their own, while the Soviets sought to prevent the Americans exploiting their technological lead to open up a costly new round of the arms race.

Similarly, there was a wish to prevent another Berlin Crisis and to stabilize the situation in Europe. Since the Potsdam Conference, Moscow had sought a peace treaty that would provide international assurances that the West would not disrupt its control of Eastern Europe (which had already been seriously challenged by the peoples of three different nations in the past decade and a half).

This tied in with Moscow's growing preoccupation with West Germany, which already in 1966 had a booming economy, a greater share of world trade than the United States, and a large and well-equipped military. There was a perception in Moscow that West Germany would continue going from strength to strength, and that Moscow therefore needed to come to some accommodation with Bonn "before it was too late."

America's European allies were particularly keen to see an easing of tension on their continent, which they knew could be rendered largely uninhabitable if war broke out there and "went nuclear." By October 1966, President Johnson was talking about the need for bridge building and achieving "the unification of Germany in the context of a larger, peaceful and prosperous Europe."[1] The Nato Ministerial Council made another major gesture to Moscow the following May when it announced that the Alliance was changing its strategy from "massive retaliation" to "flexible response" and that it intended to seek a détente in relations with the Soviet Union and Eastern Europe (see p. 194).

Problems in the Third World added to the pressures on the United States and the Soviet Union to reach some accommodation. As the situation in Vietnam worsened and opposition at home mounted, American leaders desperately wanted Moscow to help extricate the United States from the war by pressing Hanoi into a peace settlement. At the same time, an even greater problem was looming for the Soviet leadership as their confrontation with Mao Zedong intensified (see p. 154).

This achievement, however, had been accompanied by two major setbacks. The Arab-Israeli Six Day War (June 10–15, 1967) had seen the swift and humiliating rout of Moscow's key allies in the Middle East—Egypt and Syria. There had also been a dramatic reversal in Indonesia, the most populous state in southeast Asia, which had begun aligning itself far more closely with the United States following an attempted communist coup in 1965.

Economic problems at home also encouraged both sides to try to cut back on military expenditure and to develop trade. The American economy was not doing well, with Japan and Western Europe eroding its international predominance, the balance of payments worsening and the dollar in trouble. The Soviet Union's international economic problems were less visible, but at home the economic outlook was deteriorating.

As the Soviet leadership were unwilling to embark on economic reform, they decided to try to get around the problem by buying advanced technology from the West on credit and by attracting Western corporations to set up their own plants in the Soviet Union, albeit under tight controls. Exports from these projects could then be used to pay off the loans and finance the import of grain and consumer goods.

When in 1966 Rodric Braithwaite, a British diplomat in Moscow, asked why Brezhnev had just spent $1 billion on American grain, Victor Louis, a Soviet journalist closely involved with the KGB, shrewdly observed that "he could not be sure that the next time the soldiers would shoot" when people rioted over food shortages, as they had in 1962.

For the Americans, the future of the "American Century" looked distinctly less rosy than it once had. Within just five years, three leading figures had been assassinated—President Kennedy, his brother Robert, and Martin Luther King Jr., the leader of the civil rights movement. Among the American political establishment there was a growing feeling that the United States should show some self-restraint—especially as, with Khrushchev gone, the Soviet Union seemed to be a more moderate power.

Politically, the mood among the Soviet leadership was decidedly more upbeat. They already had diplomatic relations with nearly all the newly independent countries in Africa, the Middle East and Asia, with many of whom they were expanding arms sales and developing trade; their growing navy was showing the flag more frequently in the Mediterranean, the Indian Ocean and the Caribbean; and they would soon achieve parity in strategic nuclear arms with the United States.

The key characteristic of the Soviet leadership's outlook at this time was their confidence that they could gain the upper hand through more moderate policies than those Khrushchev had pursued. And given the general malaise in the West, they believed that this was a good time to start trying.

The Man Who Loved Détente

The Soviet approach to détente was greatly influenced by the personality of Leonid Brezhnev, the man who had orchestrated the coup against Khrushchev in 1964. Two years later, Brezhnev proclaimed his pre-eminence over the Soviet Communist Party by taking the title of General-Secretary, one not used since Stalin's day. But he was of a different generation than Stalin's—he was also the first leader of the Soviet Union to look comfortable in a Western suit.

Brezhnev showed few inhibitions about enjoying the good life. Before long, Muscovites were joking that when he showed off to his mother his fine dacha, his collection of imported cars and clothes, his sporting guns and his girlfriends, she said, "Leonid, this is wonderful. You have done so well. But what will happen to us when the revolution comes?"

Unlike Khrushchev, Brezhnev was consistent, could be open and convivial, disliked confrontation and wanted to keep East-West tension low. Anatoly Chernyaev, who worked in the party secretariat and saw quite a lot of Brezhnev over the next few years, told me that "Brezhnev genuinely believed in the possibility of making peace with the imperialists'" and, as such, was "a driving force for détente."

In one important respect, however, Brezhnev was like Khrushchev—he was keen to make the Soviet Union the world's pre-eminent superpower. In the five years between 1965 and 1969, one thousand additional intercontinental missiles were deployed in new bases in a vast arc along the Trans-Siberian railway, stretching from the eastern Ukraine into Kazakhstan. This was the single largest and most expensive weapons project in Soviet history.[2]

Within the Kremlin there was a growing conviction that more should be done to help history on its way. Brezhnev had always insisted that détente and "peaceful coexistence" in no way undermined Soviet support for national liberation and class struggle. This was not just driven by an ideological urge to assist those seeking freedom from colonial rule, but was part of a strategy to weaken the capitalist world and revitalize the "socialist camp" that had been so badly damaged by the Sino-Soviet split.

The Sino-Soviet Split

The United States and the Soviet Union each had fractious allies, but in every sense China was a far bigger headache for Moscow than France ever was for Washington—and, as in the case of France, personalities played their part (see p. 158). Khrushchev enjoyed agitating his adversaries, but no one succeeded in ruffling him as effectively as Mao did. In Mao, Khrushchev met his match.

The considerable efforts Khrushchev made in the mid-fifties to improve relations with Mao did pay off. The gains were short-lived, however, because the two of them had completely incompatible agendas. Khrushchev wanted to ease tensions with America and begin de-Stalinization at home. Mao, on the other hand, wanted to maintain tension with America so that he could "mobilize" the

Chinese people to develop "socialism" in China to an even greater degree than the Soviet Union.

Like Stalin in the immediate post-war period, Mao seems to have wanted no one to think that he could be intimidated by the threat of nuclear war. But Khrushchev did not think that Mao was as rational as Stalin. When Mao called the Americans "paper tigers," Khrushchev reminded him that they had "atomic teeth."

Relations were further worsened by sharp differences over China's border dispute with India (with which Moscow had good relations) and its attacks on the small "off-shore" islands still controlled by Chiang Kai-shek (which complicated Moscow's relations with Washington). Other bones of contention included Khrushchev's denunciation of Stalin (which Mao felt damaged the reputation of all communist parties), the Soviet handling of events in Poland and Hungary, as well as the lack of Soviet support for revolutionary movements in the Third World.

During Khrushchev's visits to Beijing in July 1958 and October 1959, Mao treated him with disdain. On the first occasion, Khrushchev was so keen to get along with Mao that he agreed to join him in a swimming pool, which was a big mistake—Mao was a fine swimmer, but Khrushchev, who had never swum in his life, had to wear a life belt. This was an exquisite form of water torture and humiliation. It was one of several encounters that contributed to their mutual antagonism and sparked some historic rows.

By mid-1959, Khrushchev had had enough. In June, Moscow abruptly terminated its secret nuclear weapons program with Beijing—three months before Khrushchev paid his first and much longed-for visit to the United States. The next year, all Soviet technicians were called home, leaving hundreds of industrial and infrastructure projects unfinished across China. The din of Sino-Soviet dispute could be heard around the world. The accusations and counter-charges were much more vituperative than those used in Soviet-American relations.

After the Cuban Missile Crisis, the United States became increasingly concerned at the prospect of Mao having an atomic bomb. Kennedy flirted with the idea of cooperating with Moscow to destroy the Chinese nuclear plants. Khrushchev, however, firmly rejected the idea when Harriman raised it with him in the summer of 1963.[3]

Just after Brezhnev replaced Khrushchev, in October 1964, the Chinese conducted their first atomic test. Sino-Soviet relations deteriorated further after Mao unleashed his so-called "Cultural Revolution" in 1966 and Soviet forces invaded Czechoslovakia two years later. In 1969 the Soviet Union began building up its forces along the Chinese frontier, where a series of armed clashes took place. Mao was quick to play up the Soviet threat, ordering hundreds of miles of tunnels and air-raid shelters to be dug beneath Beijing and other Chinese cities. Moscow began to fear that Mao's decision to dispute Soviet claims to large tracts of Siberia would be followed by tens of millions of Chinese civilians swarming across the border to reoccupy these historic "Chinese lands."

A few years earlier the Sino-Soviet alliance had given strength to the cause of world communism; henceforth China would undermine Soviet influence across the Third World and seriously drain Soviet military resources as Moscow built up its conventional and nuclear forces along the border from Central Asia to the Pacific.

A New Test of Containment

While Brezhnev was building up Soviet forces to hold the line against China, Johnson was considering how to shore up South Vietnam, a task becoming more difficult and damaging by the day—financially, politically, and in terms of America's credibility.

When Truman began helping the French finance their military operations against the communists in Vietnam in 1950, few Americans understood that the communists were not merely rebels. For many Vietnamese, they were the standard-bearer of the country's intensely nationalist cause that had been strengthened through a millennium of keeping the Chinese at bay and a century of opposition to French colonial rule.

The French left Indochina in 1954, after suffering a humiliating defeat at the hands of the Vietnamese communist forces at Dien Bien Phu. They had lost some 90,000 troops in less than a decade. To help reduce tension with the United States after the Korean War, Moscow and Beijing pressed Ho Chi Minh, the Vietnamese leader, to accept the division of the country at the 17th parallel, believing that within two years there would be elections that would give him control of the South.

Despite the French experience, Eisenhower backed the anti-communist regime in Saigon and the elections never took place. Instead of building a national consensus, the regime antagonized much of the population by suppressing its non-communist critics. In 1959, the North began infiltrating troops (both Northerners and Southerners) into the South, not across the fairly well-defended frontier along the 17th parallel, but along the Ho Chi Minh trail that ran through the jungles of neutral Laos.

Kennedy was reluctant to send American troops to fight in Vietnam. But despite clear warnings from General MacArthur and others that America could not hope to win, Kennedy backed large-scale counter-insurgency operations. While the number of American military "advisers" rose to 16,000, the Communist forces gained control of about a third of the country.

Even though the conventional wisdom was that the South was an essential outpost in the defense of liberty, Johnson remained skeptical about committing American troops, especially as no major ally was willing to join him. In the end, domestic political pressures persuaded him to do so. After the outrage in the United States over the "loss" of China to the communists in 1949, few American politicians wanted to be held responsible for losing South Vietnam and opening up southeast Asia to further communist victories.

Once the decision was made, Johnson exploited an incident in the Tonkin Gulf in August 1964 to obtain wide powers from Congress for the conduct of this undeclared war. An intense bombing campaign was launched against the North from aircraft carriers. This did not stop the North sending more forces into the South; nor did it deter Moscow and Beijing from increasing their military aid to North Vietnam. The following year, while the Soviet Union was providing advanced missiles and aircraft, over 300,000 Chinese support troops were in North Vietnam helping with transport and air defense.

Just over three months after being elected president in his own right with a landslide majority, Johnson began sending ground forces into Vietnam in March 1965. He also ordered the use of B-52 bombers to intensify the attacks on the North and against Vietcong strongholds in the South. This bombing campaign and the influx of half a million American troops appeared to stem the communist offensive. In January 1968, Johnson declared that America was winning the war.

A few weeks later the communists launched the "Tet" offensive across the South. They suffered heavy losses, but their attacks dramatically reinforced the view of many Americans that the war in which they had already lost some 35,000 troops was unwinnable. As American opposition exploded in student protests, congressional support slumped for this immensely costly war that it had never formally declared. The bipartisan consensus on foreign policy had virtually disintegrated by 1968.

In March 1968, Johnson announced that he would not seek a second term as president. Despite all the atrocities committed by the North Vietnamese communists in the South, Johnson had never been willing to try to force Hanoi to abandon the war by using the B-52s to attack the Red River dykes, which would create a flood that could kill hundreds of thousands of civilians and ruin much of the best agricultural land. There were limits as to what it was acceptable for America to do in war.

Nevertheless, as the Soviet need for détente grew, Moscow cajoled Hanoi into peace talks with the Americans, which started in Paris in April 1968. Washington had no doubt that success would depend on Moscow stepping up its pressure on Hanoi. And for that, the Soviet leadership would want rewards.

Ironically, it was the firmly anti-military Japanese who were the unquestionable beneficiary of the war in Vietnam. They became a major supplier of all sorts of non-military goods and equipment to both the Americans and the South Vietnamese, which did much to help the Japanese economy take off during the sixties, with its surging exports cutting into markets that America had dominated since the war. This was a turn of events that America had not foreseen.

Le General et La France

"La France" never had a more ardent modern champion than "Le General"—Charles de Gaulle, who was determined that his country should be a great power once more. Immediately after becoming president again in 1958, after an absence of twelve years, de Gaulle made nuclear weapons the touchstone of his relations with the United States.

That September, de Gaulle asked General Laurent Norstad, the American commander of Nato, whether American forces in France were equipped with nuclear weapons. When Norstad replied that, to his very great regret, he could not tell the president, de Gaulle responded icily "that is the last time . . . a responsible French leader will allow such an answer to be made."[4] De Gaulle was further angered when, in 1961, Kennedy agreed to provide the British with Polaris missiles, but not the French.

Doubting that the Americans would ever risk a Soviet missile attack on their territory in order to protect France, de Gaulle stepped up French efforts to create their own independent nuclear deterrent. By 1964, France had produced a number of atomic bombs along with strategic bombers to deliver them; meanwhile, work continued on developing a French long-range missile.

In March 1966, de Gaulle ordered Nato out of France and three months later he underlined French independence by breaking ranks and becoming the first Western head of state to pay a state visit to the Soviet Union. In Moscow, he called for a new Europe stretching from "the Atlantic to the Urals." This was the best news Moscow had had from Western Europe since the beginning of the Cold War. Moscow hoped that by cultivating France and the Western European states it could weaken Nato and possibly bring about its eventual collapse.

For all his doubts about the Americans, de Gaulle still banked on Nato being France's first line of defense. Although France had withdrawn from its integrated military structure, it remained a full member of the alliance. Military cooperation was quietly extended through a secret protocol between the Supreme Allied Commander and the Chief of the French Defense Staff. French forces remained garrisoned in Germany and the Germans continued to store "backup" military supplies in France.

The Prague Spring

The most far-reaching changes in Europe over the last two decades of the Cold War stemmed not from the General's policies, but from what became known as the Prague Spring, the brightest moment of hope that the communist world had ever experienced.

Czechoslovakia had the double distinction of being the only country in Eastern Europe not to have Soviet troops stationed on its territory and the only one to have had a democratic government after the war. When Brezhnev chose Alexander Dubcek to head the communist party in Czechoslovakia in January 1968, he wanted him to embark on much-needed economic reforms. He had not expected that those reforms would soon generate pressure for political liberalization and a lifting of press censorship.

Dubcek tried to reassure Moscow that Czechoslovakia would remain a loyal member of the Warsaw Pact, but he was not believed.[5] By the beginning of August, the Soviet Politburo had lost hope that Dubcek would reverse the ever-widening range of political and economic reforms. In a telephone conversation on August 13, Brezhnev repeatedly accused Dubcek of "deceiving us" and threatened to "resort to new, unavoidable measures."[6]

On August 21, a massive force of some 450,000 Warsaw Pact troops invaded Czechoslovakia. Apparently, if they encountered Nato forces they were to stop immediately and hold their fire. The implication was that however much

Moscow wanted to prevent Czechoslovakia's defection, it was even more determined to avoid a major war with Nato.[7]

The invasion went smoothly. Nato did not intervene, nor did many of Dubcek's countrymen resist the occupation. But the occupation was more difficult than Moscow had expected. Brezhnev's efforts to set up a regime of collaborators failed, because so few were willing to play that role. Amazingly, Dubcek had to be retained until April 1969, when he was quietly removed from office, though never jailed.

The most serious consequence of the suppression was that there was now little prospect of reform in either Eastern Europe or the Soviet Union. In Moscow, Andropov set up a new directorate within the KGB to monitor and crack down on dissent in all its manifestations.[8] Political and economic problems would become more acute and harder to resolve.

Moscow noted that although the Soviet invasion had brought a sharp chill to East-West relations, Nato had not tried to intervene. Moreover, not only was America embroiled in serious problems, but so too were some of its main allies. During the summer of 1968 there had been massive student riots in Paris and widespread student protests in West Germany. By the end of the decade, armed separatist movements were gaining momentum in Northern Ireland and Spain, and the urban terrorist group the Red Army Faction was becoming active in West Germany.

From Moscow's standpoint, these developments augured well for the negotiations towards détente. Before those negotiations began, however, Brezhnev wanted to warn the East Europeans against repeating what Prague had done. In Warsaw that November, he announced to Eastern European leaders the "Brezhnev Doctrine." Each socialist country, he said, had a duty to preserve socialism at home and to protect it abroad—which meant helping to crush any regime trying to take its socialist reforms too far.

Brezhnev hoped that this would send a message to the West that Moscow had regained control of Eastern Europe and that the West should not interfere there. In the months and years that followed, however, it was the Italian Communist Party that took the lead in challenging the right of the Soviet Union to intervene militarily "in the internal life of another communist party or another country," a move supported by other West European communist parties, who came to be known as the Eurocommunists.[9]

15 Trying to Make Détente Work

Some Headway

Richard Nixon entered the White House in January 1969 with impeccable credentials for trying to negotiate a new relationship with the Soviet Union as he had built his political career on the strength of his ardent anti-communism. He now embarked upon a radically different course with a fresh vision and with great patience—talents that, unfortunately, contrasted sharply with his vindictiveness in domestic politics.

Three years before Nixon entered the White House in 1969, he had come to the conclusion that America would have to find a way of "managing the emergence of Soviet power" and extricating itself from the quagmire of Vietnam. Given the country's problems and prevailing mood, the only possible option, he believed, was a creative form of détente.

To implement his vision Nixon chose Henry Kissinger as his national security adviser. Kissinger, a German-born professor at Harvard University, had written extensively about the balance of power and the impossibility of fighting a "limited" nuclear war. He brought to the White House a Germanic clarity of thought, along with a deep pessimism about "the decline of the West," which made him feel that Washington had to reach an accord with Moscow before its position weakened further.

Together Nixon and Kissinger set out to create a new form of détente that was, nonetheless, still rooted in the tradition of *realpolitik.* Their policy was based on a "web of interdependence" which they hoped would give Moscow a vested interest in restraint. Good behavior would be rewarded through expanded trade, generous credit, more dialogue on issues of common concern, plus wider cultural and educational exchanges. Secret diplomacy, they firmly believed, would enhance the chances of reaching agreements that would command support from the American public.

There was a palpable sense of relief within the Western alliance and the Soviet bloc when Washington and Moscow gave a renewed impetus to détente in 1969. At first progress was not rapid, but given the difficulties of earlier years it was hardly surprising that both sides wanted to feel their way forward.

Nixon soon began signaling to Moscow that the United States would be trimming its sails and turning away from the highly confrontational policies of the Kennedy and Johnson era. On July 25, the president declared what is known as the Nixon Doctrine, the essence of which was that the United States intended to reduce its involvement around the world and its allies would have to do more to defend themselves.[1]

Then, in Paris, on August 4, Kissinger and Le Duc Tho, a leading member of the North Vietnamese politiburo, started secret negotiations aimed at ending the war. Three months later Nixon announced that American troops would be withdrawn from Vietnam in phases as the South Vietnamese forces were strengthened under Washington's new policy of "Vietnamization."

Despite its many woes America still had an impressive lead in advanced technology. This was highlighted on July 20, 1969, when Neil Armstrong stepped onto the surface of the moon and took "one giant step for mankind." That was an achievement the Russians were never able to match.

At the Cusp

Each side had its own particular interests, but the one issue to which they both attached special importance was arms control. Before the negotiations started in Helsinki in November 1969, Brezhnev and Nixon had to address an entirely new series of problems over how to deter each other.

These were generated by rapid technological change, and complicated by the political and psychological aspects of deterrence. Just over two years earlier, in September 1967, Robert McNamara, who had recently retired as secretary of defense, spoke of the "mad momentum" of nuclear weaponry. "If something worked," he said, "there were pressures from all directions to acquire those weapons out of all proportion to the prudent level required." It was a prophetic warning.[2]

At that time the Americans were being compelled to rethink their strategy because the Soviets, like the Americans in the early part of the decade, were now deploying on average a new missile a day. As the United States could no longer hope to destroy all Soviet strategic nuclear forces at the outset of a conflict, McNamara advocated returning to the simpler option of threatening to devastate cities, which is what the Soviet Union could now do to the United States. Deterrence would, therefore, be based on the concept of "mutually assured destruction" and this opened up the possibility of each side cutting back its strategic nuclear forces. President Johnson liked the idea as he wanted to move away from competition and into serious forms of arms control.

Intelligence, however, showed that the Soviets were making considerable progress in developing an anti-ballistic missile (or ABM) system, which was comprised of a group of high-speed, radar-guided missiles with nuclear warheads that could intercept incoming missiles. If perfected, these systems could be used to protect cities or missile bases, with the result that destruction might not be quite mutual or assured.

When Johnson raised this issue with Alexei Kosygin, the Soviet premier, in June 1967, Kosygin told him that Moscow was not prepared to ban ABM systems, but it was willing to reduce the totals of offensive strategic missiles, so that both sides could have a deterrent at a lower cost. He left Johnson in no doubt that he believed, "defense is moral; aggression is immoral"[3]—a sentiment Reagan would echo some fifteen years later when advocating his Strategic Defense Initiative (SDI).

Nixon's Choices

"The debate in Washington centered on three big questions," Andy Marshall, who was then director of strategic studies at RAND, pointed out: "Was it to America's advantage to compete with the Soviet Union in developing antiballistic missile systems? How should the United States respond to the increasing accuracy of Soviet missiles, which before long could enable them to destroy America's Minuteman missile force? Should it seek to ban missiles with multiple warheads or should it exploit its lead in this field?"

Of these three issues, the one concerning the use of multiple warheads did the most to derail strategic calculations for the rest of the Cold War. New technology had made it possible to fit within a single missile nosecone not just one warhead, but several "multiple independently targetable re-entry vehicles" or Mirvs. They could be either nuclear warheads or decoys. They could simply overwhelm any defensive system.

"Our ABM program was progressing sufficiently well and we had intelligence that showed it was beginning to worry the Soviet leadership," Schlesinger recollected. "However, despite this opportunity," Marshall noted, "Nixon was unwilling to draw the Russians into a long and costly competition in this field, even though it would only require modest American investments." Nixon's main aim was to conclude an arms control agreement, which he hoped would increase stability and save money.

"Mirvs appeared a particularly attractive option," Schlesinger explained, "as they demonstrated America's technological superiority at a time when the Russians were still adding to their strategic missile force and we were not." At this stage, the United States had just below 2,000 targets in the Soviet bloc that were ear-marked for nuclear attack, with nearly 90% of them being military. Mirvs would not only make it possible to return to a "counterforce" strategy and attack all of these targets at the outset of a war, but one senior official went so far as to argue that Mirvs would give the United States a first-strike capability.[4]

Nixon gave the go-ahead for Mirvs in 1969 and, by 1971, the Americans had perfected the technology. As far as deterrence was concerned, it was a Pandora's box. Instead of one missile being able to destroy another, a single missile now might be able to destroy as many as the number of Mirvs it was carrying—which could be anywhere up to fourteen. This brought about a fundamental change in the calculus of deterrence.

Brezhnev's "Little Civil War"

In the Soviet Union the preparations for Helsinki sparked what came to be known as "The Little Civil War." This was a savage controversy about a very big issue—whether the Soviet Union should continue to rely on the threat of preemption to deter the United States or shift to building up the ability to retaliate. The Americans had no inkling of this debate, which revealed so much about Soviet fears of nuclear weapons.

Up to this point, the primary Soviet concern had been to catch up with the United States. Now the Soviet leadership moved to the next step, which was to seek superiority. As the distinguished Soviet strategist General Andrian Danilevich pointed out, "of course we strove to achieve superiority, just like you did. We chose different paths; we emphasized land-based systems; you emphasized sea-based systems."[5] "Superiority over the United States," General Nikolai Detinov, a leading Soviet arms control expert, explained, "was seen by Moscow as something highly valuable in political and ideological, not to mention strategic, terms."[6]

By the end of the sixties, trenchant studies by Soviet scientists were making the point that pre-emption was a dangerous illusion as, no matter who struck first, neither side could "win" a nuclear war. "Later," General Danilevich said, "the General Staff informed key members of the leadership that even if the Americans retaliated with just 10% of their missile forces that would be enough 'to put the state to death.'"[7]

Scientists also savaged the idea of launching Soviet missiles on the basis of a warning of an attack from a radar system they knew was unreliable. At one high-level meeting, an exasperated scientist blurted out, "Do you really think it possible in ten minutes to make a decision—based on the report of a general on duty looking at a radar screen—to push the button that may take millions of lives?" His outburst was met with stony silence, but many of those present knew he was right.[8]

The only sane policy, the scientists argued, was for the Soviet Union to follow the Americans and build up a force capable of retaliation. Initially, this would require new missiles that could be launched quickly from well-protected silos and early warning radars (and eventually satellites) able to detect the launch of American missiles, not just announce their imminent arrival.

Eventually, the debate focused on which missile should be the backbone of the modernized missile force. The "traditionalists" headed by Marshal Grechko, the minister of defense, favored the SS-19 because he could have more of them for the same price. The "modernists," headed by Dmitri Ustinov, the head of the military-industrial complex, and Mstislav Keldysh, the highly respected chairman of the Academy of Sciences, championed the SS-17, emphasizing the importance of housing missiles in well-protected silos, which, they argued, were worth the extra cost.

In July 1969, Brezhnev convened the Defense Council to resolve the dispute. Rather improbably, this top-secret meeting was held in a marquee in a forest clearing high above the resort of Yalta, where Brezhnev was holidaying. General Igor Illarionov, who was present, remembered that "tensions were very high." "Because of Brezhnev's indecisiveness and unwillingness to quarrel with his closest friends," the general explained, the meeting "ended up giving something to everyone."[9]

As a result, in addition to the SS-18 (the largest missile ever fielded by either side), the Defense Council approved production of both missiles, along with the first mobile intercontinental ballistic missile. The total number to be produced would be determined by the outcome of the Salt negotiations. These decisions were, in effect, part of a wider plan to move away from preemption and develop a credible retaliatory capability.

Détente, German Style

One of the most significant revelations to have emerged about the détente era concerns just how obsessed the Soviet Union was with the rising power of West Germany. It also turns out that the opening up of relations between West Germany and the Soviet Union set in motion changes that would eventually bring about the dramatic collapse of communism in Eastern Europe.[10]

After the Berlin Wall went up in 1961, Willy Brandt, then mayor of West Berlin, did not see any hope of "reunifying" all of the land that had been part of Germany before Hitler began expanding it in 1938. Sizeable portions of that territory were now within Poland, a small part had been incorporated into the Soviet Union, and, furthermore, few Germans still lived in either region. He believed, however, that in the long-term it would be possible to unite the two post-war Germanys.

Achieving this goal, however, would require a new West German policy towards the East—an *Ostpolitik*—based on a series of bilateral agreements with the Soviet Union, with which Bonn had had diplomatic relations since 1955, supplemented by others with the East European countries and East Germany, with which it did not.

Brandt's efforts to promote this prophetic vision gained momentum after he became leader of the Social Democratic Party in 1964. By the time Brandt became chancellor at the head of a new Social Democratic government in 1969, his general thinking about *Ostpolitik* had been honed into a negotiating strategy by Egon Bahr, the head of the Planning Department of the Foreign Ministry. Bahr had an extraordinary ability to see the key elements in complex issues and the trade-offs there could be.

"A fundamental, yet unspoken, premise underlay Brandt's *Ostpolitik*," Bahr pointed out. "This was that only by accepting the *status quo* throughout Eastern Europe would West Germany have the opportunity to undermine it and so create the conditions that would make it possible to unify Germany."

Westpolitik

Despite all the horrors of the Second World War, there were still many Russians who retained a respect and admiration for the Germans—not just for their efficiency and drive, but also for their culture. "Just think of it," Ambassador Vladimir Petrovsky said to me, "at the height of the battle of Stalingrad in 1943, our diplomatic cadets were still being taught to appreciate the poetry of Goethe and Schiller!"[11]

Moscow's *Westpolitik* had serendipitous origins. In 1965, a pretty girl introduced Yuri Andropov, the man then in charge of Moscow's relations with socialist countries, to her friend Viatcheslav Kevorkov, in the hope that Andropov would give him a job.

Andropov was a complex man. Knowing that the Party elders were suspicious of his powerful intellect and education, Andropov protected himself by always siding with those who advocated hard line policies, as he did when he was Soviet ambassador in Budapest at the time of the Hungarian Revolution in 1956. But Andropov seems to have understood the need to anticipate problems, not just react belatedly. In 1965, he had established a "consultants group" to give him private and honest advice on what was going on in the communist world.

Kevorkov, then in his forties, was probably the most perceptive Soviet analyst of German affairs. "At the end of the war," he told me, "I had interrogated German prisoners, including top generals, so as to understand the Germans and their outlook. Many of those I met were cultured, thoughtful and likeable. They opened my mind to thinking about Germany objectively rather than in the stereotypes generated by the war." Later Kevorkov became the KGB's leading analyst on German affairs.

"When Andropov asked me how Germany was likely to develop," Kevorkov recalled, "I seized his attention by saying that I did not think Germany could remain divided. The sense of the German nation was so strong that in time they would pull together." Andropov did not contest this assessment, but restricted himself to saying: "My task is not to unify Germany, but to shore up the German Democratic Republic. Therefore, I cannot use what you have told me."

Brezhnev had good reasons for wanting détente with both the United States and West Germany—particularly given Moscow's rising concern about China. The question was how could this best be done. For Andrei Gromyko, the foreign minister who was renowned for viewing the world "through the Stars and Stripes," this goal could only be achieved by working with Washington. Andropov's perspective was different.

Shortly after Andropov had become the head of the KGB in 1968, he summoned Kevorkov to his office and asked for his views on Germany. Kevorkov recalled that "After I had reiterated them, he asked me to set them down in a one-page memo. A few weeks later he praised my memo, adding, 'It is what I needed at this time.'" Andropov went on to explain that close relations with West Germany offered the best way to improve the Soviet Union's domestic and international situation.

"Andropov had a better idea than most about just how weak the Soviet Union was economically," Kevorkov emphasized. "He didn't think we could prevent unification. The only sensible option was damage limitation. Moscow would have to try to establish good relations with Bonn long before the two Germanys were unified. To his Politburo colleagues, however, he always spoke about East Germany being and remaining a socialist country."

Andropov's hopes of realizing this goal were raised by the first-rate reports the KGB was receiving from Markus Wolf, who almost certainly understood West Germany better than the head of any intelligence service has understood his adversary. The scale of Wolf's operations against West Germany was amazing. "By the seventies we had about a thousand sources in West Germany, of whom a hundred or so provided valuable intelligence, some of which I ran myself." He had been quick to spot, he recalled with pride, "that important changes were taking place in the Social Democrats' attitude towards the Soviet Union, especially in the shape of Brandt's ideas for *Ostpolitik*."

During the summer of 1968, the Soviet leadership gave little further thought to this matter, as they were preoccupied with the Prague Spring. Shortly after having played a leading part in suppressing the Czechoslovak reform movement, Andropov visited East Berlin. At a dinner in his honor, Erich Mielke, the minister of state security, praised the Soviet leadership for crushing the "social democrats" in Prague.

Andropov responded rather icily. The decision to intervene, he said, had been a difficult one and "as for Social Democrats, that is a subject to which we shall have to give further thought." "The temperature in the room," Wolf noted, "seemed to drop sharply as those present pondered the portent of Andropov's remarks."[12] With just a few sentences Andropov was leading sacred cows to the slaughter. The prospect of Moscow cooperating with the German Social Democrats marked a monumental shift in Soviet thinking, because the social democrats and the communists had long been bitter rivals. It showed just how desperate the Soviet leadership was to reach an accord with Bonn.

Doing a Deal

At their summit in April 1969 Soviet and Eastern European leaders had agreed that the economic success of the Soviet bloc could not be based on their economic integration, but would depend on them opening up economic relations with the West, especially West Germany.[13]

By October, Brandt was the new chancellor at the head of a coalition of Social Democrats and Free Democrats. One of his first moves was to send a secret letter to Moscow suggesting that a back-channel be opened to explore possibilities. Brezhnev passed the letter on to Andropov, with the comment that "you can use it as you wish." Andropov moved quickly, and arranged to send Kevorkov and an assistant to Bonn. Brezhnev attached such importance to this enterprise that he personally briefed Kevorkov and instructed him that "If you cannot tell the truth, keep silent rather than tell a lie."

"Bahr was rather surprised when we called to see him at his home—it was after all Christmas Eve. But as soon as I mentioned some words from Brandt's secret letter," Kevorkov recollected, "he knew we were high-level emissaries, because he had drafted those words himself."

When Gromyko got wind of what was happening, he was so outraged that he called on the Politburo to put a stop to it. At this point, Andropov sent Kevorkov to see Gromyko. Kevorkov was not simply a talented, charming KGB officer, but also a friend of Galina, Brezhnev's wayward daughter. "I managed to persuade Gromyko that he might find it easier to 'unlock' difficult problems in Washington if he also had taken advantage of keys that could open up new and friendlier links with West Germany." From that day on, Kevorkov kept Gromyko informed of what was going on, usually seeing him once a month.

Over the next few years, Kevorkov learned a lot about the thinking behind Andropov's *Westpolitik.* "At this time," he recalled "it was clear that Andropov did not expect West Germany to leave Nato or become a friend of the Soviet Union. His hope was that it would 'understand us.' He wanted to have someone to work with—not just America."

When Bahr and Gromyko had their first meeting in Moscow in January 1970, Gromyko doggedly insisted that Bonn must recognize East Germany as a separate state. "I rejected this concept," Bahr pointed out to me, "on the grounds that it would contravene the constitution of the Federal Republic, which explicitly stated that there was only one Germany. When Gromyko refused to budge, I told Kevorkov I would have to break off the negotiations."

Kevorkov was listening carefully when Brezhnev telephoned Gromyko to tell him that "What I would like is for you to handle things so that the Germans are happy." "The next day," Bahr said, "Gromyko was much more flexible. The back-channel was working effectively. In the end, Moscow accepted Germany could not recognize frontiers as inviolable, but could renounce use of force and accept that frontiers could only be changed peacefully."

The success of the negotiations owed much to the good personal chemistry between Brandt and Brezhnev. Bahr felt that "If a doctor had told them that they had to give up wine, women or song, they would have replied in unison 'song.'" Their rapport enhanced the effectiveness of the back-channel.

Intelligence helped, too. "The very good intelligence we were providing on Brandt's thinking and negotiating positions," Wolf emphasized, "helped reassure Brezhnev and Gromyko that they were on the right course. Some of this came from Gunter Guillaume, our agent, who, although not in Brandt's inner circle at this time, did provide excellent assessments of what was going on."[14]

Willy Brandt arrived in Moscow in August 1970 to finalize the Moscow Treaty. Despite unease in the Politburo over its terms and its implications, the text was agreed and the Moscow Treaty was signed on August 12, 1970. The following day the Soviet party newspaper, *Pravda*, hailed the treaty as an "acknowledgement by realistic forces in the West of post-war realities."

The Moscow Treaty provided for the mutual renunciation of force and recognized all borders in Europe—including that between the two Germanys—and declared they could only be altered by peaceful means. The other great post-war change—the shift of the Polish-Germany frontier westwards to the Oder-Neisse river—was implicitly recognized in the Warsaw Treaty, which Brandt signed during his historic visit to the Polish capital in December 1970. There Brandt reached out emotionally to the peoples of Eastern Europe, by sinking to his knees in front of the Warsaw Ghetto memorial in an act of contrition for Nazi crimes. It was during that visit that he reminded the Germans that the time had come when the results of history had to be accepted. The treaties, he said, "surrendered nothing that was not gambled away long ago."[15]

Where Will This Lead?

Gomulka, the Polish leader who was Brandt's host, thought that the future might write history very differently. In March 1969, shortly after the two Germanys had concluded a long-term trade agreement, he warned Moscow that if East Germany's economic "integration" with West Germany continued at such a pace, it would lead to German reunification.[16] Otto Winzer, the East German foreign minister, seemed to share his view. According to Bahr, "He labeled our policy 'aggression in felt slippers.'"[17]

Not surprisingly, Nixon and Kissinger were furious that Brandt had stolen the limelight in dealing with Moscow. Kissinger gave vent to his frustration that summer when he fumed to a West German official: "If there is to be a policy of détente, then we will do it, not you."[18] Fortunately, the Four Powers negotiations on Berlin that had started in March 1970, now gathered momentum with the Americans playing the leading role on the Western side.

Moscow quite quickly acquiesced to Western demands for the Soviet Union, not the Democratic Republic, to guarantee the free movement of traffic between Berlin's western sectors and the Federal Republic, as well as to improve communications between West and East Berlin. For their part, the Western Allies agreed that West Berlin would not be considered a constituent part of the Federal Republic and would not be directly governed by Bonn.

Although the Quadripartite and related treaties were meant to stabilize the situation in Europe, both Moscow and Bonn had other aims. Each understood that the other wanted to change the *status quo* to its advantage; each believed it knew how to manage that risk and was convinced fortune was on its side. But Bonn's fortune—both figuratively and literally—was stronger than Moscow's, with the result that it had growing influence in East Germany and Eastern Europe.

The discussions that Kevorkov had with Bahr and others reinforced his conviction that German unification was inevitable. One day, Kevorkov asked Bahr, "Why do you pay so much money to the GDR?" Bahr paused, then replied, "We are Germans." Kevorkov remarked, "I thought that was such a clever answer. It meant that we will be together again, that it's just a matter of time."

With the signing of the Quadripartite Agreement on Berlin in September 1971, the legal status of Berlin was finally settled after many years of controversy. Given the general improvement in relations the past two years and the headway that was being made in the arms control negotiations, both sides were edging towards a summit—the first in over a decade.

16 A Balancing Act

Moscow Wants Progress

From Moscow's standpoint, the beginning of the seventies seemed a particularly good time to try to improve relations with Washington. Besides Vietnam, Nixon faced serious economic difficulties. For the first time since 1894, the United States imported more merchandise than it exported and Japan had taken over its role as Asia's main trading partner. As the balance of payments worsened, America was forced in August 1971 to abandon the gold standard, which had been such a symbol of its international financial pre-eminence, and devalue the dollar.

Brezhnev and his colleagues had their own preoccupations. At the Party Congress in Moscow in March 1971, Brezhnev emphasized that the production of consumer goods would be a priority in the new five-year plan. This was a challenge as the Soviet Union was facing economic difficulties, the scale of which would not be widely recognized in Washington for some years to come. One of the ways of squaring this circle was to curb defense expenditure through arms control. That is why Brezhnev stressed that he hoped for better relations with America.

The Soviet leadership thought the prospects were good. In his speech, Gromyko memorably expressed the sentiment that "the existing military-strategic parity" ensured that "no question of any importance can be decided without the Soviet Union or in opposition to it."[1] The previous year, Brezhnev had set out to indicate this by following the example of what the United States had done in 1908—and sending the new Soviet navy to show the flag around the world—in all, over two hundred ships and submarines made the trip.

It was at this congress that Brezhnev launched his proposal for the convening of a Conference on Security and Cooperation in Europe, which he regarded as a key element in his overall approach towards détente. "Today in our talks with the largest states in the West," Brezhnev told his speechwriters in October 1971, "we aim at agreement, not at confrontation ... This will postpone war perhaps by twenty-five years, probably even by a century."[2]

Moscow's "peace-loving" image was seriously tarnished, however, when Oleg Lyalin, a KGB major, defected in London in September 1971. He provided details of the wide-ranging sabotage and assassination operations that the KGB aimed to carry out in London, Washington and other Western capitals in the event of an outbreak of war and in some crises short of war. The British responded by ordering 105 Soviet Intelligence officers to leave Britain, which created such a crisis in Moscow that the planning of such operations was discontinued.[3]

These events did not deflect Nato leaders from what they saw as their main task, which was to try to consolidate the positive aspects of Soviet policy into a lasting form of détente. At their meeting in Brussels in December they honored their pledge to Brezhnev and agreed to talks on the convening of a Conference on Security and Cooperation in Europe.

Nixon and Brezhnev's main preoccupation remained, however, their summit meeting, which had been set for Moscow in May 1972.

The China Card

Before agreeing to a summit, Nixon wanted to be confident that Brezhnev would put enough pressure on the North Vietnamese for the Americans to leave the South "with honor." The best hope he had of securing that support was by playing the China Card.[4]

As early as 1967, in an article in *Foreign Affairs*, Nixon had written about his long-term goal of "pulling China back into the world community—but as a great and progressing nation, not as the epicenter of world revolution." Nevertheless, when Nixon told Kissinger in the first weeks of his presidency that he wanted to open up relations with China, Kissinger said to one of his aides: "Our leader has taken leave of reality. He has just ordered me to make this flight of fancy come true."[5]

Kissinger's task was made easier when, following serious armed clashes on the Sino-Soviet border in early 1969, Premier Zhou Enlai declared that the Soviet Union was now China's "main enemy." Moscow began to suspect that there would be a shift in Chinese foreign policy when the Chinese press highlighted the fact that the journalist Edgar Snow, described as an "American friend," had

Nixon meets Mao, Beijing, February 21, 1972. (New China News Agency)

watched the National Day parade with Mao Zedong from the rostrum overlooking Tian An Men Square in Beijing on October 1, 1970.

Sino-Soviet relations were so bad that in mid-August a KGB officer in Washington raised with a State Department official the possibility of a Soviet attack on China's nuclear facilities, which the official firmly rejected.[6] Moscow did not pursue the matter further, but instead speeded the buildup of its forces along China's frontier with the Soviet Union and Mongolia, Moscow's ally. By 1972, there would be more Soviet troops facing China than there were on the frontline facing Nato. That showed whom they really feared.

Whereas Soviet leaders expected some change of emphasis in Chinese policy, they had not braced themselves for the great shift that was in the offing. Kissinger's secret visit to Beijing in July 1971 had caught the Soviets completely by surprise, as did the news that Nixon himself would be going to China—a country with which Washington did not even have diplomatic relations. The opening up of relations between the two countries had been greatly facilitated by the fact that Kissinger's main interlocutor was Qiao Guanhua, the deputy foreign minister who had studied philosophy at Tubingen University and like Kissinger thought about world affairs in terms of broad, Germanic *Gesamtkonzept*.

On February 21, 1972, Nixon arrived in Beijing, where he met with Chairman Mao and over the next few days had more detailed discussions with Premier Zhou Enlai. In the Shanghai Communique signed at the end of the visit, China and the United States declared that neither "should seek hegemony in the Asia-Pacific region and each is opposed to efforts by any other country or group of countries to establish such hegemony." Everyone understood that "any other country" was a reference to the Soviet Union. Washington's links with Beijing were given substance when Kissinger passed sensitive intelligence to the Chinese about the continued buildup of Soviet forces along the frontier.[7]

At his farewell banquet in Beijing's Great Hall of the People, Nixon said that "This was the week that changed the world." If it did not exactly do that, it did change his relations with both Beijing and Moscow.

The Moscow Summit

Nixon managed to temper Brezhnev's indignation over his China triumph by making an important gesture. Shortly after his return to Washington he told Dobrynin, the Soviet ambassador, that the time had come for political decisions. He was ready, he said, to establish parity in strategic weapons, even though this would be unpopular with some influential groups in America.[8] This is what Brezhnev had been hoping for.

How far détente would go was closely linked to events in West Germany. After the Four Powers concluded the Quadripartite Agreement on Berlin in September 1971, Brandt's government had to ask the Bundestag to ratify the related Moscow and Warsaw Treaties he had signed in 1970. In practice, these treaties not only meant that Germany was accepting the loss of much of its historic lands as a result of the Second World War, but also that it would deal with East Germany as an equal. That unleashed one of the longest and most contentious foreign policy debates in its history.

When the conservatives called for a no-confidence vote on Brandt in April 1972, Kevorkov recollected that "Andropov gave me a suitcase full of dollars—enough for four members of parliament—and told me to deliver it to Bahr. I did, but Bahr refused the money." Markus Wolf, however, came through for Moscow. "I bribed one Bundestag member and blackmailed another—both conservatives—to abstain. The no-confidence vote failed by exactly two votes. We were lucky. There was a quite a lot of bribery going on at that time."

The summit, however, was threatened by the major North Vietnamese offensive into the South in April and May, to which Nixon responded by ordering the bombing of Hanoi and mining the entrance to Haiphong, North Vietnam's main port, thereby blocking-in Soviet, East European and Chinese ships that were delivering military supplies. After a heated debate, the Politburo agreed to the summit going ahead because, in the words of Dobrynin, "the alternative would amount to handing Hanoi a veto over our relations with America."[9] On the plane to Moscow, Kissinger said to Nixon: "This has got to be one of the major diplomatic coups of all time."[10] It was.

Nixon's arrival in Moscow was a historic event—this was the first time an American president had ever paid a formal state visit to Russia or the Soviet Union since diplomatic relations had been established with Tsarist Russia in 1807. It was only the second time an American president had visited the Soviet Union; the first visit was made by Roosevelt, who had been to the Big Three conference in Yalta twenty-eight years earlier.

Broadly speaking, the summit and its documents symbolized the parity between the superpowers. It seemed to the world at large that, finally, after a quarter of a century, sanity had prevailed when Nixon and Brezhnev signed the first two arms control treaties between the Soviet Union and the United States. For Brezhnev and his colleagues, these treaties provided one great additional benefit. Instead of Moscow having to claim that it had parity, the treaties announced to the world that the United States itself recognized that, in the field of strategic weapons, the Soviet Union was a superpower equal to the United States (see below).

The other major accord signed in Moscow was on the "Basic Principles of Relations" between the two countries. This pious document contained a pledge to refrain "from efforts to obtain unilateral advantage at the expense of the other, directly or indirectly,"[11] but the drafting concealed fundamental differences of view as to what these words meant.

One of the main reasons the two sides overlooked the problems these words would create was because they were more interested by what they were saying than what they were supposed to be hearing. Genrykh Trifomenko, then a leading Soviet expert on American affairs, later pointed out that at the summit "With a view to precluding any American illusions that the Salt agreements could be exchanged for Soviet 'guarantees of stability' in the Third World, Soviet leaders stressed . . . [that] . . . the Soviet Union . . . would continue to support the struggle of the peoples for their social and national independence."[12]

Nevertheless, as Nixon had expected, his first summit with Brezhnev allowed both sides to overcome strong mutual suspicions. For his part, Brezhnev told the Politburo: "You can do business with Nixon. It's time to prepare for a return visit to the United States." Later he wrote to Nixon, saying that "a sound basis has been laid for a radical improvement in Soviet-American relations."[13]

Arms Control

The Anti-Ballistic Missile Treaty, or ABM Treaty, which was of unlimited duration, prevented a new costly arms race in a realm of technology where the Americans had a strong lead. Each side was restricted to just two ABM sites, one to protect a missile installation (so that those missiles could be used in a retaliatory strike) and the other on the nation's capital (which would give the leadership a chance to negotiate an end to hostilities). This meant that the threat of "mutually assured destruction" remained, as a full-scale missile attack would still be able to devastate the rest of the country. In the end, the United States never built an ABM system and the Soviet Union only built one to "protect" Moscow.

Brezhnev and Nixon also signed the counterpart accord—the Interim Strategic Arms Limitation Treaty (generally known as Salt-I). This was to remain in force for five years while negotiations continued on unsettled issues, including overall cuts in strategic nuclear forces. The treaty could only codify a rough parity, because the forces of each side were so different. Most of the Soviet force was land-based, whereas a large part of the American force was located on submarines and bombers. The treaty only covered strategic missiles, not bombers.

Each side's land-based missiles also had distinctly different characteristics. The Americans had invested heavily in small Minuteman missiles, housed in well-protected silos. American skills in miniaturization had made it possible to squeeze three Mirvs onto one of these missiles, but no more. Soviet missiles, on the other hand, had always been much bigger, because the Russians were not good at miniaturization. But once they had mastered the Mirv technology, they could fit far more warheads on to their large land-based missiles.

Agreement was possible because the Soviet leadership wanted to cap the American ABM system; in exchange, they were willing to cap their own strategic missile force. However, since the Americans refused to cut their existing forces and refused to include in the treaty their aircraft and missiles in Europe which could reach Soviet territory, the Russians were permitted to expand theirs, though to a considerably lower figure than they had originally planned. The Americans retained their 1,710 launchers and the Russians were allowed to increase their total to 2,240—in return for which the Americans were left free to deploy their new Mirvs on as many missiles as they pleased.

Nixon and Kissinger were delighted with the accord because they believed that the Russians had agreed to limit the number of their new "heavy" missiles, which could carry up to ten, possibly even more, warheads. This would stop them acquiring even more warheads than the Americans. Brezhnev and the Soviet military were even more delighted. In the words of Ambassador Oleg Grinevsky, the veteran Soviet arms control negotiator, "We won a victory over the Americans and this treaty gave us an opportunity to deeply change the structure of our forces."[14]

The Soviet success also owed much to the poor drafting of the treaty, which would enable Moscow to build far more heavy missiles than the Americans had expected. During the last-minute negotiations in Moscow, Kissinger had agreed that the Russians could replace their old "light" missiles with new ones that would not be significantly larger. Because his staff mistranslated the word "diameter" as "dimension," the Russians were able to introduce new missiles that were a full third bigger than those they were replacing.[15]

"Days after the summit," Schlesinger recalled, "we intercepted a telephone conversation in which Marshal Grechko assured Brezhnev that this new missile, the SS-19, would fit into the silo of the lighter missile it was to replace." Shortly thereafter, the Russians began testing the SS-19, which for all practical purposes was a "heavy" missile capable of carrying large numbers of warheads. That was in addition to the huge SS-18s, which were permitted under the treaty and could carry up to ten warheads. In other words, size had come to matter—and the Russians were turning the tables on the Americans.

Schlesinger said, "I was not alone in believing we had been hoodwinked."[16] Years later, Soviet negotiators still denied that they had done that, but they did pride themselves for having negotiated well. As General Detinov, a member of the Soviet delegation, put it, "[We succeeded through] the formulation of a clearly one-sided negotiating position and a tenacious adherence to it during the negotiations."[17]

Concealing Weakness

After the Moscow Summit Marshal Grechko invited Brezhnev and some of his colleagues to take part in a "war game," seemingly hoping to stiffen Brezhnev's resolve in dealing with the harsh realities of a nuclear war. The exercise began with generals describing the impact of a surprise attack by over a thousand American missiles. They grimly explained that 80 million people would be killed, the armed forces obliterated, 85% of industry destroyed and European Russia so irradiated as to be uninhabitable. General Danilevich recalled that "Brezhnev and Kosygin were visibly terrified by what they heard."[18]

Marshal Grechko then asked Brezhnev to push a button that would launch a "retaliatory strike," which in reality involved the launch of just three missiles with dummy warheads along a test range. Brezhnev turned pale, began perspiring and trembled visibly. He repeatedly asked Grechko, "Is this definitely an exercise?" The leadership were traumatized by this experience. None of them ever again participated in such an exercise. Brezhnev immediately ordered yet tighter controls to ensure that there could never be unauthorized use of Soviet nuclear weapons.[19]

People who worked closely with Soviet leaders on war planning believed that, in the event of a crisis, the Soviets would have entered negotiations with the Americans to avert a nuclear war and the top military would have backed them.[20] If the Americans did launch a token strike against the Soviet Union, the Politburo would insist on making their own decision in the light of the particular circumstances. The General Staff were allowed to work up options, but these were not plans that would be implemented automatically.[21]

It was clear that none of the leadership wanted a nuclear confrontation, especially Brezhnev, who was a *bon viveur* of the first order. In his diary, he often wrote little notes about lovely ladies who had made him feel good.[22] On his way to visit Nixon in 1973, he took such a shine to a Soviet air hostess that he had her made a "nurse" in his official party so that she could comfort him at night.[23] During the same visit, Brezhnev's enthusiasm for women was famously documented in a photo of him admiring Jill St. John's rear (see p. 180). This man had no wish to go anywhere near Armageddon.

While the Soviet leadership fretted over the inadequacies of their strategic nuclear forces, they had one great source of comfort—they knew that the West

Leonid Brezhnev's second glance at Jill St. John, San Clemente, June 22, 1973. (Courtesy of the Center for American History, University of Texas, Austin)

believed that before long Soviet strategic forces would have the upper hand. This was a perception that worked to Moscow's political advantage.

Playing on Gut Reactions

James Schlesinger, who became Nixon's secretary of defense in 1973, was the first who had to address the issue of how America would respond to the erosion of its unquestionable superiority. He had wide experience of strategic issues, having been in charge of strategic studies at RAND (a leading American think-tank) before becoming chairman of the Atomic Energy Commission (which produced nuclear weapons) and then serving briefly as the director of Central Intelligence.

"The long-term Soviet aim," Schlesinger believed, "was to deter the United States from threatening to use its strategic missiles for the defense of Europe. If the Germans and others, for example, came to believe that we would not use our strategic nuclear forces in defense of Europe, they would become even more wobbly. We had to persuade the Russians and our European allies that extended deterrence still worked, even though the Soviet Union could now destroy our cities."

In the sixties, Secretary of Defense McNamara had persuaded Nato to move away from a strategy of "massive retaliation" and adopt one of "flexible response," which explicitly threatened to use some of the alliance's 7,000 short- and medium-range nuclear weapons to stop an offensive by Soviet conventional forces, even by attacking their supply lines in Eastern Europe. But if that failed, or if Soviet forces made retaliatory attacks against Western Europe, many of McNamara's colleagues doubted that he would do more to protect his Nato allies.

"Every year," Schlesinger recalled, "McNamara drafted a formal defense memorandum which said 'The strategic missile force is intended for the defense of the United States.' Every year it would come back from the State Department with the addition of just three words '. . . and its allies.' This secret memorandum was never finalized or made public. Had that happened, it would have caused ructions within Nato."

Schlesinger's response was a declaratory policy of what he called "limited nuclear options." He warned the Soviet leadership that if they attacked Europe, the United States would not only respond by using tactical nuclear weapons against the Warsaw Pact forces in Eastern Europe, but would also use a few strategic missiles to strike remote targets on Soviet territory.

"The 'beauty' of this strategy," as Schlesinger likes to put it, "was that it played to Soviet gut reactions. Soviet leaders had said time and time again that they did not believe nuclear war could be restrained once it had started. 'Limited Nuclear Options' would, therefore, make them very cautious and so reinforce deterrence." At the same time, Schlesinger wanted friend and foe alike to perceive that "we are able to counter the Soviet Union in terms of strategic nuclear weapons." This was the essence of the Schlesinger Doctrine.

"The key issue, in terms of hardware," Schlesinger explained, "was for us to be confident that we could destroy all of their missile forces. Mirvs certainly would help achieve that goal and, in 1972, we produced some 7,000 of them, which was more nuclear warheads than in any other year in history."

"There was still a problem," Schlesinger continued, "because we did not think our missiles and Mirvs were accurate enough to destroy hardened Soviet missile silos. That is why, before long, Congress approved unprecedented peacetime increases in the military budget. These helped fund a long-term program for modernizing the Triad by developing a new, big land-based missile (the MX—which stands for 'missile/experimental'), more accurate and powerful submarine-based Trident missiles, the B-1 bomber and cruise missiles."

Going Our Way

Brezhnev was pleased with the way things were going on the diplomatic front. In January 1973, under pressure from both Moscow and Beijing, the North Vietnamese finally signed the Paris Accords with the United States, which offered the Americans the hope of being able to extract themselves from Vietnam if not with honor, then at least without humiliation. The prospects were good, Schlesinger also felt. "At the time the accords were signed, I was director of Central Intelligence. Like Nixon and Kissinger, I believed that in the South the Vietcong had been destroyed and North Vietnam's regular forces neutralized. With continued strong American air support the Army of Vietnam would be able to protect the South."

Considerable progress was also being made in Europe. In Prague in February 1973, Brezhnev told Gustav Husak, the Czechoslovak party leader, that the developments in Europe indicated that the "capitalists" were willing to negotiate about security. He observed that the East needed to "win the struggle with time" as "the more time we gain, the more the economy and people themselves will change to our advantage."[24]

One of the most important areas of progress had been on Germany. In December 1972, the West German parliament had ratified the Moscow and Warsaw treaties, along with the Basic Treaty through which East and West Germany recognized each other. The latter treaty opened the way for them both to join the United Nations in May 1973, the month Brezhnev traveled to Bonn at Brandt's invitation, elated at being the first Soviet leader to visit West Germany.

Brezhnev later told Kevorkov that he had been deeply touched when Franz Josef Strauss, the volatile leader of the Christian Socialist Union, said to him during the visit: "History tells us that when the Russians and the Germans worked together, there was stability in Europe; when we are in opposition then there is instability. We have, therefore, to be together." Kevorkov added, "Increasingly in Moscow there was a feeling that Germany was the only strong country with whom Moscow could speak and work. We realized this with Brandt, Schmidt and Kohl."

When Brezhnev paid a return visit to the United States in June 1973 for his second summit with Nixon, progress was made on several issues. Summits were to be held annually and agreement was reached on an outline of the fundamental principles for limiting strategic weapons under the follow-up Salt-II treaty. The two sides also agreed that talks on reducing conventional forces in Europe (the Multilateral Balanced Force Reductions talks) should begin in Vienna in October. Although no headway was made on economic cooperation, Brezhnev was optimistic that the legislation Nixon had recently submitted to Congress would be approved.

At the end of the summit, Soviet-American relations were better than they had ever been since the war, the American people felt more self-confident and détente was popular. Two weeks later, the foreign ministers of thirty-five countries met in Helsinki for the opening of the Conference on Security and Cooperation in Europe. It seemed to many that the world was becoming a safer place.

"In late 1973," Kevorkov recalled, "Brezhnev called Andropov into his office and told him that his vision had proved correct. Andropov felt vindicated. It was probably the best day of his life."

17 Expletives & Ambitions

Hardball in the Middle East

Despite their pledge at the Moscow Summit to refrain from "efforts to obtain unilateral advantage at the expense of the other, directly or indirectly," both Nixon and Brezhnev did so.

The first test case was in the Middle East, where, in 1967, the Israelis had had a series of spectacular victories against their Arab neighbors during the Six Day War. They had seized the Golan Heights from Syria, the Sinai peninsula from Egypt and the West Bank and East Jerusalem from Jordan.

During his visit to the United States in 1973, Brezhnev tried to draw Nixon's attention to the difficulty Moscow was having keeping its Arab allies in check. To avert another Middle Eastern war, he proposed that Washington and Moscow should work together to impose peace. In return for a total withdrawal from the territory it occupied during the 1967 war, Brezhnev said Israel would receive security guarantees, though these were not specified. This approach appealed to Moscow and its Arab friends, but not to Tel Aviv or Washington.

Kissinger and Schlesinger later acknowledged that they had dismissed Brezhnev's warning and those of others, even the sudden withdrawal of Soviet forces and personnel from Egypt and Syria. They simply could not believe that President Anwar Sadat of Egypt wanted to start a war he could not win. Sadat, however, was starting from a different premise. He judged that if Egypt could put up a good fight, the superpowers would have to broker a settlement on terms acceptable to Egypt.

On October 6—the day of Yom Kippur, the holiest in the Jewish calendar—the Egyptians launched a massive and extremely well prepared attack across the Suez Canal and began recapturing sections of the Sinai peninsula, while the Syrians attacked across the Golan Heights. After an initial delay, which angered the Israelis, the Americans mounted a huge airlift of arms the Israelis urgently needed.

Brezhnev's Expletives

Soviet and American efforts at the United Nations led to an agreement for a cease-fire being reached on October 22, but the Israelis were in no hurry to implement it. The following day, Gromyko, the Soviet foreign minister, went to consult Brezhnev at his dacha at Zavidovo, on the outskirts of Moscow.

One of those present was Anatoly Chernyaev, then a senior official in the International Department of the Central Committee, who recollected that "This was an extraordinary meeting." Brezhnev told Gromyko that the Soviet Union should take an active role in the peace negotiation, including guarantees on the frontiers of Israel, with whom Moscow would restore diplomatic relations. When Gromyko tried to point out that the Arabs would take offense and "there will be a great deal of noise," Brezhnev began venting his anger and frustration. "We have been offering them a sensible course of action for so many years," he said. "They wanted war and they are welcome to it. . . . To hell with them!"

"Brezhnev then swore at Ponomarev (the head of the International Department) for supporting the Arabs, and at Gromyko for wanting to keep 'our flag and bases in the Middle East,'" Chernyaev continued. "In exasperation, Brezhnev shouted at them: 'You will do as I say. We will not let these ****ing people involve us in a world war!'" The Soviet airlift of military equipment to Syria stopped abruptly that day.

By the next day, October 24, the Israelis had encircled the Egyptians' 3rd Army and Sadat pleaded with Brezhnev to help. Brezhnev sent Nixon a strongly worded message to which, at the last minute, he added a phrase proposing that Soviet and American military contingents be dispatched to Egypt to enforce and guarantee the agreed cease-fire. Brezhnev warned that the Soviet Union was ready to act alone.

To put some pressure on Washington, the Soviet navy had rapidly reinforced its fleet in the Mediterranean to the point where, for the first time, it was a match for the American Sixth Fleet. The Soviet air force mounted several symbolic exercises in the southern Soviet Union and a couple of Soviet transport aircraft flew to Cairo. Nixon politely rejected Brezhnev's proposal and, on October 25, America's armed forces (including nuclear forces) were put on a higher level of alert than normal, but still two steps below maximum readiness. The alert was revoked in less than two days.

Nixon and Kissinger claimed that the American alert had deterred Soviet intervention. "But this had had no effect on Soviet conduct," Chernyaev insisted, "as Brezhnev had already decided that the Soviet Union would not intervene."

After the crisis had passed, Nixon assured Brezhnev that "as long as I live and hold the office of president I will never allow a real confrontation with the Soviet Union." For his part, Brezhnev assured Nixon that "our determination to proceed with the radical improvement of Soviet-American relations had not diminished on account of the Middle East developments."[1] This exchange, however, in no way deflected Nixon and Kissinger from exploiting every opportunity to reduce Soviet influence in the Middle East—or Brezhnev from still hoping to gain the advantage.

Americans Turn Against Détente

Despite these frictions, Brezhnev was beginning to feel that his relationship with Nixon was working well. He was delighted that in the run-up to the June 1974 summit in Moscow—the third in three years—Nixon had agreed that détente was an "irreversible policy." As pressure mounted on Nixon over Watergate, Brezhnev sent him personal messages of support that were unprecedented in the annals of Soviet-American relations. The last one was sent after Nixon resigned the presidency in August 1974.

Opposition to détente had meanwhile been mounting in America. One of the first issues to catch the public's attention was the "great grain robbery." Following the Moscow summit in May 1972, the American government extended governmental credits to facilitate Soviet purchases of American grain over the next three years. Soviet buyers then speedily traveled around the country and, with great skill, quietly bought up 20 million tons of grain at bargain prices before the market realized what they were doing. This fine display of commercial acumen quickly contributed to the feeling that the Soviets were cheating on the Americans.

More damaging still for Nixon was that in his efforts to win support for détente he had oversold it, claiming among other things that Salt-I would help build "a new structure of peace in the world," which it did not. The main victim was the Trade Bill that was intended to offer the Soviet Union considerable economic benefits, through "most favored nation" treatment, increased trade and generous credits.

The opposition was led by Senator Henry Jackson from Washington State, who had close links to Boeing, one of America's largest defense contractors.

The Soviet Union, Jackson believed, was an implacable adversary and the White House, he argued, was gullible to think that stability could ever be achieved through "managing" the Cold War. That could only be done by gearing up for an unequivocal competition through which the United States would compel the Soviet Union to give up.

Jackson rallied those who disliked détente and repression around a new cause. Economic relations, he insisted, could only expand if Moscow permitted Soviet Jews to emigrate if they wished. Moscow refused, but because it attached such importance to détente, it gave private assurances that the number of emigrants would almost double to 60,000 a year.[2] The deal was quickly scuppered by Jackson insisting that the Soviet Union publicly commit itself to allowing that level of emigration. Then at the end of 1974, he secured congressional approval for the Jackson-Vanik amendment, which made the trade bill even more restrictive than the legislation in force before détente began and is still in force in 2008. This was an unpleasant shock for Brezhnev and his colleagues.

Third World Aspirations

"The future competition with the United States will take place not in Europe, and not in the Atlantic Ocean. It will take place in Africa, and in Latin America. We will compete for every piece of land, for every country."[3] In saying this to a closed meeting of party officials in Moscow in 1965, Andropov, who was then in charge of relations with socialist countries, was reflecting the general view of the Soviet leadership at that time.

The Americans, on the other hand, after being bogged down in Vietnam for several years, had turned away from wishing to help Third World countries develop and had put more effort into supporting rulers who stopped their countries from sliding to the left. In September 1973, the Americans had backed the Chilean military coup that ousted President Allende, whom they had accused of trying to overthrow democracy despite the fact that he was elected with only a third of the vote. For Moscow—and Cuba—this was a serious setback to its hopes of new left-wing victories in Latin America.

Soviet prospects were much brighter in Africa, especially in the southern part. The leaders of the independence movements there felt that the United States was too closely tied with South Africa and Portugal, the last major colonial power in the region, to be willing to support them. As a result, they were turning to Moscow for help.

In May 1970 Andropov, who now headed the KGB, sent a memo to Soviet leaders in which he argued that, by moving quickly, the Soviet Union would not only be able to thwart a further expansion of Chinese influence in Africa, but steal a march on the West as it was not expecting Moscow to mount a "broad offensive" in Africa.[4] Within a few months, Brezhnev had given his backing for the Soviet Union to become more actively engaged in southern Africa. Chernyaev commented to me that "Brezhnev was not driven by ideological considerations, but more by the feeling that an empire was the attribute of a great power."

The first opportunity opened up in 1974 in Angola, from which the Portuguese withdrew quickly after the overthrow in Lisbon of the dictator General Salazar. Early the following year the various factions that had been fighting to oust the Portuguese from Angola turned against each other, with the Cubans backing the left-wing Popular Movement for the Liberation of Angola (MPLA). Initially, Brezhnev flatly refused to transport Cuban troops or to send Soviet officers to serve with them in Angola.

Brezhnev's attitude changed when the South African troops intervened to help another group overthrow the MPLA, and the CIA also began providing more assistance to other opponents of the MPLA. Before the MPLA formally declared the independence of Angola on November 11, 1975, the Soviets had begun helping the Cubans fly thousands of troops into Angola, along with several dozen Soviet officers whose main task was to keep an eye on them.

After Vietnam, and with the American economy reeling from the surge in oil prices following the Yom Kippur war, Congress had no appetite for confronting communist expansion in the Third World. Nevertheless, it regarded the idea of a left-wing regime coming to power with direct Soviet backing as an anathema. From his many discussions with Kissinger on this subject, Dobrynin felt that "What really matters to Kissinger was not who won, but that none of the combatants themselves should achieve victory with the outside help of a superpower."[5]

This was not how Moscow viewed events. Boris Ponomarev, the head of the international department, told Dobrynin that as the Americans were involved in many civil wars around the globe, they could not claim that Soviet support for the newly formed government in Angola was a violation of détente. The Soviet Union simply would not yield, he said, to "American arrogance and their double standards."[6] Moscow wanted to make gains and according to Nikolai Leonov, the head of the KGB's foreign intelligence assessments, there was "a feeling that Africa could become almost a socialist continent."[7]

By the time that the MPLA had gained the upper hand in the civil war in the spring of 1976, there were some 36,000 Cuban troops in Angola. This had been a huge logistical exercise for both Cuba and the Soviet Union, which had never before transported so many men and equipment by air, let alone over such distances. Just as important was the fact that the Cubans and the Soviets had worked together well in this enterprise. The Soviet Union had, Arne Westad observed, "sent a strong message to the world of its capabilities and willingness to confront the United States and its allies in Africa."[8]

Not everyone in Moscow was optimistic about Soviet prospects in the Third World. Years later, Georgi Arbatov, the director of the Institute of the United States and Canada, claimed that he told Brezhnev at the time "if we have what seems like good luck in Angola, it'll doom us to another step somewhere else . . . till we run our head into a stone wall and have our own Vietnam."[9] Similarly, Nikolai Leonov recalled that in 1976/77 he prepared a paper for the Politburo recommending stopping efforts to expand areas of influence overseas because the Soviet Union was unable to sustain them. It should, however, back South Yemen, because of the strategic significance of Aden, and try to make Nicaragua a showcase for socialism.[10]

Blood in Vladivostok

With Salt-I, the Interim Strategic Arms Limitation Treaty, due to expire in 1977, Brezhnev and President Gerald Ford met in Vladivostok, on November 23, 1974, to agree on the guidelines for the negotiators. Besides all the antagonisms mentioned above, there was the added complication that Ford, who three months earlier had replaced the disgraced Nixon in the aftermath of the Watergate affair, was an un-elected president operating under severe political constraints.

As Kissinger told Brezhnev during the preparations for the Vladivostok summit, détente was "hanging by a thread."[11] Brezhnev, no doubt, would still have in mind the warning that Nixon gave him shortly before he resigned: "If détente fails, the hawks, not the doves, will take over."[12]

At the start of their discussions Brezhnev lamented to Ford, "We have not achieved any real limitation . . . I just don't know how much farther we can go in building up so-called security."[13] Ford shared these concerns, but the two sides had markedly different views about how the arms race could be curbed—and curbed without placing them at a disadvantage.

Not only had the Russians started producing Mirvs, but they would soon be able to put many of them on each of their new "heavy" missiles. Despite these differences, progress was made. Brezhnev agreed that both sides should have the same number of launchers, a point that Congress had insisted on. They settled on the figure of 2,400, which meant the Russians would have to forego about 300 missiles they had planned to build. Within the overall ceiling, each side would be permitted to have 1,320 Mirved missiles, which could be used on land- or submarine-based missiles as they pleased. In other words, the Soviet Union would be allowed to retain the advantage in land-based missiles, while the Americans kept theirs in submarine-based missiles.

Bombers were beginning to regain some of their former importance in strategic calculations because there was a prospect that air-launched cruise missiles could have a range of some 2,500 km (1,550 miles) and if a bomber carried several of these they would, in effect, be rather like a Mirved missile. It was accepted that this complex issue, along with deeper cuts, would have to be negotiated later.

Marshal Grechko, Brezhnev's minister of defense, had adamantly opposed many of the concessions Brezhnev wished to make, especially that which deprived the Soviet Union of the right to replace almost 40% of its intercontinental missiles. In what was probably the worst confrontation between any general secretary and his minister of defense, Brezhnev forced Grechko to "eat the Vladivostok agreement."[14] Brezhnev felt he had "paid with his blood" for that agreement.[15]

The price Brezhnev paid was more than the serious weakening of his hand with his own military. On his way back to Moscow he suffered a stroke. He continued to deteriorate both mentally and physically, and his worsening condition seriously marred the last three years of his leadership—from 1979 until his death at the end of 1982.

The Vladivostok Summit had, however, reinforced Brezhenev's conviction that his approach to détente was still bearing fruit. As Alexander Bovin, one of Brezhnev's senior foreign policy advisers, wrote in the Soviet press in February 1975, "the purpose of détente is to make the process of international change as painless as possible."[16]

At the 25th Party Congress held at the Kremlin in February 1976, Brezhnev proclaimed that for the first time the correlation of forces had "irrevocably shifted in favor of socialism."[17] In the corridors of power, Ambassador Oleg Grinevsky recalls, there was talk that "the United States is losing the arms race." Indeed, there was the widespread belief that "the Soviet Union had reached the peak of its power"—to date, that is.[18]

Détente, arms control and the American withdrawal from Vietnam had, however, combined to spark some radical thinking briefly within the Soviet General Staff. Years later, Marshall Akhromeyev, who later became chief of the General Staff, wrote in his memoirs that "A very narrow group of people began working out proposals for freezing military expenditures, chiefly by reducing mass-produced weapons."[19]

This was an extraordinary turn of events because in the past the General Staff had never taken such an initiative. By the time the proposals were ready Brezhnev was seriously ill and incapable of focusing on such a major issue. For that reason Dmitri Ustinov, the new minister of defense, said he could not put them to Brezhnev; the more likely explanation is that Ustinov himself, who had been in charge of arms production for many years, was probably not enthusiastic about this shift in policy.

Blood in Washington

Before the Senate Foreign Relations Committee on September 19, 1974, Kissinger, who was secretary of state, argued that the central challenge of détente was "to reconcile the reality of competition with the imperative of coexistence."[20] That task became yet more difficult when, in April 1975, the North Vietnamese unexpectedly poured into Saigon, forcing the remaining Americans to make a humiliating flight by helicopter from the roof of their embassy.

Although Moscow and Beijing had pressed Hanoi into signing the Paris Peace Accords of 1973, the Soviet Union had subsequently provided the arms that made possible the North's speedy takeover of the South. The North had also been helped by the congressional ban on the American government taking any further military action in Indochina. The Americans were humbled and embittered.

The military credibility of the United States had taken a hard battering. Almost immediately, Schlesinger noted, "Kim Il Sung, the North Korean leader, began to make bellicose noises suggesting that he might be able to take over the South. We had to stop him in his tracks. I broke our long-established practice and declared that we had nuclear weapons in South Korea and would use them if necessary."

For a number of years influential conservatives from both parties had accused the CIA of relying too much on the physical evidence concerning Soviet forces and not delving deeply enough into Soviet thinking. In 1976, President

Ford granted these conservatives permission to challenge three National Intelligence Estimates prepared by the CIA—on Soviet air defense, missile accuracy and strategic objectives—in what became known as the "Team-A/Team-B debate," with the CIA staffing Team-A and the conservatives Team-B.

Professor Richard Pipes, the Soviet expert from Harvard who led Team-B, did not challenge the CIA's assessment that the Americans had twice as many deliverable nuclear weapons as the Russians. Instead, Pipes reiterated his argument that the success of détente depended on completely changing the world outlook of the Soviet regime, and he had chastised Nixon and Kissinger for pursuing such a policy without having familiarized themselves with Russian history or with communist theory. The CIA was slated for not understanding the "evil genes" of the Russians and, therefore, their evil intentions.

The thrust of Team-B's report was that the Soviet Union was not seeking parity, but superiority—and was already well on its way to gaining it. Soon, Team-B argued, the Soviet Union would have so many Mirvs that it would be possible for them, theoretically at least, to obliterate the whole American land-based force in a pre-emptive strike and still have plenty of missiles in reserve.

"Theoretically" and "practically" were, however, two very different things. Moscow could never be sure that before their missiles arrived the Americans would not have launched hundreds of their land-based missiles. In any event, the Americans should still be able to retaliate with their submarine-based missiles and bombers, which were almost as potent.

In their critique, Team-B emphasized that if the Russians were believed to have that capability to launch such an effective pre-emptive strike, they would gain a great psychological advantage. Soviet leaders would become increasingly menacing as they sought to exploit this psychologically and politically. America had to respond.[21]

It later became clear that the Team's judgments about Soviet capabilities and attitudes to war were not always well grounded. There was, however, plenty of visible evidence over the next few years of the buildup they predicted. In 1990, General Danilevich pointed out that the buildup that began in 1975–76 "was stimulated above all by the desire to get ahead of American competition."[22]

18 The Mastery of Europe

Dynamic Rivalry

While the nuclear arms race attracted most of the public's attention, the conventional arms race was every bit as important—and was a saga that did much more to end the Cold War than has been acknowledged. One of the most extraordinary stories to emerge from my interviews demonstrates just how intense and dynamic the rivalry between Nato and the Warsaw Pact really was.

This rivalry absorbed a huge amount of the energy of both the military commanders and the political leaders. As Diego Ruiz-Palmer, one of the most astute observers of this era, remarked, "No other war has been so thoroughly planned and well prepared, yet never fought."

During the last two decades of the Cold War much was written and said about the strengths and weaknesses of Nato and the Warsaw Pact, but few people had a clear idea of what was really going on. Sometimes even top generals did not understand what the other side was trying to do. Now we can see that they were both seeking to ensure that if a hot war did break out in Europe it would not go nuclear.

This honorable intention sparked the greatest renaissance of military thinking in the 20th century. High-quality intelligence, in both senses of the word, shaped the actions of the two sides, and each was often very quick to adopt the other's innovations. In the arms race that followed, Central Europe gained the disturbing distinction of having the heaviest concentration on earth of conventional and nuclear weapons.

The members of Nato began to realize that the Soviet approach was not to seek a stable military balance as a pre-requisite to détente, but instead to use the East-West rapprochement in order to undermine support within the members states of the Western Alliance for its defense policies. But even at this stage, there were people in Moscow who were coming to the bleak realization that it simply could not continue to compete with the United States.

In essence, the two sides were engaged in a struggle for the mastery of Europe. It was not just a military struggle, but one that was political, psychological and economic as well. At times the relationship was fraught and unpredictable, and the stakes exceptionally high. And, for the first time, we can see how each side viewed this contest as it evolved.

Trying Not to Go Nuclear

By the mid-sixties, despite what they often said in public, neither side expected the other would start a war in order to seize territory. If war did occur, it would stem from other causes. There was, for example, the possibility of a war in the Gulf leading to tensions in Europe that then flared out of control. Or the trouble might stem from crises in Eastern Europe. General Klaus Naumann, the German chief of defense, commented that "the chief of operations of the East German Army told me that at the time of the demonstrations in East Germany, before the Wall came down, he feared Nato would attack in order to unify Germany."

Some progress was made towards preventing a war in Europe "going nuclear" when, in 1967, Nato declared that it would maintain a full range of both conventional and nuclear forces, so that it could respond to any attack "at an appropriate level." This meant that Nato no longer planned to use nuclear weapons for fighting a war, but for "war termination." In other words, Nato would respond to a Soviet conventional offensive by selectively using just a few nuclear weapons. The aim would be to bring home to the Soviet leadership the seriousness of the situation, so that they would call an end to the fighting before Nato used more nuclear weapons.

According to Sir Michael Quinlan, then Britain's chief nuclear strategist, "Nato's public declarations were carefully worded for Soviet consumption." As he explained, "We rightly believed Soviet Intelligence would obtain accounts of the policy discussions that had taken place behind closed doors, so we tried to ensure that two key messages got through to Moscow—first, Nato had faced up to the tough issues of nuclear use; and, second, Nato would not take provocative or hasty action."

"We had one great advantage," General Hans-Henning von Sandrart, the commander of Nato's central front, told me. "Despite all its knowledge of Nato, the Soviet General Staff could never be certain of the exact circumstances in which we would "go nuclear" for the simple reason that the members of Nato themselves did not know." Senior officials in Nato and the West German government provided a fine example of the difficulties Moscow faced. Nato policy, they would often say, was to use nuclear weapons "as late as possible, but as early as necessary." This was deterrence as much by default as by design.

Nonetheless, the General Staff had to try to ensure that a conflict would not go nuclear.

Moscow's Opening Move

Marshal Andrei Grechko, who had just been appointed minister of defense, soon signaled to Nato that Moscow was taking their new strategy seriously. *Dnieper '67*, a major military exercise that took place in the autumn of 1967, began with Soviet forces fighting for a week before resorting to nuclear weapons—this was a first.

Preventing Nato "going nuclear" posed a massive challenge to both sides. In Europe, Nato had 1,000 aircraft capable of carrying nuclear bombs and roughly the same number of missiles and pieces of artillery that could deliver nuclear warheads—of which they had some 7,000, mainly in Germany. This called for no less than a transformation of the way the Soviet Union would wage war in Europe.

While Soviet field commanders were still insisting that nuclear weapons would enable them to prevail in any war with Nato, some members of the General Staff doubted that was possible.[1] Their research was beginning to show that Soviet use of tactical nuclear weapons would slow their advance dangerously in open terrain and block it completely in hilly and mountainous areas. If Nato used them too, fighting would become almost impossible.

By the early seventies, Vitaly Tsygichko, a scientific analyst working in the Ministry of Defense, said that Marshal Grechko and his top generals "understood and believed that the use of [tactical] nuclear weapons by either side would be catastrophic,"[2] as that could spark a strategic nuclear conflict. In the event that Nato did use some nuclear weapons, the General Staff were considering a proportionate response, not a massive one as Moscow had long threatened. After all, the last thing Moscow wanted was to unleash a full-scale nuclear war.

Contrary to what Nato believed, the General Staff realized that it would take some years to acquire the equipment and train its forces to fight a conventional war for ten days, let alone any longer. At this stage, the main task was to begin developing a new strategy and tactics that would make it possible. Meanwhile, Soviet deterrence in Europe would remain based on the threat of using tactical nuclear weapons.

Despite the alliance's mythology, Moscow knew that in the late sixties Nato was in a sorry state, both politically and militarily. Nato forces in Germany were incapable of fighting as a single entity, their equipment was not standardized nor were their communications systems integrated. The West Germans only had enough artillery shells to fight for a week—if that. The Soviet General Staff's task was facilitated by their impressive understanding of the situation in Nato. "This was acquired," Wolf reminded me with a smile, "from much high-grade intelligence, especially the documents, provided by our agents within Nato headquarters."

Under Nato's new strategy of "flexible response" its armies would try to hold the frontline close to the Inner-German border, while its aircraft, which accounted for half of Nato's conventional firepower, remorselessly pounded the attackers. This made it very difficult for the Warsaw Pact to mass the forces they needed to push back or break through Nato's frontline.

Whatever the new Soviet strategy would be, the General Staff knew that its forces in Central Europe would need much greater firepower and mobility. Over the next few years, their firepower was increased by about 50%, while the volume and quality of their trucks (many of which were needed to carry ammunition) rose by a considerably greater factor. Paradoxically, most of the truces were produced at the new Karma River truck plant, which had been built with Western loans as one of the symbols of détente!

The aim of this buildup was to enable each division to shell the Nato frontline so heavily and continuously that it could not fire back. The Soviet air force in the forward areas, meanwhile, began to acquire large numbers of new aircraft—some designed to provide close support for ground troops, others to pin down Nato aircraft at their bases and destroy their nuclear storage sites etc.[3]

In Europe, Brezhnev and his colleagues felt that the "correlation of forces" was really shifting in their favor. In 1974, Marshal Viktor Kulikov, the chief of the General Staff, announced with satisfaction that Soviet forces were now "abreast of contemporary requirements."[4] Moscow was hoping that by gaining the psychological advantage on the military front, it would be able to prevent the West from challenging communist rule in Eastern Europe, and convince Western Europe to cooperate more fully with the Soviet Union.

The Americans Re-engage

Nato was in dire straits in the early seventies. A report on the alliance by a highly respected Belgian general was appropriately entitled *Europe without Defense.* When General Haig took command of Nato in 1974, he judged that if the Russians attacked, the American divisions under him would be hard pressed to hold the line. "Alcoholism and drug abuse were serious and widespread . . . Our state of readiness was way below acceptable standards . . . US commanders [of the three services] had seldom talked to each other in a coordinated military manner."[5]

James Schlesinger, who became the American secretary of defense in 1973, explained to me that "The American sense of weakness was reinforced by the despondency among our Nato allies. I set out to reassure them that building up conventional forces would augment deterrence, not replace it." His "Schlesinger Doctrine" helped persuade the Germans that this was feasible; so, too, did his decision to deploy nearly 7,000 troops in the narrow belt in north Germany between the Inner-German border and the major port of Hamburg. He emphasized that "This was a clear signal to Moscow that if they wanted to seize north Germany they would have to kill American troops."

This "renaissance" in thinking about strategy got underway in America as soon as the Vietnam War was over. That still left open the question of what Nato's overall strategy should be. In 1973, Schlesinger established the Office of Net Assessment (ONA), which was tasked with something no one else in the government was authorized to do—providing a comparative assessment of US-Soviet military balance, including that between Nato and the Warsaw Pact.

Schlesinger appointed Andy Marshall as its director. Marshall was one of RAND's wisest and most creative thinkers and had recently been working with Henry Kissinger. He made imaginative suggestions on how to strengthen Nato and put the Soviets on the defensive. He also invested heavily in research by consultants, scholars and the military themselves. Before long Marshall was helping mold new ideas into an intellectual offensive that focused on how Nato could win with conventional weapons.

This would be an uphill task. As the Pentagon began to focus again on Europe it was shocked to find that Soviet forces there were now far larger and better equipped. Even though the Arabs had been trounced, the Arab-Israeli war of October 1973 had shown considerable advances in Soviet strategy. The integrated use of tanks, armored personnel carriers for infantry and close air support had proved to be highly effective; so too had anti-tank weapons.

Given the likely scale of the Soviet offensive, Nato had to win the initial battle. "From the beginning," Marshall said, "we knew that would require new weapons, but I also firmly believed they could only be effective if combined with a new doctrine, based on a careful study of how Soviet forces would fight."

"We began to look more closely than others had previously done at the way Soviet forces did things, and why they did them that way," Marshall explained. "We not only monitored exercises, but studied training manuals and models or matrixes that the General Staff used to assess the balance of forces. It was clear that Soviet commanders feared that if subordinates were not pushed there would be inertia. The battle plans, therefore, had to be built around creating mass and momentum. To facilitate this, they relied heavily on standardized procedures."

General William DePuy, who headed the US Army's Training and Doctrine Command, took this work further in 1976 by effecting the biggest change in army doctrine since the Second World War. Instead of confronting Soviet forces in Europe with well-prepared static defense, the army would henceforth pursue "active defense," which meant that they could counter-attack with ground troops well beyond their own front line.

Similar changes were pushed through by General David Jones, the commander of the American air force in Europe. He realized that he now needed to concentrate on breaking up Soviet forces close to the front line, not just the reinforcements being brought up from the rear. This would require the air force to work more closely with the army. Jones initiated an intensive intelligence effort to understand how his opponent would fight, which made it possible to develop special training programs that enabled American pilots to exploit Soviet weaknesses.

One of the first ground-breaking studies commissioned by ONA was *The Comparison of Soviet and US Weapons*, which was based on a close examination of the Soviet equipment the Israelis had captured, plus details of other items acquired by the CIA. The study was led by Phillip Karber of BDM, a consultancy firm that did a lot of work for the Pentagon.[6] Joe Braddock, the head of BDM, told me: "Our report showed that new Soviet equipment was as good or better than that which the Americans were producing except—and this was a big exception—in the field of electronics. The message was clear. Nato could only regain the advantage by exploiting advanced technology."

In 1974, the Defense Nuclear Agency and the Defense Advanced Research Projects Agency sponsored a study on the revolution taking place in the accuracy of weapons. "This was extremely important," Marshall noted, "because it demonstrated that for some tasks it would soon be possible to use conventional substitutes for nuclear weapons." Within a year, work had started on a whole new range of sensors, information-management systems, along with heat-seeking and terminally guided weapons that were together called "assault-breaker." At Marshall's urging, the Defense Intelligence Agency began to work out how these weapons might be used to best effect.

The first renaissance in Nato strategy was now really underway and Moscow knew it. On December 14, 1975, Andropov, the head of the KGB, briefed the Politburo on a range of new hi-tech weapons under development in Nato. According to his reports, he said, these weapons could dramatically increase the ability of the Western alliance to mount a successful defense against a conventional attack.[7]

The Helsinki "Final Act"

While these military developments were unfolding, the first major new political accord on relations in Europe since the end of the war was being negotiated in Geneva in the Conference on Security and Co-operation in Europe.

This was the conference that Moscow had first proposed in 1954 and pressed for many times in the hope that it would result in new arrangements that would erode American influence in Western Europe and increase Soviet influence there. In 1972, the United States had grudgingly agreed to it, in part to temper the enthusiasm of its European allies for détente. At the Europeans' insistence, the work of the conference was split into three "baskets" or chapters, covering security in Europe, economic cooperation and human rights.

The most contentious issue was human rights, the subject of Basket III, which the West had insisted upon. When Brezhnev decided in April 1975 that he wanted the treaty, or "Final Act" as it was widely known, to be signed in Helsinki on August 1, his negotiators were left with an unenviable task. For over eighteen months they had made minimal concessions to the West; now the West was holding the first two baskets to ransom until it got satisfaction on the third.

Michael Alexander, the British diplomat who had led the negotiations on the Western side, told me at the time that "The Russians found themselves having to making bigger and bigger concessions as the deadline approached. As a result, we achieved a text beyond our wildest expectations." He was referring to such clauses as: "The participating States . . . will promote and encourage the effective exercise of civil, political, economic, social, cultural and other rights and freedoms all of which derive from the inherent dignity of the human person and are essential for his free and full development." In addition, every country undertook to publish the full text of the Final Act in its main national newspaper.[8]

In Moscow, there were heated debates in the Politburo over whether to sign the "Final Act." Although the Final Act enshrined the concepts of national sovereignty and non-interference, the critics argued that Basket III would legitimize the growing foreign interference in Soviet internal affairs. Foreign Minister Gromyko acknowledged that problem, but stressed that the package finally granted the Soviet Union what it had strived to achieve for thirty years—the recognition of the post-war frontiers. He won the day by making the point that Kissinger had made to him: "No matter what goes into the Final Act, I don't believe that the Soviet Union will ever do anything it doesn't want to do."[9]

The Soviet press lauded the Final Act, because the leadership liked what was said in Baskets I and II. In Moscow, it was hoped that détente would now be strengthened, as well as the Western European communist parties and the peace movements that were already active in many countries. Almost immediately the Soviet-controlled World Peace Council embarked on a costly large-scale propaganda campaign to undermine popular support for Nato's strategy of nuclear deterrence.

This was the high point of the wave of optimism in Soviet foreign policy. Following the fall of Saigon and the gains the Popular Movement for the Liberation of Angola (MPLA) was making in Angola with Soviet and Cuban backing, Moscow believed that "the world was turning in our direction."[10]

The American press trashed the Final Act on the grounds that it sold-out the Baltic republics and conceded too much to Moscow in return for intangible promises about human rights. All did not, however, go Moscow's way. In November 1975, a remarkable secret operation got underway that reduced Soviet influence in Western Europe. In this operation, which has only recently come to light, the Italian Communist Party worked with a number of European socialist parties to oust the communists from Lisbon, where they had held power since the overthrow in 1974 of the aged Portuguese dictator Antonio de Oliveira Salazar. The Italians feared that these hard-line Portuguese communists would discredit "Euro-communism" and destroy the "historic compromise" they had achieved at home.

Worse was soon to come. When one of the Polish delegates taking part in the negotiations saw the final draft, he had turned to Alexander and said, "Do you know what this means? The party secretary in Krakow will ring the general secretary in Warsaw and tell him 'you people must have been mad to agree to our signing this thing.'" The man went on to tell him, "Well, this will ensure the destruction of socialism in Eastern Europe."[11] It certainly helped.

"Final Act" was almost certainly the most prescient title a treaty has ever had. Few people realized that the trumpet call from Helsinki would soon herald the beginning of another final act—that of the Cold War.

Why Did Détente Turn Sour?

Détente turned sour because it was, in essence, a case of "one bed, two dreams." The Americans, plagued by problems and dissent, wanted to use détente to achieve a lasting accommodation on the basis of the *status quo,* while the Soviets sought to use détente to create an atmosphere in which the Americans would come to accept the Soviet Union as an equal in world affairs, with the Soviets hopefully gaining an edge over the Americans.

That said, after the intense confrontations during the Berlin and Cuban crises, both sides did share one key objective—and that was the wish to manage their relationship in a less nerve-wracking way. In many respects, Nixon and Brezhnev were well-suited to this task. They were measured in their conduct and, despite the considerable differences in their personalities, they could relate to each other as human beings. Anatoly Chernyaev, who understood Brezhnev well, commented that "if Brezhnev had retained his mental vigour and physical stamina, Soviet relations with the West would have been less fraught."

Even though the Soviet leadership did not get all the gains they had hoped from détente, they liked the way things were going; for the Americans, détente turned sour because they did not get what they wanted. On the American side, the breakdown of consensus on foreign policy stemming from the Vietnam war certainly made it harder for Nixon and Kissinger to manage their relations with the Soviet leadership, but several other factors contributed to the growing American hostility towards détente—the strategic arms race, the buildup of Soviet forces in Central and Eastern Europe and the sudden increase in Soviet involvement in the Third World. It was as a result of these Soviet actions that the West came to view the Soviet Union not just as a vague general threat, but as a growing and very specific one.

Had Washington known about Brezhnev's horror of nuclear war that might have eased tensions, but it is far from certain that it would have brought the Cold War to a speedier end, as it was a many-headed hydra. The archives show that Brezhnev's view of détente contrasted sharply with that of Nixon and Kissinger, to say nothing of the American opponents of détente. Problems in one or other area of their relationship would have quickly brought the two superpowers back into confrontation.

The Soviet leadership's biggest miscalculation was to overestimate the willingness of the Americans to accept the idea that the Soviet Union should expand its power and become the full equal of the United States. The miscalculation of most Americans was not dissimilar because they took their faith in the basic "goodness" of others to mean that others would agree with them. As a result, they expected that détente would fundamentally change the Soviet worldview and Soviet conduct.[12]

As the Americans began to feel that the Soviet threat to their country's standing in the world was growing, their attitude towards détente started to sour. To come to terms with a supplicant was acceptable, but the idea of having to make concessions to a challenger was abhorrent. This sentiment fueled the unease that a growing number of Americans felt about the ambiguities and ambivalences of détente. They longed for the simple verities of an earlier age when they were proud of being a "redeemer nation" that had a mission in the world.[13]

The issues that had complicated Soviet-American relations in the Nixon-Brezhnev era would begin to plague those between Carter and Brezhnev—strategic nuclear forces, the military balance in Europe, the political configuration of Europe and rivalry in the Third World. Over the next five years, each of these issues would become far more complex and the risk of confrontation even greater because the Soviets now considered themselves an equal power.

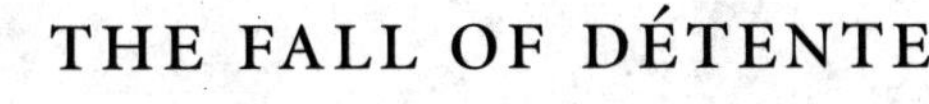

THE FALL OF DÉTENTE

As a Soviet convoy makes its way through a difficult Afghan pass, a member of the mujahedin waits for the moment to fire on it with his rocket launcher. (Igor Belov, from his website www.ruswar.com)

19 The Twilight Zone

Carter's Détente

President Carter, one perceptive commentator noted, had "the good fortune to ride into office on the waning hour of a vaguely anti-military tide of public and congressional opinion and the bad luck to take office just as the tide turned."[1]

Carter's problems were compounded by the fact that Brezhnev and his colleagues felt they were operating from a position of strength. On taking office, Carter was confronted with a stark assessment of Soviet strategic objectives from his National Intelligence Council: "The Soviets still see basic trends in the world as positive for themselves and negative for the United States."[2]

There is no doubt, however, that Carter's own inadequacies made matters worse. Carter was an unusual politician—both saintly and calculating. He often enjoyed fiddling with the details of a matter rather than making hard choices, especially if they involved the use of violence. He would take bold stands on matters of moral principle, but was easily swayed by his subordinates to be pragmatic.

The presidential election campaign had shown that most Americans felt their country had more than enough nuclear weapons. Carter responded to this sentiment in his inaugural address by pledging that: "We will move this year towards our ultimate goal—the elimination of all nuclear weapons on this earth."[3] He was the first president ever to make such a commitment.

Carter's talk of eliminating nuclear weapons, then still a radical departure from post-war policy, contributed greatly to the public impression that he was "flaky" on defense. So, too, did his continuing drive to cut the military budget, already much reduced since American troops had been withdrawn from Vietnam.

A deep reduction in nuclear weapons was at the heart of Carter's policy towards the Soviet Union. The way to deter either side from making a fatal error in a crisis, Carter believed, was to ensure that neither side had enough missiles and warheads to be confident of destroying the entire land-based force of the other. The buzzword was "build-down."

Carter hoped that the cuts themselves would stabilize Soviet-American relations, which could be further improved by widening diplomatic and trade contacts. Naively, he saw no reason why his call for the Soviet people to enjoy similar civil rights to those he had been championing for the Americans should arouse hostility in Moscow.

The Opening Salvo

The Soviet leadership attached enormous importance to arms control which Alexander Bessmertnykh, who later became Soviet foreign minister, described as constituting "95% of the total relationsip, more or less."[4] Before his election, Carter had assured Moscow that he would conclude the Salt-II negotiations rapidly.

In the hope of facilitating that process, Brezhnev made a major speech at Tula on January 18, just two days before Carter's inauguration. "Détente," he stressed, "means a readiness to resolve differences and disputes not by force, nor by threats and saber-rattling, but by peaceful means, at a conference table. Détente is a certain trust and ability to take into account the legitimate interests of the other."[5]

Carter's first letter to Brezhnev, written a month after he took office, incensed the Politburo. To Moscow's considerable annoyance, Carter had changed his position and began calling for far deeper cuts in nuclear weapons than Brezhnev had been able to persuade his own military to accept. The Politburo was equally angered by Carter's moral support for Andrei Sakharov, the leading human rights campaigner and father of the Soviet H-bomb, which they viewed as an unprecedented American intervention in Soviet internal affairs. This as a sign, they believed, that Carter was actually intent on destroying the Soviet system.

The Politburo had never been vexed so quickly by a new administration. Even before Secretary of State Vance paid his first visit to Moscow in March 1977, two leading members of the Politburo wrote a strongly worded letter to Brezhnev. In it Andropov, the head of the KGB, and Ustinov, the minister of defense, accused Carter's Administration of wanting to renegotiate Soviet-American relations from scratch. They were right.

Things went from bad to worse when Vance arrived in Moscow and presented Carter's new arms control proposals and his views on human rights. As Viktor Sukhodrev, Gromyko's interpreter, observed years later, "Suddenly, right here in Moscow—in Brezhnev's office—to talk about human rights . . . Unheard of![6]

The Politburo viewed Carter's arms control proposals as being strongly biased in America's favor.[7] The big problem was not that he wanted to cut the number of missiles from the 2,400 agreed at Vladivostok to below 2,000 a side; it was that within that total there would, for the first time, be two sub-ceilings on Mirvs—with 550 being allowed on land-based missiles and 550–650 on submarines. In addition, the Soviet Union's "heavy" missile force would be more than halved, from 308 to 150, and the Soviet Union would not be allowed to develop a strategic bomber force.

In return, the United States would be willing to agree to a ban on all new strategic missiles, which would end the development of the new American "heavy" missile, the MX (which stands for "missile-experimental"), and restrict the range of all cruise missiles to 2,500 km (1,550 miles).

To the Soviet leadership this seemed a highly unattractive package. They were being asked to make major cuts in their highly effective land-based missile force and built up a retaliatory force based on submarines carrying strategic nuclear missiles, which was where the Americans had a great advantage. The Soviets preferred land-based missiles because they were easier to control than those on submarines and land-based missiles could be made less vulnerable by moving them around the vast uninhabited regions of the Soviet Union by road or rail. They would also have known from American naval ciphers, which they were reading at this time, that the Americans believed they could destroy most of any such Soviet force at the outbreak of hostilities, even in their supposedly well-defended "bastions" of the Barents Sea and the Sea of Okhotsk.

Brezhnev and his colleagues responded sternly to show Carter that they could not be treated in this way. "We got a wet rag in the face," Vance recalled, "and were told to go home."[8] Such a tough stance gave the Politburo emotional satisfaction, but achieved little else. When Gromyko took Vance to the theater the following evening, he reiterated his well-known opinion that progress on arms control would "open the box to the keys that would unlock the solution to other problems."[9] Before long, Moscow had agreed to resume serious negotiations on Salt-II in Geneva, but within the framework of what had been agreed at Vladivostock, rather than put forward in Carter's recent proposals.

Both sides were hoping to strike a balance—on the one hand, convincing their adversary that they were ready to deter any action that had the potential to snowball into a nuclear crisis; on the other, convincing themselves that they could stand up to their adversary in a crisis. And whatever else happened, both the Soviets and the Americans wanted to feel confident that they were not at a disadvantage.

Soviet Strategic Concerns

In his speech at Tula, Brezhnev asserted that neither side could hope to win a nuclear war and that such a war should never be contemplated, let alone fought. This was not just rhetoric on Brezhnev's part. According to General Danilevich, the leading strategist of the General Staff, "By the seventies we had concluded that there was no chance in hell that we would survive" if a nuclear war started, and the leadership understood this.[10] We also now know that, in 1975, possibly earlier, the General Staff received "an instruction" from the leadership that Soviet forces were never to be the first to use nuclear weapons.[11]

Despite having reached parity with the Americans, the Soviets still felt at a considerable disadvantage in the psychology of deterrence. The nub of the matter was that the Soviet leadership had little confidence in its ability to retaliate against an American nuclear attack. There were many short-comings in its early-warning radars and satellites, as well as the command and control systems. The Soviet leadership would have great difficulty in ordering one massive retaliation, let alone carefully calculated "warning shots."[12]

To mask their insecurity, Soviet leaders, political and military, continued to threaten that if just one American missile landed on Soviet territory, they would strike back massively. To convince the Americans that they would do this, they wanted them to believe that the Soviet Union would fight and fight to win. The Party kept reiterating that in a war the communists would always "prevail." They sought to give credence to what they said by strengthening both their defenses against nuclear attack and their offensive missile force.

Since the early seventies, the Soviet leadership had been investing heavily in building bunkers to protect themselves in the event of nuclear war. The strongest of these reinforced steel and concrete structures were deep below ground outside of Moscow, accessible by special high-speed trains from a station beneath the Kremlin.

In addition, the Soviet Strategic Rocket Forces had well-protected communications and radar linked to Soviet missile fields and forces, as well as a civil defense network, which included massive bomb-proof doors at the entrances to the Moscow metro stations, so that they could be used as shelters. In parallel, the Soviet Union was, according to Aleksei Kalashnikov, one of the top missile experts in the Soviet Ministry of Defense, well on its way to creating "a superior first-strike arsenal."[13]

American Strategic Concerns

America's highly effective array of satellites and radars was constantly on the lookout for a Soviet missile attack. All the signs they detected were monitored on radar screens in bunkers deep beneath the Cheyenne Mountains in Colorado; from there, alerts were flashed to the White House.

Since entering the White House, Carter had devoted much thought to how he would respond to a Soviet missile attack. To a far greater degree than any of his predecessors, he paid attention to the mechanics of deterrence and the strategic nuclear war plan. He wanted to know what the United States was threatening to do to the Soviet Union and whether the threat was credible.

"Carter practiced taking the telephone calls telling him that a Soviet missiles had been launched against the United States," Brzezinski said. "He knew that within twelve minutes of the first report, bombers of Strategic Air Command would be airborne, within eighteen minutes the White House would be evacuated. He would remain." Up to seven minutes could elapse before it was possible to confirm that Soviet missiles really were heading towards the United States. As soon as confirmation had been received, the national security adviser would inform the president. At the most, the president would have twenty minutes in which to decide what to do.

This nightmare scenario was made all the worse by American tests showing that even fifty Soviet missiles could so disrupt communications that the president, like Brezhnev himself, might not be able to launch a retaliatory attack.[14] Work soon began on upgrading warning systems, making command posts less vulnerable to attack, and communications better able to function after one had occurred.

Despite what Brezhnev had said at Tula, concern began to grow in Washington that the Soviet leadership might not simply be indulging in rhetoric when they declared that if a nuclear war started, they would fight to win. It seemed increasingly doubtful that Moscow still believed in the concept of "mutually assured destruction," on which the Americans had bet everything.

Early in its first year, the Carter Administration began receiving intelligence that showed that the modernization of Soviet strategic nuclear forces was proceeding rapidly. In the past, the Americans had underestimated Soviet scientists and overestimated Soviet industry. Finally, Soviet production lines were working speedily and new missiles were being fitted with Mirved warheads.

This possibility gave a boost to Carter's critics, who asserted that a "window of vulnerability" was opening up. In a highly influential article in the July issue of *Commentary,* Richard Pipes, who had headed Team-B, asserted that the Soviets were capable of fighting a nuclear war not only because they had the necessary missiles, but because they were inured against the horrors of war as a result of the enormous suffering they had endured during the Second World War and Stalin's purges.[15]

Even those who did not share Pipes's view about the Soviet willingness to endure another war were deeply concerned by what satellite and other intelligence had revealed about the huge network of Soviet bunkers. "The evidence suggested," Marshall said, "that they were costing a phenomenal 1–2% of Soviet GDP." The Americans had nothing comparable, nor would they be willing to spend so much on them. It was one of the great asymmetries of the Cold War."

The Carter Administration now had to decide how to respond. Although Carter was not initially robust on defense, his secretary of defense, Harold Brown, was. He was a distinguished scientist, who for many years he had been a leading figure in the development of America's nuclear weaponry. One of the many issues that concerned him, Brown recalled, was that, "as the Soviet Union was a closed society, it was better able to launch a surprise attack than we were." That consideration did much to shape the proposals he put forward.

In the eighteen months since Carter entered the White House there had been a marked growth in opposition to détente, due not only to what was happening in the strategic field, but also in Europe and the Third World. The call-to-arms made by Team-B in the summer of 1976 was amplified by the recently established Committee on the Present Danger (CPD).

This committee was comprised of influential conservatives of both parties and led by Paul Nitze, who back in 1950 had drafted the famous policy paper NSC-68 that had called for a far more military form of containment. The CPD's well-funded media campaign began to make its mark, with papers like "Is America Becoming Number 2?" that was issued in October 1978. America, this paper argued, could not afford to lose the "battle of perceived capabilities."[16]

Brzezinski and Brown had judged that because Soviet leaders were not risk-takers, they would seek to win through intimidation. This led Brown to back a massive new missile buildup aimed at driving Moscow into negotiations; it involved the largest public works project and the most expensive weapons program in history. While Congress debated these proposals, Brown reminded them of the scale of the challenge the Soviets were posing, pointing out that "when we build, they build; when we cut, they build."[17]

At the heart of the Administration's new program was the deployment of 200 "heavy" MX mobile missiles, each with ten very accurate warheads. They were to be moved around an underground rail network in which they could be concealed in any of its 4,600 concrete shelters. Because the Soviets could never know where they were, they would not only be invulnerable to a Soviet attack, but they would also have the ability, theoretically speaking, to destroy Soviet missiles in their silos. In addition, America's submarine-based missiles would be upgraded so that they were as accurate as its existing land-based ones. This meant that America's retaliatory forces would be able to inflict almost as much damage as its land-based force.

When Brezhnev and Carter finally met in Vienna in June 1979, they signed the Salt-II Treaty, which was close to what had been agreed on four and a half years earlier at Vladivostok. The treaty, however, addressed few of the developments that threatened strategic stability, let alone resolved. Neither side yet understood the other's thinking about deterrence and both still felt vulnerable. The Russians and the Americans alike wanted to exclude from the negotiations weapons that would strengthen their relative positions. Indeed, the prevailing view in both capitals was that strategic stability only existed when one side had clear superiority over the other.

20 Battle of the Strategies

Ogarkov Makes His Mark

While Soviet developments had driven the United States to rethink its nuclear strategy, American developments had been forcing the Soviet Union to rethink how it would fight a conventional war in Europe. When Marshal Grechko died in 1976, Brezhnev was still alert enough to recognize the urgent demand for new thinking in the Soviet defense establishment on the balance to be struck between arms control and gaining the psychological advantage over the Americans.

General Jaruzelski, then the Polish defense minister, believed that "The one person Brezhnev trusted and who understood these issues was Dmitri Ustinov," the highly effective head of the military-industrial commission who had played a key part in the development and production of Soviet armaments since the early forties. Brezhnev appointed Ustinov as the new minister of defense, with the title of Marshal.

The strategy for winning a conventional war in Europe that Ustinov inherited from Grechko had obvious flaws. The speed of advance was too slow, and it did not address the problems created by Nato's rapidly growing number of anti-tank guided missiles, the increasing speed with which the Americans could airlift reinforcements into Germany, and the fact that Soviet forces remained highly vulnerable to Nato air attacks.

On top of these current failings, there was the prospect of yet another "revolution in military affairs." This was in the form of the "assault-breaker" weapons and computerized battle management systems that the Americans were developing, which would yet once more transform the balance of power in Europe. This was a daunting and costly specter.

But all was not lost, as by the latter seventies Moscow had a surprise in store for Nato. "Our new SS-20 missile," according to General Danilevich, "was a breakthrough, unlike anything the Americans had. We were immediately able to hold all of Europe hostage."[1] This was no exaggeration: the SS-20 could attack targets anywhere in Europe from deep within Soviet territory and each missile carried three Mirved warheads. The General Staff believed that they would now be able to develop a credible strategy for defeating Nato with conventional forces alone. And that could transform the psychological balance of power in Europe, by making the West Europeans doubt that the United States would be able to protect them.

Following Brezhnev's Tula speech, Marshal Ogarkov, another outstanding strategic thinker of the post-war generation, was promoted to chief of the General Staff. For some years, he had been pushing for the latest technology to be incorporated into Soviet military doctrine, recognizing that this would require changes in the way Soviet forces fought. Ogarkov tasked a team headed by General Danilevich to solve the problems Ustinov had identified.

The result of their labors was contained in General Danilevich's masterpiece, the three volume *Strategy of Deep Operations (Global and Theatre)*, which he and others had compiled between 1977 and 1986. This became the top secret "directive" that guided Soviet nuclear and conventional war planning for at least the last decade of the Soviet state. (To this day, the Russians have not published its contents).[2]

A few people in Washington, however, soon had a good idea of Marshal Ogarkov's new strategy, thanks to a treasure trove of material that had come from two CIA agents with remarkable access: Colonel Ryszard Kuklinski,[3] an officer of the Polish General Staff who was working on the Warsaw Pact's war plans, and General Dmitri Polyakov,[4] who was based at the headquarters of Soviet Military Intelligence (the GRU) in Moscow from 1976 to 1979.

The small group of people allowed to see this intelligence were stunned by the scale of Ogarkov's vision. It gave them a sense of shock and awe long before that term entered common parlance. The documents Kuklinski and Polyakov provided showed the highly offensive nature of Soviet war plans, which sought to exploit the twin elements of surprise and deception. The central concept was that the offensive would be launched from a standing start under the cover of military exercises, which would almost immediately be backed up by the rapid advance of two million well-equipped troops.[5]

"This new strategy aimed to give the Soviet Union more options than Nato," Phillip Petersen, one of the leading experts on Soviet strategy in the Defense Intelligence Agency, emphasized. "Ogarkov knew that many in Nato doubted that their political leaders would agree quickly to use nuclear weapons. A key aim, therefore, was to fight the war in such a way as to delay Nato taking the decision to use nuclear weapons until it was too late for them to be able to influence the outcome of the war."[6]

Under Ogarkov's plan, the whole of continental Europe was to be divided into three huge theaters of military operations—with each front line being up to 750 km (465 miles) wide and with operations being conducted as far as 1,200 km (745 miles) beyond it. This would be a military operation on an unprecedented scale. The great innovation was the concept of fighting an integrated air and land battle over a vastly greater area than ever before. This technique called for huge amounts of new equipment.[7]

"What really stunned us," Petersen recalled, "was that Ogarkov's opening move would be a giant air offensive, with up to 2,000 aircraft, to destroy Nato's nuclear weapons and pin down its aircraft for up to 48 hours. This was all the more important as Nato aircraft were soon expected to be carrying 'assault-breaker' munitions that would be far more effective than conventional bombs against a Soviet armored offensive."[8]

To suppress Nato defenses, which had been strengthened with nearly 50,000 modern anti-tank guided missiles, Soviet forces would subject them to such an unprecedented bombardment. The term for it in Russian suggested that it would be of nuclear intensity. Once the front line was broken, Ogarkov's new "operational maneuver groups" (OMGs) would take over. These fast-moving armored units would be accompanied by artillery and engineers with river-crossing equipment, as well as mobile air-defenses. Fighter-bombers and attack-helicopters would support their advance, as would special forces who had been airlifted behind Nato's front line.

The key task of OMGs was to penetrate deep into West Germany to disrupt the command and control of Nato forces, and to seize the remaining nuclear stores, airfields and key logistic points. Other OMGs would encircle the main Nato units, just as slower-moving Soviet forces had planned to do in the early seventies. The intent was for Soviet forces to reach the Channel in less than twenty days, without using nuclear weapons.[9]

The Poles preferred this strategy to nuclear war-fighting on their territory. After a major Warsaw Pact exercise in 1980, General Jaruzelski had written a scathing account of the destruction that had resulted from the use of nuclear weapons. "The chain of command was incapacitated by 'nuclear paralysis' and operations had grounded to a halt."[10]

Exercise Zapad-81: fast-moving tracked vehicles with surface-to-air missiles to protect rapidly advancing Soviet armored forces. (Tassphoto, Moscow)

The implication was that it would be madness to resort to nuclear weapons. One of his senior officers had earlier recommended that the only way the Polish nation could survive in such circumstances would be to build a good, solid bunker and put in it "a hundred Polish men, some sort of real good fuckers, plus two hundred women" and start again from scratch.[11]

Testing

In September 1981, on the plains of the western Soviet Union, the General Staff brought together forces for their largest military exercise since the Second World War.

This was *Zapad-81. Zapad*, which means "West," was the big annual exercise to test Soviet forces against Nato. Marshal Ogarkov used the occasion to demonstrate the brilliance of his strategy and the extraordinary power of a well-coordinated Soviet high-speed offensive using the new armored "operational maneuver groups."

"We monitored this exercise intently," recalled Diego Ruiz-Palmer, who worked with Andy Marshall at the time. "Ogarkov showed that over the past three years he had studied closely the ways in which the Americans' 'assault-breaker' would work and what action could be taken to minimize their impact."

Compared with Nato, Soviet conventional forces had never looked so good, especially in the carefully edited Soviet propaganda film that followed. Publicly, Soviet leaders were proudly proclaiming that the structure and methods of their forces had been perfected to the point where they could win a European war with conventional weapons alone.

"Experienced observers knew," Ruiz-Palmer points out, "that every part of these maneuvers had been carefully rehearsed and choreographed. Nearly all those taking part were officers and NCOs, not ordinary soldiers. This was not a military operation, it was military propaganda at its best."

Much still needed to be done before Ogarkov's concept could be realized in full. One of the biggest questions that remained for the Soviets was how to compensate for the unreliability of Poland.

Cracks in the Western Alliance

While the Americans turned against détente, the Western Europeans tried to hang on to it. The West Germans, in particular, did not want to prejudice the gains that had been made and the openings it continued to offer.

When Carter came into office, defense and arms control issues were already causing considerable frictions within the alliance. The most immediate issue facing him was that Nato did not have enough conventional forces to stop a Soviet armored offensive. He proposed using "enhanced-radiation weapons" (popularly known as "neutron bombs") that would kill the tank crews, but do little other damage.

Before public opinion could be prepared, the story broke in the *Washington Post* on June 6, 1977. The article quoted scientists involved with the project as saying that the neutron bomb was something that "kills people and leaves buildings standing," which gave a strong boost to Europe's anti-nuclear movements. These protests were openly supported by the Soviet government—and more effectively backed by the KGB taking what it called "active measures" that involved clandestine finance of foreign peace movements and feeding false stories into the Western press.

Soon thereafter, Carter—beset by moral doubts and facing much international opposition—delayed the neutron bomb program indefinitely, leaving Schmidt embarrassed politically and deeply angered by Carter's conduct. Before long, however, Carter ensured that the neutron bomb would be available should the need arise. Although he banned production of the neutron bomb in 1978, Carter secretly approved a production of the components, which in a crisis could be assembled in 48 hours and airlifted to Europe.

While Soviet armored forces in Central Europe had been growing, Nato began to notice that Moscow was embarked on a full-scale modernization of its missiles that could cover targets in Europe, but not reach the United States. The new missile that was being deployed was the SS-20, the lynchpin of Ogarkov's strategy. Chancellor Schmidt was quick to realize that this posed a serious threat to Nato. At the end of October, in an address to the International Institute of Strategic Studies in London, he robustly called on Nato "to remove the disparities of military power in Europe."[12]

Moscow paid no heed to Schmidt's warning not to provoke Nato by deploying large numbers of these missiles. Given that the neutron bomb fiasco had been a damaging blow to American leadership, other West European leaders backed Schmidt in insisting that there had to be a visible response to such a clear political and psychological challenge posed by these new missiles.

Euromissiles

Euromissiles is a term that journalists used to help readers who did not need to know the differences between the three very different types of missiles that were being deployed in Europe. The differences, however, were important.

The Soviet SS-20 was a ballistic missile with three warheads and a range of 4,500 km (2,800 miles); the American Pershing-II was also a ballistic missile, but with only one warhead and a range of 1,700 km (1,050 miles); the Gryphon (often mistakenly called Tomahawk) also had one warhead and a similar range, but it was a cruise missile. The Gryphon could avoid radar detection by flying very close to the ground, but it would take almost two hours to reach targets at its maximum range. From bases in Europe the Pershing-II and the Gryphon would be able to strike a variety of military targets in the western Soviet Union. They would not, however, be able to reach Moscow or the SS-20s, which were deployed still farther inland.

At this time, in the late seventies, Nato was already considering how it could launch carefully selected "warning shots" into the Soviet Union to "bring home," literally speaking, the risks of continuing with any offensive against Western Europe. After much debate, the Americans said they thought that two missiles they were developing—the Pershing-II and the Gryphon—might meet the European requirement. "As Western governments thought this argument too complex," Michael Quinlan, Britain's leading nuclear strategist explained, "they sold these missiles to their respective electorates as being intended to counterbalance the new Soviet SS-20s."

In December 1979, Nato announced its "twin-track" decision on what was called "Intermediate-range Nuclear Forces" or INF. Unless Moscow responded positively, Nato said it would begin deploying 108 Pershing-II and 464 ground-launched cruise missiles to Europe in late 1983. Such a large number were needed to persuade Moscow to cut the number of SS-20s it was deploying.

The scene was set for another major battle of wills.

21 The Death of Détente

Global Rivalry

Well before the confrontation over Euromissiles and the Soviet invasion of Afghanistan put several more nails in the lid of détente's coffin, détente was suffering badly in Africa.[1]

By the time Carter became president in January 1977, Soviet leaders wanted to press ahead with undermining American influence in the Third World because they felt that was the only way they could gain the overall advantage. As their economic problems mounted, however, they hoped that they would be working with groups so committed to change that they would not require much in the way of Soviet resources to achieve success.

While Carter was concerned about Soviet expansion in the Third World, the bitter experience of Vietnam made him wary of using military force and skeptical of excessive fears of what Moscow might stand to gain. He hoped that it would be possible to shore up America's position in the Third World mainly by helping to improve conditions there, not just through aid, but through emphasizing the American values of individual freedom, the market economy and political representation.

At the beginning of Carter's presidency, the spotlight was on the Horn of Africa, where the two superpowers had coexisted for nearly two decades. Somalia had aligned itself with Moscow since gaining independence in 1960, receiving training and arms for its forces in return for granting substantial facilities to the Soviet navy and air force in Berbera at the mouth of the Red Sea (which leads to the Suez Canal and is not far from the entrance to the Gulf).

Neighboring Ethiopia, one of the few independent countries in Africa, had had good relations with the Americans since the fifties. After the Emperor Haile Selassie was overthrown in 1974, the situation within Ethiopia became chaotic. America's links with Ethiopia weakened, and in 1977, following extensive human rights abuses by the left-wing Mengistu regime, arms supplies were cut off. At this point, the Somalis tried to seize the Ogaden region of Ethiopia, which they had long claimed. The resulting conflict soon reshaped alliances in the Horn.

When Mengistu turned to Moscow for a huge supply of arms, the Soviet leadership were so keen to have a former American ally align itself with them that they were willing to lose Somalia, their own first convert in the region. When Soviet arms began arriving in Ethiopia, Somalia broke off relations with Moscow and closed the naval base facilities to its ships. For its part, Washington began supplying Somalia with arms.

The scale of the Soviet airlift to Ethiopia soon worried the Carter Administration. Soviet aircraft were not merely bringing in equipment, but 1,500 Soviet military advisers (including some senior generals), plus Cuban troops, who at their peak numbered 17,000. Between November 1977 and January 1978, 225 large Soviet transport aircraft provided what was virtually an air-bridge between the Soviet Union and Ethiopia. In all, there were about 6,500 Soviet flights into Ethiopia—averaging three an hour every day for three months—plus ships bringing in heavy equipment and fighter-bombers.[2]

This operation was much bigger than the airlift of Cuban forces to Angola two years earlier—indeed it was the largest ever mounted by the Soviet Union. "We felt," Brzezinski told me, "that Moscow was deliberately giving a display of its ability to project power—and it was impressive." By March 1978, Ethiopian and Cuban forces had pushed the Somalis out of the Ogaden.

Carter accepted Brzezinski's view that the war in the Horn of Africa was a challenge to American interests in the Gulf and Indian Ocean. In August 1977, the president signed PD-18, a directive that marked a significant change in American policy towards the Third World. It emphasized "forward defense" and the creation of a rapid deployment force with global reach. This force, however, would take years to materialize.

At a Politburo meeting on June 8, 1978, Brezhnev blamed worsening relations on Carter's increasingly anti-Soviet policy and wish to return to the Cold War. The same day, in an address to the US Naval Academy, Carter claimed that "to the Soviet Union, détente seems to mean a continuing aggressive struggle for political advantage and increased influence in a variety of ways. The Soviet Union apparently sees military power and military assistance as the best means of expanding their influence abroad."[3] Moscow would have "to choose between cooperation and confrontation."

Gains and Losses

The Americans had, nonetheless, made one key strategic gain. In the summer of 1975, they had excluded the Russians from the talks that led the Israelis to withdraw from Sinai in return for the establishment of diplomatic relations with Egypt. This changed the balance of power in the Middle East, reduced Moscow's influence and enhanced America's prestige.

During Carter's first year in office, President Sadat of Egypt paid his breakthrough trip to Israel, where he addressed the Knesset (parliament). In September 1978, Carter played a bold role as mediator in securing the Camp David accords between Sadat and Premier Begin of Israel. These not only resulted in a peace settlement, but a recognition of the rights of the Palestinians. Carter's efforts demonstrated that only the United States could act as an honest broker between these two long-standing adversaries. With the United States now Egypt's main backer, the Soviet influence in the Middle East had been sharply cut back—not just in Egypt, but also in Syria and Iraq.

Carter's Near Eastern gains were swiftly offset farther east. In April 1978 radical officers had overthrown the King of Afghanistan, in June there was an "anti-Imperialist" coup in South Yemen and in Iran the Shah, America's major ally in the Middle East, was heading for his downfall—something that Khrushchev had predicted at his meeting with Kennedy in Vienna in 1961. By January 1979, he had fled into exile and the Islamic fundamentalists began to take control of the country. In November, Iranian militants seized the American Embassy in Tehran, taking 52 American hostages.

On one level, the Soviet leadership were delighted by the ousting of such a prominent American ally. However, Moscow was not making any headway at America's expense. Soviet relations with the new regime were not good. Indeed, the KGB's activities in Iran were even more constrained than they had been in the Shah's day.[4]

At another level, the aged Brezhnev and his colleagues were troubled by the rising power of this religious movement that was so alien to them. They feared that Islamic fundamentalism could well ferment unrest in Soviet Central Asia, both directly and through Afghanistan. Although Afghanistan had traditionally been a buffer state between East and West, it had since Khrushchev's visit in 1955 developed closer ties with Moscow, where Afghan army officers began to be sent for training. While the Soviet leadership were surprised when a coup brought the Afghan communist party to power in 1978, they lost no time in welcoming the new regime to the socialist camp.[5]

Unfortunately for Moscow, the Afghan communist party was notorious for the savagery of its infighting. The faction that gained power, headed by Nur Mohammad Taraki and Hafizulah Amin, made matters worse by ignoring Moscow's repeated calls for moderation. Soon their brutal efforts to enforce socialism in a profoundly Muslim country were stirring up revolts.

Moscow was also angered by the prospect of Sino-American relations moving from symbolic to substantive. In January 1979, Deng Xiaoping, the Chinese leader, visited the United States to consolidate the recent establishment of full diplomatic relations between the two counties. On February 15, 1979, the day after the expiry of the 1950 Sino-Soviet Treaty, China announced its intention to attack Vietnam for having invaded Cambodia. This was seen in Moscow as clear evidence that Washington and Beijing were beginning to collude in moves against the Soviet Union and its allies.

The boot of discomfort, however, was soon on the American foot. After the Vietnamese inflicted humiliating defeats on the Chinese, Maurice Bishop led a Marxist coup on the small Caribbean Island of Grenada in March 1979. Then in July, the Sandinistas, who had been supported by Castro and helped by the KGB since 1966, overthrew the Somoza regime, which had ruthlessly exploited Nicaragua for decades. This was the first revolutionary gain in Latin America since Castro overthrew Batista in Cuba in 1959.

Carter was not sorry to see the Somozas go. He was troubled, however, by the determination of the Sandinistas to back the revolutionaries in neighboring El Salvador and Guatemala, which lay just to its north. Gradually, the Soviet Union began providing economic and military aid to the Sandinistas. Over the next few years, this would become a serious bone of contention in Soviet-American relations.[6]

Troubles Brew in Eastern Europe

Less than a decade after the suppression of the Prague Spring, some brave Czechs once again called for greater freedom. In January 1977, 230 prominent Czech intellectuals published a manifesto announcing the formation of Charter-77, a "loose, informal and open association of people" committed to human rights in keeping with the Czechoslovak constitution and the Helsinki Accords. The signatories included the playwright Vaclav Havel, who would later become the first president of Czechoslovakia after the communists were ousted by the "velvet revolution" of 1989.

The West condemned the arrest of several of the signatories and the crackdown on dissidents that followed. In response to Carter's subsequent declarations of support for human rights in the Soviet Union, the Politburo ordered the arrest of three key members of the Moscow-based Helsinki Watch Group—Yuri Orlov, Alexander Ginsberg and Anatoly Sharansky. In the early spring, a CIA report to the White House quoted a Hungarian leader as saying that the "almost paranoid Soviet party leadership" believed Carter was pursuing "a deliberate strategy to overthrow the Soviet regime."[7]

Brezhnev and his colleagues were close to the mark, as Carter *had* just approved unprecedented proposals from Brzezinski, his national security adviser, to attack the legitimacy of the Soviet regime within the Soviet Union itself.[8] Even though these proposals were whittled down by the State Department and the CIA itself, there was a marked increase in the quantity of dissident and Western information and literature smuggled into the Soviet Union and Eastern Europe.[9]

Encouraged by Brzezinski, who was of Polish origin, Carter began to show more interest in Eastern Europe than any other American presidents had. His first state visit, in December 1977, was not to one of America's allies, but to Poland. The visit was not quite the success the president had hoped for, in part because something was "lost in translation." Carter wished to tell his audience of his "love for freedom," but unfortunately his interpreter rendered this remark into Polish as "my lust for freedom." This comic incident reinforced the impression that he was naïve and inexperienced in diplomacy.

But a month later, Carter's diplomacy hit the right note. The Crown of St. Stephen, a Hungarian national treasure that had been in American "safe keeping" since the end of the war, was returned to Budapest where it was received with popular rejoicing. Carter also began cultivating Yugoslavia (and even Romania). Funding for Radio Free Europe and Radio Liberty was stepped up to boost reception throughout Eastern Europe and the Soviet Union.[10]

Front Line Cracks

What the West did not realize at this time was the extent of Moscow's concerns about East Germany. "Tension had been building up for a decade," Markus Wolf, the head of East German Intelligence, recollected. One of Brezhnev's key objectives in pursuing détente was to ensure stability in Eastern Europe. By 1971, he had enough of the cantankerous and obstructionist Ulbricht, whose anger rose at the sight of girls with ponytails and short skirts. Brezhnev replaced him with Erich Honecker, a younger and more energetic man who had earlier been fairly successful in heading the communist youth movement.

The East German leaders were proud that they had finally acquired international recognition for their state, albeit more than twenty years after its establishment. The achievement of socialism in Germany was, they felt, symbolized by the new 368 meter-high television tower that soared over their capital of East Berlin and could be seen from every part of West Berlin. It was the tallest structure in the whole of Europe. They were less happy about the huge cross that would appear on the faceted globe that crowned it every time the sun shone. Many claimed that this was "God's revenge."

Honecker soon tired of Moscow treating his Democratic Republic as a pawn in the chess game that it was playing with the Americans in Europe. The tension that Wolf recalled was evident in 1975, at the annual commemoration at the Soviet war memorial in East Berlin. When the Soviet ambassador noticed that for the first time ever no East German officials were present, he turned to his American, British and French colleagues and said "So what! This is *our* day!"[11]

Under Honecker, standards of living and welfare improved, along with the supply of imported Western consumer goods. The amount of time people were obliged to to spend in political activities of one sort or another was reduced and they were encouraged to enjoy the traditions and simple pleasures of earlier provincial life. More visits were allowed between East and West Germany. To prevent this increasingly relaxed atmosphere from fostering instability, Honecker greatly strengthened the Stasi, the secret police. While the Stasi was quite successful in persuading people not to challenge the regime, the party had little success in stimulating support for it.[12]

After what had happened in Czechoslovakia, reform was not on the agenda for the East Germans. "The seriousness of our economic situation became increasingly clear to me from the early 1970s as we fell further and further behind West Germany," Wolf recalled, "and there were no indications that we would be able to close the gap." To revitalize the economy, the government borrowed from the West to build new factories. When those investments did not generate the profits needed to buy Western consumer goods, the government borrowed more again. Within three years, Honecker's chief financial expert was warning him that East Germany was on the road to bankruptcy.

"The truth of the matter," Wolf observed, "was that Honecker was, indeed, becoming more economically dependent on West Germany." Exports soared as West German companies had products made in East Germany and then exported them duty-free to EEC counties as West German products. In 1976, the Soviet ambassador was painting for Moscow a picture of growing threats to East German stability.[13] By the end of the decade, West Germany accounted for roughly half its hard-currency earnings.

Soviet concerns were compounded by Honecker's willingness to make concessions on travel and emigration in return for cash. Between 1962 and 1989, some 300,000 people were allowed to leave East Germany in return for a total of over $3 billion. In addition, private transfers of funds to friends and relatives in the East amounted, on average, to about $1 billion a year.

When Brezhnev visited East Berlin for the 30th anniversary of the Democratic Republic in 1979, Honecker had already run up hard-currency debts of over $10 billion. Pounding the table, Brezhnev castigated the East German leaders saying: "You can only consume what you have produced. No one can live at the expense of someone else by wanting to declare bankruptcy!"[14] Honecker ignored his protest. He told his Politburo that they had to keep borrowing because if they increased prices, the people would overthrow the regime.

In the years ahead, East Germany would become an even greater headache for Moscow and, with Moscow's approval, for the West as well. East Germany was not only providing sanctuary for West European "nihilist" terrorists, but had trained, armed and funded many of them. In particular, in June 1979, they assisted the West German "Red Army Faction" with an attack that almost succeeded in killing General Alexander Haig, the commander of all Nato forces, and, in September 1981, attempted to assassinate General Frederick Kroesen, the commander of the US army in Europe.[15]

Afghanistan

Afghanistan was Moscow's Vietnam. Even though the war was less costly in lives, it was an equally traumatic demonstration to the Soviet leadership about the limits of power.

The Soviet decision to invade Afghanistan was shaped by vague perceptions.[16] On the one hand, there was the fear of fundamentalism spreading from Iran to Afghanistan and then infecting the Muslims of Soviet Central Asia; on the other, there was fear that Amin would follow Sadat and suddenly side with the Americans.

At the beginning of 1979, the tribal revolt against the Afghan communist party's attempts to introduce socialism to the country began to gather momentum.

When an uprising broke out in March 1979 in Herat, where a number of Soviet advisers and their families died, the Afghan government called on Moscow to send troops to help suppress it. The Politburo refused—Gromyko said that sending troops would destroy the remaining gains of détente and the Salt-II arms control treaty; Andropov added that "we cannot permit" Soviet troops to "wage war against the [Afghan] people."[17]

On July 3, almost six months before Soviet military intervention began, Carter authorized the first American financial support for the mujahedin. The sum was not great, just over $500,000, but it reflected a new American determination to check Soviet expansion in the Third World.[18]

In the hope of reversing the worsening situation, Moscow decided to back Taraki, the leader of one faction within the communist party, against Amin, who led another. The plan literally misfired in October when Amin learned of this, seized the initiative and murdered Taraki. While Brezhnev took this as a personal affront to his authority, Amin tried to shore up his position by telling tribal leaders that he would distance himself from the Soviet Union. At the same time, Amin made contact with American officials in Kabul.

After the Herat uprising, Ustinov put before the Politburo a plan for an invasion. By November, the forces earmarked for this task had been brought to full readiness. The aim was to kill Amin, install Karmal (a comparatively moderate Afghan communist leader then in Prague) and stay on for long enough to bring the situation under control.

On December 6, as the Soviet leadership moved towards giving the go-ahead to this operation, it became clear that Nato would soon announce plans to deploy Pershing-II and cruise missiles unless Moscow cut back its force of SS-20 missiles targeted on Western Europe. The Soviet leadership thought that intervention in Afghanistan could not make their relations with the West any worse. As Anatoly Dobrynin later put it, "by the winter of 1979 détente was, for most purposes, already dead."[19]

As Brezhnev's grasp of reality slipped away, Ustinov and Andropov had become the main voices on Afghanistan. Andropov sent the generally cautious Brezhnev a handwritten letter to persuade him of the need for intervention. He played on Brezhnev's fears by telling him that "there is no guarantee that Amin, in order to secure his personal power, would not turn to the West." This suggestion touched on a particularly sensitive nerve. Brezhnev was in no mood to lose a recently acquired "socialist" ally at a time when the stability in Eastern Europe was becoming fragile.[20]

The Invasion Begins

When the Politburo met on December 8, Ustinov and Andropov gave this argument a new twist. They raised the possibility of "American short-range missiles being deployed in Afghanistan," which meant that they would be able to destroy strategic missile sites in the southern Soviet Union before Moscow could order a retaliatory strike.[21] By then Soviet troops had already established a substantial bridgehead in Kabul and the KGB had made one unsuccessful attempt to assassinate Amin.

The following day Marshal Ogarkov, the chief of the General Staff, not only warned the leadership of the perils Soviet troops would face in Afghanistan, but was bold enough to tell them that the fears of hostile American activities in the region were imaginary. Then, at the Politburo meeting on December 10, he warned that an invasion would "align the entire Islamic East against us" and the Soviet Union would "suffer political damage around the world." On both occasions he was told to shut up and follow the Party's orders, which he did.[22]

Intervention was approved on December 12. The members of the Politburo confirmed the decision by signing a short handwritten protocol entitled "Concerning the Situation in 'A,'" which was probably the most pathetic security measure ever taken within the Soviet bureaucracy.

On Christmas Day, Soviet troops began entering Afghanistan on a massive scale. Within forty-eight hours, Amin had been killed during a raid by KGB special forces, and Karmal brought in to head the new regime. By January, there were 85,000 Soviet troops in the country fighting the mujahedin, with the number rising to around 100,000 by the end of 1981. This was the largest Soviet military intervention beyond Eastern Europe since the Second World War.

Carter sent Brezhnev the sharpest message of his presidency. The invasion was, he said, "a clear threat to peace" and "could mark a fundamental and long-lasting turning point in our relations."[23] The president ordered the CIA to step up its covert assistance program to the Afghan Islamist rebels, withdrew the controversial Salt-II treaty that had been presented to the Senate for ratification and announced that the United States would not take part in the Olympic Games scheduled to be held in Moscow in the summer of 1980.

In his State of the Union address at the end of the month, the president went further and warned that "Any attempt by any outside force to gain control of the Persian Gulf region will be regarded as an assault on the vital interests of the United States of America, and such an assault will be repelled by any means necessary, including military force."[24] The Soviet leadership had no such intention. But this was a prudent move given what had happened when the Americans had not been explicit about their commitment to South Korea in 1950.

Brezhnev himself seems to have genuinely believed that the intervention would be a "limited operation." He told Dobrynin that he expected that the intervention "would be over in a few weeks' time."[25] Brezhnev and his colleagues were in for a nasty surprise.

The Soviet military intervention in Afghanistan was not a case of a weakened regime embarking on war before it became weaker still, but one of a sclerotic leadership desperate not to lose a recent gain, for fear that they would begin to lose all the others they had made since the war. The failure of their ill-considered enterprise gave an impetus to the demise of their empire.

The Pope's Divisions

While problems mounted in Afghanistan, Poland once again began to torment the Soviet leadership and compel them to contemplate changes they would never have countenanced in the past. These changes were necessary as the leadership considered Poland to be the pearl in the crown of the empire.

The rot had set in much earlier. Mieczyslaw Rakowski, the former leader of the Polish Communist Party, explained to me that "the main culprit was the man known in Moscow as 'The Frenchman.'" The Frenchman was Eduard Gierek who, Rakowski said, "had been a miner in France during the war and was the only East European leader not to have been trained in Moscow. His distaste for doctrinaire communism was more than matched by his love of the good life."

Gierek came to power in 1970, after a wave of strikes had brought down Gomulka. Poland became the first Eastern European beneficiary of détente, as Moscow allowed him to borrow heavily from the West. With cavalier extravagance, Gierek financed the import of consumer goods and the building of new factories. The failure of factories to generate the earnings needed to repay the loans created economic problems that in 1976 led to more strikes, in which members of the Polish intelligentsia actively helped the strikers. Brezhnev viewed these developments with mounting concern and suspicion.

"Whatever Gierek's other weaknesses," Rakowski pointed out, "he had a fine feel for Brezhnev's vanity. During Brezhnev's visit to Warsaw later that year, Gierek placated him by bestowing on him Poland's highest military award, the

Virtute Militari. This did not go down well with the Polish people, but Brezhnev was delighted. By the end of the decade Gierek had borrowed a total of $20 billion from the West."

The Catholic Church, meanwhile, went from strength to strength. Its university at Lublin, the only non-state run university in the communist world, was flourishing. The level of church attendance was the highest in the Catholic world, with Church-going not just an act of religious faith, but an expression of nationalism.

In the days when Poland had elected its kings, the Primate had acted as head of state when the country had no monarch. He was the *Interrex* in the *Interregnum* and, as such, embodied the spirit of the nation until the Poles elected another ruler of their choice. The vast majority of Poles revered the post-war Primates for championing their rights. For that reason, the Kremlin was mortified when Cardinal Karol Wojtyla, the Archbishop of Krakow, was unexpectedly elected Pope in 1978. Nonetheless, there was such an upsurge of nationalism in Poland, that even the Communist Party felt obliged to send a message of congratulation.

When the Pope returned to Poland the following year, he transformed the political landscape. An extraordinary two-thirds of the population watched his "pilgrimage" in person, the rest viewed it on television. "Drawing on communist techniques," Rakowski admiringly observed, "the Pope converted his huge open-air masses into mass rallies, which he made all the more potent through the skills he had developed as an actor in the days of his youth. The people felt they were in the presence of a moral and political giant." In Krakow, over two million people are estimated to have gathered to hear him speak—probably the largest crowd of people ever to have assembled in European history.

"The future of Poland," the Pope declared from the pulpit of his old cathedral, "will depend on how many people are prepared to be non-conformist."[26] Although he voiced no explicit criticism of the regime, his message to the people was clear: "Don't be afraid—the future of Poland depends upon you." They sensed that it did and felt empowered. As a leading Polish prelate said to me at the time, "Communism is an interesting transient phenomenon."

Solidarity

Just over a year later, in August 1980, almost 20,000 workers barricaded themselves into the Lenin Shipyard at Gdansk, on whose gates they hung a large photo of their hero the Pope. Within days these strikers, under the charismatic leadership of Lech Walesa, had created "Solidarnosc" (or "Solidarity"), Poland's

Lech Walesa (in the left foreground) and his fellow strikers at confession in the Lenin Shipyard, where an image of the Pope is displayed both on the inside and outside of the gates, August 1980. (Alain Keler, Bettmann/Corbis)

first free trade union since the war. The Pope encouraged Polish workers to hold out for the legal recognition of their union and for the first time Polish strikers received extensive support from the intelligentsia. Before long, some 300,000 workers were on strike across the country.

On August 31, after eighteen days, the strike ended. Lech Walesa announced that the negotiations had been a "success for both sides." The authorities, he said, recognized not only the right of workers to strike, but to organize independent trades unions; the strikers, for their part, acknowledged the leading role of the communist in Poland. The two delegations then stood to sing the national anthem.[27]

One of the small signs of the great changes taking place occurred in the building in Krakow that had housed the revolutionary government of 1846. There in September 1980 I witnessed a descendant of Count Potocki, one of Poland's great aristocrats, advising workers on how to negotiate with the government. It was an unforgettable sight.

As Solidarity burgeoned, Moscow began increasing economic aid to Poland. Brezhnev cut back the export of cheap oil to other East European countries and sold it on the world market to pay for Polish imports. At the same time, American economic assistance to Poland was increased while Washington advised all Poles who would listen to exercise moderation.

Moscow put increasing pressure on the Polish leadership to crush Solidarity. By December, both the Poles and the Americans had plenty of intelligence that preparations had been made for Soviet troops to take over the country.[28] On December 3, Carter sent a message to Brezhnev to assure him that it was "the firm intention of the United States not to exploit the events in Poland nor to threaten legitimate Soviet security interests in that region." The Polish people should be left to resolve their internal difficulties. But if force was used to impose a solution "our relationship would be most adversely affected."[29]

Intervention or Martial Law?

By this time Solidarity had some ten million members, a number equal to around 30% of the population and representing nearly all the workers. Many of them wanted to overthrow the regime. Stanislaw Kania, the new Party leader, warned Moscow that "if there were an intervention there would be a national uprising."[30] He was given more time to solve the problem in a Polish way.

In the spring of 1981 Moscow again pressed the Polish leadership to suppress Solidarity. "Extensive Soviet military activity began in adjacent parts of the Soviet Union and in Poland itself," Jaruzelski recalled. "At the same time," Rakowski pointed out, "Soviet intelligence officers were making sure we knew that they were 'casing' all the key locations in Warsaw and other cities."

On March 27, Solidarity staged the biggest strike in the history of the Soviet bloc. Output slumped, inflation soared and the country's hard-currency debt surged to $30 billion. The State, Solidarity and the Church agreed to try to head off the looming crisis and risk of Soviet intervention. In April, Cardinal Wyszynski, the 80-year-old Primate of Poland who was close to death, knelt before Walesa and said that he would remain in that position in prayer unless Solidarity abandoned its plans for a general strike. The dramatic gesture worked.[31]

Then on May 13, 1981, while Poland remained tense, Mehemet Ali Agca, a Turk, fired the shot that almost killed the Pope in front of St. Peter's in Rome. Although the Pope believed that Agca acted on Moscow's behalf, no conclusive evidence has yet emerged that he did. Suspicion persists, however, because two sets of documents found in the archives of the Czechoslovak intelligence service after the Cold War discussed the "physical elimination" of the Pope, perhaps with a virus contained in the lining of a wooden box.[32]

The attempt on the Pope's life provoked deep anger in the ranks of Solidarity. Had the Pope been assassinated there could have been an uprising, but as he had survived the situation merely worsened. The Church's negotiator reported to the Vatican that with Solidarity split between moderates and radicals no deal was possible and the country was becoming ungovernable.[33] At the first national congress in October, Solidarity declared that "Our union is . . . a protest against the existing form of power."[34]

At a Politburo meeting in Moscow on October 29, no one dissented from the view of Mikhail Suslov, the guardian of Soviet political orthodoxy, that "there can be no consideration at all of sending in troops" because such a step "would be a catastrophe."[35] Then, at another Politburo meeting on December 10, Andropov, the head of the KGB, declared, "if Poland falls under the control of Solidarity, that's the way it will be." Intervention would provoke the West into imposing economic and political sanctions that, he said, would "make things very difficult for us . . . we have to take care of our own country."[36] The last thing Moscow needed was for the West Europeans to align themselves firmly with Washington.

The preferred Soviet solution was the imposition of martial law by General Jaruzelski, the minister of defense, who had recently become Party leader. "I was willing to do this," he told me, "because I believed that even if Soviet forces did not intervene, the country was about to collapse into chaos. At the very least, this would lead to heavy fighting between the various factions—and that itself could have provoked Soviet intervention."

Jaruzelski expected that if he declared martial law, he would receive Soviet backing should things go wrong. At the last minute, the Soviet leadership left him in no doubt that he was on his own.[37] By December the mood in the country had changed, with officially sponsored public opinion polls showing that the vast majority of the people wanted stability.

On December 13, Jaruzelski declared martial law and put the much respected Polish army in charge of the country. The operation, which had been meticulously prepared, caught Solidarity completely by surprise. No unit in the army refused to act, nor was there any significant resistance. Some 6,000 people were detained; hundreds were charged with various serious offenses; a few were killed; and the union was banned.

To this day, debate continues over whether Poland had another realistic option. Some argue that if Kania and Jaruzelski had said "no" to the Soviet Union from the beginning, Solidarity would have had to cooperate with them to guarantee Poland's independence; others argue that this would have been a very risky strategy because it might have prompted hard-liners in the Party and the security services to seize control. At the time, however, neither the Poles nor the West knew that the Soviet leadership were willing, if they had no other choice, to accept a Solidarity government.[38]

Turning the Tide

As President Carter moved into the fourth year of his presidency he was under seige at home and abroad, as the historian Nancy Mitchell so vividly captured: "Inflation had risen to almost 20 percent, and unemployment was more than 7 percent. Americans sat in lines at gas pumps. Pummeled from the left by Senator Edward Kennedy and from the right by Ronald Reagan, Carter's quest for a second term was foundering. The Shah of Iran had been overthrown, the Soviets had invaded Afghanistan, the Sandinistas had seized power in Nicaragua, and 52 Americans sat captive in Tehran."[39]

At seven o'clock on the morning of April 25, 1980, the president addressed the nation. "'Late yesterday,' he explained, looking exhausted and grim, 'I canceled a carefully planned operation which was underway in Iran to . . . rescue . . . American hostages, who have been held captive there since November 4.'[40] The photographs of the crumpled hulks of US helicopters in the Iranian desert seared deep into the American psyche. They seemed to illustrate the absolute collapse of US power and prowess."

The tide, however, was already turning as within the Carter Administration robust new policies towards the Soviet Union were formulated, especially on nuclear strategy. The real "wake-up" call came in the form of a National Intelligence Estimate that was completed in mid-1979 which "really caused an absolute explosion" within the Carter Administration, according to Leslie Gelb, then the Assistant Secretary of State for Political-Military Affairs.[41] It noted that the latest Soviet missile warheads were more accurate than those of the Americans, that they could destroy hardened silos, and that, within five years, the Soviet Union might have 50% more warheads than the United States. (The Americans later discovered that the dramatic improvement in the accuracy of Soviet missiles owed much to the Western technology acquired by the Soviet intelligence services.[42])

The gut feeling of Harold Brown, Carter's robust secretary of defense, was that the Soviet leadership could be deterred by less than the total destruction of their country. Brown tasked Andy Marshall, the director of the Office of Net Assessment, and Walter Slocombe, the undersecretary for defense planning at the Pentagon, with working out what would suffice. "This was an issue of perceptions," Slocombe emphasized.

"The CIA could not provide any hard intelligence on the fears of the Soviet leadership, such as Brezhnev telling his psychotherapist that he would do anything to avoid the destruction of his car collection or his mistresses. The next best thing we could do," Slocombe explained, "was to use experts on Soviet affairs to try to deduce what the Soviets feared most. The experts concluded that the leadership's greatest fear was of losing control over their own country."

"Once these studies had been completed," Marshall pointed out, "we started to let it be known that one of our priorities was targeting the Soviet leadership—and we knew where their bunkers were and we had the weapons to destroy them. If they initiated a nuclear war, they would be signing their own death warrants." Thus, it was under Carter that the targeting of the Soviet leadership became more explicit than ever before.

The strands of this new approach to deterrence were brought together in Presidential Directive-59, on *US Nuclear Weapons Targeting Policy*, which was conceived and drafted by Brigadier-General William Odom, Brzezinski's assistant for military affairs. In late July 1980, Carter approved PD-59, which was leaked to the press shortly thereafter.[43] In parallel, Brown announced that henceforth America would adopt a "countervailing" strategy, so that it could match the Soviet Union at any level of nuclear warfare. "We wanted Moscow to be in no doubt," he said "that there would be no victors in an all-out nuclear war . . ."

To its considerable surprise, Moscow now saw that the United States was adopting a Soviet approach to deterrence, based on conveying the message that it was ready to fight an extended nuclear war. "The computerized studies we commissioned at the Pentagon," Slocombe recalled, "showed that under any circumstances we could inflict more damage on the Soviets than they could on us." "The Carter Administration drove home the point," Andy Marshall recalled, "by staging some major exercises by America's strategic nuclear forces. The exercises were conducted openly enough so that Soviet Military Intelligence could not fail to get the message."

Other recent events had added to Soviet unease. On three occasions during the summer of 1980, the Soviet General Staff had detected America's strategic forces being put on combat alert—what they did not know was that each case had stemmed from genuine failures in the American early-warning computer systems. The CIA learned that in June the KGB had sent a message to all its residencies abroad saying that these alerts were not an error, that they were part of a plan to lull Moscow into a false sense of security and thus provide cover for a possible surprise nuclear attack.[44]

That was not what the Americans had in mind. Nevertheless, one of the false alarms that summer brought home to them the extraordinary risks inherent in the nuclear arms race, especially at times when tensions are high. At 3 a.m. one morning, Odom awakened Brzezinski to say that 220 Soviet missiles had been launched against the United States. Some minutes later he was on the line once more, this time to say that the number had now risen to 2,200. Just minutes before Brzezinski woke the president to give the order to retaliate, Odom telephoned once again—this time to say it was all a ghastly error—a training tape simulating a massive attack had inadvertently been fed into the early-warning system.[45]

Despite all the efforts to improve the ability of the United States to fight an extended nuclear war, both Carter and Brown, his secretary of defense, were firmly agreed that nuclear weapons were for deterrence. If deterrence failed, however, they were to be used sparingly to convince the Soviets of the horrendous consequences of letting the war continue. In other words, nuclear weapons were for "war-termination."

Why Did the Cold War Drag On for So Long?

The simple answer is that neither of these two strongly motivated superpowers was able to gain the degree of advantage that would make the other give up, especially after the trauma of the Cuban missile crisis had brought home to them the dangers of trying to seize the advantage.

The Americans settled in for a policy of "containment," the aim of which was not to defeat the Soviet Union, but to outlast it. They believed that relations between the two powers needed to be "managed." This process was at times made more difficult by the competitive nature of democratic politics and the proclivity of the Americans to exaggerate their weaknesses and their vulnerabilities.

In many respects the Cold War up to this point was a classic struggle between the "over-dog" wishing to protect wide-ranging interests around the globe, and the "underdog" challenger, trying to gain advantage by clever stratagems and by probing for weak points. As the years went by, the competition expanded and, in both countries, the Cold War had become a way of life. Month after month, year after year, new tensions arose—at home, within each alliance, or between them.

Since the end of the Second World War the Soviet Union had certainly strengthened its position vis-à-vis the United States. In the seventies it did particularly well in the fields of strategic nuclear weapons, Euromissiles, conventional forces in Europe, the ability to project power and through increasing its presence in the Third World. And while the United States and the West in general were reeling from the huge hikes in oil prices in the seventies, the Soviet Union had the benefit of being an oil exporter whose output was rising strongly. In America fears were being voiced that the Soviet Union could soon be perceived by America's allies as being stronger than the United States.

Over the years, the Soviet leadership had succeeded in making a weak country *look* strong by investing heavily in military hardware. But instead of breaking free from the constraints that their ideology imposed on their economic policy, they kept putting their faith in easy options and hoping, if not for miracles, then that things would "go their way."

In Europe, for instance, Soviet leaders kept hoping that they would be able to neuter Nato, either by exploiting differences between the Americans and their West European allies or through helping the peace movements influence their respective governments. Similarly, in the Third World, Moscow hoped that the need of left-wing regimes for aid would tilt the global balance of power in its favor.

There were several reasons why the Soviet Union did not do better. First and foremost, the United States was in every respect far more of a superpower than the Soviet Union. Although the lack of an American consensus on foreign policy enabled Moscow to erode American influence abroad, it had far less chance of inflicting irreparable damage in the short to medium term.

In the developed world, Soviet attitudes made it almost impossible to sustain the policies—political, economic and cultural—needed to win over countries that were prosperous, free and fairly sophisticated. When difficulties arose, Moscow was less inclined to charm than to intimidate. In the Third World, the attraction of the Soviet system, both political and economic, had sharply diminished.

Above all, Soviet strategy was ill-suited to its purpose. Soviet leaders were slow to realize that their economy could not sustain its heavy investment in the arms race and economic and military aid to left-wing regimes (see next chapter). Their costly investments had not only failed to give them the full gains they had expected, but the speed with which they had acted eventually provoked the far richer United States into responding to their actions. In other words, the Soviet leadership were having to face the prospect that they would not get what they wanted by the risky route they had chosen.

Anatoly Chernyaev, then one of Brezhnev's speechwriters, believed that Moscow had to break out of the vicious cycle of the arms race. Having listened to Brezhnev's speech at Tula in year 1977, Chernyaev wrote in his diary: "The noise about the Soviet threat is based on facts. Periodic statements that we threaten nobody will not do the job. If we do not undertake real change in our military policy, the arms race aimed at our economic exhaustion will continue."[46]

That was a sound judgment. Nothing that has emerged from Soviet archives, however, suggests that any leader before Gorbachev was willing to contemplate abandoning the competition.

Why Did It End the Way It Did?

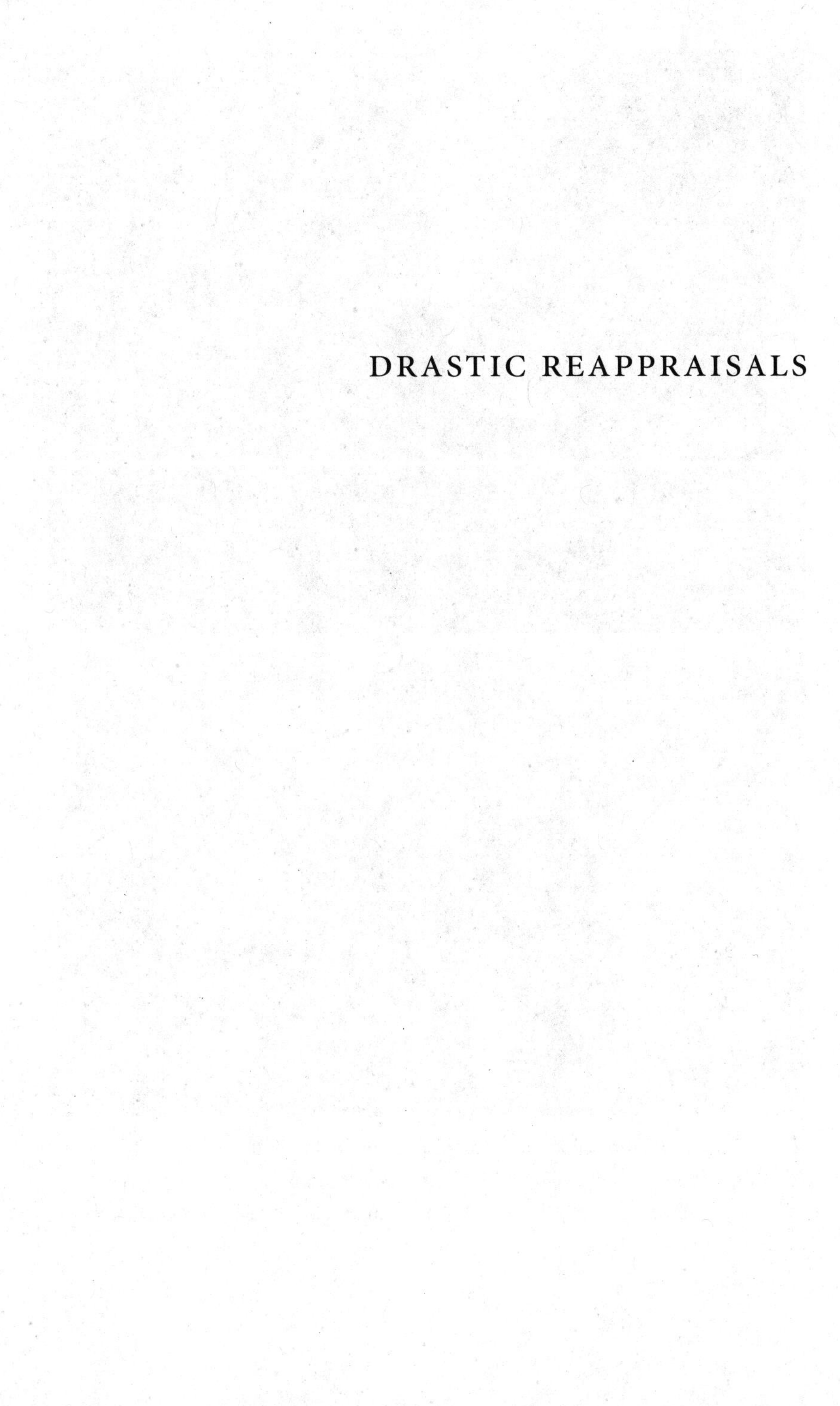

DRASTIC REAPPRAISALS

Above: Brezhnev's funeral in November 1982 (above) was followed by that of Andropov in February 1984 and Chernyenko's in March 1985. (Tassphoto, Moscow) *Below:* An energetic President Reagan and his wife at their inaugural parade, January 20, 1981. (Courtesy of the Ronald Reagan Presidential Library)

22 The Correlation of Forces

What Now?

The disillusionment over the collapse of détente was accompanied by an extraordinary reversal of fortunes. In the later half of the seventies, Brezhnev and his colleagues were confidently talking about the correlation of forces in the world having shifted irrevocably in their favor. Then, in just two years, these aged leaders found themselves on the defensive on almost every front, especially by virtue of what one might call the "three Ps"—the Pershings, the Pashtuns and the Poles. Meanwhile, with Ronald Reagan's election to the presidency in November 1980, America looked as if it had not only regained its self-confidence and dynamism, but was determined to take a much tougher line with the Soviet Union.

The implications of this shift were enormous. Given the impasse they had reached, both sides needed to consider what they would do next. Neither would find this an easy process, as every option carried considerable risks—political, economic and military. Behind the scenes in Moscow and Washington, small numbers of people had already started to make "drastic reappraisals" of the situation. This required them to take a hard look at their respective strengths and weaknesses. In Moscow, this process was called "the correlation of forces"—one of the few Marxist-Leninist concepts that has enduring value. In Washington, it had the name of "net assessment."

The Soviet Balance Sheet

The members of the Soviet regime felt that Brezhnev had ushered in a Golden Age. Throughout the world the Soviet Union was believed to be a strong and stable state, a military superpower equal to the United States with growing influence in the Third World. After the murderous uncertainties of Stalin's rule and the endless upheavals under Khrushchev, Brezhnev had brought stability.

Many Soviet citizens, especially those living in the cities, felt that standards of living and education had improved, and the system provided them with some sense of self-respect and a degree of social security. There was more personal and cultural freedom, as well as, for the more privileged, the chances of buying foreign consumer goods and, for the very privileged, visits to the West.

When Moscow hosted the Olympics in the summer of 1980 (which many countries boycotted because of the Soviet invasion of Afghanistan), the city looked its best—freshly painted buildings, newly planted flowers and many people, especially young women, attractively dressed. This was all in the old Russian tradition of the "Potemkin Villages," in which places were tarted up to look better than they were. The Soviet Union was using borrowed money to import consumer goods and hotel furnishings from Finland, Yugoslavia and some Western countries.

Behind the scenes the optimism was evaporating. Even in the upper reaches of the Party faith in ideology crumbled, with hardly anyone still believing they were building a great society. They just hoped to make the best of the "system" of which they were part. Members of the elite were becoming increasingly skeptical about Soviet prospects. For instance, Yevgeny Primakov, the deputy director of the Institute of the World Economy and International Relations, was contemptuous of those who predicted Soviet victory in peaceful competition with capitalism.[1]

One of the things holding that system together was a dogma that imposed conformity. "What we feared," Alexander Bessmertnykh, the former foreign minister told me, "was not committing heresy before God, but before the Party."[2] Mikhail Gorbachev later captured the mood of the period when he remarked that "initiative was a punishable offense."[3]

Within the leadership this atmosphere nurtured a far greater fear of popular unrest than the West ever realized. Andropov, who as chairman of the KGB was well informed about the mood of the people, reflected the party's concerns in a revealing piece of doggerel that he wrote around 1970:

> Some scoundrel blurted out one day
> That power spoils people, so to say . . .
> They do not see the other side.
> It's the people that spoil the power![4]

"Although there were probably never more than 3,000 active Soviet dissidents," according to Vladimir Bukovsky, who was one of the leading ones, "they were regarded as the early rumblings of a potentially explosive volcano.

Their *Samizdat*, the underground network of newspapers dealing with political events, was widely available.

Some members of the Academy of Sciences, Bukovsky explained, were virtually untouchable because of their standing in Soviet society. They were signing petitions and a few had even set up a fund to help political prisoners.

Because of détente, the leadership needed to be cautious about how it dealt with dissidents. Andropov tried to keep things under control by letting the KGB have "friendly chats" with tens of thousands of potential troublemakers. More serious offenders were committed to infamous "psychiatric hospitals," where they were terribly abused.

Prominent figures, however, could not be dealt with in this way. Alexander Solzhenitsyn, the renowned writer, was sent into exile in Germany, mainly because Andropov feared that "some idiot will kill him."[5] On the other hand, Andrei Sakharov, the father of the Soviet H-bomb who in 1970 had co-founded the Soviet Human Rights Committee, was sent away from Moscow and kept under close watch by the KGB because Andropov regarded him as "domestic enemy number one."[6]

The economy was the Achilles' heel of the system, with the abundance of natural resources in many respects being a curse. The Soviet economic system, like its tsarist predecessor, was far less concerned about the efficient use of resources than about the best ways to marshal them for some particular project. In fact, there is no Russian word that captures the essence of "efficiency." As a member of one of Moscow's leading research institutes put it after the Cold War: It was only because the Soviet Union was so rich in natural resources that "this crazy [communist] experiment could last eight decades. No other country could have put up with it so long."[7]

Centralized planning and production targets resulted in a prodigious waste of resources. Some armaments factories were producing spades that contained so much titanium that canny Westerners were importing them and making small fortunes by extracting that precious metal from them.

The other common denominator in so many economic problems was pricing. Without market pricing, determined by supply and demand, it was impossible to know the real cost of anything—let alone that of building one more tank, or, by extension, the overall "costs of empire." As growth slowed in the mid-sixties, several leading economists warned of further decline. With Soviet manufacturing industries only about 25% as efficient as those in the West, there was a real need for reform.[8]

One of the reasons nothing was done, according to Alexander Yakovlev, who at this time was in the Party's propaganda department, was because "almost everyone at the top was tied up in ideological knots" and the bureaucracy feared that any serious moves towards markets and private enterprise would undermine their power. In 1973, the party secretary in charge of agriculture told Yakovlev that "Every single person in the Politburo is for agricultural reform, but together we are all against it." The following year, 1974, the chairman of the state planning commission warned that the economy as a whole was already in grave trouble.

As a result of the drive for parity with the United States, the Soviet's military expenditure had been rising twice as fast as their national income. It had become, in Gorbachev's words, "a *Moloch*" with an insatiable appetite for funds.[9] General Viktor Starodubov, a military expert in the party secretariat, later explained that when Dmitri Ustinov, the head of military production, became minister of defense in 1976, he "brought the psychology of the producers of armaments into the strategic planning of the Ministry of Defense . . . there was an arms over-saturation with an unnecessary duplication of similar armaments systems . . ."[10]

Even the top secret figures shown to the general secretary (though never seen by the Politburo) greatly underestimated the real burden of Soviet defense expenditure. Nonetheless, Brezhnev realized that it had to be cut. Although the West did not know it at the time, the Soviet leadership froze expenditure on military procurement in 1976. But the real cost of procurement was almost certainly continuing to rise because the more advanced equipment being produced cost far more in real terms than the items being replaced.

Unwilling to embrace reform, the leadership pinned many of its hopes on greater oil and gas exports and on the theft of Western technology, not solely for military purposes. In the late seventies, the Soviet economy was still benefiting from a bonanza in foreign exchange earnings—partly from the hike in world oil prices, partly from the near doubling of production during the decade. Even so, the economy was hardly growing in real terms. One reason for that was that nearly all the hard-currency income from oil exports was spent on importing grain.

By this time, the comforting stability of Brezhnev's early years had become tainted with stagnation and corruption. As his health declined, he could no longer control the system and the system could not function without a strong leader. It degenerated into political baronies that were more interested in protecting their own interests than they were in making the system work effectively.

Meanwhile, thanks to détente, thousands of young people traveled to the United States and Western Europe in delegations of various sorts. Disenchanted with the Soviet failure to create a dynamic, modern culture, the young had years earlier turned to the West for inspiration. They were now copying Western fashions and reading smuggled-in Western books to a far greater extent than had been possible during the Khrushchev "thaw."

Above all, young people were listening to Western pop music to help them disengage from a system they did not admire. Some idea of the number who did so could be seen when Paul McCartney performed in Red Square in 2003. Most of the 100,000 people in the audience were now middle-aged members of the new Russian establishment—and nearly all of them were mouthing in English the words of Beatles' songs that they had learned in their youth.

While Soviet youth were borrowing Western culture, the Soviet Union and its allies were borrowing Western money. This was supposedly to finance the import of modern factories, but most was wasted on bad investments and consumer goods. By the early eighties, the Soviet bloc's hard-currency foreign debt had already surged during détente to over $85 billion.[11] This borrowing from their adversaries was already creating a dependency on the West that restricted Soviet options, which would get narrower by the year.

While problems continued to mount around them, the Soviet leadership felt increasingly besieged. The rise of Solidarity was threatening communist rule in Poland and its example could do so elsewhere. Meanwhile, Moscow's hopes of undermining the West in the Third World were fading as a hundred thousand Soviet troops became embroiled in Afghanistan.

By this time, the attitude of the aged Soviet leadership was that as the West puts pressure on us, we must by every means available maintain strategic parity and be tough with them in negotiations. "Such institutionalized confrontation with the West," Bessmertnykh, the former Soviet foreign minister, noted, "had become one of the factors assuring the survival of the regime."

Andropov recognized that détente had run its course. In October 1980, he told Pham Hung, the Vietnamese interior minister, that America and other Western countries had turned against détente because they "realized that a reduction of international tension worked to the advantage of the socialist system."[12]

The American Balance Sheet

One of the reasons the Soviet Union had been so optimistic about détente was that America appeared to be in such bad shape. The decade between the mid-sixties and mid-seventies had certainly been one of the most convulsive in its modern history.

The success of capitalism had created a counter-culture that turned the young against authority. Opposition to the Vietnam War, for which many had been conscripted or feared that they might be, strengthened the protest movement. At the same time, the large pockets of poverty that remained produced the worst American riots of the 20th century. And there was much opposition to the growing demands of the black community for acceptance of their civil rights. During these troubled ten years, dozens were killed in various protests.

On the economic front, American self-confidence was shaken once again, when the tripling of oil prices in 1973/4 plunged the world economy into recession, with the United States experiencing the worst economic downturn since the Great Depression. By 1975, unemployment had doubled to 9%. At the end of the seventies, the price of oil again tripled, pushing the economy once more into decline. Although unemployment this time only rose to 7%, inflation soared to nearly 15%. In the past ten years, more than a thousand sizeable factories had closed across the continent.

In the aftermath of Vietnam and Watergate no new consensus could be forged on the big strategic issues that had emerged during the early years of détente—either nuclear or conventional. A lively debate began on America's options. There was still, however, a strong sentiment among Americans that they had the right to total security. As General Andrew Goodpaster, a former supreme allied commander of Nato forces, said in 1983, "the concept of partial security was alien to the United States."[13]

Within the Alliance, too, there were deep divisions. The Europeans did not like Moscow's invasion of Afghanistan, but were unwilling to jettison the gains that they believed had been made during the détente years. President Giscard d'Estaing and Chancellor Schmidt would go no further in their condemnation than saying "détente would probably not be able to withstand another shock of the same type."[14]

Although during the presidential election campaign Reagan had promised that his policies would boost the American economy, there was still considerable uncertainty that they would. "Reaganomics," which was based on the theory that economic growth depended on controlling the supply of money, had yet to be tested; so had Congress's willingness to accept huge deficits.

Most people did not give enough weight to the new and most positive element in the American economic equation—the dynamic interplay between America's scientific and entrepreneurial cultures that greatly facilitated the development of information technology. In 1975, the year Microsoft was founded, the first personal computer came on the market, and by 1981, annual sales of personal computers had passed the million mark and were rising exponentially. Silicon Valley was already well-established, and the state of California alone was as wealthy as the sixth-richest country in the world.

Despite the disruptions caused by the sudden rise of oil prices, there were signs of strong growth in parts of the world economy. During the seventies, South Korea, Taiwan, Hong Kong, Brazil and Mexico had economies that were growing at over 7% a year. Moreover, the sharp decline in the value of the dollar against the German and Japanese currencies in the late sixties and early seventies was beginning to make American exports more competitive.

The new information technology was leveraging that regained competitiveness by making it possible for American companies to exploit the efficiencies of this emerging global market—through the timely delivery of components and products, both bought and sold. By 1980, American companies already had invested $200 billion overseas, some 40% of the world total, and this figure was rising rapidly, as was the inflow of foreign investment into the United States.

Micro-electronics were similarly pushing forward the "revolution in military affairs" in which the American lead would grow rapidly in the years ahead. The Americans were developing new precision-guided weapons and computerized systems that would enable them to fight far more effectively. Before long, they would be able to thwart any Soviet conventional assault into Western Europe and would have the missiles in Europe that could checkmate the advantage that the SS-20s had given Soviet forces. Together these changes would alter "the correlation of forces" in Europe—and this was a deeply disturbing prospect for Soviet leaders.

23 American "New Thinking"

An Intellectual "Revolution"

Why had it taken the Americans such a long time to realize that the United States was so strong and the Soviet Union so weak? As I explored this important but neglected subject, I discovered that behind closed doors in Washington, an intellectual revolution had quietly got underway in the late sixties.

It roots could be traced back to the fifties at the RAND Corporation, where a handful of top analysts believed that the West was far stronger than the Soviet Union and its allies—it had more manpower, greater wealth and a huge lead in technology. What it needed, they argued, was a long-term strategy that would be more effective than the policy of containment—and the will to implement it.

"Those who followed our experience in the war against Japan believed that anthropologists and historians could help them understand the extent to which the Russians thought differently from the Americans," Andy Marshall, who was then a strategic analyst at RAND, pointed out. Such people admired Nathan Leites from RAND, who in 1951 published his seminal work *The Operational Code of the Soviet Politburo.*

Few others, however, believed what Leites said about the determination of the Soviet leadership to gain ascendancy over the United States; nor did they hoist in what Kennan had said in his "Long Telegram" (see p. 44) about the many different methods they would use to attain their goals.

An extraordinary conviction emerged that these "revolutionary commies" must soon mellow, one that even the hard-headed Eisenhower accepted in large measure. Most Democrats had a more benign view than Eisenhower's, being prone to think in terms of the "natural harmony of man." They found it difficult to believe that Soviet leaders could not be coaxed into accepting a relationship with the United States that would not threaten American interests.

As America's strategic superiority increased during the fifties and extended into the sixties, scientists and economists began to dominate American thinking about the Soviet Union. They assumed that the two sides were rational and reasonable. "They were not inclined to ask," Marshall lamented, "whether there were two kinds of rationality—one Soviet and the other American, with each having its own ideology, values and preoccupations. That worried me."

Not until the late sixties, when the Americans began to feel that the Soviet Union was in the ascendant position, did some people become more interested in the workings of the Russian mind. Weakness was to become the Mother of Reflection.

Given America's trials and tribulations in the sixties and seventies, it is hardly surprising that the orthodoxy of the seventies was that the Soviet Union was strong, especially militarily, and stable. "This was the view of those who favored détente, whether they were pessimistic about America's prospects or thought that the Soviet Union would change," Marshall recalled. "This view was also shared by the opponents of détente, but they sought to galvanize the American people into repairing their military forces in order to check Soviet expansionism before it was too late. Even when that had been done, they did not expect that we would be able to prevail over the Soviet Union."

During these years, a small number of people in America came to believe that their country could gain the upper hand. Some of them began by querying whether the Soviet economy really was doing well compared with that of the United States. Others started by believing that the United States could compete because it had more resources, and technologically it could do some very clever things, both commercially and militarily. This group might best be described as "revivalists," the term used by James Schlesinger, the first leading figure to advocate such a course of action.

Schlesinger was director of strategic studies at RAND in 1968–69. He then held three posts in the Nixon Administration before serving as secretary of defense from 1973 to 1975. "I didn't think that the Soviet Union was very weak or very strong," he explained. "I simply rejected Kissinger's Spenglerian view that we have to settle now, because in the years ahead we will be weaker relative to the Soviet Union. I believed that détente would only work if it protected our interests and I had long felt that the Cold War would only end if America competed so strongly that the Soviet Union would give up."

The "revivalists" were kindred spirits rather than a group, though several of them later worked together in the Carter and Reagan administrations. They came to share three core beliefs—that the Soviet Union was weak, that the

Soviet elite had lost faith in their system, and that military competition was moving into areas in which the Soviet Union could not compete.

How Weak Is the Soviet Economy?

With Americans increasingly pre-occupied by signs of growing Soviet strength, such thinking did not attract much support. The situation began to change in the latter sixties as American analysts monitored the rapid buildup of Soviet forces.

"Even when we were together at RAND," Schlesinger told me, "Andy Marshall and I suspected that in real terms the Soviet Union must now be spending roughly the same amount on defense as the United States. As the Soviet economy was far smaller than America's, the defense burden might be so high as to be unsustainable in the long run. That possibility needed to be investigated."

Although few American economists took Soviet statistics at face value, they did not appreciate how greatly they exaggerated the size of the Soviet economy and the speed at which it was growing. The Soviet success in first putting a satellite and then a man into space had lent weight to Khrushchev's claims that before long the Soviet Union would overtake the United States economically. Since the fifties, the CIA had been running a mega-computer program to assess the strength of the Soviet economy. Although it invested a huge effort in the painstaking analysis of fragmentary information and intelligence, its conclusions were similar to the prevailing consensus.

One of the first open challenges to conventional wisdom was made in 1960 with the publication of Schlesinger's *The Political Economy of National Security*. Two years later, Warren Nutter published his taboo-breaking book on *The Growth of Soviet Industrial Production*. In it, Nutter argued that there was no reason to believe that managed economies would perform better than America's and certainly not by the high margins people were willing to accept. He was vilified by many American scholars. Then, in a 1968 paper for the RAND Corporation, Egon Neuberger predicted that "the centrally planned economy eventually would meet its demise, because of its demonstrably growing ineffectiveness as a system for managing a modernizing economy in a rapidly changing world."[1]

In the late seventies, the CIA was claiming that Soviet GNP was 60% that of the United States, with defense expenditure only amounting to 8–9% of GNP.[2] "Before long, a somewhat acrimonious debate got underway about the size of the Soviet economy and its defense burden,"Marshall recollected from

Andy Marshall with Secretary of Defense Cheney, 1989. (Private Collection)

his early years as the director of the Office Net Assessment at the Pentagon.

From their research and travels in the Soviet Union, some American economists felt that real Soviet GNP was only around 40% that of the American figure. Meanwhile, Pentagon studies on the Soviet military were beginning to suggest that the real defense burden was far higher than the CIA's estimate. These high figures were seen as an indicator of the extent to which Moscow was willing to pay any price for military superiority.

Leading Soviet economists who had been able to emigrate to the United States during the détente years accepted the dictum of "lies, damned lies and statistics." Igor Birman, for instance, explained that one of the fundamental flaws in published Soviet figures was that without market pricing you could not do serious economic calculations. This meant that no one would ever be able to establish for sure just how big the Soviet economy was, nor just how heavy a defense burden it was carrying.

Birman went on to argue that the Soviet economy was running into serious problems, and they were likely to get worse. At the same time, diplomatic reports of conversations at cocktail parties in Moscow quoted Russians as saying that "we can't go on like this; we can't compete with the Americans."

"By the early eighties," Marshall believed that "it was increasingly clear that the CIA had got both the nominator (the size of the Soviet economy) and the denominator (defense expenditure) seriously wrong." The Pentagon's own studies also came to the conclusion that the Soviet economy was only 40% as large as that of the United States. That reduction automatically pushed up the burden of defense expenditure. Further research by the Office of Net Assessment into the hidden military costs and those of maintaining the Soviet empire increased the total "defense" expenditure even higher. "The new figures indicated that Soviet defense expenditure, broadly defined, was really around a whopping 30% of GNP," Marshall said.

Sustaining such a level of expenditure would be difficult for a strong economy and almost impossible for one that was as inefficient and riddled with problems as the Soviet Union's. Over the next few years, this radically different view of Soviet economic strength would shape American policy.

This issue, however, was closely tied to the question "How strong is the American economy?" Despite the periods of high growth there had been since the Great Depression, most Americans harbored doubts about the long-term prospects of their economy.

At the end of the sixties, respected economists such as Paul Samuelson were still asserting that planned and managed economies would perform better than those based on free-market principles. The post-war slump, the collapse of the dollar in 1971 and the high inflation that followed the oil crisis of 1973 all helped keep American concern alive through the détente era. So, too, did the growing competition from Germany and Japan. In addition, the riots of the late sixties vividly brought home the fact that sizeable parts of the population remained poor even when the economy was thriving.

On July 14, 1975, *Time*'s cover story was "Can Capitalism Survive?" Following a visit to Moscow in 1982, the historian Arthur Schlesinger was dismissive of "those in the U.S. who think the Soviet Union is on the verge of economic and social collapse . . . Each superpower has economic troubles; neither is on the ropes."[3] It would be over another decade before the free-market views of Hayek and Friedman became part of the accepted wisdom. Meanwhile, the "revivalists" kept arguing that the American economy was far stronger than that of the Soviet Union, and that the gap would widen in the United States' favor.

How Weak Is the System?

"At the beginning of the Carter Administration," Brzezinski told me, "Jim Schlesinger and I headed a group that concluded that the Soviet Union could face a serious economic crisis in the mid-eighties—and that could be speeded and exacerbated by cutting off their access to certain types of Western technology and know-how."

By 1980, William Odom, Brzezinski's military assistant, was writing: "The Soviet Union . . . suffers enormous centrifugal forces . . . .The dissolution of the Soviet empire is a not a wholly fanciful prediction for later this century."[4] "This led to a covert program," Brzezinski said in 2001, "which the CIA undertook, euphemistically and elegantly called a program for the 'delegitimization' of the Soviet system. It was designed to exploit national tensions within the Soviet Union."[5] "Later in 1980," Odom told me, "I recommended in a strategy memo that if Carter was re-elected he should compete selectively and make the Soviet Union face the full military, economic, political and ideological power of the United States."

American scholars of Russian cultural history were among the first to find evidence that the Soviet elite had little faith in Marxist-Leninist ideology and corruption was on the rise. For example, James Billington, one of America's top Russian scholars, who is now the Librarian of Congress, told me that "during my visits to the Soviet Union in the seventies, I was fascinated by signs I saw of a growing interest in religion."[6]

"At first," Billington explained, "party officials were collecting icons and there were official workshops at which these could be repaired. As the decade progressed, many of them talked about religion. On his death-bed, Brezhnev agreed to return to the Church the Danilov Monastery, the oldest in Moscow, for the city's 800th anniversary. Shortly thereafter, Mrs. Brezhnev publicly crossed herself at her husband's funeral."

By the early eighties, Billington also observed, the elite were increasingly concerned by their children's lack of purpose and drift towards debauchery. Some called for greater discipline; even more called for the Church to be brought back into national life, as Stalin had done when facing the trauma of the Great Patriotic War. This time, it was needed not so much to provide solace as to reintroduce some moral fiber into Soviet society.

Billington's accounts lent credence to other reports reaching Washington, such as one George Shultz had seen in August 1982 that quoted remarks by

Andropov to a visiting Polish delegation. Andropov had reportedly admitted that the Soviet economy was not in much better shape than Poland's. He added, "The Soviet Union faces a serious and increasing problem with [our] youth, who are becoming apolitical, pacifistic, and interested only in themselves." The Soviets had a "church problem," he said, "with more and more young people seeking out the church, perhaps as a means of dissent."[7]

The elite were no longer optimistic about catching up with the West, let alone overtaking it. Some economic managers, for example, were complaining that the country lacked the material resources to compete with the West and Soviet targets could only be met if the Russians worked as effectively as the Germans or the Swiss—which was not going to happen under the Soviet system.

Population experts, such as Murray Feshbach, highlighted the implications of Soviet population trends. The most notable of all was that by the year 2000 a third of the total population would be Muslim.[8] From many other sources there was growing evidence that a deep sense of malaise pervaded Soviet society (see p. 284).

Undermining Soviet Confidence

Within the American government, the first serious efforts to get inside the Soviet mind were on the military front. Pioneering work was done on how the Soviet military thought about war, how they measured the strength of their opponent and what the Americans could do to get a better score. Studies were also done on the various powerful players within the Soviet military to understand their preferences and their instinctive reactions to new challenges.

"From Schlesinger, through Rumsfeld to Brown," Andy Marshall pointed out, "American secretaries of defense pursued a policy of developing weapons that would force the Soviet Union to change its strategy in ways that would make it less worrying to the United States." In an attempt to persuade Moscow to reduce the number of its ten war-headed SS-18 missiles, which particularly troubled them, the Americans dramatically improved the accuracy of their own missiles to make the SS-18s far more vulnerable to an American attack.

This approach was also used to keep the B-1 bomber project alive during the late seventies and early eighties. The Soviet air defense forces leapt to the bait. Billions were spent by the Soviets on developing the Mig-25 and new surface-to-air missiles to meet a threat from a supersonic bomber that would never materialize. The strategists in the Pentagon preferred to see Soviet money spent this way, rather than on more offensive weapons.

In Europe, similar efforts were made to use new technology to improve the rating that Nato forces would get from the Soviet General Staff. Nato exercises that were attended by Warsaw Pact observers after 1986 (as part of the "confidence building measures") were often designed with this in mind.

These new strands of thinking on how the United States could deal with the Soviet Union tied in closely with those of Reagan, who in his own intuitive way had come to the conclusion that the Soviets were weak.

24 Soviet "New Thinking"

The Seeds of Change

"We're preparing mankind's suicide. It's insane!" Anatoly Chernyaev exclaimed to himself as he listened to Marshal Akhromeyev, the chief of the General Staff, briefing members of the Central Committee secretariat on "The Threat from the West" in 1984.

"I wanted to ask the Marshal," Chernyaev said, "'What if we just destroy all those weapons . . . Would the Americans attack us in an instant?'"[1] He did not know how the Marshal would respond, but he knew that he would from that moment on be treated as a "nutcase." After all, he was the deputy chief of the International Department of the Central Committee of the Soviet Communist Party!

Chernyaev was one of a number of "new thinkers" who thought that the Soviet Union needed reform, and that the West was not a military threat to their country. They felt the Soviet Union had to rethink its relationship with the West. They refined their ideas and waited patiently for the opportunity to press their case.

Some of the new thinkers in the Soviet Union came from cultured families that valued intellectual integrity and remembered the pre-revolutionary days when Russia had been part of Europe; others came from less privileged backgrounds. At university, nearly all of them were taught by professors who managed to pass on the tradition of intellectual enquiry that had characterized the best Russian universities before the revolution.

Most of the families of the future "new thinkers" had suffered at the hands of Stalin. Fighting alongside ordinary soldiers during the "Great Patriotic War" opened their eyes even further to the brutality of Stalin's rule. When the war finally ended they were all horrified to see Stalin treat returning Soviet POWs as criminals, who were either executed or sent to slave labor camps, where they often died.

The doubts of these future reformers about the communist system were reinforced by the shockwaves that surged through Soviet society from Khrushchev's revelations at the 20th Party Congress in 1956 about the enormity of Stalin's crimes. The "thaw" which followed made them feel that they had been right to hope for better things.

Prague's Revenge

For the West, the 1948 communist takeover of Prague, then the most cultured city in Eastern Europe, was a defining moment in the Cold War. Ironically, it was there, just a decade later, that several of the future "new thinkers" came to believe that the West was not a threat, and that the Soviet system was fundamentally flawed.

They were some of the brightest young members of the Soviet Communist Party, who had been sent to Prague to work on the newly established journal *Problems of Peace and Socialism.* Because Khrushchev wanted to use the journal to spread the gospel of communism to a wider international audience, the staff had considerable freedom to travel to Western Europe and talk with non-communists. They saw for themselves what life, politics and "civil society" were really like in Western Europe. A popular destination was Amsterdam, where the "red light" district was admired, among other things, as a symbol of the tolerance of social democracy.

In 1965, the Central Committee's first international affairs consultant group began work under Yuri Andropov, who was then in charge of relations with the other socialist countries. One of the reasons Andropov set up this group was the he, too, had earlier had the benefit of some intellectually rigorous training. The consultants Andropov selected were young scholars and journalists from outside the Party apparatus. Among them were three who had earlier been together in Prague—Georgi Shakhnazarov, Oleg Bogomolov and Georgi Arbatov.

Arbatov recalled that members of the group "stood out by virtue of their independent minds, unusual talents, and thirst for change . . . It was an outstanding oasis of creative thought." Andropov encouraged them to give of their best: "In this room," he told them, "you can come clean and speak absolutely openly—don't hide your opinions."[2] He kept his word, they kept their heads.

To survive in the ruthless Soviet system "new thinkers" required prudence and a willingness to lead a double life. As Alexander Yakovlev, who had studied at Columbia University before becoming deputy head of the Propaganda

Anatoly Chernyaev and Mikhail Gorbachev, the Gorbachev Foundation, Moscow, March 1, 2006. (Private collection)

Department of the Central Committee, later said: "I lived a double life of agonizing dissimulation."[3]

In the mid-sixties, encouraged by Premier Kosygin, Professor Liebermann and several distinguished Soviet economists proposed market-oriented reforms to reverse the decline in economic growth and improve the poor quality of most of the non-military items it produced. Little came of their ideas because of opposition from the bureaucracy and fears within the leadership that such changes would, as in the case of the Prague Spring, soon get out of control.

The suppression of the Prague Spring in 1968 came as a terrible shock to all those who after 1956 had hoped that there would be genuine reform in the Soviet Union. Yakovlev had the unenviable task of being sent to Czechoslovakia to oversee Soviet journalists reporting from there after Soviet troops had allegedly been invited into the country at the request of the people. He saw effigies of Soviet soldiers hanging from gallows and people shouting "Fascists! Fascists!" Such scenes, Yakovlev recalled, were "An important school for me . . . it had a great sobering effect."[4] In a similar vein, Anatoly Chernyaev, one of those who had worked on *Problems of Peace and Socialism* in Prague, told his daughter, then still a schoolgirl: "Always remember this, a great country has covered itself with shame and will never be forgiven."[5]

"New Thinking" Gathers Pace

Scientists who had developed thermo-nuclear weapons were the first to express reservations to Soviet leaders about the rationality of an unrestrained arms race with the United States. They did not hesitate to express ideas similar to those in the Russell-Einstein Manifesto of 1955, which argued that in a thermonuclear age new thinking was required because any war could have horrendous consequences.

In 1961, Andrei Sakharov, the father of the Soviet H-bomb, took issue with Khrushchev over his decision to continue testing nuclear weapons in the atmosphere. Then, in 1968, he circulated through *samizdat*, the underground network of newspapers, a far more wide-ranging memorandum giving his *Reflections on Progress, Coexistence and Intellectual Freedom*. In it he proclaimed that in the thermonuclear age salvation lay in a steady "convergence" of the socialist and capitalist systems, which in turn, was a precondition for "the resolution of the world's global problems."[6] The ideas of other courageous dissenters also gave an impetus to new thinking.

As the Soviet Union embarked on détente with the West, the main research institutes linked to the Central Committee grew in importance. Their directors did better than most of the Soviet establishment in understanding what was really happening in the world. Their openness of mind and academic training helped them benefit greatly not only from their privileged access to Western books and newspapers, but also their meeting with foreigners.

In their overt publications these "institutniks," as they are often called, followed the party line, while in their classified research papers they voiced many heresies. Such papers were highly appreciated by the small group of fellow "new thinkers" dealing with international affairs within the party secretariat (including Chernyaev, Shakhnazarov and Yakovlev), the Ministry of Foreign Affairs and even the military establishment.

At this time, however, the "institutniks" had little influence on policy. Less than a month after Soviet troops invaded Afghanistan, for example, Oleg Bogomolov, then the director of the Institute of Economics of the World Socialist

System, sent a note to the Central Committee and the KGB entitled "Some Reflections on the Foreign Policy Results of the 1970s" highlighting the fact that the demise of détente started from "our military actions in Angola" and warned that the Soviet Union would pay a heavy price for its intervention in Afghanistan.[7] Bogomolov was right, but it was a long time before the leadership began to change course.

New ideas were, nevertheless, being generated in discussions with foreigners. One of the leading Soviet participants was Georgi Arbatov, the director of the Institute of the United States and Canada. Participation in prestigious international conferences helped boost his standing and contacts, while Western governments resented the skill with which he exploited these occasions to put across the Soviet case. But Arbatov, along with his colleagues from other institutes, was also listening to what the Westerners were saying and learning from them. He described new ideas being "born from collective experience and in open, honest and sometimes heated debate."[8]

From Arbatov's discussions with Social Democrats, on the Palme Commission (an independent group working on disarmament and security issues) and at the meetings of Socialist International (which brought together social democratic, socialist and labor parties), he gained many ideas on how the Soviet system could be reformed. Through the Pugwash and Dartmouth conferences, which focused on nuclear and military matters, Arbatov became intrigued with the idea that security should be based on an entirely defensive strategy, not one that required such massive forces for a counter-attack that they actually threatened the security of others. Later, at the Palme Commission, this evolved into the concept of "common security," meaning that the security of one state should not come at the expense of another.[9]

25 The Reagan Challenge

The Making of an American Radical

Reagan's hostility towards the Soviet Union sprang from the leading role he played in ousting the communists from the Screen Actors Guild in Hollywood, at a time when the communist-led film unions there were trying to dominate the industry. During these troubled years he carried a gun.

Over the next decade, Reagan gained an extraordinary understanding of the American people through his work for General Electric. He traveled around the country talking to them about their concerns and aspirations, giving pep talks at the company's plants and hosting its popular television show. He began honing his skills as "the great communicator"—skills which later helped him to become governor of California, then president.

Long before he entered the White House, Reagan believed that détente was nothing less than "a satanic device . . . to blunt our sword" while the Soviet Union "moved in for the kill." He despised all those who had advocated it, especially Nixon and Kissinger. The world would only be safe, he kept saying, when America had won the Cold War—either by persuading existing Soviet leaders to take a more constructive approach or by getting them replaced by others who did.[1]

Way back in 1963, twenty years before he announced "Star Wars," Reagan explained how he would achieve this goal: "in an all-out race our system is stronger, and eventually the enemy gives up the race as a hopeless cause."[2] Unlike most experts, Reagan believed the Soviet leadership no longer had any real ideological fire in their bellies. James Woolsey, who became director of Central Intelligence in 1993, told me that he admired Reagan "not only for understanding Soviet weakness, but for his intuitive sense of how vulnerable it made them. I think the Irish can hear voices others can't."

By the time Reagan became president he seemed determined to "lean on the Soviets until they go broke."[3] Reagan believed that if America were to win, so too would the Soviet Union. However, Richard Allen, a close associate and future national security adviser, pointed out that there was one unspoken proviso—"although he was willing to make compromises on the basis of his terms, he was unwilling to do so on theirs." In other words, the Soviet Union would have to be willing to change along the lines that Reagan wanted. That would only happen, he knew, if he succeeded in persuading the American people that they were threatened and had to prepare themselves for action. America, he warned the electors, faced a "window of vulnerability" to a surprise Soviet missile attack that could only be closed by using America's full technological might.

Reagan was the first American president to believe that the United States could force the Soviet Union to end the Cold War. After he was elected, in 1980, he would begin to pursue this goal with steely determination.

Raising Hackles

In American presidential elections, the Soviet Politburo usually had a preferred candidate. In 1980, that was not the case. As Brezhnev said, "Even the devil himself could not tell who is the better—Carter or Reagan."[4] By a modest majority the American people chose Reagan.

Nearly all of Reagan's advisers believed that the Soviet Union was strong and the Cold War would still have to be managed, but they could rely on him to be tough in doing so. They were, however, deeply split between these hard-liners and the small though influential group of what one might call the "confrontationalists." Reagan played both sides to his advantage, listening to them when it suited him and ignoring them when it didn't. Even in Reagan's inner circle, few people understood his determination "to end this thing" *and* rid the world of nuclear weapons. At times, his actions caused as much surprise in the White House as they did in the Kremlin.

The main architects of confrontation were Bill Casey (the head of the CIA, who had been Reagan's campaign manager); Herb Meyer (Casey's special assistant, the former editor of *Fortune* who in the early eighties had predicted the collapse of the Soviet Union); Gus Weiss (Reagan's adviser on intelligence and technology); Professor Richard Pipes (the Soviet expert on the NSC, who in 1976 had headed Team-B) as well as three people from the Pentagon—Fred Iklé (the Undersecretary for Policy); Richard Perle (the Assistant Secretary for Security Policy) and Andy Marshall, the director of the Office of Net Assessment.

The confrontationalists, along with their supporters outside the Administration, faced one particularly tricky issue. While they were avid collectors of information about Soviet weakness, their strategy was based on rallying support against the "Soviet threat." They made great efforts to persuade the public that the Russians were spending huge sums on armaments and determined to pay any price to ensure their superiority. Any information to the contrary was unwelcome.

Although Reagan had been an apocalyptic ideologue during the campaign, the aging leaders in the Kremlin hoped he would prove to be a pragmatist as president. They were outraged that in his first press conference he accused them of being willing "to commit any crime, to lie, to cheat" in order to promote world revolution. Uneasy about this remark, Reagan telephoned Alexander Haig, his secretary of state, to say that it was "not meant to offend anyone in Moscow," but just an expression of his "deep conviction." Dobrynin, the Soviet ambassador, commented rather tartly that "the clarification only made things worse."[5]

Dobrynin felt that the two features of Reagan's policy that annoyed the Soviet leadership most were "his apparent determination to regain military superiority" and "his determination to launch an ideological offensive against the Soviet Union, and foment trouble within the country and among Soviet allies."[6]

Don't Overreact

When the Politburo met on February 11, they were "emotional and angry" and vented their fury over Reagan's unprecedented and sudden worsening of relations. Nevertheless, they decided that they should still seek an accommodation with the new administration; Brezhnev sent Reagan a letter to that effect, in standard but measured terms.[7]

Two outside voices influenced this decision, the first being that of Dobrynin, who had been Soviet ambassador in Washington for almost twenty years. He quietly urged the Politburo to adopt a wait-and-see attitude toward the Reagan Administration. Andropov respected Dobrynin's diplomatic skill and judgment, but seems to have been influenced to an even greater extent by Dmitri Yakushkin, the head of KGB operations in America, a man fascinated by the big issues in East-West relations.

Yakushkin was far from being a typical member of the Soviet establishment or *nomenklatura.* One of his aristocratic forebears had been executed by the tsar in 1825 for wanting to reform Russia on Western lines, and Dmitri's own father, a member of the Academy of Sciences, had passed on to him what was possibly the finest private library in the Soviet Union. According to one of his close friends in Washington at the time, "Yakushkin prided himself on his breadth of knowledge and for being able to keep abreast of all the best books on America."[8]

Yakushkin's understanding of America was not only enhanced by the intelligence he collected, but by his extensive travels through the United States. As Kevorkov, one of his colleagues put it, he had "not only penetrated state secrets, but had grasped above all the driving forces that kept the flywheel of this gigantic state machine in motion." Yakushkin warned against provoking "the American lion into a fury" that would drive it to mobilize the full resources of its economy against the Soviet Union.[9]

The Kremlin seems to have made a distinction between not wishing to provoke the American lion and stopping its alluring words being heard by more and more people across the Soviet empire through the broadcasts of Radio Free Europe and Radio Liberty. On February 21, a small terrorist group, backed by the KGB and the East German secret police, detonated 20 kilos of plastic explosive at the headquarters of Radio Free Europe and Radio Liberty in Munich before slipping back into East Germany. The blast did $2 million of damage to the building and shattered windows a mile away.[10]

While recovering from an attempt on his life by a deranged young American, Reagan made an emotional gesture towards the Kremlin. On March 31, 1981, despite opposition from his advisers, he sent a personal, handwritten letter to Brezhnev expressing the hope that they could establish a private dialogue. The letter did not go down well in Moscow, however, because, in it, Reagan implied that Soviet conduct was the source of the problems between the two countries.

When Reagan saw what he rather unfairly described as Brezhnev's "icy" reply, he remarked, "Well, we did not want an arms race, but if there is to be one, the United States is not going to lose it."[11] But even if Brezhnev's tone had been friendlier, there was virtually no chance they could have found common ground at that stage.

Although Reagan believed that building weapons of mass destruction was fundamentally immoral, he thought it was legitimate to have them as bargaining tools to secure disarmament. To this end, he authorized the largest peacetime buildup since the end of the Second World War.

Seeing the Light

"The intelligence we were carrying was so sensitive," Phillip Petersen recalled, "that General Rogers, Nato's Supreme Commander, had to send his personal plane to collect it from Washington at the close of 1981 and bring it to his headquarters at Mons in Belgium." The material in question was that provided by Kuklinski and Polyakov on Marshal Ogarkov's new strategy.

In the most secure briefing room at General Roger's headquarters, Petersen and John Hines, another expert from the Defense Intelligence Agency, gave him their presentation. "As I finished, Rogers told me," Petersen recalled, "that 'For the first time in my career I really feel I'm seeing the battle from inside the mind of my adversary.'" Rogers took his time absorbing what he was being told, despite the fact that dozens of generals were waiting for their meeting with him.

Despite the weight and credibility of the intelligence, the idea that Ogarkov's forces would only use conventional weapons to defeat Nato was dismissed out of hand by some of the most influential members in the American intelligence community. They still firmly believed that Soviet forces would use nuclear weapons from the outset. One senior Soviet specialist reportedly accused those who accepted the intelligence of being wimps who "don't have the balls to push the button." Exceptional efforts were made to prevent the Joint Chiefs of Staff being told what General Rogers had just learned.[12]

Nato's New Dynamism

Having understood Ogarkov's intentions, General Rogers quickly came to the conclusion that Nato had much to learn from him.

"The ground had been well prepared," General von Sandrart, the commander of Nato forces on the central front during the last years of the Cold War, told me, "by the discussions that senior American army officers had been having with old German generals since the late seventies. They explained to the Americans that they had treated the whole Eastern Front as a single, huge 'theater of military operations,' in which the army and the air force worked closely together. This had only been done in the east, where the Germans were fighting across a far greater expanse than elsewhere."

The Americans also asked Dr. Ferdinand von Senger und Etterlin, then the senior German general in Nato, for his advice on fighting the Russians. The clock had turned full circle. The general had started his career in the Wehrmacht, had gained much experience of armored warfare on the Eastern Front, risen in the new

Bundeswehr modeled on American lines and, now, as a top Nato commander he was coaching the American army on how to think about large-scale operations—just as the Wehrmacht and the Red Army had done in the days of his youth.

While Nato's new strategy was being developed, American forces had been revolutionizing their tactics and training. In 1975, the air force opened its "Red Flag" training school in Nevada. A mini-Soviet air force was established with captured Soviet aircraft, the help of a pilot who had defected with the latest Soviet interceptor, and that of Israelis who had fought both Soviet and Soviet-trained pilots over the Middle East.

By following the special instructions they were given those pilots flying American aircraft became highly skilled at getting the better of their "Soviet" adversaries. Few of these macho men knew that they were being guided to victory by an attractive American air force officer, Reina Pennington, reputedly one of the greatest aerial tacticians of modern times.

Within a few years the army had a similar institution out in the desert of California, where a "Red Division," equipped with captured Soviet tanks, fought like Russians. American units that trained against them always lost. They were relieved to learn that the Reds won in large part because they had fought more "battles" together than any of the teams that took them on. Practice made perfect.

Proposals for re-equipping American forces and developing weapons based on "emerging technologies" had received strong backing from key players in the Carter Administration. This new equipment would certainly strengthen Nato forces, but Nato still had to devise a strategy for defeating an Ogarkov offensive.

To help its Nato allies understand the seriousness of the Soviet threat and the desirability of deploying Pershing-II and cruise missiles in Europe, the Pentagon accepted that it would have to share some of the their special intelligence with their allies. The Pentagon's public diplomacy office put Petersen in charge of a group that was tasked with giving well-informed briefings to the political elites and media in Nato countries. Their briefings were linked to the publication of many articles that were based on recently de-classified intelligence.[13]

Although de-classification was easier following Kuklinski's defection to the Americans in December 1981, many in the intelligence community objected. "Fortunately, the public diplomacy project," Petersen pointed out, "was overseen by General Richard Stillwell, the head of intelligence in the Pentagon, a man not inclined to take 'no' for an answer. In his old soldier's voice he would say 'I cannot make you lift your objection to releasing this material, but I can certainly make you wish that you had.'"

British Sparks

In reshaping the way that Nato would respond to a Soviet offensive in the eighties, one British officer played a crucial role. This was General Sir Nigel Bagnall, who early in his military career established a reputation both as a "fighting" soldier (who had twice won the Military Cross in the jungles of Malaya) and as an intellectual who thought deeply about his profession. In 1972 he was sent to Oxford University to spend a year studying under Michael Howard, one of the great historians of warfare, and later became the first regular officer to be elected an honorary fellow of Balliol College where he had studied.

"Bagnall had a major impact on Nato's operational thinking and its General Defense Plan for West Germany," according to Field Marshal Lord Inge, who served as Bagnall's chief of staff in Germany. When Bagnall returned to Germany in 1981 he first commanded the 1st (British) Corps, a force of some 40,000 troops that was part of Nato's much larger Northern Army Group which was tasked with defending the north German plain. Then in 1984 he took command of the Northern Army Group itself.

"At that time, Nato's General Defense Plan was based on deploying significant forces close to the Inner-German border in order to give the impression that Nato forces would fight for every inch of German soil. This deployment," Inge pointed out, "had several disadvantages—it lacked depth, significant armored reserves and, to an extent, played to the Soviet strengths. It also meant that Allied airpower was used piecemeal rather than in a concentrated way. In Bagnall's view it also would have required the political authorization of the early use of tactical nuclear weapons, which very understandably he thought was unrealistic. He firmly believed that Nato would have to take a far more innovative and flexible approach to thwarting a Soviet offensive."

Any changes to the General Defense Plan were a politically sensitive issue and Bagnall realized he would have to persuade the politicians that what he wanted to do was realistic. In this task he was greatly helped by his fluency in German and the close relationships he had established with two senior German officers—General von Senger und Etterlin, the commander of Allied forces in Central Europe, and General Hans-Henning von Sandrart, the chief of staff of the German army. "Their support," Inge stressed, "was crucial in winning approval for the military-political changes that Bagnall wanted to make and in implementing them. They were not only very important in persuading the Germans to agree to Bagnall's approach, but also the Americans, the Dutch and the Belgians."

Bagnall also recognized that he had to spread the word more widely and educate officers in key appointments throughout the chain of command. He established what became known as the "Ginger Group." This name was chosen not only because of the color of his hair and his nickname, but more importantly for its role in generating new ideas and spreading the "word."

The group included officers from the air force as well as from the army. Bagnall loved leading his enthusiastic protégés around the battlefields of Europe, where he showed them how small forces had been able to defeat far larger ones. Inevitably this group was resented by those officers who were not "invited" to become members, but it undoubtedly played a key role in educating the officer corps and led to senior officers being given more training in higher command.

A fresh input to the group came from Christopher Donnelly, an engaging lecturer at the Royal Military Academy at Sandhurst. Donnelly understood the Soviet military so well that even before the Cold War ended, a colonel in Soviet Military Intelligence wrote that Soviet officers could learn a lot about themselves and their army by reading Donnelly's book *Red Banner: The Soviet Military System in Peace and War*. Donnelly enjoyed reminding his audiences that the etiquette taught to Soviet officer cadets was almost identical to that at Sandhurst, except that they had compulsory dancing lessons.

An Afghan Shock

The Afghans had taught the British some harsh lessons in the 19th century, but few people know what a humiliating defeat an Afghan colonel inflicted on the British army in Germany in the 20th century.

Colonel Ghulam Dastagir Wardak had studied at the Voroshilov General Staff Academy in Moscow from 1973 to 1975. "After the Soviet invasion of Afghanistan in 1979, I first escaped to Pakistan," he told me, "then I returned to collect the dozens of notebooks containing detailed accounts of all the lectures I had attended at the Academy that I had buried in my garden. I had written out my notes in a little known Afghan script and then smuggled them back to Kabul in the Afghan diplomatic bag."[14]

"Wardak was a wonderful source because he had a deep understanding of Soviet strategy and tactics—he knew how to think like a senior Soviet officer," Petersen recollected. "His most direct contribution to Nato strategy came in 1983 when General Bagnall invited him to the headquarters of the 1st British Corps to command a full Soviet army in a war game."

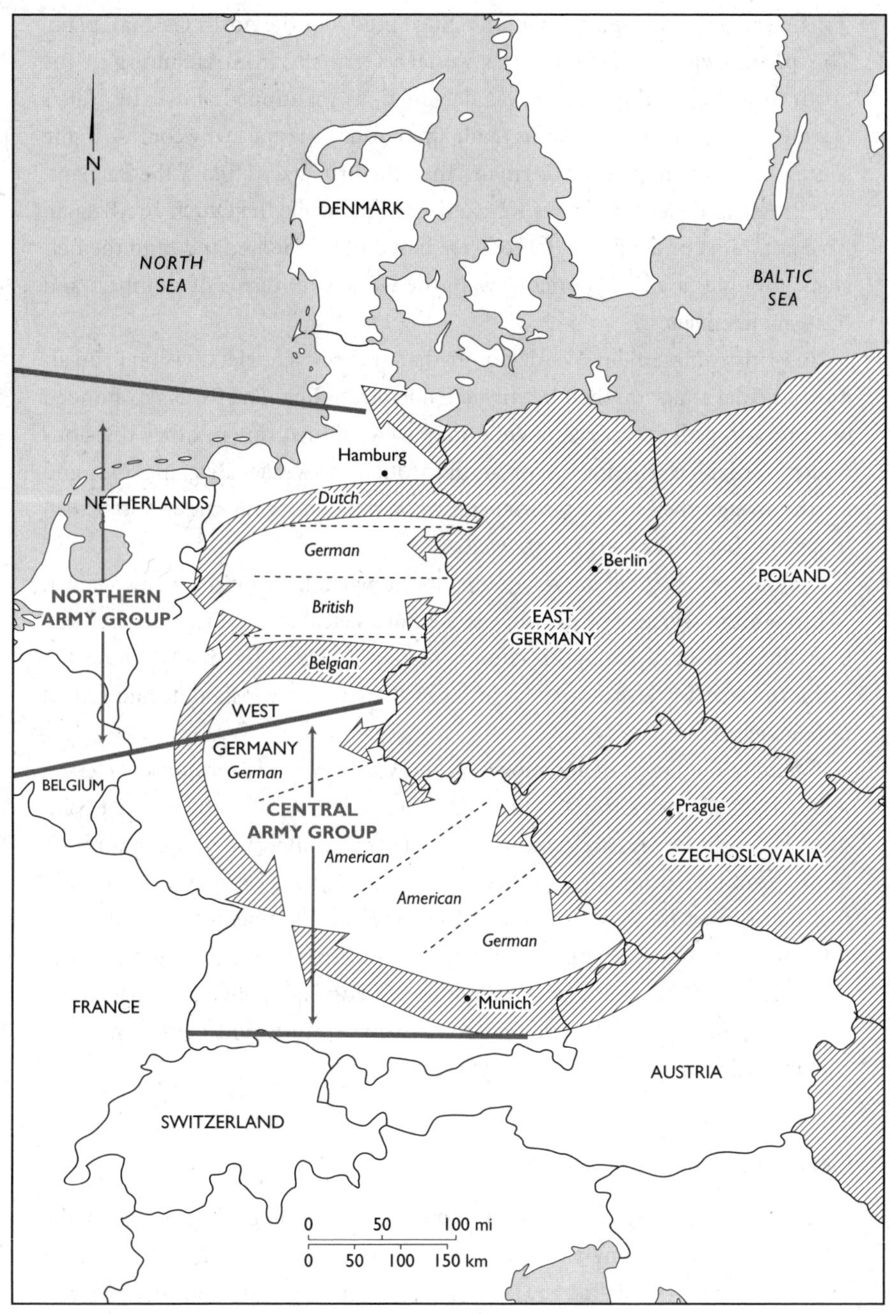

How Forces in West Germany Planned to Encircle Nato Forces. (Courtesy of Phillip A. Petersen)

The war game was played out on a huge model of the north German plain. This plain—which stretches across western Germany from Hamburg in the north to Kassel in the south—was defended, as mentioned above, by Nato's Northern Army Group. This was made up of four separate army corps—to the south of the Dutch were the Germans, then the British and finally the Belgians. The British and German forces were quite strong, while the Dutch and Belgian were not. Most of the Dutch forces were based in the Netherlands and the Belgians, though based in Germany, were the weakest in terms of numbers and combat effectiveness.

To British amazement, Wardak immediately threw a Soviet division in an almost suicidal attack on their heavily defended front line. The British responded by commiting their reserves. While they were pinned down, other divisions under Wardak's command swept south through the weaker Belgian sector and north through the Dutch sector, thereby encircling not only the whole British force, but that of the Germans as well.

Wardak left Bagnall in no doubt about what he would be up against: "Through the sacrifice of one division, I have defeated the British army." For Bagnall, the pain of seeing his commanders humiliated by an Afghan on the plains of Germany was more than offset by the vivid new insight he had gained into Soviet thinking.

"Wardak's account of his moves in the war game was masterly," Petersen pointed out. "Wardak told the Brits that the General Staff, knowing that Nato thought Soviet forces would mount a concentrated offensive to break through Nato's front line, would do just that. As Nato committed its reserves to prevent that happening, the Soviet commander would do the unexpected and break through the less well-defended parts of the front to encircle the stronger Nato forces. I believe that that war game reinforced Bagnall's conviction that to defeat such a highly coordinated Soviet offensive, Nato would have to have an equally well coordinated defensive strategy."

German Reinforcements

"German thinking had been evolving on similar lines, but we faced the major problem that any war, conventional or nuclear, would be conducted on German soil," according to General Hans-Henning von Sandrart, who was then chief of staff of the German army. "For political reasons our traditional operational concept had been to try to hold the line of defense as close to the

Inner-German border as possible, along with our American and other Nato allies."

"The key point," von Sandrart explained, "was to gain the time needed for the political leadership of the Alliance to invoke nuclear deterrence by the measured first use of nuclear weapons, if political means had failed to stop the war. With Ogarkov's new strategy in mind, however, we in the German military realized that we needed a new and credible operational concept—one that would enable us and our allies to fight a coordinated defensive battle in depth and launch massive counter-attacks."

"My task was all the more difficult," von Sandrart explained, "because some members of the Social-Democratic Party were deeply suspicious and accused me of being a war-monger who was undermining the coherence of deterrence. It took much hard work to convince them that improving our operation approach to defense was part of a credible deterrence. By 1983, when Bagnall became commander of Nato's Northern Army Group—which comprised British, German, Dutch, Belgian and American troops—we were able to work closely on developing a common operational concept."

"Bagnall's great achievement in the North Army Group," Inge emphasized, "was in leveraging the power of ground troops and airpower. Within three years Bagnall had them fighting as one army, exploiting their superior flexibility, concentration of force and surprise. He told his commanders to 'use your initiative, don't follow my orders.'"

Nato could never win, however, unless it had strong reserves. Work soon began on integrating Nato's nearly 2,000 helicopters in Europe into eight airmobile divisions. The first was the French *Force d'Action Rapide*, which combined large numbers of helicopters and fast-moving wheeled armored vehicles. This new concept gained real weight when General Rogers began increasing the number of American troops flown into Europe each year for the annual training exercises. Most of these were earmarked to be part of the reserve force and they included an airmobile division.

Setbacks for Ogarkov

While Nato's optimism was rising, that of the Warsaw Pact was on the way down. When its defense ministers met in Moscow in December 1981, just three months after *Zapad '81*, the outlook was not good—technologically, economically or in terms of the reliability of its allies. Marshal Ustinov conceded that the balance of power between Nato and the Warsaw Pact was "at the moment not in our favor."[15]

This sudden change of outlook is most likely to have stemmed from a full assessment by Soviet Military Intelligence of the implications of the new "revolution in military affairs" that the Americans were pioneering. They were now pushing the competition into a realm beyond Soviet reach—that of microelectronics.

The Warsaw Pact itself was also in trouble. Although General Jaruzelski's declaration of martial law on December 13 had stabilized the situation in Poland, the events there over the past two years had fundamentally weakened the alliance. In a crisis, the Poles might even impede the movement of troops across their country to East Germany. As if that was not bad enough, Marshal Ogarkov had just learned that Colonel Kuklinski, who knew so much about Soviet war plans, had defected to the Americans.

"Ogarkov's strategy was brilliant," according to Diego Ruiz-Palmer, one of the key analysts who monitored it closely. "But its implementation," he recalled, "would be difficult." He pointed out that in developing the main concepts the elite of the General Staff had "continued to rely on hierarchical rigidity and the discipline of the system to enhance effectiveness. The strategy, however, required an intensity of coordination never previously seen in Soviet operations. And this was no longer just about traditional staff work, but called for initiative and flexibility."

Nato's new strategy created major problems for the Soviet General Staff. After attacking Soviet armored forces with its new "assault-breaker" weapons, Nato would then launch major ground offensives that would compel whole Soviet armies to fight defensively—something that was incredibly alien to their usual way of fighting war. Ogarkov recognized that his forces needed to be smaller, more professional and better trained, changes that would shake the foundations of the Soviet military establishment.

Come the Revolution

The Soviet General Staff were rightly concerned by the military implications of the new technology. The hundreds of articles about "assault-breakers" that appeared in American military journals gave Soviet Military Intelligence a good idea of what to expect.

The Americans were already developing many different types of precision-guided munitions that could break up a Soviet armored offensive. In addition, within two years they were expected to bring into service cruise missiles with a range of 2,500 km (1,550 miles). These were intended to destroy hardened targets that were previously only vulnerable to a nuclear attack. This meant that the whole territory of the Warsaw Pact would be exposed to a speedy conventional attack from the outbreak of hostilities.

Soviet Military Intelligence grossly overestimated the pace at which "assault-breaker" munitions would be deployed. Joe Braddock, a leading consultant to the Pentagon who had been closely involved in their development, thought that this happened for two reasons: "First, the United States, Britain and Germany had indeed rapidly developed and fielded the first generation of precision-guided munitions; second, the advertising for the next generation combined reality with hype. The second generation of precision-guided munitions, however, would be far more complex and take longer to develop because they were intended to be even more precise and lethal over a wider area and so would be highly efficient."

The brochures drew heavily on a film produced in 1979 that showed aircraft dropping hundreds of "bomblets" whose heat-seeking sensors enabled them to home-in on tanks with devastating effect. The film, however, was a cleverly edited version of the first test of the new weapons a year earlier.

"Each of the 'bomblets' was hand-made and cost a fortune" according to Phil Karber, one of Braddock's assistants on this project. "They were strung on wires across a canyon directly above lines of tanks that were not moving. They worked, but it would be years before they could be mass-produced and dropped from aircraft."

"Soviet Military Intelligence," Braddock surmised, "had also probably learned that the Americans had been testing helicopters in Germany with radar that could identify moving objects 30–40 km (19–31 miles) beyond the front line. This would make Nato air strikes even more effective." It was not until 1990, however, that Nato began deploying J-STAR aircraft, which could detect movements up to 400 km (310 miles) away.

The Soviet General Staff were in no doubt that the Soviet Union faced a major challenge. To date, they had done remarkably well. While the Americans were developing anti-tank guided missiles, they were already protecting their tanks with a new "reactive" armor. And by the early eighties, they had fielded more anti-tank guided missiles than Nato.

Soviet Intelligence was still doing well in acquiring samples and blueprints, but now Soviet industry often could not manufacture the parts. Even when it could, it would always be at least one step behind the Americans. An equally serious problem was that Soviet society would have to be transformed before it could acquire the computer skills that were widespread in America.

By the end of 1982, Ustinov was referring rather coyly to "unsolved problems and difficulties" in the development of the Soviet economy.[16] There was little doubt that, unless the economy was revitalized, the Soviet Union would not be able to match the new American weaponry. Over the next two years the Americans obtained information that Ogarkov was criticizing the apportionment of too many resources to weapons for a nuclear war that could never succeed, while allowing the Soviet Union to fall dangerously behind in the new technology for conventional weapons that was likely to be decisive for the war that might be fought.

26 Vulnerability

The Risk of War

At a top secret KGB conference in Moscow in May 1981, Yuri Andropov declared, "The United States is preparing for nuclear war."[1] This was one of the most dramatic statements made by a chairman of the KGB since the Cold War began. The gravity of Yuri Andropov's remarks was attested to by the presence of Brezhnev himself at the conference.

This was not a bolt out of the blue. In February 1980, Andropov had met with Markus Wolf, the head of the East German Foreign Intelligence Service. "I had never seen Andropov so somber and dejected," Wolf later wrote. "His sober analysis . . . [was] . . . that the US government was striving by all available means to establish nuclear superiority over the Soviet Union," and he cited statements by Carter, Brzezinski and Pentagon spokesmen that included "the assertion that under certain circumstances a nuclear first-strike against the Soviet Union and its allies would be justified."[2]

A particularly worrying aspect of this shift in policy was Nato's threat, made just two months earlier, to deploy nearly 600 intermediate-range nuclear missiles—Pershing-IIs and Gryphon ground-launched cruise missiles—in Western Europe at the end of 1983 if Moscow did not eliminate its similarly sized force of SS-20 missiles. Nato believed the SS-20s undermined its strategy and thus would give the Soviet Union a psychological advantage in a crisis.

The Americans had carefully designed the Pershing-II missile to have a range of 1,700 kilometers. They did this because they did not want it to be regarded as a strategic missile on the grounds that it could destroy the Soviet capital. Nevertheless there was "a very genuine fear" in the Soviet General Staff that the Pershing-IIs could do just that.[3] This opened up the horrendous possibility of the United States "decapitating" the Soviet political and military leadership in Moscow in just some ten minutes. That undermined the very foundation of

Soviet deterrence, which was based on the assumption that strategic missiles launched from the United States would take roughly thirty minutes to reach the Soviet Union and that would give the leadership just enough time to launch a retaliatory attack.

During his first four months in office Reagan had shocked the Politburo with the staggering scale of the military buildup he was calling for and with his increasingly confrontational attitude. Although American reconnaissance aircraft had for years probed the periphery of the Warsaw Pact as they gathered intelligence on its air defenses, sizeable numbers of military aircraft were now flying straight towards the Soviet or East German frontiers, only turning away at the last minute. And off the coast of Italy, one aircraft had recently buzzed the flagship carrying Admiral Gorshakov, the founder of the modern Soviet navy.[4] The General Staff's "warning indicators'" were surging upwards.

Operation RYAN

Faced with the appalling prospect of the United States "preparing for nuclear war," Andropov said the Politburo was ordering the KGB and Soviet Military Intelligence (the GRU) to cooperate in a worldwide operation to collect intelligence on indicators-and-warning of war. This was *Operation RYAN*, the Russian acronym for "Nuclear Missile Attack." Military Intelligence would concentrate on the military indicators; the KGB on the political ones. It was the first time that the two services had been tasked in such a detailed and coordinated way. "The slogan," General Kalugin of the KGB vividly remembers, was "'do not miss'—don't miss the moment when the West is about to launch war."[5]

The roots of *RYAN* went back a long way. Given what had happened in 1941, it was hardly surprising that Soviet leaders and the General Staff shared a deep-seated fear of an unexpected attack. "As soon as Andropov came to office in 1967," a senior KGB officer recalled, "one of our major preoccupations was to organize our intelligence activity to assess the progress of [American] planning with regard to the *possibility* either of a first-strike or of a limited strike . . ." (emphasis added).[6]

Since then, through a series of outstanding Soviet and East European intelligence operations, Moscow had acquired thousands of Nato documents on war plans, including top secret/cosmic ones on the procedures leading to the decision to use nuclear weapons and how they would be used.[7] By this time, one of Markus Wolf's agents alone had probably provided a thousand of them![8] East

German intelligence officers understood Nato thinking and were well-placed to detect any changes.

Soviet Military Intelligence had the added benefit of being confident that it could detect changes in Nato's alert status and moves towards the release of nuclear weapons in Europe. The chances of detecting a strategic strike from the United States were not so good. The ability of Soviet Intelligence to read American naval codes could have alerted them to preparations for war, as could their ability to intercept sensitive telephone communications in the United States, but Soviet Intelligence did not have the comprehensive coverage of communication in the United States that it had in West Germany.

The anxiety of the General Staff and the Soviet leadership was compounded by the continuing problems with their early-warning satellites and radars; these problems were far more serious than the Americans knew. The fact that the Soviets might not have time to retaliate against a surprise American nuclear missile attack had a profound effect on the way they thought about deterrence.[9]

Andropov understood that what the Soviet leadership needed was not intelligence that a missile attack was about to begin, but for Soviet Intelligence to detect political and economic indications that a decision to launch a war was under consideration. Only this intelligence would grant the Soviets the time required to try to prevent war through diplomacy, and to remind the Americans of the terrible risks of launching an attack.

In his speech, Andropov had chosen his words carefully. Although he had accused the United States of "preparing for war"—he had not gone so far as to accuse it of planning to initiate one. *Operation RYAN* was not launched in panic, but with prudence. Within KGB headquarters, work began on turning Andropov's concerns into an operational plan.

Disconcerting Shocks

The United States had "in effect already declared war on us," Marshal Ogarkov told the Warsaw Pact chiefs of staff in September 1982.[10] That was an exaggeration, but Washington certainly was stepping up the pressure.

In August–September 1981 a battle group of over eighty Nato warships passed through the Greenland-Iceland-UK Gap in radio silence and came close to Soviet territory before they were detected. Four American surface warships, for the first time in twenty years, then moved forward into the Barents Sea, supposedly the "bastion" in which Soviet submarine-based missiles were safe from

Nato attack.[11] When they were about 20 km (12 miles) from the main Soviet naval base at Murmansk they switched on all their electronic equipment. The message was loud and clear—"We can run rings around you!"

At the end of the year, the General Staff had another wake-up call. This time, they discovered that the Americans were tapping their naval communications cables that ran across the Sea of Okhotsk, which faces into the Pacific. Like the Barents Sea, which leads into the Arctic and the Atlantic, this was a highly defended "bastion" where a large number of Soviet strategic nuclear submarines were based. Another Soviet weakness had been exposed. What the Russians did not know was that the Americans were also tapping one of the Soviet's main naval communications cables, which ran across the Barents Sea and proved to be a rich vein of intelligence.[12]

Soviet Intelligence had details of the Americans' new and more aggressive Air-Land Battle strategy, which involved attacking targets far into Warsaw Pact territory at the outset of a war.[13] British airbases in Germany were now so well-trained that they could reload their fighter-bombers, of which they had more than sixty, with nuclear weapons in just 6 ½ minutes.[14] Mrs. Thatcher's swift and decisive response to the Argentine invasion of the Falklands in 1982 left little scope for doubt over her willingness to use armed force should the need arise.

Moscow was stunned by the scale of the American military buildup. In October 1981, Congress approved a defense expenditure of $1.5 trillion over the next five years. The strategic nuclear forces were to receive 100 MX missiles, six new Trident submarines with a total of 96 D-5 missiles, 3,000 air-launched cruise missiles and 100 B-1 bombers to carry them.

The General Staff were shaken, according to Vitali Kataev, a leading Soviet missile expert, when analysis showed that the improved accuracy of these missiles "increased the power of the American arsenal by a power of three."[15] Taken together, these new missiles would be able to inflict terrible damage on the Soviet political and military leadership, their systems of command and control and the new mobile missiles that Moscow hoped would strengthen its ability to deter the United States.

Preparing for the Worst

Administration officials were saying that the purpose of using force was not to prevent defeat, but to prevail. Once a war started, there would be no return to the *status quo*; the situation would be resolved on new terms. In addition, steps were taken to upgrade America's command, control and communications networks so that they had a better chance of functioning after a nuclear attack.

What riled the Kremlin was that Reagan had rallied support for this buildup on the grounds that the Soviet Union believed that it would win a nuclear war. The Soviet leadership, however, did not consider their forces could do that or that they were deployed aggressively. Their mobile missiles remained in garrison except when on training exercises; their aircraft were never on airborne-alert with nuclear weapons on board and only 10% of their submarine fleet was at sea at any one time, compared with 50–60% of the American fleet. In military training, General Makhmut Gareev recalled, "we were forbidden to exercise the initiation of nuclear use."[16]

A furious Brezhnev responded to recent American actions and statements through *Pravda* on October 21. "Only a suicidal maniac," he fumed, "could begin a nuclear war in the hope of emerging victorious." The most important task, therefore, was make sure that the Soviet Union could respond with a devastating counter-attack even in the event of surprise nuclear attack.

By the early eighties, the General Staff had made considerable progress in developing this capability. According to General Varofolomei Korobushin, the former deputy chief of staff of the Strategic Rocket Forces, "our control system was so well prepared that . . . it took just 13 seconds to deliver the decision from Moscow to all launch sites in the Soviet Union."[17] That was an enormous improvement, but the leadership still needed adequate warning of an attack.

But just in case this system failed, Dr. Viktor Surikov, a top Soviet defense scientist, had been tasked with designing a "Doomsday Machine," like the one so frighteningly portrayed in the film *Dr. Strangelove* in 1964.[18] It was, according to General Korobushin, "to launch all missiles remaining in our arsenal even if every nuclear command center and all our leaders were destroyed." Appropriately, it bore the morbid name of "Dead Hand."[19]

Breaking Up the Soviet Empire

In the White House, work was underway to weaken the grip of the increasingly decrepit Soviet leadership over Eastern Europe, where the weakest point was Poland. To this end, in May 1982, Reagan signed a secret "national security decision directive" that authorized a range of economic, diplomatic and covert measures. During a private meeting at the Vatican on June 7, Reagan and the

Pope agreed to undertake a clandestine campaign to hasten the dissolution of the communist empire.

Richard Allen, Reagan's first national security adviser, described this as the beginning of "one of the great secret alliances of all time."[20] Although it now seems that this alliance was not very secret as far as Soviet and Polish leaderships were concerned, it was certainly "great." After all, in Poland the Pope had many "divisions"—so to speak—as well over half the population took communion every week. From the Vatican's well-filled coffers and those of the Reagan Administration, tens of millions of dollars were secretly channeled through to Solidarity.

In his address to the British Parliament on the day after his audience with the Pope, the president spoke for the first time about the "crisis" in the Soviet Union. The outcome of the struggle with communism, he said, would not be determined by "bombs or rockets, but a test of wills and ideas . . ."[21] He urged the West to encourage democratic change in communist countries. This, the president believed, was the essence of his Reagan Doctrine.[22]

Besides providing funding for Solidarity and other democratic groups in Eastern Europe, Reagan funded new powerful transmitters for Radio Free Europe, Radio Liberty and Voice of America so that more people could listen to their broadcasts across Eastern Europe and the Soviet Union. America's annual funding for these projects probably exceeded that which the Soviet Union and East Germany were channeling into the West European peace movement.

From the outset, the Administration had been trying to deny Moscow access to advanced Western technology and restrict its ability to earn hard currency. Reagan's determination to do this was reinforced by the *Farewell Dossier* that President Mitterrand gave Reagan in July 1981.[23] *Farewell* was the code name of the Soviet intelligence officer who had revealed to the French the Soviet Union's extraordinary success in acquiring advanced Western technology, both legally and illegally.

"This information reinforced what Vladimir Treml, a Soviet émigré, was telling the White House about Moscow being critically dependent, not just highly dependent, on its hard-currency earnings from the export of oil and gas," Andy Marshall, the director of the Office of Net Assessment at the Pentagon, recalled. His judgment added to the importance of the efforts by Casey and others to persuade the Saudis to push down the price of oil. Not only would that give a much-needed boost to the flagging American economy, but it would also slash Soviet foreign exchange earnings.

In parallel, Richard Perle, the assistant secretary for defense, worked hard to close the technology loopholes. Reluctantly, Western countries began to restrict sales of advanced technology to the Soviet Union. However, American efforts to bloc a major oil/gas pipeline deal sparked a highly acrimonious transatlantic dispute, which ended in the Americans having to back down in exchange for further talks on such issues. Nonetheless, Moscow's economic problems mounted, in part because of the sanctions the Administration imposed on Poland following General Jaruzelski's declaration of martial law at the end of 1981. "They soon began inflicting a heavy burden on Poland and the Soviet Union," the General said. "They cost us alone some $12 billion."

While Nato governments began expelling most of the Soviet intelligence officers engaged in the illicit acquisition of technology, Gus Weiss, Reagan's intelligence adviser, took a different approach to exacerbating Soviet problems. Working with the CIA he set out to ensure that some items did get through. These items included software that had "bugs" hidden deep in their programs. On one occasion, in June 1982, a "malfunction" generated such a huge pipeline explosion that it could be seen from space via American satellites.[24]

Reagan was equally determined to reverse Soviet gains in the Third World—especially in Afghanistan, Angola and Cambodia, along with those in Central America. The key issue in Central America was Nicaragua, where the Sandinistas had come to power in 1979, the first successful revolution in Latin America in twenty years. The Sandinistas soon began supporting revolutionary movements in El Salvador and Guatemala, with Soviet and Cuban backing.

During his first year in office Reagan ordered the CIA to organize and support a Nicaraguan counter-revolutionary force, the "Contras," which by the late eighties was about 15,000 strong. At the same time, the Americans stepped up pressure on the Russians in Afghanistan, through arming the mujahedin. Moscow responded by increasing aid to Nicaragua. It was not willing, however, to give them combat aircraft as that would have caused trouble with other Latin American governments.

Malaise & Vulnerability

The Soviet leadership had every reason to feel vulnerable. Well-sourced accounts reaching Washington about the depressed mood of the Soviet elite had considerable influence on the strategists in the Administration and, of course, the president.

On August 3, 1982, Casey sent the president a report from British Intelligence that strengthened his conviction that his adversary was on its last legs. It was entitled *The Malaise of Soviet Society*. "It was one of the best reports we had seen in years" recalled George Kolt, a Soviet expert on the National Intelligence Council at the time.[25] He went on, "Nothing illustrated more graphically the crumbling of the Soviet system—the extensive corruption, including in Brezhnev's own family; armed gangs raiding railway trains; the vandalism done to historic sites in Leningrad; fine fur hats being stolen from right outside Andropov's office in the Lubyanka; one of his deputies being murdered as he walked home; and a blind-drunk man being found on a window-ledge of the Lubyanka—a crime made all the more heinous as he did not work for the KGB!"

"The main message," Kolt said, "was that public discontent was mounting and the cohesion and discipline of Soviet society had been seriously weakened. In a crisis, for example the mishandling of industrial unrest, people below the age of 45 might well challenge the leadership of the party and the authority of the state."

A second British report, on Soviet difficulties in foreign policy, was also considered extremely important. Kolt remembered that "it highlighted the fact that the Soviet leadership had seriously underestimated Western reaction to its moves in the Third World and the Soviet military buildup. According to the report, the big increases in American defense expenditure were placing a heavy strain on the Soviet economy. At the same time, the Soviet Union had paid too high a price for détente, which had already weakened the levers of political control. Western influence now posed an even greater threat to the ideological stability of the regime."

The Reagan Administration was keen to exploit these Soviet vulnerabilities. By this time, however, they too were coming under pressure.

27 Changing Tack

Abolishing Nuclear Weapons

Before becoming president, Reagan visited America's missile-tracking headquarters deep beneath the Cheyenne Mountains in Colorado. He was depressed to learn that the United States could still do nothing do to stop a Soviet missile attack. Having won the election, Reagan did not like what he was told about his options for responding to an attack. The thought of pushing the button "sent shivers up his spine."[1]

Reagan, however, would continue to insist that the United States was developing the capability to fight a nuclear war. In June 1982, General David Jones, the outgoing chairman of the Joint Chiefs of Staff, said publicly that planning for a protracted war would be throwing money down a "bottomless pit," adding, "I don't see much of a chance of a nuclear war being limited or protracted."[2] Although Jones's remarks were a serious breach of protocol, they tallied closely with the president's private sentiments.

Since Hiroshima, Reagan had openly voiced his wish to see the abolition of nuclear weapons and, during his first year in office, he called for plans to "abolish all nuclear weapons." None were forthcoming because his staff thought this was just another of his dotty ideas. Later George Shultz would remind them that the president had been twice elected on that platform: "I cannot get it into your heads that this man is serious." They should, he said, think creatively as to how the president's wishes could be implemented.[3]

While they were not thinking creatively, Reagan's fears about nuclear war were increasingly nurturing his deeply emotional dream of creating a "shield" that would protect the American people against a Soviet missile attack. In October, Reagan authorized a "vigorous research and development program" and over the next year set about winning the support of the Joint Chiefs of Staff for what later became known as his Strategic Defense Initiative (SDI) or more popularly as "Star Wars."

"Bud" McFarlane, his national security adviser, was not worried about the feasibility of this project. If the research effort could be traded for deep reductions in Soviet strategic missiles, that would be "the greatest sting operation in history."[4] He did not, however, put this point to the president, who showed every sign of firmly believing in SDI.

The following month, the hawks in Reagan's administration did make a proposal on Euromissiles that the president liked, which was called the "double-zero" option. Nato, they argued, should cancel its deployment of Pershing-II and cruise missiles if Moscow dismantled all its SS-20s and older similar systems. Secretary of State Haig thought it was "absurd to expect the Soviets to dismantle an existing force of 1,100 warheads . . . in exchange for a promise from the United States not to deploy a missile force that we had not yet begun to build and has aroused such violent controversy in Western Europe."[5]

While those who backed the "double-zero" option had rightly judged that Moscow would reject the idea out of hand, they had failed to understand why the president had backed it enthusiastically—because he hoped that, as the pressure on the Soviet leadership built up, they would come to accept it.

In the spring of 1982, the focus shifted to strategic nuclear forces where Reagan, like Carter, called for deep cuts. Moscow accepted Reagan's proposal that the name of the negotiations on strategic nuclear forces, scheduled to start in Geneva in June, should be changed from SALT, which were about "arms limitation," to START, which were intended to bring about "arms reduction." As the two sides continued to have fundamentally different views on the nature of the reductions, the omens were not good.

The Soviet military were determined not to be seen to bow to American pressure. In June, they harassed the Americans in a number of different ways—they fired a laser at the space shuttle *Challenger*, which interfered with communications and gave the crew some physical discomfort; bumped an American submarine; fired on a helicopter flying along the Czechoslovak-German border; and interfered with commercial flights into West Berlin.[6]

During the same month, the Soviet General Staff conducted an unprecedented exercise simulating a "seven hour nuclear war" that featured an all-out strike against the United States and Western Europe, including the almost simultaneous launch of intercontinental and intermediate-range missiles as well as submarine-launched ones.[7] The General Staff rightly assumed that the

United States would monitor this exercise. The NSA did and, according to one senior official dealing with this subject at the time, it was considered to be "political dynamite" because it looked like a response to "Reagan, the war-monger." "No formal assessment was ever issued. At NSA, the one copy that could be consulted by those who had to know became very thumb worn."[8]

At the Pentagon, no one wanted to fight a nuclear war, but officials were becoming increasingly confident that they could deter one. A top secret and highly restricted review of the strategic balance "demonstrated convincingly," Marshall explained to me, "that the United States was already in a rather good position and that was set to improve." Caspar Weinberger, the secretary of defense, had to be given a special, private briefing about a few other highly sensitive projects not mentioned in the report, but which further strengthened the American advantage. One of these was the B-2 "stealth" bomber.

Need for a New Approach

The growing strength of the peace movement came as a nasty shock to the Reagan Administration. Some one million people took part in anti-nuclear rallies in October 1981 in Amsterdam, Bonn, London, Rome and Brussels—the capitals of the countries in which the missiles would be deployed. In Germany there were fears that the ruling Social Democratic Party would no longer back the deployment of Pershing-II missiles in Germany.

Less than a year later, the peace movement was becoming a force in American politics. In June 1982, three-quarters of a million people gathered in New York to call for an immediate nuclear "freeze." This was the largest political demonstration in American history. Some congressmen were also calling for a declaration that the United States would not be the first to use nuclear weapons. The American public's support for increased military spending had slumped.

Every bit as worrying for the Reagan Administration was the split in Congress over what form deterrence should take. The biggest problem of all was that Congress refused to back the development and deployment of 200 MX missiles, with ten warheads apiece, that were intended to redress Moscow's advantage in land-based intercontinental ballistic missiles.

Faced with this damaging impasse, the president cleverly passed the task of creating a strategic consensus to a blue-ribbon presidential commission headed by the much respected Brent Scowcroft, a retired air force general. In essence, this required bringing to an end the fractious debate over the "window of vulnerability" that Reagan himself had fanned during the presidential campaign. "Brent set about doing this," his deputy Woolsey pointed out, "by skillfully combining the interests of the arms controllers with those who wanted more accurate offensive missiles that could attack Soviet missile sites etc."

Enter Andropov

As the Scowcroft Commission began work in Washington, in Moscow, Yuri Andropov was making his mark as the new leader of the Soviet Communist Party following the death of Leonid Brezhnev in November 1982. Brezhnev, for reasons of infirmity and senility, had been a considerable embarrassment to his colleagues for the past few years.

Andropov brought a renewed vigor and keen intelligence to the leadership. He enjoyed classical music and literature; unusually for a Soviet leader, he had a talent for writing doggerels and was a teetotaler. Whatever else he was, he was not a closet liberal. He had led the KGB's intense and ruthless clampdown on dissent over the past decade and even criticized his own son for being a social democrat.[9]

Although Andropov was almost certainly the best-informed member of the leadership on Soviet weaknesses at home and abroad, he had no wish to reform the system. His goal was to make it work effectively. He believed a long period of careful economic reform would be needed before there could be any significant political change.[10] For this reason, Andropov liked Ostrovsky's famous play about 19th-century Russian merchants in which one declares that "In Russia there never was public opinion and there never will be."[11]

As the disastrous consequences of the Soviet intervention in Afghanistan that he had pressed for became clear, Andropov was forced into the painful realization that the Soviet Union was now well-and-truly on the defensive. He understood better than anyone else in the leadership that the "correlation of forces" had turned irrevocably against the Soviet Union, which had few ways to reduce the imbalance, let alone reverse it.

On January 4, 1983, after some six weeks in office, Andropov gave East European leaders in Prague an unemotional assessment of the shift that had taken place over the past four years. He began by looking back to the golden years of the seventies, when "our dynamic policy of détente" had led to "substantial positive shifts" to Soviet advantage. Now, however, the West was responding by seeking to exploit the economic and political difficulties of the socialist states.

Anti-war demonstration in Berlin, 1982. (Courtesy of the German Information Service)

In essence, Andropov said, "we are faced with one of the most massive efforts . . . to stop the progress of socialism or even roll it back, at least in some areas."

The American buildup of new military capabilities intended for fighting a protracted nuclear conflict was particularly worrying. It was "difficult to say where the line lies between extortion and actual preparations to take a fateful step." Despite American hostility, the Soviet Union was willing to "go very far" to end the arms race. To that end, Andropov would try to get relations back on a better course and to reopen a "dialogue of equals" with Reagan.[12]

Andropov seems to have realized that the Soviet Union had little hope of winning the psychological battle for pre-eminence in Europe, where there were now three of the most robust anti-communist leaders since the war—Francois Mitterrand, Helmut Kohl and Margaret Thatcher. But there was always the possibility that through bad leadership the Americans would lose.

Andropov's main hope was that the peace movements in Germany and elsewhere would be able to force Reagan to be less confrontational. Moscow continued channeling more money to some of the peace groups that had sprung up spontaneously in West Germany, where the deployment of Euromissiles remained highly controversial. Meanwhile, East German Intelligence set up and supported "Generals for Peace" there. To date, however, these campaigns had failed to deliver any clear gains.

Since the early seventies there had been a buildup of East Germany's "special operational forces" and new guidelines for its cooperation with "patriotic forces" in peace time, crises and war. In early 1983, we now know, Moscow made preparations for attacks on British, American and Nato targets in Europe. As part of this effort, the KGB identified places in bars and restaurants near American bases in West Germany to conceal explosives that when detonated would make it look as if there had been a terrorist attack.[13] When, in October 1984, Honecker discussed with Gromyko the failure of the peace movement to prevent the deployment of Euromissiles, Honecker said that this was due to the fact that the protests had remained non-violent.[14] Moscow may have hoped that the peace campaign would turn violent, but was unwilling to take the lead in provoking it.

To the considerable annoyance of the East German authorities, the Euromissile crisis had sparked the growth of an independent peace movement in their own state. "The churches," Markus Wolf recalled, "were calling for disarmament and an end to military education in schools. The Stasi seized the badges worn by these church groups—which depicted swords being made into ploughshares." "This was ironic," he noted, "since the badge was based on a Soviet sculpture at the United Nations."

Time to Talk

When he spoke in Prague, Andropov had assessed Reagan's intentions remarkably accurately. Two weeks later, on January 17, after much heated debate within his administration, Reagan had signed National Security Decision Directive 75, which focused on reversing Soviet expansionism abroad and promoting a more pluralistic society within the Soviet Union. A third element of this policy was to engage the new leadership in Moscow in negotiations to protect and enhance American interests. This was not just the most robust declaration of "containment" ever made by an American administration, but more akin to a secret declaration of economic and political war. It was the first time the United States had set out to change the Soviet regime.

The first real achievement from Reagan's point of view came on February 11, 1983, when he won backing from the Joint Chiefs of Staff to explore "strategic defense." Over dinner the following evening, with the president elated by the decision of the previous day, Secretary of State Shultz tactfully suggested that contacts should be expanded with the Kremlin on four main issues—human rights, regional issues, bilateral economic issues and arms control—and work towards a summit should begin. "The latter idea appealed to Reagan," Richard Allen, his first national security adviser, explained. "He felt he had outwitted the communists in Hollywood. Now he relished the prospect of negotiating with Soviet leaders themselves." This opened up many new possibilities.

Four days later—and unseen by the media—Shultz discretely brought Dobrynin into the White House, where he had a two-hour meeting with the president. This was Reagan's first substantive conversation with a senior Soviet official. The main point that he asked Dobrynin to convey to Andropov was "I don't want war between us . . . We should make a fresh start."[15]

On Febuary 17, the day after Dobrynin's report reached the Kremlin, the KGB residencies in Nato and some other countries received—perhaps coincidentally—their first detailed instructions on *Operation RYAN*. These explained how KGB officers should seek "to uncover Nato preparations for a nuclear missile attack on the USSR," a task of "growing urgency" given the expected arrival of the new Pershing-II and Gryphon cruise missiles in Western Europe towards the end of the year.[16]

Few KGB officers serving in the West are likely to have known of the top secret "psyops" being mounted against the Soviet Union, or just how apprehensive the Soviet leadership was becoming. Although the underlying concept of *RYAN* was sound, some of the information KGB officers overseas were told to look for made them dismiss the whole operation as being ludicrous. Most of them ridiculed requests to watch for such things as lights on in ministries late at night and hospitals collecting more blood. However, knowing they would be severely reprimanded if they detected no signs, KGB officers began to make them up, uncertain of what impact, if any, their reports would have on KGB headquarters.

Striking the right balance between relaxing tension and maintaining vigilance would never be easy for the Americans. As Richard Perle told *Newsweek* at this time, "Democracies will not sacrifice to protect their security in the absence of a sense of danger, and every time we create the impression that we and the Soviets are cooperating and moderating the competition, we diminish the sense of apprehension."[17]

Just three weeks later, on March 8, Reagan delivered a speech not only conveying the harsh essence of NSDD-75, but adding that the Soviet Union was an "evil empire." When his wife urged him to cut back on such rhetoric, he retorted: "It is an evil empire. It's time to close it down."[18] The Soviet leadership, General Kalugin of the KGB later recalled, "was shocked . . . and said we are to expect something terrible from this reckless president."[19] But as Ben Fischer, CIA's former chief historian points out, "Although Reagan's rhetoric was often brilliant and rattled the Soviets, it rarely surpassed them in distorting the facts."

If closing down the Soviet empire would be a long haul, at least Reagan could take comfort in the fact that Scowcroft had managed to create a new consensus on strategy. Scowcroft's key proposal was to put just 100 MX missiles into silos and develop a small and mobile single-war-headed Midgetman missile that would be less vulnerable to attack than silo-based missiles. In parallel, the United States should seek arms control agreements that would ensure neither side would have an incentive to strike first in a crisis. This involved reducing the number of warheads on each missile so that one missile would not have the potential to destroy, say, ten of the other side's.

The arduous task of winning congressional support was eased by the wording of the commission's report, written by Scowcroft's deputy, James Woolsey. Woolsey drew on ideas and language crafted by his friend Michael Quinlan, the British government's high priest of nuclear theology. The result, elegant and exquisitely balanced, was one of the most articulate documents of the Cold War.[20]

The Scowcroft Commission submitted its report on April 6, 1983, and Congress approved it. Then on May 4, the "nuclear freeze" resolution passed the House. "This reinforced the Commission's message," Woolsey said, "that arms control was the *quid pro quo* for congressional cooperation on the strategic buildup."

The "window of vulnerability" was now considered to be closed, even though none of the new weapons could be ready for several years. It was all a matter of perception and domestic politics.

The Shock of SDI

The Scowcroft Report aroused little interest in the Kremlin, where Soviet leaders were still reeling from the speech Reagan had given on March 23, 1983, to launch his Strategic Defense Initiative. He called on scientists to render nuclear missiles "impotent and obsolete" by developing an impenetrable network of ground and space-based systems that could destroy missiles in flight.

Reagan hoped that SDI would serve as a catalyst for the elimination of all nuclear weapons, especially as he had offered to share the technology with the Soviet Union. Four days after Reagan's speech, Andropov accused him of "deliberately lying" about Soviet military power to justify SDI, which would open up an arms race in space. Reagan's aim, he concluded, was to invent "new plans on how to unleash a nuclear war in the best way, with hope of winning it."[21]

In the months that followed, the Americans acquired much intelligence that confirmed the fact that the Soviet leadership was deeply troubled by the prospect of the arms race moving into space.[22] Shortly after Reagan's announcement a telling insight into Soviet weakness came from a conversation that Marshal Ogarkov had with a former American arms-controller. Ogarkov told him, "In America, small children play with computers . . . for reasons you know well, we cannot make computers widely available in our society. We will never catch up with you in modern arms until we have an economic revolution. And the question is whether we can have an economic revolution without a political revolution."[23]

While top Soviet scientists started to assess the feasibility of SDI, the KGB was hit by a bombshell of a very different sort. In early 1983, Markus Wolf forwarded to Moscow what he described as the "the most depressing insight yet into the state of the Warsaw Pact." This was MC-161, Nato's top secret annual assessment of the East-West balance of global power that, in his view, gave "a masterful analysis of the weaknesses of the Soviet system and its decline in military efficiency and economic power."[24]

Wolf said that he "labored with my brightest young team" to ensure that the covering note "would neither veil the bleak picture presented by the Nato study nor express any high-handed *Schadenfreude* about the miserable portrayal of the Soviet Union." That report must have made deeply depressing reading for those who saw it in Moscow.

Meanwhile, Andropov continued to hype the threat from Pershing-II missiles. At one point he admitted to Honecker that he did not really consider that Pershing-II would change things much as the Americans already had plenty of missiles with which to attack the Soviet Union and East Germany. The real reason for focusing on these missiles, he explained, was "to raise the struggle against the whole course of militarization onto a higher level" and "should the deployment take place, and everything indicates that it will, then the struggle against militarization would nevertheless continue."[25] In other words, Andropov's aim was to strengthen the peace movements in the West in order to undermine popular support for Nato's strategy of nuclear deterrence and SDI.

Regardless of how poor Reagan's judgment was on the possibilities of creating a defense against ballistic missiles, he had shown a profoundly shrewd instinct for how the project would be received.

Still Trying Not to Overreact

Soon after Reagan's announcement on SDI at the end of March, it became clear that the peace movements had failed and Nato's Euromissiles would begin to be deployed on schedule in November. When the Politburo met on May 31, Andropov asked them whether American policy makers would use the Euromissiles without being provoked. Gromyko rightly replied, "I think they wouldn't dare to use nuclear missiles without sufficient reason."[26]

At a meeting with Warsaw Pact party leaders shortly thereafter, Andropov accurately summed up Reagan's policy as being to "radically change the international situation to its advantage in order to dictate to us how to live and how to handle our own affairs." The Soviet people, he said, would have to make sacrifices "in view of the war danger that is a threat to the nation."[27]

Despite these developments, Moscow and Washington worked to normalize relations. By the summer, some progress was being made. A group of Pentacostalists who had been given sanctuary in the American Embassy in Moscow since 1978 were allowed to emigrate from the Soviet Union, as Reagan had requested in his first meeting with Dobrynin; the Soviet Union had agreed to buy American grain, and talks were underway on improving the hot line between Washington and Moscow.

On June 15, Shultz set out for the Senate Foreign Relations Committee a forward-looking statement on policy towards the Soviet Union. "Strength and realism can deter war, but only direct dialogue and negotiation can open the path toward lasting peace."[28] In July, Reagan sent a personal, handwritten letter to Andropov expressing a wish for arms reductions. Although there were doubts in the Politburo about Reagan's motives, his tone was not confrontational. On August 1, Andropov responded positively, suggesting that a back-channel be opened to explore the possibilities.

KAL 007

While SDI was being evaluated in Moscow, the General Staff were confronted with yet more American military "psyops." The biggest came in April-May 1983, when the US Pacific Fleet moved towards Petropavlovsk, the main naval base on the Soviet Pacific coast and, for the first time, openly sent submarines, supported by aircraft, into the Sea of Okhotsk, where they had earlier been secretly tapping Soviet naval communications (see map on p. 28). Since then Soviet air defense forces in this region had been on high alert.

Subsequent American intelligence gathering flights close to the Soviet frontier had made them increasingly edgy.[29] On the night of September 1, a Soviet fighter shot down an aircraft that had flown over Petropavlosk, then continued over the island of Sakhalin. The attack, which probably took place in international airspace between Sakhalin and the Soviet mainland, killed all 269 people aboard, including many Americans. This was Korean Airlines flight KAL 007, which had inadvertently strayed into Soviet airspace on its way from Alaska to Seoul.

Washington immediately embarked on a worldwide campaign to condemn the Soviet action. The following day, the CIA informed the president that throughout most of the incident Soviet air defense thought that they were tracking an American reconnaissance plane that had earlier been in the area to monitor an expected Soviet missile test.[30] While the campaign continued, President Reagan used the incident to persuade Congress to increase defense spending.

In Moscow on September 9, Marshal Ogarkov, the chief of the General Staff, appeared in uniform at a prime-time televised press conference at which he used maps to argue his case that the plane was unquestionably on an intelligence mission. The local air defense commander, he said, had acted rationally and the blame lay with the United States. The tapes he played of what the pilot had reported to his ground controllers had, however, been doctored to remove mention of two key facts—the aircraft had two rows of lighted windows (because it was a Boeing-747) and its wing lights were flashing, neither of which was compatible with a spy flight.[31]

Behind closed doors in Moscow, Andropov raged against "those blockheads of generals" who in a trice had destroyed all his efforts to improve relations with Reagan. He feared that as a result of this "gross blunder . . . it probably will take us a long time to get out of this mess."[32] It was over a month before the Soviet Union would acknowledge that it had shot down a passenger plane.

After the vituperous exchanges sparked by the KAL 007 incident, Andropov issued a statement in *Pravda* on September 29 that was unprecedented in the annals of Soviet diplomacy. He declared that "[I]f anyone ever had any illusions about the possibility of an evolution to the better in the policy of the present American administration, these illusions are *completely* dispelled now," with "*completely*" being italicized in *Pravda*. Thus, Moscow saw no hope of improving Soviet-US relations while Reagan remained president.[33]

Georgi Arbatov, the director of the Institute of the United States and Canada, put it better when he said that "the danger of war in U.S. policy lay in the conduct of policy as if there was no danger of war."[34]

False Alarm

An even greater jolt to the Soviet system came on September 26, 1983, at the recently established satellite early-warning center outside of Moscow. That night (as I described briefly at the beginning of this book) the monitor screens showed that five American Minuteman missiles had been launched against the Soviet Union. The officer on duty, Stanislav Petrov, quickly decided this was a false alarm. First, he did not believe the Americans would launch a surprise attack on such a small scale, and secondly, the ground-based radar was showing no signs of the missiles coming over the horizon.

As we know from General Valerii Yarynych, the former long-term head of nuclear command and control on the Soviet General Staff, these sorts of alarms were quite frequent because the early-warning systems were unreliable. However, they were resolved quickly, without much fuss. Yarynych insists that although such incidents posed risks (especially at times of tension), he and others in charge certainly would not have thought that an alert showing just five missiles was a real attack.[35] Nevertheless, the incident confirmed what some experts had said—the system was unreliable. The Soviet leadership would have to be ultra cautious.

The president was beginning to sense the need, too. Two years earlier, he had been told at a meeting of the National Security Council that at least 150 million American lives would be lost in a nuclear war with the Soviet Union, even if America "won." On October 10, he had a private viewing of *The Day After*, an American television docu-drama that showed just how horrendous a nuclear exchange with the Soviet Union would be. That night he confided to his diary that the film had been "very effective and left me greatly depressed."

28 War Scare?

Growing Anxiety

By brilliantly exploiting the downing of KAL 007 the Reagan Administration did much to discredit the peace movement, especially the strictly pro-Soviet or anti-American elements. This made it possible for more West European politicians to support the deployment of Euromissiles—the very issue in the battle of wills with Moscow.

Even so, on October 22 and 23, 1983, in cities across Western Europe, two million people demonstrated against the imminent deployment of those missiles. Their general message was that Reagan's arms buildup was unnecessary and that the deployment of Euromissiles and Reagan's "aggressive" attitude towards the Soviet Union greatly increased the risk of war. As final decisions on the deployment of missiles in West Germany and Italy still had to be taken by their respective parliaments, the protesters hoped to step up the pressure on governments in the weeks ahead.

Since 1980, the last year of the Carter Administration, the Soviet media carried more and more reports asserting that the United States was a growing threat to peace. Most Soviet officers and senior officials were not immune to this mixture of genuine anxiety and propaganda. In the run-up to the deployment of Euromissiles in November, concerns within the General Staff about the threat from the United States soared. According to General Gelii Batenin, one of the key missile experts working with Marshal Akhromeyev, "There was a great deal of tension in the General Staff at the time and we worked long hours, longer than usual. I don't recall a period more tense since the [Cuban Missile] Crisis in 1962."[1]

The KGB issued a top secret report to leading members of the Party and government stating that the United States had "prepared everything for a first-strike."[2] According to Soviet Military Intelligence, American "strategic forces" would be involved in *Able Archer*, Nato's annual exercise, which was due to start in early November.[3]

Over the past two years the Soviet media had whipped up fears that Reagan was pushing the world towards war. In the autumn of 1983 civil defense exercises were carried out, with air-raid and gas mask drills being practiced. Officially organized peace rallies were held in Moscow. A diplomatic interpreter returning to Moscow from abroad in November 1983 described the atmosphere as "pre-war."[4]

In Washington on October 28, Secretary of State Shultz had told Dobrynin, the Soviet ambassador, that "We are headed into a dangerous period, and we are not well equipped to manage it." He emphasized the importance of keeping open communications and keeping them private.[5]

Able Archer-83

Crises seemed to be breaking out everywhere. In late October, 241 American service personnel and 58 French paratroopers had been killed when suicide bombers attacked their barracks in Beirut, where they were part of a UN peacekeeping mission; in the Caribbean, American troops had just begun invading the island of Grenada to overthrow its extreme left-wing government and, in Vienna, the Russians had withdrawn from the negotiations on reducing conventional forces in Europe.

In this strained atmosphere, Nato went ahead with its preparations for exercise *Able Archer-83*, which would run from November 2–11. This was one of those annual "war games" that tested procedures and communications but without any weapons being involved. Each year the scenario was different, but always led to the Supreme Commander requesting permission to use nuclear weapons and receiving it. The exercise ended with him issuing "dummy" orders to fire "tactical" missiles, not American strategic ones.

Since General Rogers became the Supreme Allied Commander Europe in 1979, he had been keen to involve political leaders in this type of exercise because, as he later explained, "getting the political decisions made in time is not as predictable as I would like to believe or like to see."[6] In 1983, for the first time, top political and military leaders were going to take part, with the president, Mrs. Thatcher and other heads of government being involved in the opening phase. However, because of the tensions in East-West relations only officials, not politicians, took part. This was widely known in Nato circles and therefore to the Soviets, which should have calmed them somewhat.

Given all the tensions leading up to *Able Archer* in 1983, however, it is hardly surprising that the Soviet leadership took a much more active interest in *Able Archer* than in previous years. From the considerable amount of once highly secret intelligence that has emerged since the end of the Cold War, we can now see fairly clearly what was happening on both sides.[7]

In the West

The Nato participants in *Able Archer* did not think that the Soviet General Staff would be concerned about their exercise because they had been monitoring this and other Nato exercises for years. However, hardly any of the analysts in the West who monitored Soviet military activity knew either of the exercise or of the psy-ops that had preceded it.

The first indication of Soviet concern about the exercise came from Colonel Oleg Gordievsky, a senior KGB officer in London who was Britain's top Soviet agent.[8] He had been keeping British Intelligence informed about *RYAN*, the KGB's operation aimed at detecting signs that the West was preparing to launch a surprise nuclear attack against the Soviet Union. Since February, KGB headquarters had been sending its residencies in Western Europe more detailed briefings about the way Nato worked and instructions on the information they were to begin reporting. Then, out of the blue, on November 8 or 9, when *Able Archer* was almost over, KGB residencies abroad received a "most urgent" telegram from headquarters.

The telegram claimed that American forces had been put on "alert," when in fact the Americans had simply been tightening security at their overseas bases since the recent massacre in Beirut. The most interesting feature of this telegram was that it listed several possible explanations for this so-called "alert," one of which was that the countdown to a nuclear first-strike had begun under the cover of *Able Archer.* Residencies were instructed to confirm the alert and evaluate the hypotheses.[9]

In the East

The Soviet General Staff had little enthusiasm for war, but they had always hoped that, in a crisis, they could gain the upper hand through deception. As a result, they were prone to think that their adversaries would turn the tables on them.

In talking about the events of 1983, Colonel-General Ivan Yesin, of the Soviet Strategic Missiles Forces, explained that "these large-scale military exercises that they [Nato] conducted were just fraught with possibilities that under the cover of such an exercise an unexpected nuclear missile strike could be launched."[10]

The General Staff shared such concerns. On the day that *Able Archer* began, November 2, it now seems certain that Marshal Ogarkov moved to his war-time command bunker deep beneath Moscow and ordered a "heightened alert" for some of his forces. This was done in the greatest secrecy, as Ogarkov was not willing to take action that would itself generate new tensions.[11]

"Although our warning system was not perfect, we were receiving an extraordinary range of intelligence on Soviet and Warsaw Pact military activities," according to Fritz Ermarth, the senior Soviet expert on the National Intelligence Council. "This would show whether their forces had been put on a higher alert, were on the move or were readying for a major offensive. We had been highly successful in tracking Soviet preparations to intervene in Afghanistan, but like members of the General Staff we did not think that the Politburo would be so dumb as to take that fatal step. None of the details detected at the time of *Able Archer* crossed the thresholds that would have made our warning lights begin to flash."

What the CIA could not "see" was that at least part of the land-based Soviet missile force went on heightened alert. This included SS-19s, an intercontinental ballistic missile with ten warheads, which remained hidden in their silos, as well as seventy-five of the mobile SS-20 missiles that were targeted on Western Europe, which had been moved out of their garrisons to well-camouflaged wartime firing positions. "This fact," General Yesin said, "was not communicated to the rest of the armed forces."[12]

In 2006, both General Yesin, who had commanded the SS-20s, and Viktor Tkachenko, a captain in charge of ten of the SS-19s, said that they knew that this was part of an elaborate training exercise. As General Yesin put it: "we knew that Nato were doing an exercise, not really preparing for the nuclear blow, although of course we couldn't fully eliminate the possibility that the nuclear strike might have been delivered."[13]

The senior members of the General Staff viewed things somewhat differently. General Andrian Danilevich, the renowned Soviet strategist, acknowledged in 1992 that the early eighties were a "period of great tension." He added that, "despite all the propaganda, we did not really believe that you would attack, although there were some frightening situations." Even so, in 1983, there was never a "war scare" in the headquarters of the General Staff, where he was working at this time. "No one," he said, "believed there was an immediate threat of a nuclear strike from the United States or Nato."[14]

The absence of panic in Moscow is attested to by Rainer Rupp, the star agent of East German Intelligence at Nato headquarters. He was not contacted by East German Intelligence about *Able Archer* until November 9, the same day that KGB headquarters had sent out its "most urgent" request for information. He responded immediately, saying that "There was no indication that Nato was preparing for war at that time." He was never contacted on this matter again.[15]

In that frame of mind, Soviet Military Intelligence, as always, assiduously monitored Nato communications. In addition, other Soviet Military Intelligence officers roamed around Western Europe in cars with listening devices to intercept any other communications they could and, above all, to make sure that *Able Archer* was still an exercise, not a guise for launching missiles. Meanwhile, in West Germany, many of East Germany's "over 500 very important" spies were also on the lookout for unusual activity.[16]

At dawn on November 11, the command post for *Able Archer* signaled the order for nuclear missiles to be launched against targets in Eastern Europe and the Soviet Union. Soviet Military Intelligence did not flinch, because they knew they were monitoring an exercise. As General Gelii Batenin, Marshal Ogarkov's deputy, explained, "We had confidence in our knowledge of when Nato was preparing to launch nuclear weapons. We would detect mating of warheads to missiles and uploading of nuclear bombs and artillery. We listened to the hourly circuit verification signal on your nuclear release communications systems and we believed we would recognize a release order."[17]

Protest & Pragmatism

Meanwhile, in London, Gordievsky was telling SIS about the "most urgent" telegram that had arrived from KGB headquarters during exercise *Able Archer*. "I felt that this was a further and disturbing reflection of the increasing paranoia in Moscow," Gordievsky told me some years later, "but not a cause of urgent concern in the absence of other indications, especially as Moscow was pumping out a lot of what I knew was war-scare propaganda at this time."

In his memoirs, President Reagan wrote that, on November 18, he had had "a most sobering experience . . . a briefing on our complete plan in the event of a nuclear attack. Simply put, it was a scenario for a sequence of events that could lead to the end of civilization as we knew it." That night, he noted in his diary, "George Shultz and I had a talk about . . . setting up some channels. I feel the Soviets are . . . so paranoid about being attacked . . . that we ought to tell them no one here has any intention of doing anything like that. What the h—l have they got that anyone would want."[18]

The timing was good as Moscow would soon vent its frustration at its failure to thwart the arrival of cruise and Pershing-II missiles in Europe. In a statement published in Moscow on November 25, two days after the arrival of the first Pershing-II missiles in Germany, Andropov lambasted the Reagan Administration for being "bent on world domination" and wanting to "launch a decapitating nuclear first-strike." He pointed to "the dangerous consequences of that course."

The statement also announced military counter-measures, including the deployment of even more Soviet missiles in East Germany and Czechoslovakia, along with the redeployment of Soviet submarines carrying ballistic missiles closer to the United States, from where they would be able to strike targets with little warning.[19] The Soviet delegation had already walked out of the INF negotiations, saying they would never return while those American missiles remained in Europe. Shortly thereafter they suspended the negotiations on strategic nuclear forces and conventional forces in Europe.

When Ambassador Oleg Grinevsky, the Soviet arms control expert, was summoned to see Andropov in hospital in December, he found him deeply depressed. The United States, Andropov told him, "wanted to . . . have the opportunity of striking the first strategic strike." He went on to lament that "our economy is in a pitiful condition" and that the Americans were doing everything possible to tie the Soviet Union down in Afghanistan. "We were unable to stop them from placing their medium-range missiles in Europe. Frankly, we lost that battle."

Then very appropriately Andropov, the well-educated former head of the KGB, went on to quote a popular French song about an aristocratic lady telephoning her chateau to ask how thing are and being told, "Tout va tres bien, Madame la Marquise," before the butler goes on to tell her of one disaster after another. "The Americans," Andropov said, "will be playing the song . . . and you will be made to sing the chorus."[20]

As Andropov's condition continued to worsen, a new air of pragmatism began to emerge in Moscow. Shortly after *Able Archer*, Wolf told me, "one of my senior officers returned from Moscow with the message that not only was *Operation RYAN* no longer such a high priority, but the threat from the West had been downgraded."

This turnaround in Moscow's attitude had been confirmed by a speech given by Marshal Ustinov, the Soviet defense minister, in Moscow on December 14, 1983. He said that, "no matter how complicated the military and political situation, there is no point in dramatizing it" and the Soviet Union was not frightened by threats.[21] Reagan also noted that Ustinov had proposed a ban on nuclear weapons.

Three days before Christmas, Bill Casey, the director of Central Intelligence and one of the president's close friends, told him that the CIA had just received a report from one of its sources saying that in November, Soviet Military Intelligence had instructed all posts to obtain early warning of enemy military preparations so that the Soviet Union would not be surprised by the actual threat of war.[22]

Casey's intelligence reinforced the president's conviction that the time had come to take a more conciliatory line. In a television address to the American people on January 16, the president stressed that the foremost interest of the two countries was "to avoid war and reduce the level of arms." There was no alternative to finding areas of "constructive cooperation." He ended with a touching, folksy tale about the longing of ordinary Russians and Americans for peace.[23]

By Reagan's standards, Dobrynin observed, this was "a remarkably conciliatory message."[24] The Soviet leadership as a whole were well on the way to realizing that they would have to make far greater efforts to end confrontation with the United States and try to reform their country.

Sharing Concerns

"Since the Falklands War, Mrs. Thatcher had given a lot of thought to the Soviet Union," according to Charles Powell, her private secretary dealing with foreign affairs. "Buoyed by that victory, she felt the time had come to move beyond the rhetoric of the 'evil empire' and think how the West could bring the Cold War to an end."

Andropov's death on February 9, 1984, provided a welcome opportunity for

Thatcher to go to Moscow to meet the Soviet leadership, which was now headed by the aged Konstantin Chernyenko. As the funeral cortege passed through Red Square on Febuary 14 Vice President Bush, President Mitterrand and Chancellor Kohl chatted among themselves, while Mrs. Thatcher, clad in black, stood in respectful silence, like the Soviet leaders themselves.

In discussions with Chernyenko and his colleagues after the funeral, each of the Western leaders reiterated their willingness to open up a dialogue with the Soviet Union. No one surprised the Soviet leaders more than the "Iron Lady." She spoke in seductively breathy tones about the importance of "peace." In doing so, she was not only exploiting her charm, but the fact that among the Western leaders, she knew the most about Soviet paranoia—thanks to the reports she was receiving from Oleg Gordievsky.

"Meanwhile," Gordievsky told me, "an important piece of new information prompted a serious discussion about how my very sensitive intelligence could be used most effectively. In January, my British friends told me that 'the experts' had detected some military indications which suggested that Moscow might have been really nervous about what would happen during *Able Archer* and, much later, I learned that one of these was that Soviet aircraft 'capable' of carrying nuclear weapons had been placed on runway-alert in East Germany."

"Although that crisis seemed to have passed, I felt that Soviet-American relations remained very fraught and there was much that the Americans still needed to understand about Soviet activities and thinking," Gordievsky continued. "I welcomed their suggestion to pass some of my reports, carefully disguised, to key players in Washington."[25]

On the day of Andropov's funeral, February 14, the first report from British Intelligence on the "war scare" reached Washington. One former senior CIA officer recalled years later that this top secret report "quoted a Czechoslovak intelligence officer as saying that for over a year his service had been tasked with monitoring major Nato exercises, which Moscow feared could be used as cover for the preparation of a pre-emptive nuclear strike."[26]

"About a month later," according to this officer, "we received another report from the British about Soviet perceptions of the military threat from the West. What really caught our attention was that, on at least two occasions during 1983, this Soviet official said he had seen documents which betrayed a genuine nervousness that such a pre-emptive strike could take place at any time, for example under cover of a routine military exercise. The official explained that although very few Soviet officials with direct experience of the West took the threat of an American first-strike seriously, such a fear was widespread in senior Party circles. The Soviet military, too, had a simplistic view of the West."

When Robert Gates, at the time the Deputy Director of Intelligence at the CIA, saw these reports, he realized that the source was well informed, but he did not know that it was Gordievsky. In 2006 he recalled that "My first reaction to the [Gordievsky] reporting was not only that we might have had a major intelligence failure, but further that the most terrifying thing about *Able Archer* was that we may have been at the brink of nuclear war and not even known it."

Extensive research was already underway in Washington on what the Soviet response to *Able Archer* had been, with Fritz Ermarth, the Soviet expert on the National Intelligence Council, leading the project. Senior members of the Administration were kept abreast of the evolving analysis. When the Special National Intelligence Estimate on the *Implications of Recent Soviet Military-Political Activities* was issued on May 18 it concluded with the carefully balanced judgment that the Soviet Union did not foresee "an imminent military clash but a costly and—to some extent—more perilous strategic and political struggle over the rest of the decade."[27] That was spot on.

Gordievsky recalled that "From early in 1984 through Gorbachev's early months as leader, many more of my reports were passed to Washington—on several important aspects of Soviet foreign policy." Gates emphasized the importance of the role Gordievsky played, pointing out that "he was giving us information about the thinking of the leadership, and that kind of information was, for us, scarce as hen's teeth."[28] According to Bud McFarlane, the national security adviser, the president was "very moved" when he saw the summaries of Gordievsky's reports.[29]

In April, following discussions with the prime minister, the British told a few key people in the Reagan Administration that the available evidence appeared to reflect a disturbing state of mind in the Soviet leadership. Gordievsky's reports reinforced Reagan's conviction that a greater effort had to be made not just to reduce tension, but to end the Cold War.

Will "Our Germans" Betray Us?

Since the beginning of the eighties, Moscow's relations with East Berlin had gone from bad to worse. "Once Brezhnev was gone," Wolf said, "Honecker saw himself as one of the elder statesmen of the socialist bloc and was even less inclined than before to do as he was told." Above all, to keep East Germany going,

Honecker required continuing support from West Germany. "In the traditions of Faust," Wolf laughingly observed, "Honecker believed he could get the better of the West German 'devil,' but Moscow did not."

To win public support at home and with West Germany, Honecker had been making East Germany more "German." Historic buildings were being restored, the statue of Fredrick the Great was returned to its former pride of place in the Unter den Linden, television programs were made about Prussian military heroes and the 500th anniversary of Martin Luther's birth was celebrated. Once again, Honecker held out the possibility of unification were West Germany to become more socialist.

Honecker's domestic policies were rapidly increasing East Germany's indebtedness. His childlike faith in new technology made him bet heavily on being able to create an electronics industry that could rival Japan's. Wolf's intelligence service acquired detailed accounts of the management processes IBM used to develop new products. "However, our very talented East German industrial managers who traveled abroad knew," Wolf said, "we simply could not implement the plans unless we changed the system itself. But Honecker was not willing to accept such advice."

As a result, East German microchips were forty times more expensive than those available on the international market. On one occasion, Honecker presented Gorbachev with an advanced microchip that he claimed had been produced in East Germany. Wolf felt that Honecker was losing his sense of reality because, as he told me, "that chip wasn't produced here, my service had acquired it abroad."

In the absence of reform, stagnation soon led to atrophy, then disillusionment. By the early eighties, key groups—teachers, professors, business leaders, writers—were losing faith in the regime. So, too, were senior people in the party. East Germany seemed locked into a precipitous spiral of decline. "We would joke," Wolf laughingly recalled, "that the seven people who took our TV programs seriously were all members of the Politburo; everyone else watched West German TV."

At this time, Helmut Kohl, West Germany's mainstream conservative chancellor, began to pursue his *Deutschlandpolitik*, which reflected his belief that the Federal Republic's ties with the West would not remain healthy without a corresponding effort to expand ties between the two Germanys.[30] He set out to improve the lot of East Germans, alleviating the personal hardship created for families by the division of Germany and fostering the "unity" of the country. In 1983, Kohl arranged a $400-million trade credit for East Germany.

In return, Honecker agreed that landmines and automatic firing devices would be removed from along the East German side of the border. In September 1983, just two months before Euromissiles would be deployed in West Germany, the East Germans began talking about the need to establish "a coalition of reason." Honecker did not want a souring of East-West relations to deprive him of the economic assistance from West Germany on which he was now so dependent.

Moscow's suspicions were mounting, fueled by reports that another huge West German loan was in the offing. "At one of our regular sauna sessions," Wolf recollected, "two top party officials told me that Chernyenko distrusted Honecker." He feared that Honecker was trying to foster a pan-Germanic identity that would supersede socialist solidarity.[31]

East Germany was not Chernyenko's only headache. Both Hungary and Romania also wanted to preserve détente. Indeed, relations were so bad within the Warsaw Pact that no meeting of its Political Consultative Committee was held in January 1984—which was the first time that had ever happened. Shortly thereafter, East Germany received an even larger credit from West Germany than the previous year. In August 1984, Chernyenko humiliatingly ordered Honecker to cancel his plans to visit West Germany. Honecker was told that the Soviet leadership did not share his view that a persistent "peace" effort might eventually alter the political course of the Federal Republic.[32]

Reestablishing Contact

Andropov's death had not removed the pile of contentious issues in Soviet-American relations, but both sides did edge towards a resumption of discussions and arms control negotiations. Meanwhile, Reagan, like Nixon and Carter before him, sought to keep up the pressure on Moscow by developing links with China, which he visited in April 1984. The Chinese and the Americans were cooperating on the collection of intelligence on Soviet missile tests, helping the mujahedin in their fight against Soviet forces in Afghanistan, and expanding trade.

Reagan believed Soviet intervention (along with that of the Cubans) was the source of social unrest and revolution not solely in Afghanistan, but also in Angola, Nicaragua, Ethiopia and other parts of the Third World. It was America's moral duty to break the communist grip so that such countries could move towards—or return to—democracy and capitalism. America's ousting of the communist regime in Grenada in 1983 convinced him that this could be done.

Reagan's chief adviser on this subject was Casey, his friend and head of the CIA. In early 1984, Casey believed the Soviet Union was tremendously over-extended and vulnerable. If America could "bloody Russian noses in Afghanistan" that would shatter the myth that history was going their way, and seriously undermine Soviet credibility.[33] At first, he had hoped merely to contain the Soviet Union in Afghanistan; now he was confident that they could be defeated there and in Nicaragua.

After all the tension in Soviet-American relations in recent years, there was a groundswell of opinion in America for serious efforts to be made to open a dialogue with Moscow. The clearest manifestation of this came in June when the Senate passed a resolution calling for the earliest possible Soviet-American summit. Two months later, the White House invited Gromyko to resume his annual autumn visits for a discussion with the president. The Politburo considered this meeting to be so important that, for the first time, special instructions were drafted for Gromyko.

When Gromyko arrived in September, Reagan treated him more like a visiting head of state than a foreign minister. Both of them worked to improve the atmosphere. Reagan reiterated that his dream was a world without nuclear arms and Gromyko agreed that should be their eventual goal. Each of them emphasized their wish for "peace."

While chatting with the First Lady, Gromyko asked her to whisper "peace" in the president's ear every night. "Of course," she said, "and I'll whisper it in yours, too," whereupon she rose on tiptoe and did just that. It seems to have given him an unexpected thrill. He recounted this incident to the Politburo "with great animation."[34] At times in diplomacy, personal contacts do matter!

Following Gromyko's return home, the Politburo embarked on a "painful reassessment" of its policy.[35] At the end of November, the Soviet Union and the United States announced that they had agreed to begin a new set of arms control negotiations on strategic weapons, Euromissiles, and weapons in space. Shultz and Gromyko met in Geneva at the beginning of January 1985 to set the agenda.

Painful Reassessments

By the autumn of 1984, leaders in both Moscow and Washington were increasingly aware of just how great a shift in the balance of power had taken place.

The American economy was growing well, the standard of living was rising and exports booming; defense expenditure was soaring, with new major weapons systems being deployed and yet more advanced ones being developed; Western Europe was also doing well economically and despite strong protests by the peace movements Pershing-II and Gryphon cruise missiles had been deployed there.

The Soviet outlook, on the other hand, was depressing. The economy had stopped growing and was possibly shrinking; new weapons systems were still being produced, but the cost was imposing an intolerable burden on the Soviet economy; while Soviet troops were bogged down in Afghanistan, popular discontent was rising in Eastern Europe; and both the Soviet Union and the countries of Eastern Europe were increasingly dependent on borrowing money from the West.

The root cause of this historic shift in the balance of power was that the great experiment Lenin had embarked on in 1917 had been fundamentally flawed, especially in the economic domain. Fearful of reform, Lenin's successors kept hoping for economic miracles that never came. According to his son, Lavrenti Beria, the head of Stalin's secret service, believed that "the whole of economics was to be found in Adam Smith," not Karl Marx.[36]

By the mid-eighties, the weakened state of the Soviet economy owed much to Brandt's *Ostpolitik,* which was far more Machiavellian than is often realized. He had lured the Soviet and East European communist countries onto the road to perdition by getting them addicted to borrowing heavily from abroad—not from their friends, but their enemies. By 1985, the Soviet Union's foreign debt was already over $30 billion and that of Eastern Europe allies in excess of $70 billion, with both rising steeply. The constant need to borrow more money created a dependency on the West that restricted Soviet options and so, gradually, set political changes in motion across Eastern Europe.

Brent Scowcroft, President Bush's national security adviser, firmly believed, he told me, that "The notion that we spent the Soviet Union into bankruptcy is a fallacy; they had already done that to themselves and their system was doomed." Ben Fischer, a former chief historian of the CIA, put it yet more graphically when he said that "even before Gorbachev came into office in 1985 I felt that the Soviet 'knight' was, in John Le Carre's elegant metaphor, 'dying in his armor'—though with his last gasps of breath still being able to produce yet more potent weapons."

It was in 1985 that the Soviet leadership came to the conclusion that they could no longer afford to compete with the United States militarily—not simply on SDI, but also in the "revolution in military affairs," based on "smart" conventional weapons that could destroy tank armies in battles where the American commanders' power would be leveraged by computer technology. In the grand and costly tournament of military chess, there was little hope they that would be able to prevent the Americans from saying "Checkmate!"

In the late sixties and early seventies Washington had been the "*demandeur*" for détente; now that uncomfortable boot was firmly on the Soviet foot. This would be a painful experience, but the Soviets hoped that, by making some concessions to the Americans, they would agree to "live and let live." The Soviets still had not comprehended just how determined Reagan was to force the Cold War to an end, period. Reagan was managing to change the rules of the game that had already stretched out for more than three and a half decades. The remaining big question was the terms on which it would be settled—and this subject would dominate the Gorbachev era.

TRYING TO END THE COLD WAR

On his way to Washington Mikhail Gorbachev stops briefly in Britain to see Margaret Thatcher, December 7, 1987. (Courtesy of Graham Wiltshire)

29 The Gorbachev Response

The Making of a Soviet Radical

During his first term as president, Reagan was fond of saying that he would be happy to settle down to talk with Soviet leaders but "they keep dying on me." On March 10, 1985, Konstantin Chernyenko became the third Soviet leader to die in a space of two and a half years. The following day, the Politburo elected the 54-year-old Mikhail Gorbachev, thereby clearing the way for a fresh dialogue between the Soviet Union and the United States. In nominating him for the post of general secretary, Andrei Gromyko assured the Politburo that Gorbachev could be very tough.

At Moscow University, Gorbachev studied law under old professors whose intellects had been honed in pre-revolutionary Russia and pushed their students to think for themselves. They opened up, he recalled, "the history of human thought, a world we had not known, [and this] excited our minds."[1] He became what was known as "one of the children of the 20th Party Congress"—those who hoped that Khrushchev's denunciation of Stalin in 1956 would lead to the creation of "socialism with a human face."

Working for the party in Stavropol over the next two decades, Gorbachev was constantly reminded of the harsh realities of day-to-day life and the inability of the Soviet system to reform itself. The country was run, he later said, as a "hierarchy of vassals . . . it was a caste system based on mutual protection."[2] His wife, Raisa, shared his concerns and helped him to understand many local problems through the sociological research she was doing in the region.

The Gorbachevs had a prescient discussion about how socialism could be reformed with Zdenek Mlynar, one of their best friends from university, who came to stay with them in 1967. Mlynar insisted that socialist societies could never flourish unless they became genuinely democratic, a goal he tried to achieve the following year when he rose to prominence as one of the leaders of the Prague Spring. When Gorbachev visited Czechoslovakia after the Soviet suppression of that reform movement, he was deeply affected by the Czechoslovakians' hostility towards his country. He realized that what the Soviet press had been saying about Soviet troops being invited in at the request of "the people" was lies.[3]

Gorbachev's window into the outside world grew even wider when, in 1971, he became a member of the Central Committee. He could now order from a long list of foreign books that had been specially translated for the Soviet leadership—including Western ones about the Soviet Union, Euro-communism and the West itself. Besides receiving uncensored translations of the foreign press, he also read the banned underground Russian newspapers: *samizdat (*newspapers compiled in the Soviet Union) and *tamizdat* (which were smuggled in from abroad). These were full of information that rarely appeared in party publications.

As a rising young member of the Central Committee, Gorbachev was sent on a number of visits to Western Europe. Anatoly Chernyaev, who became his foreign affairs adviser in 1986, accompanied him on his first trip to the West—to Belgium and the Netherlands in 1972. As they drove across the country, Gorbachev went on and on about how important it was to do this or that in Stavropol. "He wasn't intrigued by the Amsterdam sex shops . . . He was embarrassed . . . But he didn't say anything," Chernyaev recalled.[4] Raisa later accompanied him on some of his trips to France, Germany and Italy, where they saw for themselves the many appealing qualities of Western life.

Gorbachev was particularly influenced by the flair the Italian communists had shown in adapting to new circumstances. Few events imprinted themselves on his mind more than the funeral of Enrico Berlinguer, the leader of the Italian communists, which Gorbachev attended in 1984. The Italian president and all the other leading politicians were present, along with over a million people, many of them not communists. This, he felt, was a mature civil society that respected different points of view.

It was through these travels and contacts that Gorbachev came to believe that only by cooperating with the wider world would the Soviet Union manage to undo the autarky and isolationism that had blighted it for so long.

Gorbachev Stakes His Claim

Gorbachev ran the Stravropol region so well that, in 1978, he was promoted to be in charge of agriculture at the party secretariat in Moscow. Yuri Andropov had been instrumental in his appointment. Just two years later, Gorbachev became a full member of the Politburo, where from close quarters he watched the Soviet political system become dysfunctional as one ailing Party leader replaced another. By the spring of 1984 he rose to be the party secretary in charge of ideology and, as such, effectively No. 2 in the Party.

To improve his chances of becoming the next Soviet leader, Gorbachev needed to show that he could handle world affairs. Soon after he arrived in Moscow, he started inviting top academics for regular discussions on a wide range of international topics, an unprecedented practice for someone who was not responsible for these matters. By the time Mrs. Thatcher invited a Soviet "parliamentary" delegation to visit London in 1984, he was able to arrange for himself to head the delegation; the instructions the Politburo approved for his discussions with Mrs. Thatcher and others gave him no difficulty—after all, he had drafted them.[5]

"When the smiling Mr. Gorbachev and his wife strode confidently into the great hall at Chequers, Mrs. T.'s official country residence, you could see at a glance, that this was someone different," according to Charles Powell, her private secretary. "The four-hour discussion between Gorbachev and Mrs. Thatcher," he said, "marked the beginning of the first real dialogue between the Soviet Union and the West. Over lunch they talked incessantly, hardly touching their food."

With charm and an engaging frankness, Gorbachev showed himself to be refreshingly open-minded; he clearly wished to explore ways of easing East-West tensions. The nuclear age, Gorbachev said, demanded new thinking, and security was a political problem that could only be solved by political means.

In a speech to British parliamentarians, Gorbachev reiterated these thoughts, adding that "Whatever is dividing us, we live on the same planet and Europe is our common home"—words that were much quoted.[6] His statements in London encapsulated the ideas that would characterize his foreign policy once he became Soviet leader.

There were several reasons why Gorbachev's visit to London went so well, but one factor that has generally been overlooked is the very constructive use that the British made of intelligence. As Gordievsky explains in his memoirs, "my friends in the British Service let me see the brief which the foreign secretary [Geoffrey Howe] would be using" in his talk with Gorbachev. Gordievsky later added that his friends had also helped him write a highly illuminating and positive account of Mrs. Thatcher for Gorbachev, while, for his part, Gordievsky had provided her with Gorbachev's brief for their meeting at Chequers.[7]

Mrs. Thatcher told the world that Gorbachev was a man she "could do business with" and privately urged President Reagan to meet him.[8] "She said to Gorbachev," Powell recalled, "'You may regard Reagan as a monster, but he is not. He is a reasonable man who wants to reach an understanding with the Soviet Union. You must talk with him, but don't think you can ever drive a wedge between us, because we are absolutely at one.'"

Such an "understanding" for Mrs. Thatcher, as for Reagan, Powell emphasized, would mean the end of communism, though that was something that she never expected to see in her lifetime. "She always said to Gorbachev that communism was a hopeless system; if you want to try to reform it, go ahead, but that will never work. The consequences of reform she said, very perceptively, will be the end of communism."

As Mrs. Thatcher was a kindred spirit who shared many of the president's convictions, he accepted her judgment of Gorbachev and hoped that he would become the next Soviet leader. There was also an item in the British press that caught the president's eye and made him hope that Gorbachev would be the next Soviet leader: it was Gorbachev's remark that "The Soviet Union is prepared to advance towards the complete prohibition and eventual elimination of nuclear weapons."[9]

Taking the Reins

On March 11, 1985, the day he became the new Soviet leader, Gorbachev told Raisa "we can't go on living like this."[10] He wanted to revitalize the Soviet system, thereby securing for the Soviet Union an honorable place in the vanguard of world history.

Gorbachev embarked on this task buoyed by a great self-confidence in his own ability to shape events. His strategy was to lead this transformation from the top, and to implement it through the party machine that ran the country, while keeping close to both the army and the KGB, two powerful consituencies that could derail his plans. Gorbachev's policy of *perestroika,* or "restructuring," attracted support both from the party conservatives who believed that it would help preserve the existing system, and from the liberals who hoped that it would lead to real democracy and a more dynamic economy.

Shortly after taking office, Gorbachev told his colleagues that, as he saw it, the problem was that "we are encircled not by invincible armies, but by superior economies."[11] "He was absolutely right," Vadim Medvedev, a member of his

Politburo, told me. "Real growth rates had been close to zero for some years and average Soviet living standards were only somewhere around those of Portugal, the poorest country in Western Europe. Qualitatively we were lagging some 15 to 20 years behind the West." One indication of this was that in 1985 there were probably just 50,000 PCs in the Soviet Union, mostly of poor quality, while in America the number was closer to 30 million and the quality far superior.[12]

The stoic Soviet people, however, were not demanding change. As a result, Gorbachev was able to focus on what he saw as the key issue, which was to free them from the siege mentality that constrained innovation. And for that to happen, the Cold War had to be ended.

In the hours following his election Gorbachev took a sheet of paper and wrote down what he considered to be his major objectives in foreign policy—"stop the arms race, withdraw from Afghanistan, change the spirit of relations with the United States, restore co-operation with China."[13] At meetings with foreign leaders after Chernyenko's funeral, Gorbachev emphasized that it was necessary to settle disputes by political means, with each nation allowed to "live as it wishes."[14]At this stage, according to Anatoly Chernyaev, who was soon to become his principal foreign policy aide, Gorbachev believed that "scaling down the Cold War meant basically scaling down the arms race."[15]

Gorbachev's "new thinking" on foreign affairs reflected his deep aversion to violence and his rejection of the idea that there really was an "imperialist threat." The military and the military-industrial complex, however, adamantly refused to lower their guard. Alexander Yakovlev, a leading member of Gorbachev's Politburo told me that "every week they would put forward some new proposal . . . always claiming that there was some new threat."

Gorbachev was able to make some headway because, as Marshal Akhromeyev, the chief of the General Staff later put it, "Those who knew the real conditions of our government and its economy in the middle of the 1980s understood that there had to be major changes in the foreign policy of the Soviet government. The Soviet Union could not continue the confrontation with the United States and Nato after 1985. The economic resources for such a policy had been practically exhausted."[16]

In April, for the first time publicly, Gorbachev declared that defense should be based on "sufficiency" and he halted the deployment of more SS-20 missiles. Reshaping Soviet policy would take time, in part because he needed to maintain Soviet military morale and to show Reagan that the Soviet Union would not be pushed around. Meanwhile, costly new weapons continued to be developed and produced, including mobile intercontinental ballistic missiles, modernized submarines that carried more effective ballistic missiles, and a far more advanced type of aircraft carrier that would help project Soviet power overseas.

Although Gorbachev derived considerable power from being general secretary, he needed time to establish his authority. Easing Cold War tensions was not just a matter of figuring out what he and his supporters were willing to settle for, but what the "system" would tolerate. As a result, Gorbachev was the first Soviet leader who was obliged to act like a Western politician, carefully choosing his words to keep the support of different groups. Gorbachev's statements on a whole range of issues confused many Western observers, and provided ammunition to those who argued that his primary intent was to make the Soviet Union strong again.

Heading Back to Geneva

Initially, Gorbachev tried to exploit the distaste some West European governments had for Reagan's policies by linking his diplomatic initiatives to propaganda campaigns aimed at the peace movements that were calling for a nuclear freeze. Gorbachev took this approach during his visit to Paris in October, his first to the West since becoming Soviet leader. Although the French gave Gorbachev a warm welcome, President Mitterrand did not break ranks, choosing instead to push ahead with modernizing France's nuclear forces.

In his diary Chernyaev observed, "Yet another effort in Russia's centuries-old attempt to embrace Europe. And again—irony, coldness, and polite condescension . . . We're in danger of going back to historic bitterness, especially if the Geneva meeting with Reagan does not work out." To give that summit a better chance of success, Gorbachev gave an interview to *Time* magazine, in which he spoke with refreshing openness and clarity about the need for the United States and the Soviet Union to "live-and-let-live."[17]

Gorbachev was in no doubt that his first meeting with Reagan would be far tougher than his encounter with Mrs. Thatcher at Chequers. It was not until July 1 that these two men agreed to meet in Geneva in November. On that very day, Gorbachev signaled that important changes were in the offing by appointing a like-minded friend named Eduard Shevardnadze to replace Andrei Gromyko as foreign minister. Gromyko had been set in his ways for too long.

In preparing for Geneva, Gorbachev's room for maneuver was limited by two considerable constraints. First, in order to facilitate reforms at home he needed to halt the arms race quickly; and second, for domestic political reasons he could not make unilateral concessions on such contentious issues as arms control. The only way out of this conundrum was to persuade Reagan to end the arms race and agree to deep cuts.

For the Soviet leadership, Reagan's Strategic Defense Initiative (SDI) was unquestionably the key issue. Gorbachev accepted the view of his scientific advisers that SDI was probably unfeasible and certainly did not constitute an imminent danger. If the Americans went ahead with it, however, they might be able to develop something that would undermine Soviet security. Counter-balancing SDI could take a decade and cost tens of billions of dollars, even if the main thrust of the counter-measures was through the modernization of Soviet intercontinental ballistic missiles.[18]

"It was absolutely clear" to Gorbachev, Chernyaev recalled, that "he would have to go very far" to secure an agreement with Reagan.[19] When Shevarnadze called on the president on September 27, during his first visit to Washington, he proposed 50% cuts in strategic nuclear arsenals, far deeper than the Soviet side had ever offered before. Secretary of State Shultz recognized that they marked a breakthrough even though the formula Shevardnadze had used to calculate the cuts was strongly skewed in Moscow's favor, and the cuts themselves were conditional on a complete ban on SDI.

The other issue Gorbachev was determined to resolve was Afghanistan. In the spring of 1985, shortly after taking office, he jotted on his working pad that "the conflict should be resolved in stages."[20] That summer, however, Gorbachev approved a surge in the war against the mujahedin, in the hope that it would create a breathing space for the Afghan regime to consolidate its position.

Whereas Gorbachev wanted an agreement banning SDI, Reagan wanted one that would accept it and was desperately seeking advice on how this could be sold to Gorbachev. Suddenly, on September 12, Bill Casey, the director of Central Intelligence, felt that he might be able to get some "inside" advice on this and other subjects. That day the British informed him that Gordievsky, who had recently returned to Britain after making a dramatic escape from Moscow, was the source of the very sensitive reports on Soviet paranoia and policy that he had seen over the past year and a half. Casey immediately flew to Britain to ask Gordievsky what he could tell the president about how Gorbachev was likely to approach the summit.[21]

Gordievsky offered Casey valuable insights into Soviet thinking. "I explained to him that Moscow was so keen to thwart SDI that Gorbachev might agree to eliminate all the Soviet SS-20 missiles in Europe and make deep cuts in strategic missiles forces." He went on to warn Casey, however, that "Gorbachev would view any offer to share SDI technology as a trick to drag the Soviet Union into massive and wasteful expenditure and provide an opportunity to spy on what technology it might have."

"That meeting with Gordievsky made a deep impression on Casey," one of his staff recalled; "so, too, did the hundreds of pages of reports summarizing Gordievsky's intelligence that a special courier had delivered to Casey's office in Washington while he was in London."[22] Four days later, at a meeting of the National Security Council in Washington, Casey forewarned the president and Shultz of the line that Gorbachev would take.[23] The private briefing the president received from Casey reinforced his conviction that, in the absence of Soviet acceptance of SDI, arms cuts should not be agreed to until it was clear that Gorbachev was really changing the Soviet Union and virtually every aspect of Soviet foreign policy.

The atmosphere for the summit improved as the result of an inspired discussion that Shultz had with Gorbachev in Moscow shortly beforehand. Contrary to the advice of his staff, who thought it would be patronizing, Shultz made time to explain to Gorbachev that the changes in the world economy were being driven by an information revolution and for any country to benefit from it, its scientists would have to be in constant touch with the "thinking community" around the world. "Shultz's approach," Gorbachev's interpreter Pavel Palazhchenko pointed out, "really gave Gorbachev the sense that the two sides could discuss big issues of common concern and gave an impetus to his reflections on the reforms he needed to pursue."[24] But this did not mean that the talks at the summit would not be tough.

30 Getting to Know You

The Geneva Summit

When Gorbachev and Reagan first met, at the elegant lakeside Villa Fleur d'Eau in Geneva in November 1985, they still had many reasons for distrusting each other. The message Gorbachev wanted to convey to Reagan was "we have to learn to live together," while Reagan's was "we can live together, but only on my terms." Despite this great divide, they both needed to be seen as capable of doing business with each other, not only by their respective colleagues and allies, but in the case of Reagan by the American public.

The process was complicated because Reagan was keen to exploit every chance to gain the psychological advantage, especially the moment of their first encounter at the entrance to the villa. Sergei Tarasenko, who arrived with Gorbachev, recalled "I saw President Reagan coming out to greet Gorbachev in a well-tailored suit . . . He projected an image of a young, dynamic leader. And Gorbachev came out of his tank-like limo . . . in a standard Politburo hat, in a scarf and . . . a heavy overcoat, looking like an old guy." This was all the more remarkable because, at seventy-four, Reagan was twenty years older than Gorbachev.[1]

Once inside, the two men settled down with their interpreters for what was supposed to be an initial friendly chat. Reagan immediately launched into one of his jokes. "An American and a Russian meet. 'My country is best,' the American says, 'because I can walk to the White House and tell the president he is doing a lousy job.' 'Big deal,' responds the Russian. 'My country is just as good. I can go to the Kremlin and tell Gorbachev the same thing: 'Reagan is doing a lousy job.'" Gorbachev laughed politely at this joke, but barely smiled at the increasingly barbed ones that followed.[2]

In retrospect, Gorbachev felt "It was like 'No. 1 Communist' and 'No. 1 Imperialist' trying to out-argue each other."[3] Reagan set the ball rolling. For years Reagan had relished the thought of telling the leader of the Soviet Union:

"Enough is enough."[4] He launched off with "Let me tell you, Mr. Secretary General, why we fear you and why we despise your system." Gorbachev did not overreact.[5]

As expected, the main bone of contention was SDI. Allowing SDI to go ahead would, Gorbachev insisted, foment mistrust and drive the arms race into the more dangerous realm of space. He tried to assure Reagan that once the development of "space weapons" had been banned, the Soviet Union would be willing to embark on deep cuts in strategic nuclear weapons.

Although this friction would plague their discussions over the next few years, these two men were bound together by their profound antipathy towards nuclear weapons. Chernyaev, who would soon become Gorbachev's foreign policy adviser, noted that Gorbachev had a "dogged determination to prove to all that nuclear weapons were an absolute evil and unacceptable foundation for world politics." The first breakthrough came with their agreement that "nuclear war cannot be won and must not be fought" and "We shall not seek superiority over each other . . ."[6] The latter phrase proved to be one that unlocked the door to serious discussions on arms control.

On the highly sensitive issue of Afghanistan, Gorbachev said Soviet forces did not intend to remain there. He refused, however, to abandon Nicaragua's Sandinistas, whose cause he felt was just. Recently he had increased Soviet aid to Nicaragua by 40%, in large part to offset the American trade embargo and in part as retaliation for American aid to the mujahedin in Afghanistan.

Reagan left Geneva with respect and liking for Gorbachev. And by the small gesture of including in his toast a quote from the bible ("For everything there is a season . . ."), Gorbachev had shown just how different he was from his predecessors. Gorbachev was less positive, initially describing Reagan as a "dinosaur" to his staff. But on his return to Moscow he told his Politburo colleagues that the two sides would have to find a way to get along together.[7]

"This was a defining moment," Chernyaev recollected. "Gorbachev had decided to end the arms race no matter what . . . Equally importantly, he decided to abandon our traditional approach of trying to isolate the Americans and focus on negotiating directly with Reagan."

A Change of Attitude

Back in Moscow, Gorbachev devoted much attention to preparing for the first party congress he would preside over, which would take place in February

1986. The practical task, as he saw it, was "to search for a realistic way to end the Cold War and find a way out of the mistrust, hostility and confrontation."[8]

As part of the preparations for the congress, Gorbachev issued a "program" that emphasized the "interconnectedness, interdependence and integrity of the world" and called for a nuclear-free world by the year 2000. The military had proposed the idea, rather like the American "hawks," in the mistaken belief that the other side would never accept it.[9]

By the spring, Gorbachev was telling his Politburo that "We have to stop being afraid of SDI." Weeks later he made it clear to the military that he did not accept that there would ever be a war with America, so "Don't put any war-fighting plans on my desk."[10] In the same vein he told them that "We want Europe to be completely free of these [SS-20 missiles] because the Pershing-II missiles are like a pistol held at our head."[11] The General Staff was soon tasked with preparing a new "defensive strategy" for the Warsaw Pact.[12]

The accident at the nuclear reactor in Chernobyl in April 1986 resulted in the death of twenty-eight people within weeks and many more over the next few years, with winds spreading increased levels of radiation across large parts of Europe. This terrible accident, which could have been a true catastrophe, brought home the sheer horror that nuclear weapons could cause and left no one in any doubt that Europe was a single continent, not one divided by an impenetrable wall between East and West. Yevgeny Velikov, one of the leading scientists in the Soviet Academy of Sciences, observed that "Chernobyl pushed Gorbachev towards 'a great instinctive leap' to break the deadlock in Soviet-Western relations."[13]

Gorbachev's determination to secure deep cuts in armaments was also heightened as he came to see that the Soviet defense establishment was a far more voracious "moloch" than he had previously thought. It was behaving as "a state within a state."[14] "Eventually, Gorbachev received a top secret briefing," Chernyaev told me, "that suggested 'defense' was consuming around a third of national income. And to make matters worse it was also employing some 75% of the country's best brains."[15]

"In a 'secret' speech to top Soviet diplomats in May 1986, Gorbachev charted a new course in our foreign policy," Chernyaev, the drafter of the speech, recalled. Gorbachev told them that their main task was to secure national security by political means, rather than pouring the nation's resources into preparations for an improbable conflict with some potential aggressor.[16]

To Reykjavik

After Geneva, Reagan's advisers remained deeply split. Weinberger, Casey and Perle pointed to strong historical precedents for refusing to believe that Gorbachev was operating in good faith. Shultz, on the other hand, was convinced that Gorbachev's initiatives were a prelude to radical changes in Soviet policy at home and abroad. He also felt that "1986 would be our year of maximum leverage," as support for the defense budget had peaked and that for SDI would decrease. "We had twelve months or so to achieve significant arms reductions . . ."[17]

Reagan kept up the pressure on Gorbachev. After a new round of American nuclear tests, Reagan accused Moscow of breaching the Salt-II treaty and said that the United States would no longer be bound by it. Next, American warships for the first time entered the twelve-mile territorial waters claimed by the Soviet Union along the Crimean coast of the Black Sea. On April 15, 1986, following a Libyan terrorist attack on American servicemen in Berlin, an attack that was facilitated by the East Germans, the Americans bombed Libya—despite its close ties with Moscow.[18] Gorbachev was livid, telling his Politburo "We cannot cook anything with this gang."[19]

"On the day of the bombing, Reagan met at the White House with four experts who had been researching Soviet weakness," Andy Marshall, the director of the Pentagon's Office of Net Assessment, recalled. "We told him that the Soviet economy was far smaller than the CIA was claiming, the defense burden was extremely heavy, the cost of empire was a serious strain and the country was more critically dependent on its dollar earnings from oil and gas exports than we had earlier thought. These judgments certainly reinforced Reagan's determination to intensify the pressure."

In the Kremlin, meanwhile, Gorbachev was surprised and annoyed by the West's unenthusiastic response to his bold proposals, failing to realize, as Chernyaev pointed out to me, that "they often had similarities with earlier Soviet initiatives aimed at wrong-footing Western governments with their own people." Fortunately, through his discussions with foreign dignitaries, Gorbachev came to understand this and began refining his proposals. Meanwhile, Alexander Yakovlev, Gorbachev's leading reformist adviser, explained that "I wished the Americans would stop their anti-communist propaganda, because it was hindering our own efforts to dismantle communism."

From Jack Matlock's position as the Soviet expert in the National Security

Council, it appeared that although "there was plenty of communication . . . both [sides] seemed to be talking past each other." Matlock believed that, before Gorbachev could get on with reforms at home, he had to convince his own people that Reagan was willing to wind down the arms race without demanding military superiority over the Soviet Union. To get this point across, Matlock sent the president spoof memos (clearly labeled as such) from Chernyaev to Gorbachev, purportedly giving advice on how to deal with Reagan. These memos not only appealed to the president's sense of humor, but also helped get the point across that he was dealing with a fellow politician.[20]

In September, Reagan agreed to Gorbachev's suggestion that they meet at Reykjavik in October to try to break the deadlock on arms control and open the way to a broader rapprochement. Their Icelandic hosts put at their disposal Hofti House, a property distinguished by its Nordic charm, not the scale of its conference facilities. Indeed, at no other summit have the participants been packed in so tightly—some of the participants were at one point ensconced in a bathroom trying to draft agreed texts.[21]

At Reykjavik

Gorbachev was in no doubt about the urgency of curbing the arms race. As he told his Politburo before Reykjavik, the Soviet financial crisis "has clutched us by the throat."[22] For that reason, should a new round of the arms race begin, "the pressure on our economy will be unbelievable."[23] "If you want to understand what happened at Reykjavik you have to realize," Chernyaev explained to me, "that Gorbachev's approach to the summit was to 'sweep Reagan off his feet' by making him an offer he could not refuse."

"In contrast," Matlock later observed, Reagan's proposals were basically "designed to be incremental."[24] Although the president was interested in an agreement on Euromissiles, he was not interested to the exclusion of regional, bilateral and human rights issues, which were an integral part of his policy to "change the Soviet Union" and end the Cold War.

From the outset, Gorbachev seized the initiative. He not only offered to slash strategic nuclear weapons by half in five years, and eliminate them entirely in ten, but also "to cut in half all the legs of the strategic triad," including Soviet "heavy" missiles, which the Americans regarded as particularly threatening. He even went so far as to express his willingness to eliminate all intermediate-range nuclear missiles in Europe, which in fact was his immediate priority. Had negotiations continued he would have made additional concessions.[25]

This was close to fulfilling Reagan's dream of eliminating all nuclear weapons. He and Gorbachev agreed that work should begin on preparing the appropriate treaties that the two of them would sign when he visited Washington in the not too distant future. There was, however, Gorbachev said, one condition: SDI research and testing had to be restricted to laboratories for the next ten years, during which time the cuts would be made.

Reagan was furious, feeling that he had been led into a carefully prepared trap. He insisted the systems had to be tested, but that they would not be deployed. Gorbachev retorted that this could allow America to perfect the system before all of its missiles had been destroyed, and so give it dominance over the Soviet Union. If he agreed to that, Gorbachev said, he would be regarded in Moscow as "a dummy, not a leader."[26]

"Gorbachev was right," Alexander Bessmertnykh, the deputy foreign minister who was at Reykjavik, explained. "He had little room for maneuver. The military had insisted that SDI had to be confined to laboratories. They had, however, left Gorbachev freedom to offer a separate deal to sharply cut back the number of Euromissiles. Gorbachev did not do so, because he felt that would be too big a concession when Reagan was offering nothing in return."[27]

Reagan's national security adviser, "Bud" McFarlane, was appalled that the president had turned down Gorbachev's offer. According to McFarlane, Gorbachev's proposal "was exactly what I was aiming for. Once we had an agreement on reductions, ten years [of delays on SDI testing] was fine. It was crazy to turn that down."[28] But McFarlane was one of those who regarded SDI as a bargaining chip. For his part, Shultz believed that if SDI did not have some teeth, Soviet concessions on strategic arms cuts could easily wither away over the next decade.[29]

On October 12, the last day of the summit, Gorbachev and Reagan glumly parted ways. Soon, however, both men came to recognize that they had made real headway. Gorbachev took the lead at the press conference he gave before leaving Reykjavik: "In spite of all its drama, Reykjavik is not a failure—it is a breakthrough, which allowed us for the first time to look over the horizon."[30] "Indeed, they had," Bessmertnykh said to me. "In agreeing to eliminate nuclear weapons Gorbachev had exceeded his instructions."[31]

America's allies were also shocked by this prospect, which fundamentally changed the whole nature of deterrence that they had accepted since the Cold

Reagan and Gorbachev part glumly at the end of the Reykjavik Summit, as Pavel Palazhchenko interprets their last exchanges, October 12, 1986. (Courtesy of the Ronald Reagan Library)

War began. Mrs. Thatcher said she "felt there had been an earthquake beneath my feet" as for one moment it looked as if they had agreed to surrender all nuclear weapons.[32] The insouciance of the American approach to this high-level horse trading was almost the most alarming aspect of the affair. Nothing had been thought through. Reagan was later readily persuaded by Mrs. Thatcher that nuclear arms cuts must take account of imbalances in conventional forces and chemical weapons.

Reflecting on the summit several years later, Matlock observed that the agreement being attempted was "too ambitious to be practical" as neither country "could undertake such a rapid and radical degree of disarmament unless a lot of other things fell into place, many of which were beyond their control."[33]

"Despite the lack of practical results," Chernyaev insists that by this time "Gorbachev felt Reagan was a moral person concerned about real human issues. He was convinced that the United States would never pre-emptively strike at the Soviet Union, nor did it wish to find itself at war with the Soviet people." This was another psychological breakthrough—and one that made it possible to reach a deal in the future.

"After Reykjavik," Bessmertnykh recalled, "there were many high-level meetings in Moscow. We realized that after the Republicans lost control of the Senate in November 1986, Reagan would find it much harder to fund the development of SDI. We also recognized that the near agreement on the elimination of all nuclear weapons opened up entirely new prospects. Not only could there be deep cuts to reduce the number of strategic weapons by more than 50%, but the deeper the cuts the less of a chance that Reagan would be able to implement SDI."

"As difficult as it is to do business with the United States," Gorbachev told the Politburo in February 1987, "we are doomed to do it."[34] Despite his failure to secure restrictions on SDI at Reykjavik, Gorbachev was not willing to let SDI thwart his whole reform program. He accepted that he would have to decouple the Reykjavik package. On March 1, 1987, Gorbachev announced that he was willing to agree to a treaty on intermediate-range nuclear forces (INF), without it being tied to other disarmament issues. Among the military there was much opposition to such a unilateral concession, which Marshal Sokolov was denouncing to anyone who would listen as "a state crime!"[35]

31 Progress & Crumbling

Breakthroughs in Europe

With his decision to seek a separate treaty on intermediate-range nuclear forces (INF), Gorbachev pushed aside decades of thinking about the Cold War, in which gains for one side were losses for the other. He now set out to bring the whole thing to an end.

"Two people played a special role in helping Gorbachev make this transition," Pavel Palazhchenko, Gorbachev's interpreter, pointed out. "Gorbachev particularly valued George Shultz for patiently explaining American thinking and consistently facilitating agreements and Mrs. Thatcher because she spoke to him more frankly than anyone else." Mrs. Thatcher was, however, prone to do so at length. On one occasion, Charles Powell, her private secretary for foreign affairs, felt so sorry for Gorbachev that he passed her a note that read, "Prime Minister, I think you're talking too much," to which she added, "I know," and continued talking.

Gorbachev accorded Mrs. Thatcher, the "Iron Lady," the honor of being the first foreign leader ever to be interviewed live on Soviet television, where she was able to say things publicly that he could not. "Her interviewers had some tough questions, but they had no experience in dealing with a world-class parliamentary debater," Powell recalled. "In no time at all, she had got them so flustered that one of them knocked over the vase of flowers on the table between them." In reporting to the Politburo on his discussions with the prime minister, Gorbachev said, "She emphasized trust . . . This is really something to ponder, comrades. We can't brush it aside."[1]

Gorbachev had been fairly quick to recognize that the European Union "is a giant rising in our neighborhood." It was, however, his discussions with Thatcher that persuaded him major changes were required in Soviet policy towards Western Europe. "We haven't studied Europe enough," he pointed out to the Politburo. "We must lower military confrontation as much as possible . . .

Our main goal is to utilize the scientific and technological potential of Western Europe . . . And remember, Western Europe is our basic partner."[2]

Gorbachev moved quickly. At a speech in Prague in April 1987, he began to speak at greater length about the need to create a Common European Home. Then, in May, he told his colleagues that if they wanted better relations with Europe they would have to admit that there was a massive preponderance of Soviet conventional forces in Europe and reach agreement on the basis of major asymmetrical reductions.

Gorbachev's meeting with East European leaders in East Berlin on May 28 ended with a call for reductions in conventional armed forces and armaments to a level that would preclude surprise attacks and "offensive operations in general." During that meeting, he also emphasized that the Soviet Union would not intervene militarily in Eastern Europe.[3]

"The focus on Europe was timely," Chernyaev pointed out, "as the issue of German unification was once again coming to the fore." In front of the Brandenburg Gate in Berlin on June 12, 1987, Reagan called on Gorbachev to "tear down this Wall." This was a highly sensitive matter for Gorbachev, whose relations with Honecker were increasingly fraught. When Gorbachev met with von Weizsäcker, the West German president in July, he tried to sideline the issue, saying it would be settled by history, perhaps within fifty years.

Headway in the Third World

In the autumn of 1985 Gorbachev won unanimous support from the Politburo to start elaborating a plan for withdrawing troops from Afghanistan. At another Politburo meeting on November 13, 1986, just over a month after the Rejkyavik Summit, Gorbachev made an angry speech about the hopeless situation in Afghanistan. His conclusion marked a dramatic shift in Soviet policy: "Our objective is to have a friendly, neutral Afghanistan so that we can get out."[4] Gorbachev would, however, find it as hard to withdraw from Afghanistan as Nixon had from Vietnam.

In mid-February 1986, the United States had decided in principle to supply shoulder-launched "Stinger" missiles to the mujaheddin, which began to be used in Afghanistan the following year. Despite changes in Soviet tactics, losses of Soviet aircraft and helicopters remained high. This was a further blow to the morale of the Soviet troops, over 13,000 of whom had already died in the conflict and 2,000 more would do so before they withdrew on February 15, 1989.

When Shevardnadze privately informed Shultz in September that Soviet troops would be withdrawn from Afghanistan "in the immediate future," Shultz instantly recognized that this was "a development of immense importance—and a dramatic moment." Shevardnadze asked Shultz for help in dealing with the threat of the spread of Islamic fundamentalism: "A neutral, nonaligned Afghanistan is one thing, a reactionary fundamentalist Islamic regime is something else."[5] There was, however, no response from Washington.

Real progress also began to be made on two other contentious regional issues—the ending of the civil war in Angola and helping Namibia towards independence, both of which required the Soviet Union to deal with the West and with South Africa. Reaching a settlement in Nicaragua and El Salvador took longer as Reagan was on the defensive in Central America. In 1987, Congress had cut off further military aid after learning that profits from the Administration's secret sale of arms to Iran were being used to finance the 15,000 Contras, the right-wingers who were fighting the left-wing government of Daniel Ortega in Nicaragua.

Gorbachev's Washington Triumph

Gorbachev had his third summit with Reagan in December 1987 in Washington, which was the first time he had visited the United States. The centerpiece of his summit was the signature of the INF Treaty, which set a new precedent by banning a whole category of nuclear weapons. At the signing ceremony Reagan once again quoted the Russian proverb "*doveryai, no proveryai,*" meaning "trust, but verify." Gorbachev interjected, "You repeat this phrase every time we meet," to which Reagan answered, "I like it."[6]

The treaty also marked the end of Soviet efforts to split Europe off from the United States. For that reason, some of Reagan's advisers felt the INF treaty was better than a 90% reduction in warheads on strategic missiles.[7] The deployment of SS-20 missiles had, Gorbachev and his colleagues agreed, been an "unforgivable adventure" that they were glad to bring to an end.[8]

Marshal Akhromeyev, the chief of the Soviet General Staff who accompanied Gorbachev to Washington, was considerably franker. In a conversation with Shultz he said, "my country is in trouble . . . That is why we made such a lopsided deal on INF, and that is why we want to get along with you. We want to restructure ourselves and be part of the modern world. We cannot continue to be isolated."[9]

"During the year," Bessmertnykh recalled, "we had noted that Americans were voicing more and more doubts about the feasibility of SDI. That encouraged us to press ahead with preparations for deep cuts." At the summit, the two sides signed a "framework" for the negotiations on a Strategic Arms Reduction Treaty, known as START, under which they would each cut their strategic nuclear arsenal to 4,900 warheads, with particularly deep cuts being made in SS-18s, the Soviet missile that most troubled the Americans. The Soviet side could not get a guarantee to block SDI, but as relations had improved in many other areas they were now willing to accept a face-saving solution on this issue.

Gorbachev's visit was a public relations triumph, reinforced by his telling Reagan that he would never again view the United States in the same way. Gorbachev felt that "perhaps for the first time, we understood how important the human factor is in international politics."[10] At last, it looked as though the two sides had come to trust each other.

It was only after the Washington Summit, Chernyaev recalled, that Gorbachev "became convinced that without a solution to the human rights problem the Cold War could not be brought to an end."[11] It was also Gorbachev's conviction that "we had lost the ideological war . . . not just because of technological or economic inferiority, but because the ideology that underlay it was wrong."[12]

Back in Moscow

Increasingly, the problems Gorbachev had to contend with were not abroad, but at home. At a public meeting in Leningrad at the end of 1986 a distinguished economist had said that "the experiment has failed," meaning that socialist economics was unworkable and far-reaching reforms would be needed. As the economy plunged into dire straits the minister of finance starkly informed the Politburo in April that "our financial position has reached the point of crisis."[13]

Political tensions were mounting, too. For the past two years, Boris Yeltsin, a member of the Politburo, had been struggling to revitalize the communist party in Moscow. Having concluded that this was an impossible task, he condemned Gorbachev for the slow pace of reform in front of a full meeting of the Central Committee in October 1987. Angry at having been openly challenged in this way, Gorbachev had Yeltsin ousted from the Politburo, an action that eventually resulted in the embittered Yeltsin becoming the standard bearer of the radical reformers.

Within months Gorbachev responded to Yeltsin's goading by beginning to push through political changes that within just three years transformed a highly authoritarian political system to one in which there was political pluralism and much greater personal freedom. Gorbachev's aim was to transfer power from the party to state and legislative bodies that he hoped would be more amenable to reform. The obedient totalitarian party did what was asked of it.

When Reagan paid a return visit to Moscow in May 1988, he received a warmer welcome than had any foreign leader before him. When asked whether he still considered the Soviet Union to be an "evil empire," he replied with a chuckle that "that remark belonged to another era." He praised the changes that had taken place under Gorbachev, but took no credit for them, and spoke of his admiration of the Russian people and their culture.[14]

Reagan's visit gave a considerable boost to Gorbachev's popularity at home and reinforced his argument that the Soviet Union was no longer under threat from the West and so could now embark on reform. At the Party Conference in July 1988, Gorbachev said the aim was to make a "peaceful, smooth transition from one political system to another."[15] When the conservatives within the party realized the implications, they turned against their leader whom they now viewed as a heretic.

Poland—Breaking the Mold

Even though the Soviet Union was providing subventions of between 5 and 10 billion dollars a year, Gorbachev knew Eastern Europe was unstable. According to Vadim Medvedev, who was at the time the member of the Politburo responsible for the region, "Gorbachev believed the way forward was for it to be run by 'mini-Gorbachevs.'" He understood that change in Eastern Europe depended crucially on what was happening in the Soviet Union. Among the East European leaders, however, only General Jaruzelski in Poland and Janos Kadar in Hungary favored reform. But even they wanted to see how far Gorbachev would go in the Soviet Union before following suit.

Hungary's once-promising economic reforms had lost their momentum some years earlier as a result of pressure from Moscow. The Hungarians now had the sad distinction of having the slowest rate of growth and the highest per capita foreign debt in Eastern Europe.

The situation in Poland was strange to say the least. Martial law had been followed by stalemate. While the government lacked the popular support needed to carry out reforms, Solidarity was too weak to overthrow the regime. By the mid-eighties, however, although Solidarity was still banned, it was operating openly in many factories. Jaruzelski decreed a general amnesty for all political prisoners in September 1986.

Jaruzelski felt that the Pope understood the complexity of the Polish situation and made his points tactfully through historical analogies. "When the Pope returned in June 1987, he reiterated his hope that socialism in Poland would become more humane. He urged me more strongly than before to engage in a dialogue with Solidarity. Shortly thereafter I told our party leadership that the time had come for us to take that step."

Then, in October, deputy prime minister Rakowski, a well-known reformer, warned that a dialogue with Solidarity would not be enough. In a memorandum to the Politburo on *The Crisis of Socialism in Poland*, Rakowski argued that history had shown that socialist economies could never compete with market economies and the party alone could not represent society. Poland had to find a political solution to its problems and that, Rakowski made very clear, would require a multiparty system.

When Gorbachev visited Poland in late July 1988, he was still cautious about change. "I assured Gorbachev that he had no cause for concern," Jaruzelski said. "After all, Solidarity was still weak. My plan was to give those members of Solidarity who 'accepted the reality of the existing situation' a limited role in the Polish parliament."

Although sporadic contacts then took place between the government and Solidarity, little progress was made until increasing economic hardship again led first to widespread strikes, then to two important announcements. In September, Rakowski was promoted to prime minister and a senior Soviet official said publicly that Moscow "would not be frightened if Solidarity re-emerged."[16] The Polish government told Walesa that if he could stop the strikes, it would agree to re-legalize Solidarity and engage in Round Table talks, together with the Church. Uncertainties about the future of reform in the Soviet Union made all concerned cautious.

East Germany—Losing Control

Moscow's relations with Honecker worsened sharply as Gorbachev unveiled his new policies and hiked the prices of oil and other raw materials exported to Eastern Europe, which hit the East German economy badly. Suspicion was becoming ever more poisonous. "Few in the Soviet Union," Medvedev explained to me, "realized the scale of East Germany's links with West Germany. The East Germans were playing a double game—opposing Gorbachev while becoming more indebted to West Germany."

Since 1983 Honecker was in increasingly frequent telephone contact with the West German chancellor—first Helmut Schmidt, then Helmut Kohl. When Timothy Garton Ash visited Honecker in a prison hospital in Berlin in 1992, Honecker gave him a touching glimpse of how much importance he had attached to those calls. He "pulled out of the pocket of his pyjamas a slightly dog-eared card on which his (former) secretary had once typed for him the direct telephone number of the chancellor's office in Bonn. They used to call each other quite often, he said. On occasion he had even dialed the number himself."[17]

Alexander Schalch-Golodkowski, Honecker's financial "fixer," led him to believe that East Germany could still borrow its way out of this crisis, just as he had earlier ones. Not all his colleagues agreed. In May 1986, Willy Stoph, the prime minister, warned Gorbachev that the situation was becoming extremely serious and Honecker was in secret negotiations with Bonn to obtain even greater trade credits than those of 1983/84.

Among Gorbachev's advisers there was increasing concern that East Germany could "lose its socialist character." Shevardnadze called for research to be done on the pros and cons of a German unification.[18]

Gorbachev had no plan for dealing with East Germany, preferring his actions to be shaped by developments. With close friends he would go so far as to say that"to force a great nation to remain indefinitely divided is wrong."[19] By July 1987, Chernyaev explained, "Gorbachev was convinced that the Cold War could never be ended without a resolution of the German question and the establishment of good relations between West Germany and the Soviet Union."

That October, Honecker was finally allowed to visit West Germany. President von Weizsäcker welcomed his opposite number to Bonn as "a German amongst Germans." But not all Germans were equal. While West Germany was prosperous, East Germany was on the verge of bankruptcy. By the following year, 1988, the service charge on East Germany's hard-currency debt was equal to one and a half times its annual exports to the West; more than half of East Germany's enterprises were already bankrupt and the prospect of massive unemployment loomed larger and larger.

To secure further loans from West Germany, Honecker was willing to allow more people to emigrate and more visits between East and West Germany. In

1988, there were over 12 million visits—either of East Germans visiting West Germany or West Germans traveling to East Germany, with the result that East Germans were having an extraordinary level of contact with their West German friends and relatives, though these only represented some 15% of the population. The shortage of medical staff, teachers and skilled workers was now creating serious problems. The East German authorities were losing control of events.

In a secret memorandum to Gorbachev and the Politburo in October 1988, Georgi Shakhnazarov, Gorbachev's chief adviser on Eastern Europe, warned that "social instability and crisis might engulf the whole of the socialist world simultaneously."[20] Gorbachev and all of his advisers on Eastern Europe wanted to avoid military intervention at all costs. Their only hope was rapid transition to a new political order in Eastern Europe on the lines of what they were pioneering at home.

32 Checkmate

The Arms Buildup Continues

Gorbachev "hated" Marshal Ogarkov, the chief of the General Staff and one of the architects of the strategy that bears his name. The main reason was that Ogarkov wanted to pour yet more money into revamping Soviet conventional forces in readiness for a war that Gorbachev was determined would never be fought.[1] Gorbachev had been delighted that shortly before his death in December 1984 Marshal Ustinov, the minister of defense, had demoted Ogarkov.

Ogarkov had been transferred to Legnica in Poland, where he had earlier established the headquarters of the "Western Theater of Military Operations," from which any future war in Europe would be directed. Given the doubts about the reliability of Polish forces, Ogarkov had concentrated on strengthening the Soviet forces in East Germany. He hoped that he could depend on the East Germans, who, with Prussian efficiency, could field nine divisions in just four days—twice as fast as Nato thought possible. The East Germans had already made boxes of medals—named after Marshal Blucher, the Prussian hero of the Napoleonic Wars—to be awarded to their valiant troops!

From Nato's perspective, the scale of the Soviet buildup was such that quantity acquired a quality of its own. Ogarkov, however, was worried by the deficiencies of his forces. He had little hope of acquiring the highly accurate conventional missiles needed to render Nato air bases unusable, and it would still take some years before he had enough of the right types of advanced aircraft to launch the giant air offensive that was to be the dramatic opening move in his grand strategy. To make matters worse, it was increasingly likely that the orders he had placed for the new aircraft would be cut back because the party leadership were belated in realizing that they were roughly eight times as expensive as the old ones.

There were also serious problems with the highly innovative "operational maneuver groups," on which the success of Ogarkov's ground offensive depended. Although they were being equipped with impressive new tanks, few of these groups had developed the dynamic flexibility needed to implement his strategy. In most training exercises, the tanks were still advancing in close formation, which made them highly vulnerable, and the air force rarely practiced giving them close support.

The decision to go to war, Ogarkov believed, would grow out of a crisis that would inevitably have put Nato on its guard. He had hoped, nonetheless, that through deception and surprise he would be able to seize the advantage when the fighting started. He was confident that Nato did not know of the network of 11,000 km (6,800 miles) of concealed trails that ran through the woods in a huge reversed "E" shape from the Polish frontier to the Inner-German Border.[2] To exploit this option, large numbers of units would have to be moved into the forward area in the right order under cover of darkness. Such a maneuver would be difficult because Soviet forces did little logistical training.

Despite these difficulties General Batenin, who had been Ogarkov's deputy in Moscow, later recalled that by mid-1987 "many in the General Staff thought that all the components necessary for conducting deep operations, were in place at last."[3]

Gaining the Upper Hand

Meanwhile, Nato's "revolution in military affairs" was gathering momentum. "Nato's new strategy provided an intellectual framework in which the latest American technology could be adapted to the realities of the European battlefield," Ruiz-Palmer, then one of the top analysts of Nato-Warsaw Pact relations, explained. "The key task was to break the assault by Soviet armored forces and close down the airfields from which air support was provided."[4]

This strategy, adopted in 1985, was called Follow-on Forces Attack (or FOFA, for short). For the first time, the commander of Nato would be able to coordinate conventional attacks across East Germany and deep into Poland. By using "assault-breaker" and other precision-guided munitions Nato aircraft would be able to destroy up to a hundred more targets than with previous conventional munitions.

Efficient targeting was essential, as the initial attack alone could involve 40,000 tanks, armored personnel carriers and artillery systems. "Through careful research," Joe Braddock explained, "my teams had already identified the routes along which Soviet and Warsaw Pact forces would advance and how that advance would be phased. This made it possible to monitor much smaller areas."

Ted Warner, a defense expert who rose to be Assistant Secretary of Defense for Strategy, emphasized that, at the time, "one of the greatest innovations was what we called the 'recce-strike.'" Nato was now developing surveillance aircraft that could identify targets on the ground up to 250 kms away. High-powered computers could then locate aircraft already in the air that were near the target and had the right munitions—and then flash them the coordinates for the attack.

Warner went on to relate how "As Nato acquired such aircraft there would be little prospect of moving tens of thousands of vehicles without them being detected. And even if deception and surprise worked, the 'assault-breakers' could quickly wreak havoc on the Soviet vanguard." "For the first time in our conventional rivalry with the Soviet forces," Andy Marshall, the director of the Office of Net Assessment in the Pentagon, observed, "the Americans were really moving towards gaining the upper hand—not in defense, but in attack."

Nato Shows Its Strength

The Warsaw Pact and Nato now faced each other on a much more level battlefield, with Nato's strength growing month by month. The Americans were now confident that in just ten days they could fly in five extra divisions to join up with their equipment which would be waiting and ready for them in Europe. That represented a formidable addition to their capability.

During the autumn of 1987, Nato set out to undermine Soviet confidence by staging the largest and most innovative exercises they had ever held. In northern Germany, General Bagnall's concept of using large armored reserves to launch a counter-strike against a Soviet breakthrough was tested in *Exercise Certain Strike,* the biggest field exercise since D-Day. It involved nearly 80,000 men, 35,000 of whom were reinforcements flown in from the United States. For the first time, all of these forces, from five different countries, were under the commander of Nato's Northern Army Group, not their respective national commanders.[5]

In southern Germany, there was a similar exercise, *Bold Sparrow,* in which the French sent 20,000 troops to support the West Germans who were at-

"Assault-breaker": A fighter-bomber drops its "bombs," each of which then releases hundreds of bomblets that then home in on their targets. (U.S. Department of Defense)

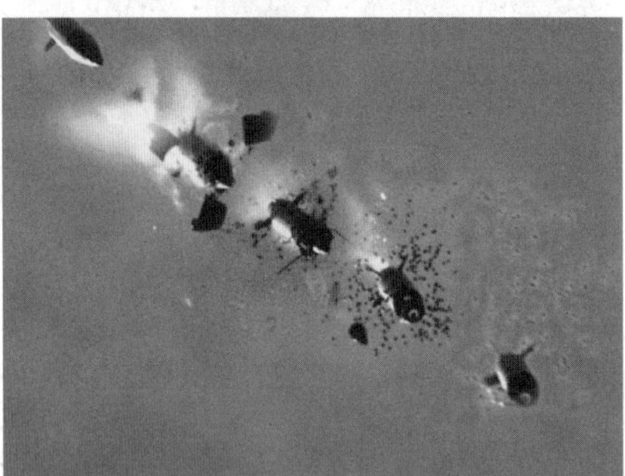

tempting to counter a Soviet-armored offensive. This was the largest ever contingent of French reinforcements to be deployed to Germany in support of Nato and the first time that France's new *Force d'Action Rapide* had crossed the Rhine.[6]

Under the new arrangements agreed at the Conference on Disarmament in Europe in September 1986, each side was allowed to send observers to view any large-scale military exercise. General von Sandrart, who was about to take command of all Nato forces on the central front, was very pleased that one of the Soviet generals who attended *Bold Sparrow* had been "amazed by the realism of the exercise, the high number of Nato tanks and armored vehicles that had survived the first day's battle, and by how skillfully a French brigade had replaced a German one on the frontline in the heat of battle." They were also struck by the close bond between officers and men. One senior East German officer later told Field Marshal Inge that "I have to say it's the first time I've ever seen generals talking to soldiers!'"

Within months of *Bold Sparrow*, secret Soviet military journals were carrying articles warning that new technology was threatening tanks with obsolescence. The new Soviet minister of defense, Yazov, compounded the depression of his colleagues when he lamented that the West had developed electronic warfare capabilities that the Soviet Union could not match. This was probably a reference to reports from an American agent that the United States could now insert false messages into the Warsaw Pact communications networks.[7]

Shortly after taking command of all Nato forces on the central front, General von Sandrart issued the first "Operational Guidance for the Central Region." This document pulled together the main elements of the new, dynamic strategy. Nato drove home the message about its growing strength in the fall of 1988 by conducting *Reforger 88*, the biggest single exercise it had ever held, involving over 120,000 men. One full American army corps (of about 60,000 men) faced another of a similar size that was playing the role of Soviet forces.[8] Nato tested its "recce-strikes," its "assault-breakers" and other new equipment.

Nato leaders felt that they had finally gained the upper hand. They had admired Ogarkov for thinking big and coordinating his operations across a huge theater of military operations; now they had shown that they could not only respond in a similar way, but had the ability to defeat forces much larger than their own. As Ruiz-Palmer graphically put it: "In military terms, this was the public execution of Marshal Ogarkov outside Nato headquarters."

Is the Soviet Threat Really Ending?

After the Washington Summit there was considerable euphoria in the West. Not only were many people claiming that the Cold War was virtually over, but there was also soon a growing number of politicians who were calling for a "peace dividend." This was to be based on immediate and unilateral cuts in Western defense expenditure, with the savings being redirected to deal with urgent economic and social issues.

Several Western leaders and their military advisers were alarmed by this prospect. First and foremost, they pointed out, the Warsaw Pact buildup was continuing and it had massive preponderance of conventional forces in Europe. Terminating Nato's own long-planned buildup, in which a huge amount of money and political capital was invested, would leave the alliance at a grave disadvantage in the event that the Soviet Union rejected Gorbachev's approach and relations became confrontational once more. Nato was also keen to see deep cuts in Soviet forces in Eastern Europe so that these countries would have a better chance of regaining their freedom.

Work was progressing well on the Strategic Arms Reductions Treaty, but it was clear that the Senate would not be willing to ratify the treaty until major cuts had been agreed on conventional forces in Europe, negotiations on which were to resume in Vienna in March 1989. Gorbachev did not object to this because as part of his efforts to build a new relationship with Western Europe, he also wanted such an accord. Just as importantly, deep cuts in conventional forces would free up more resources for the Soviet economy than would cuts in strategic nuclear missiles.

The way to such cuts had already been opened by his decision in early 1987 to negotiate an INF Treaty that abolished Euromissiles. These, of course, included the Soviet SS-20 missiles, the very ones that had made Ogarkov's strategy possible in the first place.

At the end of their meeting in East Berlin on May 28, 1987, the leaders of the Warsaw Pact called for reductions in conventional armed forces and armaments to a level that would preclude surprise attacks and "offensive operations in general." That very day, Mathias Rust, a 19-year-old West German, flew a Cessna light aircraft a thousand kilometers across the Soviet Union and landed it right in Red Square, close to Gorbachev's office in the Kremlin—without anyone trying to stop him.

In his memo to Gorbachev on the incident the following morning, Chernyaev wrote that "A great military power was reduced to a joke in the space of a minute."[9] Gorbachev sacked the minister of defense and many senior officers, making it easier for him push forward the reform of Soviet strategy in Europe. Just ten months later, the Warsaw Pact staged its first large-scale exercise that was purely defensive, followed by a limited counter-offensive over a three-week period that halted after Nato forces had been expelled from Eastern Europe. "This period," Marshal Akhromeyev said, "would have provided leaders on both sides with ample time to terminate the war."[10]

The Warsaw Pact, however, was not marching closely in step. "What really amazed us," General Naumann, the German chief of defense, told me, "was that after unification we discovered documents that showed that one year after the Warsaw Pact had said it was going on the defensive, the East Germans conducted an exercise in which forty nuclear weapons were fired at the Hamburg region to close off Nato's northern flank." At least it was "command post exercise," not a "field training" one in which weapons are moved into firing positions and notionally fired.

With military expenditure continuing to rise, Gorbachev told his colleagues in February 1988 that "It's clear now that without substantially cutting military expenditures we cannot solve the problems of perestroika."[11] The crucial question that Gorbachev had to address urgently was how big were the cuts he wanted—and whether he thought the military would accept them.

Pressure and Trust

Reagan came into office in 1981 determined that the Cold War would not be ended through compromise, but only on his terms. He built up the pressure on the Soviet Union in the military sphere through massive increases in expenditure and by exploiting America's great lead in technology, by "Star Wars" and many other initiatives. After Gorbachev came to power in 1985, the pressure was increasingly applied on the economic front.

The success of the global market had already played a key role in destroying the credibility of "socialism." Economic reform was well underway in China and one of the greatest ironies of the war in Vietnam was that the defeated South Vietnamese were now introducing capitalism to the victorious communist North. Gorbachev and his supporters recognized the need for economic reform, but they faced an immense challenge because "socialist" economics and dislike of enterprise were deeply ingrained in their country.

Gorbachev's task was made all the harder as the prices of gold and primary products had been falling since the early eighties, when the US Federal Reserve Bank adopted a restrictive monetary policy. The ensuing reduction in Soviet foreign exchange earnings was greatly exacerbated by America's success in persuading Saudi Arabia to increase oil production in 1986, and by the discovery of oil on Alaska's north shore. The resulting sharp reduction in the world price gave a much-needed fillip to the American economy, while slashing Soviet hard-currency earnings by nearly half and before long sending the Soviet economy reeling towards collapse.[12] In the five years since Gorbachev came to power Soviet hard-currency debt had doubled to over $50 billion and was now surging upwards.

Unquestionably, the cumulative effect of Reagan's policies *increased* the pressure on Gorbachev not just to seek a rapprochement with the West, but to end the Cold War. By the time Gorbachev came to power, he might have resisted the momentum to end the Cold War, but he could not have stopped it. In November 1988, after reorganizing the leadership, Gorbachev felt he could press his colleagues harder to accept arms reductions. "Our military expenses," he complained to the Politburo, "are two and a half times those of the United States." Soviet forces needed to be reduced and restructured for "purposes of security, not intimidation."[13]

Gorbachev had already shown himself to be the first Soviet leader who was willing to engage in serious discussion and to look at old issues in new ways. One of the main hopes of the détente era was that there would be scope for what diplomats call "the cumulative effect of little differences" to ease tensions and open the way to a more stable relationship. Gorbachev understood this well, along with the related need to build trust—a process greatly helped by the perceptive and sensitive diplomacy of George Shultz.

Through Gorbachev détente was finally beginning to pay its dividend, but that was something very different from ending the Cold War. Before any significant progress could be made in Europe, Gorbachev had to find a way to break the deadlock in the long-running negotiations aimed at cutting conventional forces in Europe (or CFE as they were known). Seeking balanced reductions had proved impossible as for years the Soviet Union had always refused to accept that the Warsaw Pact had far larger forces than Nato. Gorbachev came up with a very imaginative solution to the problem.

CLOSURE

The end of the Berlin Wall, November 9, 1989. (Courtesy of the German Information Service)

33 Accelerating & Braking

Pushing for a Settlement

In his historic address at Westminster College in Fulton, Missouri, in 1946, Churchill spoke of the Iron Curtain that had cut Europe in half. When Gorbachev gave his first speech to the United Nations, in December 1988, he wanted to show that he was now lifting that curtain.

In his speech, Gorbachev first emphasized the importance of the global interests of humanity, then went on to make the dramatic announcement that, over the next two years, Soviet forces would be cut by 500,000 men, and six of its armored divisions in Eastern Europe would be disbanded. Moscow, he assured his listeners, was not going use force against Eastern Europe or anywhere.

Gorbachev received a standing ovation. As Anatoly Chernayev, his foreign affairs adviser, later told me, "Gorbachev wanted to cause a sensation—and he did." He also caught the American establishment off-guard, though Secretary of State Shultz later recalled feeling that "if anybody declared the end of the Cold War, [Gorbachev] did in that speech: It was over."[1]

Few Western leaders went so far as Shultz, publicly or privately, but most accepted that Gorbachev was moving briskly in addressing some of the remaining contentious issues of the Cold War. The large, unilateral cuts he had announced in Soviet conventional forces would put Nato and the Warsaw Pact on a more equal footing.

The immediate gain was that when the negotiations on reducing conventional forces in Europe resumed in Vienna in March 1989, there was now hope of a real breakthrough. For the first time, the Soviet Union was likely to table credible figures on the number of its troops and the equipment it would have in Europe once the announced unilateral cuts had been implemented. That would provide a realistic basis on which the two sides could discuss deep and rapid cuts.

Wanting Rapid Progress

As has often been said, 1989 was a year that changed the world. But it has been less often remarked that it was Gorbachev who repeatedly took the lead in bringing about dramatic transformations, pressing on with radical changes despite the obstacles he faced both at home and abroad. His outlook came more and more to resemble that of the European social democrats.

After Gorbachev gave his speech at the United Nations, he had a warm farewell meeting with Reagan on Governor's Island and his first with president-elect Bush. Bush took the opportunity to warn Gorbachev that there would have to be a "pause" while his incoming administration reviewed policy.

In the spring of 1989, while the policy review got underway in Washington, the Soviet people held their first largely free elections in seventy-five years and the first in Eastern Europe since 1948. They elected a Congress of People's Deputies, with each republic having its own democratically elected parliament. The first meeting of the national-level congress, which ran through May and June, was a major landmark in pushing forward Gorbachev's policy of *glasnost* or openness.

Just as progress was being made on the political front, popular discontent over economic problems was coming to the fore. Over the past five years, the Soviet people had become the poorest in the whole Soviet bloc—a terrible indictment of the system and its leaders. Oleg Bogomolov, one of Gorbachev's economic advisers, urged him to follow "the Chinese example and begin the process of reform in the agricultural sector." Gorbachev thought that this was too risky politically, because Soviet hostility towards enterprise and incentives was far more deeply entrenched than that of the Chinese. Much needed imports could only be sustained by drawing down Soviet foreign exchange reserves, which by then were less than $25 billion.

"The empire-federation," Chernyaev observed, "was falling apart." The party was in disarray, having lost its place as a ruling, dominating and repressive force, and government authority had been shaken to breaking point. The conservatives began digging in their heels.[2]

In their presentations to Gorbachev, both the KGB and the GRU were urging "extreme caution," as the United States was said to be intent on destroying the Soviet Union. This was not strictly true. The Americans were not out to destroy the Soviet Union, but the old Soviet system. Few in Soviet Intelligence, however, were willing to recognize that essential distinction, which is hardly surprising given that without the old system neither the "union" nor the outer Soviet empire in Eastern Europe could be sustained.

New President—New Approach

When Bush came into office in January 1989, he was keen to show that his policies would not simply be a continuation of Reagan's. As a liberal Republican, he had been badly scarred by détente, to the point where he shared the widespread feeling in Congress that Reagan had been a political romantic. Lt. General Brent Scowcroft, Bush's national security adviser, who for years had watched the Soviet Union carefully, said, "I kept reminding people that the Cold War was not over, and I doubted whether Gorbachev really wanted to end it."

The president was less skeptical, but still cautious. So far, however, he saw few signs that Gorbachev's reforms had changed the basic elements of Soviet defense policy. Indeed, there were numerous indications that Soviet forces would continue to be modernized. And in Moscow, billboards continued to proclaim: "The main goal of *perestroika* is to strengthen military preparedness!"

Soviet activities in the Third World still aroused suspicion, albeit less than in earlier years. On February 16, 1989, after all his men had left the country, General Boris Gromov, the Soviet commander in Afghanistan, made his much-televised march over a bridge and back into the Soviet Union. Soviet military aid, however, continued to pour into Afghanistan, helping to keep Najibullah's regime in power for the next three years. Although in mid-May Gorbachev had informed Bush that he was stopping shipments of weapons to Nicaragua, Washington believed that Cuba and East Germany were taking over as the main suppliers of arms and assistance to both Nicaragua and El Salvador.

Bush also felt Gorbachev was still hoping to fracture Nato's cohesion and there was a chance that he might succeed. In Europe, Gorbachev's popularity exceeded that of any 20th-century Western leader. Several European governments were keen to cut their defense budgets, even though there had been virtually no cuts yet in Soviet forces. At the end of a meeting devoted to discussing American policy in Europe, Bush told his advisers in a resigned tone, "If we don't regain the lead, things will fall apart."[3]

While the policy review dragged on, major changes were unfolding in the Soviet Union and Eastern Europe and Bush was beginning to be accused of "sleepwalking through history." On May 12, in his first major speech on relations with the Soviet Union, he declared that his policy was to go "beyond containment" and seek to integrate the Soviet Union into "the community of nations."[4]

"We in the Bush Administration," Secretary of State Baker explained some years later, "knew we could not reform the Soviet Union. But we realized nonetheless that we could assist the process."[5] Economic aid, however, would not be available to encourage economic reform. It would only be extended to reward a new Soviet Union that had embarked on serious reforms.

Dennis Ross, the head of Baker's policy planning staff, elaborated: "Our aim was to facilitate a 'soft landing' for the Soviet Union, as we brought the Cold War to an end on American terms." President Bush realized that this would not be easy because, as he mentioned to me, he was "not at all sure" about what the Soviet Union "might do to keep the Warsaw Pact intact and preserve its superpower status."

Before responding to Gorbachev's initiatives, the Administration had already been addressing its top priority—the re-establishment of a bipartisan consensus on foreign policy. This had been weakened by Reagan's policies on his Strategic Defense Initiative, Latin America and the related "Iran-Contra" affair. The considerable effort that Bush invested in this task paid off. He won support for a new policy towards Central America, which later extended to general backing for his policy towards the Soviet Union.

Bush also set about rebuilding a consensus within Nato, where a real crisis had developed over the modernization of short-range nuclear missiles, especially in West Germany. As Hans-Dieter Genscher, the foreign minister, would often point out, "the shorter the range, the deader the Germans." The sensitivities of the allies had been revealed in March in one of Nato's annual exercises, Wintex-89, which involved the use of nuclear weapons to stop the advance of Warsaw Pact armies into Germany. This war game, scheduled to last eight days, came to a fractious end after just six.

General Klaus Naumann, then the overall chief of the German armed forces, explained: "The problem was that Germany was particularly sensitive about the use of nuclear weapons on German territory—East or West. The German officials who were 'playing' this war game eventually agreed that nuclear weapons could be used against targets on the Polish-Soviet border. When Chancellor Kohl heard of this he said the whole thing was politically unacceptable and had to stop." Bush and Baker knew they had to forge a new consensus in Nato before its summit meeting in May.

The End of Eastern Europe

Gorbachev's view was that whatever happened, the East Europeans "will have to decide themselves how they will live." "He still expected that 'reformed communist parties' would be in charge," recalled Vadim Medvedev, a member of the Politburo who advised Gorbachev on Eastern Europe. From reports reaching the Politburo, however, it was becoming increasingly clear that these regimes were already quietly rejecting socialism and were "in the powerful magnetic field of the West."

In January 1989, as President Bush was taking over the reins of power in Washington, a Politburo commission began working with Soviet think-tanks on the worsening situation in Eastern Europe. One memorandum submitted by Oleg Bogomolov, the director of the Institute of Economics of the World Socialist System, concluded that if the ruling parties did not make concessions to their opponents, there could be "cataclysms."[6]

In Poland, serious efforts to avoid such an outcome were reaching a critical stage. The party, Solidarity, and the Catholic Church started Round Table talks in February. When they ended in April, Solidarity had been legalized once more and an agreement had been reached on elections. But Solidarity was not the force that it had once been—its membership was now two million, a mere fifth of what it had been in 1981.

Jaruzelski flew to Moscow at the end of April to explain to Gorbachev that, "as Solidarity would not have more than 35% of the seats in parliament, we would only have a restricted form of pluralism." "I assured Gorbachev," he told me, "that the situation would not be allowed to get out of control."[7] Jaruzelski believed that "we had such a good chance of making progress with economic reform, that we would win real popular support and the free elections that we had agreed would take place in four years' time." Then Jaruzelski added wryly, "This was a miscalculation. The elections came much earlier and we lost!"

Meanwhile, in Hungary, preparations for multiparty elections were well underway. In March, Gorbachev had told the Hungarian leadership that "the safekeeping of socialism" was "the limit" of reform.[8] Since then, the pace had quickened. During the early summer the barbed-wire fence along Hungary's frontier with Austria was removed and the remains of Prime Minister Imre Nagy, who had been executed on Soviet orders after the Hungarian Revolution of 1956, were reburied in June with lavish ceremony and deep emotion. The party agreed to disband itself and hold free elections because reliable polls indicated that a reformed party would remain the dominant force in Hungarian politics for several years to come.

Although these changes had so far gone fairly smoothly in Poland and Hungary, there was much that could still go wrong there, to say nothing of East

Germany and the other countries of Eastern Europe. Bush was worried about the unpredictability of such rapid change. He did not wish, as he later wrote, "to encourage a course of events which might turn violent and get out of hand and we then couldn't—or wouldn't—support, leaving people stranded at the barricades."[9]

After the Nato summit, Bush visited Germany where he declared that America wanted to see "a Europe whole and free." "The Cold War began," he said, "with the division of Europe. It can only end when Europe is whole."[10] He was the first American president to set that condition. Meanwhile, he decided to seek closer ties with local reformers in order to speed the withdrawal of Soviet troops from the region. This is what led to his visits to Poland and Hungary in July 1989.

In the elections in June, Solidarity won all but one of the seats open to it in the Polish parliament, plus all of those in the Senate (on which there were no restrictions). The smaller non-communist parties that had existed under the old system now sided with Solidarity and gave it a majority. "This came as a shock to both Walesa and me," the general pointed out. "We now had to negotiate on what sort of government would rule the country."[11] They responded to the challenge with much good sense, as did Gorbachev.

Gorbachev recognized that he would have to accept a Solidarity government: "Poland has $56 billion debt. Can we take Poland on to our balance sheet in our current economic situation? No! And if we cannot—then we have no influence."[12] As soon as Solidarity gave assurances that it would honor Poland's obligations to the Warsaw Pact, Moscow declared that "political arrangements in Poland are solely for themselves to decide, without influence from any quarter."[13]

On July 9, Bush arrived in Warsaw and two days later went on to Budapest. There he stressed to the Polish and Hungarian reformers that Gorbachev's success in the Soviet Union was essential for the advancement of their own democratic reforms. At the end of the month Shevardnadze privately assured Baker that force would not be used to deal with problems in Eastern Europe or at home.

Although there was some recognition of this point, Walesa, the leader of Solidarity, raised the stakes at the beginning of August. He called for a new Solidarity-led government under a communist president, a proposal which he encapsulated in the slogan "Your President, our Prime Minister." Rakowski, who was now the leader of the communist party, knew this would involve some hard bargaining. "When I telephoned Gorbachev at the end of August to inform him of the negotiations with Solidarity, his response was that 'this is a new situation, of which you will have to take account.' He ended by telling me 'We support you and all that you will do.'"

On September 12 the Poles formed the first non-communist government in Central Europe since 1948. The new government contained four communist ministers, including those of Defense and the Interior. Following calls from both Walesa and Bush, Jaruzelski agreed to be president—his considerable powers included being commander-in-chief of the armed forces.

These events came as a shock to many communist reformers in both the Soviet Union and Eastern Europe. It showed how difficult it would be for a communist government to remain in power. Worse was yet to come.

34 Maltese Breakthrough

Preparing for Malta

After his visits to Poland and Hungary Bush was convinced that Gorbachev really did want to terminate the Cold War and was a force for stable change. On his way home, he drafted a personal message to Gorbachev proposing an informal summit. Eventually, they agreed to meet at Malta in early December.

"For us, the continuing changes in Eastern Europe were reshaping our relations with Moscow," Dennis Ross, Secretary of State Baker's assistant, pointed out. Ross stressed that: "An even bigger breakthrough came during Shevardnadze's visit to America in September. He deeply impressed Baker by talking extremely frankly about Soviet problems."

According to Bessmertnykh, Shevardnadze's deputy, "Headway was made on arms control when the Americans indicated that Soviet heavy missiles, which we viewed as a possible counterweight to SDI, would not have to be destroyed. At last we felt the log-jam could be broken." This shift in the American position enabled Shevardnadze to de-link the negotiations on the strategic arms reductions treaty from those on the Strategic Defense Initiative. He also pledged to dismantle the Krasnoyarsk radar, which the United States had long and rightly claimed was a violation of the anti-ballistic missile treaty.

Baker understood that these were serious concessions. He began to signal that the United States now saw the prospect of "a whole new world." In a major speech in Berlin that December, he began to speak of a new security zone that stretched from Vancouver in the west to Vladivostok in the east.

Since the beginning of the year, Gorbachev had, in a similar vein to Baker, been pushing forward his idea of a "Common European Home." When Gorbachev paid his first visit to West Germany in June 1989, he received an extraordinarily warm welcome. Gorbachev and Kohl agreed that their paramount objective was to work together to build a Common European Home "in which the United States and Canada also have a place." "This was all the more urgent," Chernyaev pointed out, "as East Germany was collapsing and decisions would have to be taken quickly on German unification."

In a private conversation with Gorbachev in his garden overlooking the Rhine, Kohl said that he told Gorbachev that the river of history was flowing towards German unity and could not be stopped. In Kohl's recollection, Gorbachev silently registered the statement. Then he spoke of the Soviet Union's economic difficulties; he asked Kohl whether, if it should come to pass that he would have to request urgent economic help, the chancellor would be willing and able to give it. Kohl said yes.[1]

Kohl considered Gorbachev's visit to have been "the decisive moment" on the road to German unity. "So did I," Chernyaev told me. Nevertheless, at that stage, both Kohl and Gorbachev still apparently expected that unification would be a gradual process, beginning with moves towards a confederation.

Trouble Brewing

Meanwhile, a rising tide of nationalist sentiment was beginning to crack apart the Soviet Union, which was still basically a land-based empire. Within the Russian Republic, some 80% of the people were Russians, whereas in the country as a whole they only amounted to just over 50%. A few years earlier, Andropov pointed out the potentially explosive consequences of this to Markus Wolf, the head of East German Intelligence: "Too many groups have suffered under the repression in our country . . . If we open up all the valves at once, and people start to express their grievances, there will be an avalanche and we will have no means of stopping it."[2] His judgment was sound.

Gorbachev had no strategy for dealing with these potentially explosive issues. On the one hand, he had such an abhorrence of violence that he was unwilling to crack down hard on nationalist protests from the outset; on the other, he did not act swiftly to defuse tensions by offering greater independence within a somewhat looser Soviet federation.

Gorbachev was not responsible for the crass mishandling of protestors in Georgia in April 1989 that resulted in the death of a dozen people and fueled nationalist sentiment. Nationalist sentiment was already far stronger in the Baltic republics, which had been forcibly incorporated into the Soviet Union in 1940. In August 1989, the Balts highlighted their demands in an extraordinary dramatic gesture—two million of them formed what was virtually a human chain that stretched some 500 km, about 300 miles, from Vilnius through Riga to Tallin.

As Bush prepared to meet Gorbachev in Malta, the CIA was expressing its belief that Gorbachev's policies were "certain to make the next few years some of the most turbulent and destabilizing in Soviet history."[3] The National Security Council set up a secret "contingency planning group" to study the implications of a Soviet collapse.

"Despite these and other warnings," Ross explained, "Bush insisted he would work with Gorbachev, telling his staff 'Look, this guy is *perestroika.*'" Ross noted at the time that "The bad impression Yeltsin made when he visited Washington in September reinforced Bush's decision. So, too, did the uncertainties about the future. They spurred us to conclude as many agreements as possible before a change of leadership occurred."

But the Bush Administration knew that its policies would put a lot of strain on the Soviet Union. National Security Directive 23, in September 1989, for example, called for "the integration of the Soviet Union into the existing international system," which required "fundamental alterations in Soviet military force structure, institutions, and practices that can only be reversed at great costs, economically and politically, to the Soviet Union."[4]

The Price of Indebtedness

Pressure for change was also intensifying in East Germany. During the first nine months of the year, some 200,000 East Germans (including many party members) had left the country. Most had gone on "holiday" to Hungary—where since August the Hungarian authorities had allowed passage into Austria and on to West Germany. Hungary's reformist leaders had not consulted Gorbachev on the grounds that they did not wish to embarrass him; nor did they mention that their decision had been facilitated by a payment from Bonn of DM 1 billion (US $600 million).[5]

Many Soviet experts on Germany were in no doubt as to what was happening. In September, for example, the KGB in East Berlin reported to Moscow that "the process of the reintegration of the German nation is underway . . ."[6] Chaos was also looming.

When Gorbachev arrived in East Berlin for the celebrations to mark the 40th anniversary of the German Democratic Republic on October 7, he warned Honecker and his colleagues that "Life itself punishes those who delay."[7] That evening it did just that as thousands of people marching past the podium began chanting "Gorby, help us!," "Gorby, save us!" Rakowski, the leader of the Polish communist party, leaned over to Gorbachev and said, "These are party activists. This is the end!"

The next day, peaceful demonstrations that included large numbers of Protestant churchgoers were forcibly broken up in Dresden and Berlin. Plans to use troops to smash the much larger protests expected in Leipzig were abandoned when Moscow made it clear that Soviet troops would not back such action. On October 25, Gorbachev's spokesman, Gennady Gerasimov, reinforced this point when he told reporters that Moscow had replaced the Brezhnev Doctrine, which justified Soviet military intervention in Eastern Europe, with the "Sinatra Doctrine," a play on the singer's signature ballad, "I did it my way."[8]

Following discussions with Moscow, Honecker was ousted and replaced by Egon Krenz. When Krenz arrived at the Kremlin on November 1, he implored Gorbachev to help East Germany and asked him "what role the Soviet Union ascribed" to the two Germanys in the future "all-European house."[9] Markus Wolf thought that shoring up East Germany had become an impossible task: "The Poles and Hungarians could adapt to the new situation by becoming more democratic and pursuing market-oriented economic reforms, but we East Germans could not. Our *raison d'etre* was to be different from West Germany."

To make matters worse, East Germany was on the brink of bankruptcy, with hard-currency debts already over $26 billion and rising rapidly as the trade deficit for 1989 was a staggering $12 billion. As a member of the Politburo remarked a little later, "an officer in Imperial Germany or Tsarist Russia would have shot himself" in similar circumstances.[10] As Moscow could not afford to bail out East Germany, the writing was, so to speak, on the wall. Nonetheless, Kohl thought that German unification "would probably not come in our lifetime."[11]

The Wall Comes Down

The very next day, the "cock-up theory of history" produced one of its finest examples. At a press conference in East Berlin, an East German government spokesman announced that, effective immediately, all citizens would be able to obtain visas to visit relatives in the West. This was a momentous announcement as it lifted the restrictions that had been in place since the Berlin Wall went up nearly thirty years earlier. This information was not supposed to have been disclosed until the following day, by which time the government hoped to have formulated more restrictive conditions for these visits and made the necessary administrative arrangements.

Within ten minutes, the news was broadcast on East German television and East Berliners began gathering at the crossing points. The guards did not know what to do, but before long, they began letting people through. The news spread rapidly. That night alone some 40,000 East Berliners visited West Berlin; within days the number of East German visitors to West Berlin had topped the million mark. Just before Gorbachev set off to meet Bush in Malta, the KGB informed him that "there was not a chance of preserving [East Germany] as an independent sovereign state and a member of the Warsaw Pact . . ."[12]

On November 16, just one week after the collapse of the wall, Czechoslovakia's "velvet revolution" began with protestors demanding free elections. Day by day, the crowds swelled, with eventually 800,000 people massing in the center of Prague. A general strike briefly brought the country to a standstill. On November 28, the communist party agreed to give up its monopoly of power. By the end of December, Vaclav Havel, who had helped launch the Prague Spring and was a founding member of Charter-77, had become the first democratically elected president of the country since 1948.

The collapse of the Berlin Wall was not, Chernyaev noted in his diary, simply the end of "this entire era in the history of socialist system . . . [but] . . . the end of Yalta . . . of the Stalinist legacy [in Europe] and the 'defeat of Hitlerite Germany.'"[13]

On his way to Malta, Gorbachev paid a visit to his much-beloved Italy. The rapturous welcome he received cheered him greatly and kept alive his hopes of creating a Common European Home. His European credentials were further strengthened by being the first ever Soviet leader to have an audience with the Pope, who congratulated him on what he had achieved and wished him well.

Malta

The planners of the Malta Summit showed appalling judgment. They assessed the risk of bad weather in December to be low and ignored how great the danger could be if they were wrong. Bush and Gorbachev arrived in Malta to find they were in the midst of a sudden, dramatic winter storm. Unfortunately for them, they were not meeting in some comfortable palace, but at sea, so as to avoid the press and the usual rituals of summits. The original plan was to hold one day of talks on a Soviet warship and one on an American warship, both

Presidents Gorbachev and Bush meet aboard the Soviet cruise ship, the M.S. *Maksim Gorky*, Valletta Harbor, December 2, 1989. (Courtesy of the George Bush Library)

anchored just off the coast. The continuing storm made that impossible, but they were able to meet on the Soviet cruise ship that was serving as Gorbachev's hotel and which was comfortably anchored in Valetta harbor.

Despite the inconvenience, Bush and Gorbachev managed to have a historic summit at which they each demonstrated a great flair for friendship.[14] Bush quickly set the tone by telling Gorbachev that he firmly believed that "The world will be a better place if *perestroika* succeeds."[15] He undertook to try to persuade Congress to allow an expansion in Soviet-American trade and the extension of credit to the Soviet Union. For the first time, the Americans made a commitment to give economic support to *perestroika*.

"The real breakthrough in strategic arms control," Ross pointed out, "came when the president said we would no longer insist on banning Soviet mobile intercontinental missiles, which were to be the mainstay of Moscow's retaliatory force." Work soon began on drafting the treaty.

For his part, Gorbachev announced an important shift in Soviet policy in the Third World by canceling shipments of weapons to the Sandinistas in

Nicaragua. This was welcome news to Bush, as the Americans had just persuaded the anti-Sandinista opposition to back one candidate—Violeta Chamorro, who won a narrow victory the following February.

Europe featured prominently in the discussions, with Gorbachev reiterating that the countries of Eastern Europe were free to choose their own political systems, which was something they had been doing quite effectively over the past year. For his part, Bush agreed to stop talking about uniting Europe on the basis of "Western values" and to use the more neutral phrase "democratic values."

Their two countries, Gorbachev told Bush were "'doomed' to talk, cooperate, and collaborate." He emphasized that it was important for the future of Europe that the United States remained there, and, by implication, remained engaged in European affairs politically, militarily and economically. He then went on to say that "We don't consider you an enemy anymore."[16] "This was not a new sentiment," Chernyaev pointed out, "but he had never said that explicitly before." It marked a reversal of decades of Soviet efforts to evict the United States from the continent.

Gorbachev welcomed Bush's assurance that he would avoid doing anything that would damage Gorbachev's position in the world, like "dancing," metaphorically speaking, on the Berlin Wall to celebrate its end. He added that he would continue to act with restraint regarding German unification. When Gorbachev floated the idea that "Maybe a united Germany should be neutral," Bush let it pass.[17]

First, a German Confederation

Moscow hoped that unification would come gradually. One week after the summit, however, Kohl announced his terms for rescuing East Germany. He offered "a completely new dimension of aid and cooperation" in return for a free press, free elections and a free market. He was saying, in effect, that the people of East Germany would know best when they wanted unification.[18] Gorbachev, Chernyaev remembered, was "furious," because Kohl was forcing the pace of unification and calling on the East German people to decide the matter for themselves, rather than leaving Bonn to negotiate it with Moscow and East Berlin.[19]

Gorbachev knew that most of his compatriots were not ready to abandon East Germany, where, at such appalling cost, the front line of Soviet security in Europe had been established over forty years earlier. But "few top officials understood that Moscow simply could not afford to keep East Germany," Chernyaev explained. "Gorbachev could not talk about this publicly, because to do so would further undermine his position. The big question was how hard a bargain could he drive for agreeing to such a historic change?" Gorbachev seems to have believed that the tougher the Soviet approach to a settlement, the less likely it was that there would be the overall relationship that he wanted with Western Europe and the United States.

To make matters worse, Gorbachev was in a weak position. In early January 1990, as the shelves emptied in food shops in all the major Soviet cities, he had to ask Kohl for urgent help. Kohl kept the promise he had made in June, and within two weeks had arranged to deliver $100 million of food.[20] None of the Soviet leadership believed that process of unification could be stopped, but they all hoped it could be controlled. On January 27, 1990, they decided to back a confederation of the two German states, with preparations soon getting underway for the withdrawal of Soviet troops from Germany.[21]

Although Bush did not exacerbate Gorbachev's problems in public, in private he strongly backed Kohl's plans for incorporating East Germany into both West Germany and Nato. When Bush met with Kohl in February he said: "The Soviets are not in a position to dictate Germany's relationship with NATO . . . We prevailed, they didn't. We can't let the Soviets clutch victory from the jaws of defeat."[22]

Rapid Unification

For Bush the unification of Germany would truly mark the end of the Cold War. Ross explained: "When Thatcher argued that 'we can't do this to Gorbachev,' Bush's response was that it was beyond the ability of the West to control what happened in the Soviet Union. The West could, however, shape a new Europe in which a united Germany was imbedded in well-established Western institutions." That, Bush and Baker believed, would provide stability and open the way to new partnerships with the Soviet Union.[23]

Events continued to drive policy. A confederation soon seemed increasingly unlikely once East German demonstrators changed from chanting "*WE* are the people!" to "We are *ONE* people."[24] To minimize the impression that unification was a "defeat" for the Soviet Union, Bush was willing for Nato to declare that it no longer viewed the Soviet Union as an enemy. But he refused to avoid doing what he believed was necessary because it might be seen as a "loss" for Gorbachev.

The train of German unification was "leaving the station," Baker told Shevardnadze, and if it left without the Soviet Union aboard, the Soviets would get nothing. The way forward, he argued, was to discuss the best deal Moscow could get. At the beginning of February, Baker deployed two arguments that Gorbachev found convincing: "The first," Ross said, "was that if Germany became neutral it might become less predictable and could one day be tempted to develop nuclear weapons; the second was that if Germany did enter the Alliance, the West promised that Nato would not extend its military presence into eastern Germany," a point which was of great importance to the Soviet Union.

By the middle of the month Baker and Shevardnadze had agreed that the details of unification would be worked out by the "two-plus-four" formula. This formula recognized that there were still two Germanys, who would deal with the internal arrangements, while the Four Powers dealt with those that touched on their own interests after unification.

Gorbachev cooperated closely with the Americans not only in the hope that the process would be peaceful, but that it would respect the interests and dignity of the Soviet Union. "We also had to work hard," President Bush told me, "to convince the Poles that, once unified, Germany would enter into a treaty guaranteeing peaceful borders for Poland."[25] In the end, the Germans went further, promising to limit the future size of a German army and not to station nuclear weapons in East Germany.

In the East German elections in March 1990, the Christian Democrats won an overwhelming victory and there was a vote for rapid unification. In April, Kohl had swiftly granted Gorbachev the DM 5 billion ($3 billion) credit that he requested.[26] Just before the "two-plus-four" negotiations began in May, however, Gorbachev told the Poliburo that there was absolutely no way the Soviet Union could let a reunified Germany be in Nato. He said he would even go so far as to break off all the arms control negotiations, "but I won't let this happen."[27]

But Gorbachev had a great ability, Chernyaev noted, to "take realities into account."[28] At his second summit with Bush, in Washington in May 1990, he unexpectedly agreed in principle that the Germans had the right to decide their own future. The West responded with some helpful gestures.

35 Riding the Tiger

Disintegrating

Timothy Garton Ash, a leading chronicler of the collapse of communism in Europe, noted that in "Poland [it] had taken ten years, in Hungary ten months, in East Germany ten weeks and in Czechoslovakia ten days."[1] In Romania—the bloody exception to the rule of peaceful transition—the end had come more swiftly, with the execution of Ceausescu and his wife on Christmas Day, 1989, an event which was televised around the world.

At the beginning of 1990, the only communist party leader who remained in power in Europe was Gorbachev—and his problems were mounting rapidly. Within the Soviet Communist Party, the conservatives believed that they would end up on the scrap heap of history unless they compelled Gorbachev to change course. Yakovlev, the most radical reformer in the Politburo, urged Gorbachev "to abandon the communists and lead a new democratic party."

Gorbachev was not willing to take the risk of letting "this lousy, rabid dog" off the leash. "If I do that, all this huge structure will be turned against me."[2] Instead, he tried to regain the initiative by strengthening his personal executive power. In March 1990, he had himself elected president of the Soviet Union—though by the new Soviet parliament, not by popular election. His new presidential cabinet was made up of a balance of reformers and conservatives.

Although the constitution had been amended to eliminate the communist party's monopoly on power, protests continued. Many of those who marched through Red Square in the May Day parade carried banners reading "Down with Gorbachev!," "Down with the Soviet Communist Party—robber and exploiter of the people!" and "Freedom to Lithuania!" Gorbachev was jeered off the reviewing stand.[3]

Gorbachev's difficulties were compounded by the slump in living standards, which began to unravel the social fabric. At the end of May, the leaders of the world's seven major developed economies gathered in Houston for the G-7 Summit. Through Kohl, Gorbachev informed them that he was embarking on radical, market-oriented reforms and requested over three years some $60 billion in support.[4]

"Some members of the Bush Administration," Ross recalled, "really did argue for a substantial aid package. On balance, however, Western leaders were simply not convinced that Gorbachev would make the tough decisions required." There were also growing doubts about his chances of survival. The best the Bush Administration could do for him was to secure a $4 billion line of credit from the Saudis and Kuwaitis, which was supplemented by some European credits.

At the Party Congress in early July the conservatives ferociously attacked Gorbachev for letting the Baltics move towards independence, weakening the Warsaw Pact, "losing" East Germany and undermining the ideological foundations of the Soviet Union and the party. In the end, however, Gorbachev out-maneuvered the hard-liners and was re-elected general secretary. To the amazement of most observers he persuaded the Congress to adopt his statement on "Towards a Humane, Democratic Socialism," which was in essence a social-democratic platform.

Despite these achievements, Gorbachev's position was weakening and Yeltsin's was strengthening. In May, Yeltsin had been elected chairman of the Supreme Soviet of the Russian Republic, which two weeks later declared that Russia was "sovereign" and would decide which Soviet laws to implement. Then at the Congress in July Yeltsin lambasted the Party for failing to embrace genuine reform, stormed out of the Congress and resigned from the Party.

The risk of instability rose sharply during the summer as soaring inflation provoked massive strikes, while the catastrophic depletion of the state's food and hard-currency reserves continued. Gorbachev used special powers granted him by the Supreme Soviet to reimpose administrative controls on the economy and rejected a 500-day plan to reform it along market lines. The intelligentsia now flocked to support Yeltsin whom they regarded as a champion of the reform who had shown the courage of his convictions.

Germany and Nato

At the Congress Gorbachev counter-attacked his critics by pointing out that Nato leaders had just, for the first time, referred to the Soviet Union as a "partner." Nato's new attitude and his success at the Congress enabled Gorbachev to make his biggest gesture on Germany. "Whether we like it or not," Gorbachev declared at a press conference in Moscow on July 16, "the time will come when a united Germany will be in Nato, if that is its choice . . . [and if it is] . . . Germany can work together with the Soviet Union." Kohl, who was present, thought that this was "a fantastic result."[5]

With the introduction of the West German Deutschmark into East Germany two weeks earlier, the German Democratic Republic effectively ceased to be a sovereign state. Kohl eased the pain for Gorbachev by undertaking to pay the cost for moving Soviet troops and their families—some 420,000 of them in all—from East Germany and resettling them in the Soviet Union. Some Soviet officers also brought quite a lot of money back with them, having sold off weapons, stores and property on a massive scale: most, however, received little help from the Soviet government.

Germany was unified and regained full sovereignty on October 3. Whereas in the West, this decision was widely regarded as a great triumph for Western policy, for most people in the Soviet Union it was "one of the most hated developments in the history of Soviet foreign policy," Alexander Bessmertnykh, who replaced Shevardnadze, later noted.[6]

Although Kohl provided new grants and loans on favorable terms—in all, some $12 billion (DM 20 billion)—most Russians and many Westerners believe that he could have squeezed far more from Nato had he played a tougher hand in the negotiations, instead of expecting to be rewarded later for the cards he gave away.

As a result of deep cuts agreed in the Treaty on Conventional Forces in Europe that was signed in Paris later that month, there was no longer a Soviet military threat to Western Europe. Soviet forces had already withdrawn from Czechoslovakia and Hungary; they were withdrawing from East Germany and would soon be committed to be out of Poland by the end of the following year.

One of those at the signing ceremony was Dmitri Yazov, the Soviet minister of defense. As a young colonel, in 1962, he had been in command of the tactical nuclear missiles in Cuba, which unbeknown to the Americans were targeted on their base at Guantanamo Bay. Yazov could not contain his fury at what he was witnessing and ranted to his colleagues that "This treaty means we have lost World War III without a shot being fired."[7] Gorbachev's critics were gaining popular support.[8]

Iraq

Saddam Hussein's unexpected invasion of Kuwait on August 2, 1990, confronted Gorbachev with yet another issue that would be contentious within the party. The Soviet Union had long had close ties with Iraq which, like the United States, it had backed against Iran. Some 9,000 of its citizens were working in the country and Iraq owed nearly $13 billion for Soviet arms. Nonetheless, Gorbachev and Shevardnadze decided that the thrust of their new thinking required them to join the United States in condemning Iraq.

Having failed to persuade Saddam to pull out of Kuwait, Gorbachev felt compelled in November to support the UN resolution authorizing the use of force against Iraq. Ross emphasized the importance of the new relationship between Bush and Gorbachev, which, he said, "made it possible for the United States to transfer a substantial part of its forces from Germany to the Gulf." Meanwhile, Gorbachev, who was keen to resolve the issue without a war, increased his efforts to persuade Saddam to pull out of Kuwait.

Once the war began, the Americans quickly destroyed much of the advanced weaponry that the Soviet Union had sold to the Iraqis in recent years. Gorbachev's opponents felt that the Soviet Union had become a silent partner in Baghdad's humiliation.

Breaking Down

At the same time, nationalist sentiment was rising across the Soviet Union. In January 1990, communal violence between Azerbaijanis and Armenians and its suppression by the Soviet authorities led to two hundred more deaths. That same month, the Lithuanian Communist Party renamed itself the Lithuanian Democratic Labor Party; within months Lithuania proclaimed its independence, the first Soviet republic to do so.

In December, Gorbachev appointed a hard-line minister of the interior because, he said, the country "needed firm executive rule to overcome the threat posed by the dark forces of nationalism."[9] He also chose as his vice president Gennadi Yanayev, who assured everyone that he was a communist "to the depths of my soul." Shevardnadze, Gorbachev's foreign minister and friend, resigned warning that dictatorship was near. In his traditional New Year's address to the Soviet people, Gorbachev lamented that 1990 had been "one of the most difficult years in our history."[10]

Worse was in store. Gorbachev seems to have believed the KGB's argument that the majority of the Balts wanted to remain in the Soviet Union and that a crackdown on the independence movements would swing opinion in Moscow's favor. On the contrary, the killing of twenty people by Soviet troops in January 1991 reinforced the Balts' determination to gain real independence from Moscow. At the end of the month, Gorbachev asked Matlock, the American ambassador, to "tell my friend George Bush: whatever pressure is put on me regarding the Persian Gulf, the German question, or the ratification of the conventional arms treaty, I'll keep to our agreements. My deepest desire is to keep our radical changes from drowning in blood."[11]

Throughout the year, Gorbachev tried to prevent the breakup of the Soviet Union. In March 1991, nine of the fifteen republics backed a proposal that would give them greater powers—but nationalism and pressure for reform were growing, especially in Russia. At the end of the month, despite a ban and the presence of 50,000 troops in the capital, mass demonstrations were held in Moscow in favor of Yeltsin, with a bloody confrontation only narrowly averted.

Gorbachev was now more desperate than ever for economic aid. At the G-7 Summit in London he tried once again to secure a huge Marshall Aid-type package. "Gorbachev believed," Chernyaev said, "that this would give him the leverage needed to persuade the republics to agree to some new form of federation." The Soviet Union, however, was not like Western Europe in 1947. It was not a market economy needing foreign exchange to revive production; it was a malfunctioning, struggling state-controlled economy that needed the money to keep afloat. Soviet hard-currency debt was now approaching $80 billion.

Ross acknowledged that "Gorbachev was embittered by the West's lack of support, especially after all he had done on Germany and Iraq." While Gorbachev was losing credibility, Yeltsin was gaining it, most significantly because, on June 12, 1991, the people of Russia, not the Supreme Soviet of the Russian Republic, elected him president of Russia. This gave him the political legitimacy that Gorbachev so lacked.

The United States continued to recognize the Soviet Union as a superpower, but less out of respect for its strength than for concern over the security implications of its weakness. As Baker put it, the task of American policy was to create a "soft landing, for a collapsing empire."[12]

At the summit meeting in Moscow on July 31, which was to be their last, Bush and Gorbachev signed the START-I treaty. For the first time, the two superpowers agreed to deep cuts in strategic nuclear weapons. Over seven years, each side would reduce its total number of strategic warheads to 6,000, deployed on no more than 1,600 missiles or bombers. These cuts would greatly reduce the chances of one side being able to destroy the land-based strategic missiles of the other in a pre-emptive strike.

On his way home, Bush stopped in Kiev, where in keeping with Gorbachev's wish he tried to persuade the Ukrainians to remain within the Union. But it was far too late for that. His speech did not go down well in the Ukraine—nor did it in America, where it was ridiculed as "Chicken Kiev."

The Demise of the Soviet Union

Although there were disturbing signs of trouble brewing within the Supreme Soviet and warnings of a coup from the Americans, Gorbachev paid no attention, still believing he could find a political solution to the country's problems. He expected the breakthrough would come on August 20 when he was due to meet with the leaders of the nine republics to work out a new Union Treaty.

Before that could happen, a group of hard-liners within Gorbachev's government mounted a coup while he was holidaying at the Black Sea in August. Gorbachev refused to cooperate with them and denounced their actions. Many people in government, the army and the KGB withheld support for the coup.

Yeltsin rallied over 50,000 people around the White House, the Russian Parliament building in Moscow. Although this was a small number in a city with a population of 10 million, it was enough to unnerve the plotters. Within four days, the coup had collapsed and Gorbachev returned safely to Moscow on August 23.

While Gorbachev had triumphed over the hard-liners, Yeltsin was about to triumph over him. On the day of his return Gorbachev was jeered in the Russian Parliament, after which Yeltsin launched into a humiliating denunciation of him. The following day, Gorbachev resigned as head of the communist party, which within days ceased to exist. Gorbachev's political power was fading fast. At the Cabinet Office in London, Sir Percy Cradock, the chairman of the Joint Intelligence Committee, invited the other members to join him for a glass of champagne, not to celebrate, but "To commemorate the demise of Soviet Communism."

The Bush Administration had difficulty in responding to the rapid pace of events. "The truth of the matter," Ross explained, "was that eighteen months of relentless work on Germany and Iraq had left our foreign policy team almost exhausted. They saw no way of reviving Gorbachev's fortunes." Yeltsin had not impressed Bush, but he was a force to be reckoned with. Bush and Baker were agreed that they had to be on the right side of the nationalist forces that were breaking the Soviet Union apart. The question of how "Soviet" nuclear weapons would be controlled became more urgent.

When Baker visited Moscow in September, he met with Yeltsin and the heads of the republics. "Baker offered principles," Ross recalls, "that would help a peaceful transition—change should be peaceful, borders should be inviolable unless changes were agreed through negotiation; economies should be free-market and civil and human rights should be protected."

In mid-November, as the specter of the breakup of the Soviet Union loomed larger and larger, Gorbachev wondered what he could possibly do to stop it. When he consulted Yevgeni Shaposhnikov, his minister of defense, Shaposhnikov warned him that it was too late for a military crackdown and the army must not be called on to resolve internal political disputes. "After reviewing these options," Gorbachev later said, "I decided we could not risk civil war."[13]

The disintegration of the Soviet Union was ultimately driven by Ukraine's bid for independence in the aftermath of the aborted coup. While Gorbachev was still trying to find a formula for preserving the Union, Yeltsin and the leaders of the Ukraine and Belarus signed a pact ending the Soviet Union and creating instead a Commonwealth of Independent States. They first telephoned Bush to tell him what they had done; then they informed Gorbachev. Although this "soft-landing" was acceptable to the West, it was not what Gorbachev had striven for.

On December 25, 1991, the Soviet Union came to an end. That evening Gorbachev handed over control of the "nuclear button" to Marshal Shaposhnikov. Shaposhnikov, accompanied by two colonels, who operated the device, then disappeared into the corridors of the Kremlin in search of their new boss—President Boris Yeltsin of Russia.[14]

In his farewell address to the nation later that evening, Gorbachev gave a perceptive analysis of why change had been needed and the broad historic and political reasons why it had not been possible to achieve what he had hoped. Nonetheless, he pointed out, there had been great achievements. Totalitarianism had ended, and there had been a breakthrough towards democracy, economic reform and a new relationship with the outside world.[15]

Not surprisingly, there was much that Gorbachev did not say. He had shown extraordinary determination in pushing forward reforms at home and in changing Soviet foreign policy. He lacked, however, the foresight and ruthlessness to deprive his adversaries of their power before it was too late.

Had Gorbachev chosen to be elected president by the Soviet people in March 1990, he would have had a better chance of sidelining his opponents and building a new power-base. His failure to do so, which left him little choice but to try to keep control of the country with the help of the old guard, did much to tarnish his reputation, especially within the Soviet Union. But even if he had followed the advice of his liberal minded advisers, he would not necessarily have succeeded. Ironically, by keeping some control over the party Gorbachev gave Yeltsin a greater chance of reforming Russia.

With the lowering of the Red Flag over the Kremlin at midnight, the Soviet Union, the world's last remaining great empire, was no more and its borders returned to where they had been in 1653, long before Russia became a great power in Europe. The fact that this happened with so little violence was one of Gorbachev's greatest achievements.

"Amid the squalor and poverty of everyday life," Pavel Palazhchenko, Gorbachev's interpreter, reflected, "many people had found refuge and relief in the fact that they were citizens of a superpower that was respected and even feared by the rest of the world."[16] Now they had not only lost that sense, but they were even poorer. There was much bitterness.

A New Beginning

After the collapse of the Soviet Union Gorbachev frequently said that "The end of the Cold War is our common victory."[17] It was, but for those of us who have not grown up within the Soviet system it is not always easy to understand the full extent of the intellectual journey that Gorbachev had to make for that to be possible.

Few statements bring home the point so clearly as the "repentance" speech made to the Politburo in 1988 by Andrei Gromyko, who during his thirty years as foreign minister had played an important part in shaping Soviet policy:

> In Khrushchev's time we produced 600 nuclear bombs. Khrushchev himself from time to time asked the question: "When should we stop?" Later under Brezhnev we should have taken a more reasonable position. But we remained attached to the same principle: since they [the US] are running ahead, we should do the same, as if it was a sports competition . . . That was . . . [a] completely erroneous position. And the political leadership was fully responsible for it.[18]

Recognizing the mistake was one thing, changing policy was another. As Gorbachev pointed out, as "rising up against our efforts were not only old habits but also real social forces linked by material interests with the old ways of doing things—from the generals . . . to the scientists, all of whom had made their careers on the basis of 'demonstrating' the irreconcilable nature of the 'two camps in the world.'"[19]

In Washington Cathedral on June 11, 2004, Gorbachev attended Reagan's funeral as the official representative of Russia. During his visit he spoke with warmth and admiration about the late president. It will still be a long time before most Russians speak about Gorbachev in the same way. But as the years go by, an increasing number of Russians are likely to recognize the longer-term benefits of the transformation Gorbachev began and the potential it still has for further change.

The day after Gorbachev stepped down as president of the Soviet Union he gave an interview to Italian journalists. Democracy and human rights, he told them, were important everywhere, but "We have our own reality, inspired by tradition, history, a unified country that has formed by a natural process. Yes, like many of my compatriots, I have spiritual ties to Europe, but I am no less bound to the East . . . these disparate trends have always been present and at odds with Russia's spiritual and political culture. Russia must recognize that it is a bridge between the two cultures, that of Asia and that of Europe, and, simultaneously, part of human civilization."[20] This subject—the identity of Russia and its links with Europe—was one that had been in the mind of Tsar Alexander I as he marched into Paris in 1814 and one that has yet to be resolved.

36 Looking Back

Although this *Journey Through the Hall of Mirrors* has addressed the three big questions of the Cold War—why it started, why it lasted so long and why it ended the way it did—at the end of it we are left facing the biggest and most important question of all: How did we survive without blowing ourselves to Hell?

Here, after all, we had a massive confrontation of geopolitics, ideology and military power. Enormous human energy was spent in mobilizing resources. During the course of the Cold War, the two sides manufactured something on the order of 100,000 nuclear weapons. At any one time, many tens of thousands were deployed as artillery shells, bombs and missiles that could be launched from land, sea or air. Even though the leaders on both sides wanted to prevent any unauthorized use of nuclear weapons, the risks of that happening remained despite the safeguards they put in place.

The specter of miscalculation cast some disturbingly dark shadows. Points of potential conflagration studded the globe: from Check Point Charlie in Berlin, to the jungles of the Third World, to the back alleys of Moscow and Washington and Vienna, to the depths of the Seven Seas. In the early years of this epic confrontation, certain very sage people—Bertrand Russell, for one—were sure that we would soon perish in a thermonuclear holocaust. But we did not.

One afternoon, I walked along the Mall in Washington with Fritz Ermarth, a distinguished Soviet expert who, during the last years of the Cold War, had chaired the National Intelligence Council, which coordinated intelligence assessments for the president. I asked him how he thought the world had been able to avert disaster.

Ermarth paused a moment, as if to respect the gravity of the question, then offered his reflection: "Despite all their rhetoric, both sides were basically cautious and risk-averse. And, just as importantly on the Soviet side, with the obvious exception of Stalin, they were animated and restrained by common human fears." Ermarth felt that in this domain Khrushchev was, in some ways, the most conflicted personality: "Although he was bold to the point of adventurism, a moral sense was at work during the Cuban missile crisis and also in de-Stalinization." Like Anatoly Chernyaev, Gorbachev's foreign affairs adviser, he felt that Gorbachev was a moral man.[1]

I had noticed, I said, other reflections of these common human fears and moral concerns. It seemed to me that however scared Soviet leaders were, and despite the many weaknesses in the Soviet satellite and radar early-warning networks, they kept two robust safety-catches on the gate that opened the way to Armageddon.

The first, was that while the Soviet General Staff was excessive in its efforts to avoid a repeat of 1941, they understood the horrors that another war would entail; they were exceedingly cautious in their judgments about the imminence of war. Even though the Politburo had bunkers that afforded them far more protection than those available to American leaders, they were even more risk-averse than the military; they regarded nuclear war as simply a collective form of suicide.

The second and equally robust safety-catch was at the technical level. While the Soviet leadership were determined to maintain a credible deterrent, they did not want anything to go wrong. They invested heavily in controls to ensure that nuclear weapons could never be used without their explicit authorization. While the General Staff was always wanting to work out how to respond to various eventualities, its top members shared the Politburo's deep distrust of automatic responses, let alone decisions made by machines. For instance, it was Marshal Akhromeyev, chief of the General Staff under Gorbachev, who blocked work on the "Doomsday Machine," or "Dead Hand." He did so on the advice of one of the people responsible for ensuring that the Soviet Union could retaliate if attacked—General Varfolomei Korobushin, the deputy chief of the Strategic Rocket Forces.[2] The Politburo were in no doubt that the decision to initiate war was far too important to be left to the military

As we walked past the White House, which would have been the No. 1 target in any Soviet missile attack, my conversation with Fritz Ermarth rather appropriately turned to the impact that the existence of nuclear weapons had had on strategic thinking. I told Ermarth what Joe Nye—who had himself chaired the National Intelligence Council in 1993–94—had said about "the crystal ball effect" of nuclear weapons when he spoke at a seminar President Gorbachev hosted in Moscow in 2006.

In the past, Nye pointed out, the outcome of any given war had always been uncertain. None of Europe's leaders could foresee the results of the wars that began in 1914 or 1939. But once both superpowers had the ability to kill millions of each other's people in moments, decision makers shuddered at the thought of nuclear war, especially as they might be one of its first victims. "It was this specter," Nye said, "that made them risk-averse."[3]

Ermarth agreed, but added that strategy itself had played a key role in keeping the peace. "I think nuclear strategy was rather like the Roman god Janus, whose two faces looked in different directions," he said. "After all, nuclear war was not 'unthinkable'—in fact we thought about it a lot. But the arms race itself made it unworkable from any point of view."

"As time went by," Ermarth recalled, "we moved away from simplistic notions of 'minimum assured destruction' to robust and large forces, with well-protected command and control systems, which could not be entirely eliminated even by a surprise attack. It was difficult and expensive. But it foreclosed illusions about cheap-shot concepts of victory and made for a much more durable and stable structure of deterrence than would have obtained if many of its critics had been in charge. The Americans developed this logic; then, grumbling all the way, the Soviets accepted it too. So, while both sides saw advantage in being perceived to have the strategic 'advantage,' they were both deeply scared about nuclear war."

As we parted ways, Ermarth offered a last reflection, which I thought encapsulated his line of thinking rather well. "I say it was Janus-faced because one face was demonic—that of the so-called 'Wizards of Armageddon' who thought about how to fight and win a nuclear war. But there was also another face that was at least human, if not angelic."

Among Western leaders Prime Minister Thatcher was well known for her insistence that, should the need arise, she would "press the button." In private, other concerns tugged at her heart strings. In his memoirs Rodric Braithwaite, who served as British ambassador in Moscow during the latter Gorbachev years, noted that she had remarked to him in 1980 that "she was not at all sure that, in the event, she could press the button: 'I want grandchildren too.'" He felt this was "an endearing flash of humanity."[4]

As we now know, whenever the leaders on either side thought of the blinding flashes that would herald a nuclear Armageddon, they were always struck by a similar mix of human fears and hopes that it would never happen. Ensuring that nuclear deterrence continues to work will be one of the greatest challenges of the 21st century

Lessons

LAST REFLECTIONS

"Our real first line of defense, wouldn't you agree, is our capacity to reason."

37 Reading Their Mail

The Thoughts of Others

"One of the things that kept the Cold War scary," Robert Gates, a former director of Central Intelligence, recalled, "was the lack of understanding on each side of the mentality of the other."[1] Milt Bearden, a key figure in the CIA's Soviet operations, responded more pithily when I asked him what he thought had been the West's greatest intelligence failure during the Cold War: "We didn't realize just how f***ing scared Soviet leaders were of us!" And on the Soviet side, it was not until Gorbachev came to power that the Soviet leadership were willing to accept that the Americans had cause to be scared of them, too.

Through the amassing and analysis of secret intelligence, each side attempted to make things a little less scary. Since the end of the Cold War much has been written about espionage, intelligence services and agencies, and the methods they use. There are some fascinating collections of documents now available, and a few senior people from both the Soviet and the American sides have been willing—off the record, at least—to throw additional light on this subject.[2]

Still, the overall picture remains fragmentary, and many mysteries remain unsolved. There is plenty of scope for debate over the impact of intelligence, especially in terms of how directly it influenced decision making. Before considering this question in more detail, I would like to look briefly at some of the difficulties each side faced—both in trying to collect intelligence and determine its significance—because they have a considerable bearing on the lessons to be learned from the Cold War.

What Washington Wanted

After four years of wartime cooperation the Soviet Union was not quite the "riddle wrapped inside a mystery inside an enigma" that it had been when

Churchill used those words to describe it in October 1939. Nevertheless, it was still a closed society and there was much the Americans did not know about the Soviet Union, its outlook and intentions.

In seeking to understand Soviet thinking on foreign policy, American leaders had to contend with a complex mixture of revolutionary ambition, legitimate security interests, and Stalin's paranoia, all of which could be confounding. Americans also wanted to know about the current military and economic strength of the Soviet Union, and how forcefully it could pursue its objectives. The question at the forefront of their minds, however, was whether war was likely.

Although the Americans and the British did manage to recruit a small number of ideologically motivated Russian and Eastern European agents in the early Cold War years—and considerably more during the détente era—they never had enough. "But what saved us," James Schlesinger, who served briefly as director of Central Intelligence before becoming secretary of defense in 1973, emphasized, "was the determination with which we developed and exploited new intelligence technology. Both intercepts of various kinds and overhead photography began providing invaluable intelligence."

What Moscow Wanted

By contrast, the Soviet Union confronted a country that was an open society, overflowing with information from the press, as well as congressional and governmental reports. Soviet intelligence officers could learn valuable details about American missiles and planes for the price of a copy of *Aviation Week*. To acquire comparable Soviet details, the CIA would probably have to spend millions of dollars.

Moscow's primary aim was to determine the lengths America was intending to go to in trying to "contain" the Soviet Union. Would it accept the Soviet Union as a great power and seek to avoid war? Would it try to "roll back" communist regimes that Stalin had established at the end of the war? Or would it go even further and attempt to eliminate the Soviet "threat" by launching a pre-emptive nuclear strike against it?

The military capabilities of the United States and its Nato allies were, of course, the other top priority. Soviet leaders sought information about the kinds of weapons—both nuclear forces and conventional ones—that existed, and about how to design such weapons themselves. Finally, over the years, Moscow made greater efforts to determine the opportunities for the expansion of

Soviet influence in the Third World, which was seen as the weak underbelly of the West and the place where Soviet gains could help Moscow win the Cold War.

As the Cold War got underway, many of Moscow's top American and European agents (of whom there had been dozens, all ideologically motivated) were betrayed or unmasked. This was a setback, but it was not a disaster for a country that had spied so successfully for so long. Soon, the lax (at times extraordinarily lax) security systems of open societies enabled Western mercenaries and misfits to provide Moscow with an extraordinary range of high-grade military and technological intelligence; yet it was that very openness that proved to be one of the West's greatest strengths.

Cryptography, too, helped offset Moscow's intelligence losses. Cracking foreign ciphers was a Russian skill dating back to tsarist times and one that reached new peaks of achievement in the Soviet era.[3] During most of the Cold War, it seems, Moscow's cryptographers managed to read a considerable amount of the world's diplomatic traffic, not only that of that of most Third World countries, but also that of the French, the Italians and, at times, the Germans as well.[4] On the military front, too, Soviet intelligence had some extraordinary cryptographic triumphs.

Reading Intelligence

In both Moscow and Washington there was a high degree of confidence that they would be able to detect preparations for war by the other side, though not necessarily those for a surprise attack. As James Woolsey, who was closely involved with the intelligence community in the seventies before becoming director of Central Intelligence in 1993, explained: "We could read a lot of their mail." The Soviets could also read a lot of theirs, too. With help from the Walker brothers, who were serving in the US Navy, the Soviets were able to read the American naval codes for over eighteen years, from 1967 until 1985.[5]

The value of intelligence, of course, lies not solely in the quality of the material. Great intelligence rarely comes neatly packaged with a clear explanation of its significance. As every society and bureaucracy has its own mantras, rhetoric, and conventions of political correctness, intelligence needs to be read with care.

One of the many contributions of Oleg Gordievsky, Britain's most valuable source in the KGB, to our understanding of the Soviet Union was through teaching us how to find the real meaning in Soviet documents. "Soviet speeches are comprised of three elements: rhetoric, which is to make us feel good; propaganda, which is to make you feel bad; and some substance." KGB plans, he pointed out, generally tell you far more about what the Soviet Union would like to achieve, than they do about the KGB's capabilities. (With a wry smile he would also point out that "Many Western speeches, it seems to me, have similar characteristics to Soviet ones!" He was not far off the mark.)

Secret documents, by their nature, are not intended to be read by "the other side," though Nato's Nuclear Policy Committee wisely took the precaution of spelling everything out for the Russians, whom they did expect would get copies of their proceedings. The sources in Nato providing top secret documents to East German Intelligence were regularly asked to explain what they meant—for the very simple reason that only the "Nato-ese" could fully understand "Nato-speak." The Americans had similar problems. "Even when Colonel Kuklinski gave us the new Soviet war plans," Phillip Petersen recalled, "it required a major effort by those of us analyzing them in the Defense Intelligence Agency to understand what they really meant."

Presenting Intelligence

The ways intelligence was presented in Moscow and Washington were decidedly different. American leaders received "National Intelligence Estimates" that tried to coordinate the views of all the intelligence agencies and the main policy-making departments. The fact that Soviet leaders had no such system stemmed in part from Stalin, who believed that only he had the intellect and judgment to assess intelligence properly.

The main reason that Stalin's successors followed his example, however, was that none of them wished to be confronted with a coordinated assessment prepared by others that either conflicted with their own views, or would make it difficult to maintain a consensus in the Politburo. They preferred to receive separate assessments and reports from the KGB, the GRU (Soviet Military Intelligence), and the Foreign Ministry. The KGB and the GRU were competitors in the field of foreign intelligence, with the KGB's agents often reporting on military matters and the GRU's on political ones.

For both sides intelligence was often a political issue, but at the Kremlin it was a far more sensitive topic. As head of the KGB, Andropov was willing to submit intelligence to the Politburo that challenged established views, but he was careful not to confront his Politburo colleagues with information in a form they would find unacceptable.

Some of Andropov's assessments for the Politburo were well-informed, unbiased and concise. On November 5, 1968, for instance, he submitted a remarkably blunt report on the reaction of Soviet students to the Prague Spring and its suppression. It referred to their profound cynicism towards the official ideology and propaganda, their receptivity to Western culture and ideas, the resentment that most students felt toward Moscow's "fraternal allies," the high incidence of excessive alcohol consumption and sexual promiscuity and entrenched anti-semitism.[6] Before long, this and other reporting led to a major new effort by the KGB to control dissent.

Assessments that conflicted with decisions already taken were given short shrift. When top members of the General Staff voiced their opposition to plans for the Soviet invasion of Afghanistan, key members of the Politburo told them, in no uncertain terms, to shut up. It remains a moot point whether they would have had a better chance of being heard if they had started making their case earlier.

Gorbachev reacted similarly when intelligence reports challenged his reformist policies. Leonid Shebarshin, one of the KGB's most senior officers, later complained: "When the information confirmed Gorbachev's views, it was welcome. But when policy and reality started to diverge, with the situation in the country going from bad to worse, Gorbachev did not want to know."[7]

The directors of Central Intelligence were far more inclined to pass to America's leaders intelligence that went against the grain. Even so, intelligence was not supposed to get in the way of policy. Douglas MacEachin, the CIA analyst who gave the daily intelligence briefings to the secretary of state and the vice president during the early Reagan era, recalled that "On no subject were we at the working level in the CIA subjected to more virulent attacks than those we received for our papers describing the collapsing Soviet economy, the disintegration of Soviet society."

"The most vehement criticism came in 1982," MacEachin recalled, "when we said that our revised estimates showed that Soviet expenditure on the procurement of weapons had not increased since 1976 and the growth in total defense expenditure had slowed significantly in real terms."[8] These estimates were criticized for underplaying the threat from a Soviet Union that was continuing to produce impressive new weapons systems and whose defense expenditure figures, some analysts argued, were not worth the paper they were written on.

"Getting policy makers to focus on rapid change could be every bit as difficult," MacEachin explained, referring to the Gorbachev era when he was in charge of the CIA's analysis of Soviet affairs. "The changes during Gorbachev's first three years had been so great that our biggest challenge had been getting people to understand that this was a historical watershed in the making, with the changes in prospect likely to be even more dramatic. And that meant we would face a yet greater challenge in communicating the overall picture to them."

"I faced a long struggle," MacEachin recalled, "before I was able to issue a paper in June 1988 that concluded 'there is a good chance that Gorbachev will by the end of the decade turn to unilateral defense cuts.'"[9] As MacEachin was about to make this point to a Senate sub-committee on December 7, 1988, he was informed that was what Gorbachev had just announced in his address to the UN in New York. "Well, Senator," he said as he began his opening statement, "we just learned that one of my analytical judgments is going to be borne out." The timing, however, was not ideal, as the incoming Bush Administration was far more skeptical about Gorbachev's intentions than Reagan had been.

Assessment, Soviet-style

In Moscow and Washington intelligence was assessed in markedly dissimilar ways, both in terms of the processes used and the mindsets that shaped the analysis. One crucial thing, however, was true for both sides—in making sound assessments it is, of course, not only the quality of the intelligence that counts, but also the sophistication of the analysis and the rigor of the judgments drawn from it. For that reason "intelligence failures" are just as likely to result from the intellectual failures of those interpreting and assessing the intelligence, as it is from the quality (or lack of it) of the intelligence reports themselves.

"One of the things to understand about the KGB that made it different from American Intelligence," Robert Gates points out, "is that it really had no analytical capability. You had all these spies out there reporting information and there was no one analyzing it for accuracy or for whether it was real or not."[10] However, the biggest obstacle the Soviets faced in assessing Western policy was that they had, as Percy Cradock put it, to "force an excellent supply of information from the multifaceted West into the oversimplified framework of hostility and conspiracy theory."[11]

While that was true, it seems that the system often coped with this matter fairly well in its own distinctive way. The first-rate report that Andropov submitted to the Politburo on April 19, 1971, on the American position in the anti-ballistic missile negotiations suggests that he had some highly experienced officers working for him on this subject in Moscow, as well as others in the Soviet delegations to these negotiations and to those on strategic arms control.[12] During the early eighties the KGB began putting more effort into assessments.

One of the few places in Moscow where there were lively debates about both the assessment of intelligence and its implications for policy was within the military.[13] While the political leadership kept a tight control over any decision concerning war, they mainly left it to the "military intellectuals," in the General Staff and Soviet Military Intelligence, to develop strategy and identify what was needed to implement it. Operational issues were often examined and debated with remarkable frankness in the top secret and secret editions of the General Staff's journal *Military Thought.*

Through most of the Cold War, the main preconceptions of the Soviet leadership reflected the traditional Soviet faith in communism being the wave of the future, something which the hard facts of life made increasingly hard for them to sustain. This made them overplay their own successes and exaggerate the weaknesses of the West. The second highly influential preconception was that any problems that the Soviet Union faced, be they abroad or at home, were the fault of subversive forces, not the failings of the regime's own policies or actions.

According to Alexander Yakovlev, a leading member of Gorbachev's Politburo, the reports received in Moscow during the Cold War reinforced the hostile image of the West by blaming the Americans for everything. "People were not praised for their objectivity, but for providing information that was in line with policy, which we call 'loyal information.'" There were, however, different strands of reporting. The GRU, being the intelligence branch of the Soviet armed forces, did much to bolster belief in the military threat from the West; the Foreign Ministry, generally speaking, tried to protect itself from criticism by blaming the West for everything, while the KGB did—at times—give a fairly accurate description of events.

Assessment, American-style

In trying to interpret Soviet actions the West faced its own problems. One of the biggest was they were trying to draw sound conclusions and projections on the basis of information and intelligence that was often fragmentary. And it was not just Soviet assessments that were affected by preconceptions; Western assessments were, too.

American assessments were afflicted by two decidedly different preconceptions. The first of these was "mirror imaging," which came to the fore after the Cuban Missile Crisis when the Americans wanted to ease tensions and "manage" the Cold War. In the absence of convincing intelligence about how Soviet leaders viewed their rivalry with the United States, many Americans were inclined to assume that Soviet leaders were, at heart, not so different from themselves and they would react to events much as they would. Well into the seventies, there was a widely held feeling that Moscow would be so happy just having "military parity" that it would not directly challenge American interests. This led to some nasty surprises.

The second preconception, which was the very opposite of "mirror imaging," was less widely held, but at times highly influential. It was claimed that the horrendous suffering and endurance of the Soviet people during the Second World War showed that Moscow would be willing to accept unimaginable losses in order for communism to prevail over the West. That could hardly have been farther from the truth; the Soviet leadership were deeply averse to the risks of nuclear war, as I have shown in earlier chapters.

The critics of the Soviet Union were on firmer ground when they slated the CIA for not understanding what they called the "evil genes" of the Soviets and, therefore, their evil intentions. One of the reasons why the CIA "neglected the seamier side of Soviet activities around the world," Robert Gates explained, was that its analysts were focused on relations between countries.[14] The operational side of the Agency had the details, but they had not been sharing them with the analysts.

Once the gap had been bridged, it became clear that the Soviet and East European intelligence services were much more engaged in subversive activities than most analysts had appreciated. These activities included providing support to terrorists (including the Red Army Faction in West Germany), left-wing political parties and "peace" movements, as well as conducting so-called "active measures," usually in the form of fabricated information aimed at discrediting Western policies. Although no hard evidence has emerged, most Western experts believe the KGB master-minded the attempted assassination of the Pope in May 1981.

By the end of the seventies, for the first time since the fifties, a broader and more hard-nosed consensus was beginning to re-emerge among most American experts about the mainsprings of Soviet conduct, though major uncertainties remained. In part, these stemmed from the unwillingness of the White House, along with the State and Defense departments, to share with the CIA information that was germane to their assessments. For example, the failure to inform the CIA of the psy-ops being conducted against the Soviet Union, contributed to analysts underestimating the nervousness of the Soviet leadership in 1983.

When the analysts began assessing Gorbachev's foreign policy two years later, another problem arose. This time, they were not given the details of the contacts American leaders had with their Soviet counterparts—and those contacts provided indications that Gorbachev was willing to make greater efforts to reach an accommodation with the West than was apparent from his public statements.[15]

Errors and Successes

In the sphere of economics both sides made costly errors. In the early to mid-seventies, the GRU estimated that, in the first year of a war, the United States could produce an extraordinary 70,000 tanks. In making this assessment, it committed sin of extrapolation—projecting the prodigious increase in America's armaments production at the beginning of the Second World War forward over the next thirty years. By the time the GRU discovered that because of the complexity of modern tanks the Americans could only produce a fraction of that number, Soviet industry was already churning out excessive amounts of all sorts of equipment so that Warsaw Pact forces would have an unquestionable superiority.[16]

Soviet Military Intelligence was not alone in having difficulty with long-term projections. Although satellite photography and the interception of communications of various sorts made it possible for the Americans to have a fairly accurate count of the numbers of various types of weapons the Soviets *had,* estimating how many they *would have* in the future was a far more hazardous venture. Having underestimated how quickly the Russians had built up their strategic missile forces during the sixties and early seventies, perhaps it was hardly surprising that until 1986 the CIA overestimated the pace at which the Russians would be able introduce new missiles or improve existing ones.

But in terms of the overall assessment of the Soviet Union, a far more important error concerned its economy. The CIA had a creditable track record in identifying trends and problems, but not in establishing the size and strength of the economy. For far too long, official Soviet statistics were taken seriously and not enough attention was paid to the massive distortion to those figures created by prices being fixed by bureaucrats and not by the market. This led the CIA to overestimate significantly the size of the Soviet economy and underestimate the burden of defense expenditure. As a result, the scale of Soviet arms production was long viewed as an indication of economic dynamism, rather than the costly addiction of a weak regime.[17]

Despite the lack of a coherent system of analysis in the Kremlin, Soviet leaders were at times perceptive in assessing the information and intelligence they acquired. The most notable occasion was in developing relations with West Germany in the late sixties and early seventies, which paved the way for détente. The opening up of that relationship owed much to East German Intelligence.

During one of our long talks, Markus Wolf recalled a meeting he had with the KGB in Moscow in 1969 or 1970 on Brandt's *Ostpolitik.* "They said, 'Comrade Wolf, you give us such a clear picture of what is happening, but this information is not in any of the reports you have passed to us.' 'Oh yes, it is,' I replied. 'It's all there. But what I am saying is my analysis not only of that material, but what is being said openly in the West German press, which I have had years of experience interpreting.'"

Wolf went on to explain that he invested heavily in assessing developments through a close study of both overt material and secret intelligence. "We capitalized on this by building up expertise within our service. Indeed, we rewarded expertise so highly that even when people had the opportunity to take up posts overseas, many preferred to remain at home." This was a remarkable achievement, as turning down an overseas posting was virtually unheard of in the communist world.

38 How Did It Help?

The Early Cold War Years

Historians have had difficulty assessing the contribution intelligence makes to the conduct of hot wars. In the Cold War, however, intelligence unquestionably had a powerful impact, because each side had time to check whether its judgments were well founded and to make the necessary adjustments to its policies and forces.

The first big post-war gains were made by Soviet Intelligence, which received outstanding reports from several American and British citizens who were spying for Moscow. Soviet Military Intelligence (the GRU) even managed to put its own man into the Manhattan Project—George Korval—who passed back to Moscow the details of how to produce enriched uranium and plutonium. This enabled the Soviet Union to test their first atomic bomb in August 1949, much earlier than they could otherwise have done.[1]

On the diplomatic front, the negotiations on a post-war settlement were more antagonistic than they need have been because neither side understood the limited nature of the other's short-term objectives. Stalin and Molotov, unlike the West, at least had the benefit of good intelligence. "The KGB was stretched to the limit, and the demands on our agents in London were heavier than ever. [Molotov] flew into blind rages when he felt he was not sufficiently informed. 'Why,' he roared, 'are there no documents?'"[2] Soviet Intelligence also enabled Stalin to call off his efforts to press the Turks into making territorial concessions before he sparked a war with the Americans.

On the Western side, the main fear after the end of the war was that Stalin would use his huge advantage in conventional forces to seize Western Europe. Thanks to an agreement reached in 1946, American, British and French "military liaison officers" were allowed to travel around East Germany, while Soviet "liaison officers" could do likewise in the Western sectors. Initially, their reporting, along with that of German and Austrian agents run from Berlin and Vienna, confirmed that Soviet forces were being rapidly demobilized, although they remained much larger than Western forces and, seemingly, well beyond what would appear to be legitimate defensive needs. Later, intelligence from these sources and British taps on Soviet military telephone lines in the Austrian capital gave reassurance that no Soviet offensive was imminent.

Generally speaking, Soviet Intelligence served Stalin well in the early years of the Cold War as he sought to consolidate his grip on Eastern Europe. But in 1950, as Stalin began to brace himself for tougher times ahead, he made his most disastrous mistake since 1941, by backing Kim Il Sung's invasion of South Korea. In the absence of reliable intelligence on the thinking that underpinned NSC-68, Stalin totally misjudged how the United States would respond and the long-term price the Soviet Union would pay for his mistake.

Missiles, Berlin and Cuba

After Stalin's death, Washington gained a good understanding of Soviet forces in Europe from a colonel in Soviet Military Intelligence, and from an Anglo-American operation that tapped Soviet military telephone and telex cables in Berlin from 1954 to 1956.[3] The monitoring of Soviet military radio communications, which the Americans and British began shortly after the war, was a crucial source of intelligence on Soviet military activities.

Despite several highly damaging betrayals, the Americans successfully exploited their technological advantage and managed to develop new techniques of collection. The Allied intercepts were not only of communications, but also the electronic signals from Soviet missiles tests, radars, etc. Aerial photography, first from aircraft and later from satellites, also provided invaluable details about targets and about the development of missiles and other weapons.

The U-2 spy flights that started in 1956 had no sooner closed the so-called "bomber gap" than the "missile gap" was alleged to be opening up. The intelligence that Penkovsky provided in May 1961 reinforced the CIA's assessment of the U-2 photography taken up until April 1960, which was that the Soviet strategic missile force was a shadow of what Khrushchev was claiming. It also led, according to one senior analyst, to the "critical" conclusion that the Soviet missile program was "proceeding much more slowly than we had forecast."[4]

Just over a month after the confrontation between Kennedy and Khrushchev in Vienna in June 1961, Penkovsky provided details of the steps Khrushchev intended to take to oust the allies from Berlin. This intelligence, taken together with that on the weakness of the Soviet missile force, encouraged Kennedy to take a firm line with Khrushchev and to declare West Berlin a "vital" American interest. The result was that, rather than try to eject the allies from the city, Khrushchev opted to build the Wall.

Shortly after the Berlin Crisis ended, America's first photo-reconnaissance satellites finally established that Khrushchev had very few missiles—and that they were all liquid-fueled and took a long time to ready for firing. From then on, thanks to the huge technical intelligence effort by the CIA and NSA, Washington probably knew as much about the capabilities of Soviet missiles as Soviet leaders did themselves. This incredible achievement continued through to the end of the Cold War.[5]

Had the U-2 spy-plane not revealed what was going on in Cuba at the end of August 1962, Khrushchev might have set up his new missile bases there before the Americans realized what was happening. In deciding how to react, Kennedy found Penkovsky's information about the time it took to prepare Soviet missiles for firing most valuable. It saved him being pushed into launching air attacks against the sites, which could have triggered at least a Soviet retaliation against American missile sites in Turkey, if not a wider conflagration.

During the Berlin Crisis of 1961, and the Cuban Missile Crisis the following year, Khrushchev's decision to back down was influenced by intelligence reports. In the first case, he received one from East German Intelligence that said the Allies planned to resort to nuclear weapons if their access to Berlin was blocked, and in the second, that the Americans were on the verge of invading Cuba. Although neither was strictly accurate, they did point to the very real dangers that lay ahead and added weight to Khrushchev's decision to avoid further confrontation.

In the sixties, the extensive and reliable intelligence that Khrushchev had on Nato enabled him to begin slashing Soviet conventional forces. He understood very well that Nato's reliance on tactical nuclear weapons showed that its strategy was defensive, as without substantial conventional forces it could not hope to attack and hold Eastern Europe.

Had Khrushchev not been ousted in 1964, the prospects for arms control in Europe might have been brighter. Ironically, it was Nato's decision in 1967 to try to prevent any war in Europe going nuclear that led Brezhnev to embark on a costly strategic rivalry with Nato—one that contributed greatly to the bankruptcy of the Soviet Union.

The Détente Years

The normalization of relations with West Germany had paved the way for détente was a far-sighted Soviet diplomatic initiative by Brezhnev, in which Andropov and his KGB played a crucial part. But it was East German Intelligence that opened Soviet eyes to the possibility of doing so.

No intelligence service had a deeper understanding of an adversary than the East Germans had of West Germany. East German Intelligence had close to 500 important spies in West Germany—in government, politics, the armed forces, the intelligence agencies and business. In addition, they also operated a massive and highly effective operation to intercept the communications used by Nato forces in West Germany and the West German government.[6] In East Germany some 2,000 people were employed to listen in to about 100,000 West German telephone lines.[7] By the Cold War's end, so much material had been collected that some of what had gone unread dated back seven years.[8]

Through 1973, the CIA was gaining some insights into the Soviet leadership by intercepting the calls they made from the radio telephones in their limousines as they drove around Moscow. "We received considerable intelligence on their personalities and their personal relationships," Gates recalled. "It was principally of value in giving us a feel for them as human beings . . . ,"[9] but there were some other nuggets, especially on Soviet plans to expand their "heavy" missile force.

The following year the Americans began receiving a less personal but in some respects more valuable flow of intelligence from Alexander Ogorodnik, which continued until 1977. He provided copies of much of the important telegraphic traffic between the Soviet Foreign Ministry and its embassies abroad. These included top secret documents that gave unprecedented insights into Sino-Soviet relations and Moscow's negotiating positions during the strategic arms talks that led to Brezhnev and Carter's signing of the Salt-II Treaty in Vienna in June 1979.[10]

The Americans may not have been the only ones to have good intelligence on arms control. When Nixon and Brezhnev signed the Salt-I Treaty in Moscow in May 1972, the Russians thought they had scored an enormous success. While it is true that they had negotiated well and the Americans had made a serious mistake at the last minute, one cannot help wondering whether the Russians did have good intelligence about the American negotiating positions, especially given the quality of a report that Andropov sent the Politburo in 1971. We now know that they gained much valuable intelligence from monitoring radio telephone conversations in the United States (as well as titillating details about the private lives of some leading figures in the Nixon Administration).[11]

In the mid-seventies the Americans also gained an insider's view of Soviet foreign policy from Arkady Shevchenko, who had been one of Gromyko's top assistants before being appointed undersecretary general at the UN in New York.[12] The material from Ogorodnik and Shevchenko contributed to a growing understanding of how Moscow was hoping to use détente to gain advantage over the United States.

During the détente years the Soviets were able to buy much sensitive technology from the West, especially the West Europeans and the Japanese. They were also remarkably successful in stealing both military and civilian technology. Generally speaking, however, no one in the Soviet leadership was willing to act on the numerous classified (sometimes highly classified) American and Nato assessments detailing the myriad weaknesses of the Soviet economic system and their implications, because such issues could only be addressed by changing policy.

The one major exception appears to have been made after Moscow received detailed American assessments, issued in 1977, showing that Soviet oil production was set to fall. In this case, the Soviet Ministry of Energy heeded the warning and the Politburo approved major new investments to boost output, which helped keep the Soviet Union going for several more years, even when the price of oil started to fall.[13]

Military Strategy

One of the ironies of the détente era is that the best intelligence available to both sides was about military matters. From the research that Vojtech Mastny and the members of his Parallel History Project on Nato and the Warsaw Pact have done in the East German archives it is clear that practically every Western military secret of any significance was betrayed.[14]

Through the Hungarian Intelligence Service, for example, Moscow had access to one of Nato's most secret documents: the General Defense Plan. Nato has never released the details of this plan, though copies found in Warsaw Pact archives are now on the web.[15] During the tense decades of the seventies and eighties, the Soviet General Staff had extensive details of how Nato forces would seek to counter a Soviet offensive. General Glen Otis, who commanded the US Army in Europe during these years, once said that, had war broken out, "the consequences would have been calamitous."[16]

At the beginning of the eighties, as the Americans started responding to Marshal Ogarkov's new strategy, they had the benefit of first-rate intelligence from a number of sources, including: Ryszard Kuklinski, a Polish colonel who liaised with Moscow on war planning; Dmitri Polyakov, a general in Soviet Military Intelligence; Mihai Pacepa, the deputy head of the Romanian intelligence service; and Ghulam Dastagir Wardak, an Afghan colonel who had studied at the Soviet General Staff Academy. The Americans also had access to remarkably high-grade satellite photography and a very good understanding of the Warsaw Pact's communications network.

Besides providing a wealth of new intelligence, Kuklinski was able to give the Americans a much deeper appreciation of Soviet thinking on war in Europe. Kuklinski's insights helped the Americans make sense of the intelligence they had from other sources. Ben Fischer, a former chief historian of the CIA, told me that "thanks to this Polish colonel our civilian and military analysts could now interpret what satellites might be able to 'see' and 'hear,' but not comprehend—and this made it possible for them to discern the difference between a routine exercise and preparations for a massive surprise attack."

Since the sixties, high-grade satellite photography and intercepts of Warsaw Pact communications had enabled the Americans to build a very good understanding of the Soviet threat in Central Europe. A major breakthrough came in the late sixties when, as the buildup of Soviet and East European forces got underway, intelligence from a Pole working for the British provided valuable help in tracking developments in the Warsaw Pact.[17]

During the late seventies and early eighties, it seems that Kuklinski and Polyakov told the Americans virtually all they needed to know about the communications networks through which the Soviet General Staff would run the Warsaw Pact in wartime. In addition, Kuklinski gave the Americans the details of the measures the Soviets would use to disrupt Nato's communications in wartime and conceal their military activities from prying American satellites.

Kuklinski also provided the locations of the underground bunkers that would be used by top military commanders in wartime.[18] After the Cold War had ended, Marshal Kulikov, who had been commander-in-chief of the Warsaw Pact, was shocked to hear from Brzezinski that within three hours of the outbreak of hostilities these bunkers would have been destroyed and the entire Soviet command dead.[19]

The reporting from East Germany by the staff of American, British and French "liaison missions" earned high praise in Nato. Over forty years they provided a steady flow of meticulous reports on the "showcase" Soviet forces on the front line in East Germany, their strengths, weaknesses and the equipment they used.

Some of the reports from the British came from what might best be described as low-level operations. The British, influenced by classical archaeologists, believed treasure could be found in muck. The shortage of toilet paper among Soviet forces suggested to them that more than newspapers might be being used as a substitute.

Protected by arm-length plastic gloves, the British rummaged in insalubrious places. One military document they found revealed that several of the Soviet units were hugely undermanned, which meant that the arrival of reinforcement could be an important indicator that an offensive was being prepared. Amongst the muck the British also found a tape recording that embarrassed as it showed that due to poor "voice security" the Soviets were listening in to some British military communications.[20]

"We also learned much about Soviet forces from watching them in Afghanistan," according to Milt Bearden, who had been coordinating the CIA's support to the mujahedin during the latter 1980s. "They had some very good equipment, but terrible logistics; troops often could not move because they could not get new batteries or tires."

Weaponry

Both sides knew a lot about the other's military equipment. One of the greatest Soviet gains—from the Second World War through the early eighties—came from the illicit acquisition of Western military technology, some of which was acquired by their spies and much of it was sold to them by venal Westerners. As Nato countries were developing anti-tank missiles, the Soviets were already producing a new type of armor that would reduce their impact.[21] Without access to this technology, the Soviets would probably have lagged far behind the United States.

The Americans, too, learned a lot about Soviet weaponry, with Kuklinski alone providing details of two hundred advanced weapons systems. They received an extensive range of Soviet equipment that the Israelis had captured from the Egyptians and Syrians in the wars of 1967 and 1973. Later, more modern equipment was bought from Soviet troops through intermediaries in Afghanistan and the almost bankrupt East European governments who were at times willing to sell items to international arms dealers without asking too many questions about who was the real buyer.

A critical piece of intelligence came from Viktor Rezun, a Soviet Military Intelligence officer who was working for the British in the late seventies. "What I was able to tell the Americans eventually convinced them that Soviet tanks could already out-gun the American one then being developed, and this," Rezun explained, "led them to spend billions of dollars on upgrading the caliber of their new tank's gun, from 105 mm to 120 mm, so that they would regain the advantage."[22] The British military "liaison" mission further helped this American research by providing a sample of the latest armor, which they had prized off of a Soviet tank in East Germany.

During the late seventies the Americans had such detailed intelligence on Soviet weapons programs that according to James Woolsey, who was working at the Pentagon at the time, they could "fine-tune the speed at which we would have to introduce counter-measures, sometimes shifting items in the defense budget from one financial year to another." This excellent intelligence did, however, lead the Americans to overestimate future Soviet defense expenditure because, given the nature of the Soviet system, many of the R&D programs and development projects were never brought to fruition.[23]

Ending the Cold War

For Moscow and for Washington, intelligence and sound, broad assessments contributed to a peaceful ending of the Cold War.

At the beginning of the eighties, it was becoming increasingly clear that the balance of power had fundamentally shifted to America's advantage. There was a growing realization within the Politburo that steps would have to be taken to ease tensions with the West and make the Soviet system work.

In monitoring the buildup of American forces, the Soviet leadership judged Reagan correctly. His actions—such as the psy-ops, the military buildup and

SDI—and confrontational statements at times made them nervous, especially during 1983, but they rightly concluded that although he was determined to neuter the Soviet Union, he was not on the point of going to war.

"Gordievsky's perceptive insights into the Soviet leadership's profound sense of insecurity was of real value to both Mrs. Thatcher and President Reagan," according to Charles Powell, her private secretary who handled that material. The intelligence and advice he provided not only helped both of them reduce East-West tensions before Gorbachev came to power, but also facilitated their subsequent dealings with him.

Mrs. Thatcher had four meetings with Gordievsky, whom she regarded as "a true hero."[24] And Gordievsky had the honor of being received by both President Reagan and President Bush, the only Soviet or East European official who had worked with the West ever to have had that honor.

Shortly after Gorbachev became leader in 1985, he criticized the poor quality of the reporting he was receiving from the KGB (and almost certainly that of Soviet Military Intelligence, the GRU, as well).[25] That same year Soviet Intelligence regained some of its kudos with two impressive breakthroughs—the first came when Aldrich Ames, who worked on Soviet operations at CIA headquarters, sold the names of most of the CIA's Soviet agents to the KGB. Months later, Robert Hanssen, an FBI officer, began selling the KGB a far wider range of material, including American assessments of Gorbachev and his policies, as well as more highly sensitive material about how the American government would function in a crisis that could lead to nuclear war.

Gorbachev and his close associates have never been willing to talk about what the Soviet Union gained from the exceptional intelligence they were receiving. However, one American familiar with what Ames and Hanssen revealed to the Soviet Union believes that although the intelligence might have eased Gorbachev's concerns over SDI, it would also have strengthened his conviction that he needed to come to terms with the United States.[26]

This message was certainly reinforced by the great discomfort that enviable intelligence was provoking among the Soviet General Staff. At first, Soviet and East German Intelligence felt that they had been enormously successful when they learned the details of American plans in time of war to disrupt the Warsaw Pact's ability to communicate with its front-line forces or, even worse, issue confusing commands to them.[27] But it did not take long for the kopek to drop. Yes, they could take counter-measures, but it was becoming clear that the

Americans were so far ahead of them in this field that, one way or another, they would soon be able to re-establish their advantage.

By the mid-eighties, there was tremendous pressure on the Soviet leadership to rethink its entire policy towards the West. Adding to it was the intelligence that the Hungarians had been acquiring for years about Nato's war plans. According to General Janos Kovacs, the head of Hungarian Military Intelligence, this information "helped prove that there were no offensive Nato plans. This led sober-thinking people to reassess the situation and to develop a new approach."[28] And this is precisely what happened under Gorbachev.

There is little doubt that this new material speeded up Gorbachev's efforts to reach agreement with Reagan, though it is less clear whether or not it enabled him to secure better terms. Gorbachev's main initiatives in foreign policy derived from another sort of intelligence—that of his advisers, whose knowledge and appreciation of Western concerns, and the scope for negotiation, was often extremely perceptive.

Trust and Verify

Intelligence played a key role in verifying compliance with painstakingly negotiated treaties of the Cold War era. Although the Soviet satellite technology lagged behind that of the Americans, it was good enough for the Soviets to agree to Salt-I and Salt-II, which required each side to use its "national technical means" to monitor the implementation of these arms control agreements.

At times, violations were detected. "The most serious by far," Fritz Ermarth, the Soviet expert and later chairman of the National Intelligence Council, pointed out, "came in 1989, when intelligence from our satellites and other intercepts revealed that Moscow had missile warheads filled with two deadly viruses—plague and smallpox—against which the West had no defense. This was in direct violation of the Biological Warfare Convention of 1972." At around the same time a Soviet expert, who had defected to the British, provided convincing evidence that the Soviet Union had been developing biological weapons on a vast scale since 1974.[29]

This intelligence confirmed the fears of those who had doubts about Gorbachev's intentions or his control over the military. Protests from Mrs. Thatcher and from President Bush resulted in Gorbachev agreeing to inspections of the Soviet facilities in 1991. In March 1992, shortly after becoming president of

Russia, Yeltsin banned all biological weapons-related activity, though doubts persist in the West over whether that ban was ever completely effective.

For his part, Gorbachev was keen to know whether the Americans were cheating him over arms control. This was a particularly sensitive subject given that he had agreed to the elimination of all of the Soviet SS-20 medium-range missiles, was negotiating on deep cuts in strategic nuclear forces and was still fearful that the Americans would push ahead with the development of Reagan's Strategic Defense Initiative. In January 1989, Gorbachev told Leonid Shebarshin, whom he had just appointed head of the KGB's foreign intelligence directorate, that detecting violations of arms control agreements was to be his top priority.[30]

Keeping the Peace

At the strategic level, each side knew that the other's early-warning systems, despite their weaknesses, would almost certainly give them the time they needed to respond to an attack—and that any retaliation could be devastating. As a result, pre-emptive attacks were not a realistic option.

When I asked Ermarth about the contribution the intelligence community had made to keeping all-out war from breaking out, he said that he believed that intelligence had been crucially important: "It made the Cold War essentially transparent on the most dangerous fronts, despite massive efforts, especially on the Soviet side, to keep dangerous things secret."

Confidence that war was not imminent was possible on both sides largely due to various forms of intelligence—satellite imagery, the interception of communications, the regular coverage of East and West Germany by each side's so-called "military liaison missions" and, of course, the intelligence gathered by secret agents.

When I spoke with him, Markus Wolf, the East German spy-master, was always keen to emphasize the contribution that his agents made to keeping the peace. So, too, was James Woolsey, a former head of the CIA, who said of Dmitri Polyakov, the general in Soviet Military Intelligence: "What . . . [he] . . . did for the West didn't just help us win the Cold War, it kept the Cold War from becoming hot."[31] Both sides realized that to avoid war, every effort would have to be made to prevent a smaller crisis from burgeoning into conflict and then escalating into war.

The collection of good intelligence and the sound assessment of it was a major undertaking. Ermarth believed that, on the Western side, "the lion's share of the credit goes, of course, to the United States and its main allies, especially our British comrades. This effort was not easy; it was not cheap; it was not flawless. But, as the saying goes, it was 'good enough for government work' and extremely valuable. Intelligence was every bit as important to the Soviets, though in somewhat different ways."

39 Looking Forward

Slaying the Myths

When the Cold War ended, many celebrated, some lamented, but few reflected. With the passage of time, it has become easier to think about the lessons we can learn from the intense confrontation that took place over nearly half a century, though one always has to bear in mind that many of the challenges confronting the West in the first part of the 21st century are very different from those of the latter half of the previous one.

Deciding what those lessons are is never easy for as Brent Scowcroft rightly points out, "History does not share its alternatives with us." Or, as Alexander Chubarian, the director of the Institute of World History in Moscow, likes to put it, "In the language of history there is no conditional tense." But before one can get to grips with the lessons it is important to clear away the five myths about the Cold War that I mentioned in the Prologue, because although they do not correspond to what really happened, their persistence is dangerous.

The first myth that needs to be slain is that the Soviet Union was not ever a real threat to the West. On the contrary, as I have shown, it was a serious threat. The danger of this contention is that it deflects attention from the sustained and complex efforts required to deal with adversaries driven by deeply rooted hostility. Such efforts are costly financially, and, to have cumulative value, they cannot simply be a series of short-term responses; they have to be part of an overall strategy—though not necessarily a "war"—a strategy that requires careful thought and much discussion.

Looking back over the long years of the Cold War, Scowcroft said, in his distinctively measured way, that he felt "it was truly remarkable that the West did prevail." He observed that, "in the early years of the Cold War, many believed that conflict with the Soviet Union was inevitable. Such apocalyptic visions were rejected. Those who said that the West needed to maintain containment won the day and over the years it learned the value of patience and caution."

The next troubling myth on my list was the idea that détente could have worked in the sixties and seventies. As I highlighted earlier, the archives are rich in material showing that at that stage the Soviet Union was still hoping to prevail over the United States. Détente only became feasible under Gorbachev. The failure of détente was a salutary reminder of the need to look carefully at the assumptions underpinning policy.

Policies that involve any sort of combat need particularly careful thought—about objectives, feasibility, sustainability and the responses that will come from those being attacked. We should never underestimate the inventiveness of the "underdogs" or their flair for striking back where it really hurts.

Strengths and Weaknesses

A third distorting myth is the notion that the United States prevailed because it was strong, its people were united and its allies supportive. This was manifestly not the case. There were times when the Soviet leadership rightly felt that it was gaining the strategic and political advantage, not just because of its military superiority, but also because of the divisions within American society, the considerable tensions between the United States and its allies, and the lack of will in the West.

The proper lesson to be drawn here is that, in any such competition, you need to understand not only your adversary's strengths and weaknesses, but also your own. This is what the Soviets called "the correlations of forces" and Americans refer to as the "balance of forces" or "net assessment."

America was certainly economically stronger, better at generating wealth and technologically more inventive. It was a more dynamic society that better met the wishes of its citizens. Democratic politics, however, made the Americans particularly prone to overreact to any Soviet success—for example, *Sputnik*—while their own insecurities led them into exaggerating their own problems.

Sudden developments, such as military setbacks or oil price hikes, cannot be ignored, but they do need to be looked at in a long-term perspective. The forces that shape the correlation, however, often have little to do with things that governments control. Broad trends such as technological innovation, economic growth, demography, the changing character of society and the shifting levels of public confidence can have a great effect. In America, there were many mood swings before Reagan became president.

The big question that follows is whether any long-term policy being advocated is sustainable. Eisenhower rightly judged that economic strength was a pre-requisite for success, but he also recognized that democratic societies are only willing to sustain a modest burden if they believe it is important to do so. The other side of the coin was that America could never hope to prevail in the Cold War unless its policies commanded the support of its allies.

Those who exaggerate the strength and cohesion of the "Western Alliance" during the Cold War do a serious disservice to the conduct of current policy because this myth creates unreasonable expectations in Washington of what an alliance can deliver. One has to face the fact that Nato, after all, was never an alliance of equals. The Americans paid most of the costs because they feared that if they did not, some of its allies would slip towards neutrality. The Europeans often had to be "dragged, screaming and kicking" into accepting policies and contributing towards them.

Over the years the Cold War had morphed into a psychological battle that the Soviet Union had no hope of winning, but the disputatious West could well lose. The United States did succeed in keeping the alliance together by investing heavily in conveying a sense of purpose, clarity of vision and an ability to sustain competition. Throughout the Cold War, every American president was frequently in personal contact with other Western leaders. It was a classic case of the United States leading by example and commitment.

The Americans not only led, they listened. They valued the insights, experience and judgments that their allies were able to contribute on a wide range of issues—from the wording of Nato declarations, to nuclear strategy and arms control—and often adjusted their own original position. Scowcroft emphasized that, when there were disputes, the discussion would return to the question "What is the Alliance trying to achieve?" The Allied leaders all acknowledged that their aim was "to hold this beast at bay until it changes its ways." "Without such a consensus," Scowcroft said, "attempts at joint action could not be effective."

The last two myths are more directly linked with the ending of the Cold War. While some Russians believe that the collapse of their state happened as a result of their own efforts at reform, most attribute it to Western intrigue and domestic treachery. The archives, however, contain a fair amount of material showing that American pressure did play a major part in the process. The lesson for the

West, I feel, is that the Soviet Union did not come to an end as a result of sharp and powerful pressures from outside, but as a result of external ones building up over many years that created real incentives for change.

The fifth and last of the myths I mentioned was that Reagan played a far greater part than Gorbachev did in ending the Cold War. The danger with this one is that it leads people to concentrate on the application of pressure, rather than the resolution of problems and the ending of confrontation. What did become clear during Gorbachev's relations with Reagan and Bush was that long-term hostility can only be overcome through the building up of trust—and that requires dialogue.

Getting Inside Their Mind

Generally speaking, the actions of the Americans and the Russians were largely shaped by preconceptions, or by what Walter Lippmann, the distinguished American columnist of the early Cold War years, liked to call "the pictures in our heads."

Scowcroft told me that he felt that, out of all his long years of work throughout the Cold War, "one lesson stands out above all others—and that is that neither side was infallible in the judgments they made about their adversary." Whatever shortcomings there were, the record shows the value of looking closely at history in its broadest sense, exploiting the potential of intelligence and asking fundamental questions.

Incoming administrations are invariably confronted with important issues that are developing day-by-day and difficult to deal with politically at home and diplomatically abroad. Even when the new administration is familiar with an issue, it is often prone to focus on the short-term manifestations. There is nothing wrong with that, but there is also much to be said for making time to look at the historical roots of issues, because they can inform longer-term strategies that are likely to give better results.

Dealing with someone from a very different culture is a major challenge, where mirror-imaging and unfounded assumptions are almost always seriously misleading and at times dangerous. Looking back over America's conduct of policy during the Cold War, Milt Bearden, one of the CIA's most experienced operational officers, told me he felt that "we made the problem worse for ourselves because we went too far in demonizing the Soviets."

While recognizing that demonizing one's adversary can be very effective in making one's own troops give their best in battle and in rallying political support in prolonged confrontations, Bearden stressed that "it also erodes common sense, reduces our chances of understanding the human foibles of our enemies, the way they think and what motivates them." The result is that policy options are restricted and those that remain are often unnecessarily expensive.

That is one of the reasons why high-level meetings are important. "The only real value that came out of summit meetings," Robert Gates believed, "was that these leaders got to take the measure of each other as men . . . and somebody they could actually communicate with—whether through the hot line or later on by telephone—and . . . [these summits] were immensely valuable in reducing the margin of misunderstanding and the potential for miscalculation."[1] Similarly, Gates believed that arms control negotiations had given each side a sound understanding of the other's capabilities, strategy and military philosophy.

Summits alone were not enough. "To get inside the mind of another leadership," Andy Marshall has always explained to his staff in the Office of Net Assessment at the Pentagon, "you really do have to start from scratch. It is not just a question of how their history and culture make them different from us, but the ways in which the structure of their regime affects the way they view the outside world and respond to developments."

Attention to Detail

Some of the biggest American breakthroughs in thinking about the Soviet Union emerged from the painstaking analysis of information and intelligence from many sources. A new generation of American analysts, who had studied Soviet affairs at university, had learned to look at what was really happening, and to avoid the pitfalls of preconceived notions, e.g. that Warsaw Pact forces were so strong and so large that Nato would only be able to stop them with nuclear weapons.

Their growing understanding of the weaknesses of Warsaw Pact forces opened up the way for the American scientists to exploit new technology to develop a range of conventional munitions that could thwart a Soviet conventional offensive. In doing so, they affected a "revolution in military affairs" that led the Soviet high command to recognize that they could no longer compete with the United States.

When I pursued the subject further with him, Marshall stressed that "valuable insights can of course be gained by closely observing what the other side does, but the real gains come from asking why they have done it—and done it in that particular way. It may not seem reasonable to you," Marshall chuckled, "but it probably does to him. Rationality, after all, can come in many different forms."

When Soviet troops began to pull out of eastern Germany in 1990, for example, it was discovered that they had nearly three times as much ammunition as Nato had estimated. By far the biggest factor contributing to this error was that Nato assumed that Soviet forces stored it according to Nato's own strict safety measures. They did not; they stuffed it right up to the ceilings of their ammunition bunkers.

For similar reasons, Soviet and American analysts came to very different assessments about the vulnerability of each other's missiles. In the mid-sixties, Soviet experts concluded from their tests that if missile silos were less than two kilometers apart, an incoming missile warhead exploding *on the ground* could render two silos inoperable. As a result, they judged that America's Minuteman missiles—which were placed in not very well-protected silos that were fairly closely grouped—were intended for pre-emptive strikes, not retaliation.

That was not the reason. The Americans believed that exploding missile warheads *above* silos, rather than on the ground, was the most effective way of destroying missiles in them. So by placing their silos close together, they were trying to maximize the chance of what the professionals call "fratricide"—of the first Soviet warhead to explode destroying the others just behind it that were heading for the same missile field. In other words, "scientific" explanations do not always provide the answer; usually, much more research needs to be done to explain why the other side has done things in a particular way.

In intelligence work while it is, of course, important to understand the political and military culture of your adversaries, artistic culture should never be neglected. I remember my friend Ernst Gombrich, the Viennese-born art historian whom I mentioned in the Prologue, telling me about the night of May 1, 1945, when he was the duty-officer in charge of monitoring German radio broadcasts for the British government. He and his colleagues were on tenterhooks as the German Home Service had just informed its listeners that there would soon be an important announcement.

To the ordinary listener the music that followed was serious, fittingly so, as Soviet troops were already on the outskirts of Berlin. "But why," Ernst asked, "have they chosen Bruckner's 7th Symphony?" One of his colleagues replied, "That's the one he wrote on learning of the death of Richard Wagner."

While the music continued Ernst wrote on one slip of paper "Hitler resigns/deposed"; on another just the two words "Hitler Dead." When the announcement finally came that Hitler had "died in the struggle against Bolshevism," Ernst pointed to the second slip and the news was phoned through to Churchill in Downing Street.

Ernst's action did not change the course of history, but it did show how understanding culture in the widest sense can give important insights into what is happening.

The Importance of Human Sources

As I hope this book has shown, good intelligence and sound assessments are particularly important when dealing with a long-term confrontation. Without good intelligence, policy is all too easily shaped by fear, ignorance or optimism. While the Cold War showed the value of satellite photography, the intercepts of various sorts and copies of your adversary's secret documents, it is important that we never lose sight of the special quality of intelligence and information that only people can provide.

Sometimes important intelligence is not to be found in documents or intercepts because it is so secret that it is not committed to paper. But even if one's agent is not a member of the inner circle, he or she may still be able to learn what is going on through the indiscretions of those that are, as did Penkovsky.

There is also another valuable vein of intelligence that is rarely reflected in intercepts or documents—and that is the things that are so well-known to those concerned that they never need to be spelled out—for example, their view of the world, their preoccupations, their assumptions, why they always react in certain ways. After all, it is not only important to know "Why the dog barked," but also "Why the dog isn't barking."

Some emigres have much to offer on these matters, though their personal and political agendas need to be understood and kept in mind. For example, Soviet economists who managed to emigrate to the West helped the Americans understand how misleading Soviet economic statistics were, and the huge cost of Soviet defense and "empire." They also helped Americans to see through the maze of the monstrously large Soviet military-industrial complex and identifying those "nodal points" whose destruction would impair any Soviet military offensive.

Everything Sends a Message

In this *Journey* I have often cited the diaries of Anatoly Chernyaev and my discussions with him. Chernyaev has not only provided remarkable eye-witness accounts of what has gone on over the years, but he has also been extraordinarily detached and perceptive in his reflections on the conduct of his own side, its efforts to bring about change and its failure at times to understand why it was not making headway. He understood to an extent that few others did, that everything one does sends a message.

When someone asks "Why did our adversary do that?" bureaucracies almost always reply, in a rather child-like way, "It wasn't our fault. We didn't do anything." While no one likes to accept blame, it is often deserved.

One somewhat extreme example vividly demonstrates this point. In the sixties, the FBI and US Army Intelligence began feeding false information material to Soviet Intelligence with the aim of diverting scarce Soviet resources into an unproductive effort to develop advanced chemical and biological weapons. Contrary to expectations, Soviet scientists were highly successful. Even after these operations were halted in the early seventies, Soviet leaders doubted, right through the nineties, that the United States was complying with the Biological Warfare Convention of 1972, with the result that the Soviet Union invested massively in developing biological weapons of almost unimaginable horror.[2]

This story is a painful reminder of what can happen when deception goes wrong. But even when no explicit attempt is being made to deceive—for instance, in making an announcement of a new weapons program or a speech to one's own supporters—one always has to ask, "How will an adversary interpret that?" There is much to be said for having specialists in the subject who track and analyze the responses over the years.

Given the pace of events and the need to be up to date, the value of intelligence collected in the past is often neglected. But as Ben Fischer, the CIA's former chief historian, put it: "From time to time one should walk down the memory lane of past cases and past events. You'll often find clues, even answers, to current questions—things that never attracted much attention at the time."

The Last Judgment

One of the biggest risks any committee faces in assessing developments stems from becoming stuck in the rut of conventional thinking or, just as

A quiet moment with my wife and Sir Humphrey, the Cabinet Office cat, during a busy weekend of assessments, August 1991. (Private Collection)

bad, becoming bogged down in a debate where departments and agencies are more interested in protecting their own political interests (and their budgets) than they are in knowing what is really happening. One also needs to bear in mind that the participants bring with them not only their expertise but also what the French call their *déformation professionelle*—their professional bias. This means that the military are prone to place too much emphasis on threats and risk, the intelligence agencies on the value of their product, and the diplomats on the ability of their profession to avoid a crisis or at least find a way out of it.

I doubt if risks and distortions can ever be entirely removed, but they can be significantly reduced if the "intelligence community" keeps asking the big questions—What is happening? Is it different from what we have seen before? Why are our rivals doing what they are doing, and why in that way? What are the implications?

Answering such questions is much easier if analysts have been given time to do serious research and test a range of hypotheses. From the fifties through the mid-seventies, the CIA actively encouraged in-depth research on Soviet and Chinese internal politics and Sino-Soviet relations. The resulting analytical papers pointed to a deepening split in Sino-Soviet relations and generated heated debate in Washington. Before long the slanging match that broke out between Beijing and Moscow showed just how right the analysts had been.[3]

While expertise is always to be highly valued, innocence is at times worth its weight in gold. Few things can more quickly open up a discussion than a non-expert saying "I don't understand why . . ." But unless the asking of such questions is institutionalized and accepted as part of the culture, dissent can all too easily be treated as disloyalty.

The Joint Intelligence Committee had a praiseworthy track record for its hard-headed assessments of the Soviet Union and Soviet policy. I recollect, however, that on one occasion the committee responded very negatively to an assessment highlighting the major and positive changes in Gorbachev's policies. In exasperation, the member of my staff who had drafted the paper waved a finger at the assembled grandees and said, "The trouble with you lot is that you don't like the message." There was nervous laughter around the table. Had I spoken in such terms I would have been in serious trouble. Fortunately, the speaker was an attractive woman with a winning smile. Some discussion did ensue.

Reflecting on the Cold War after it was over, a senior Soviet Military Intelligence officer said, "The Americans beat us not because they had more tanks, but because they had more think tanks."[4] There was more to it than that, but he was right to underline the power of careful thought. We should all be thankful that on both sides there were people like Anatoly Chernyaev and Andy Marshall who thought long and hard about how the Cold War could be brought to a peaceful close.

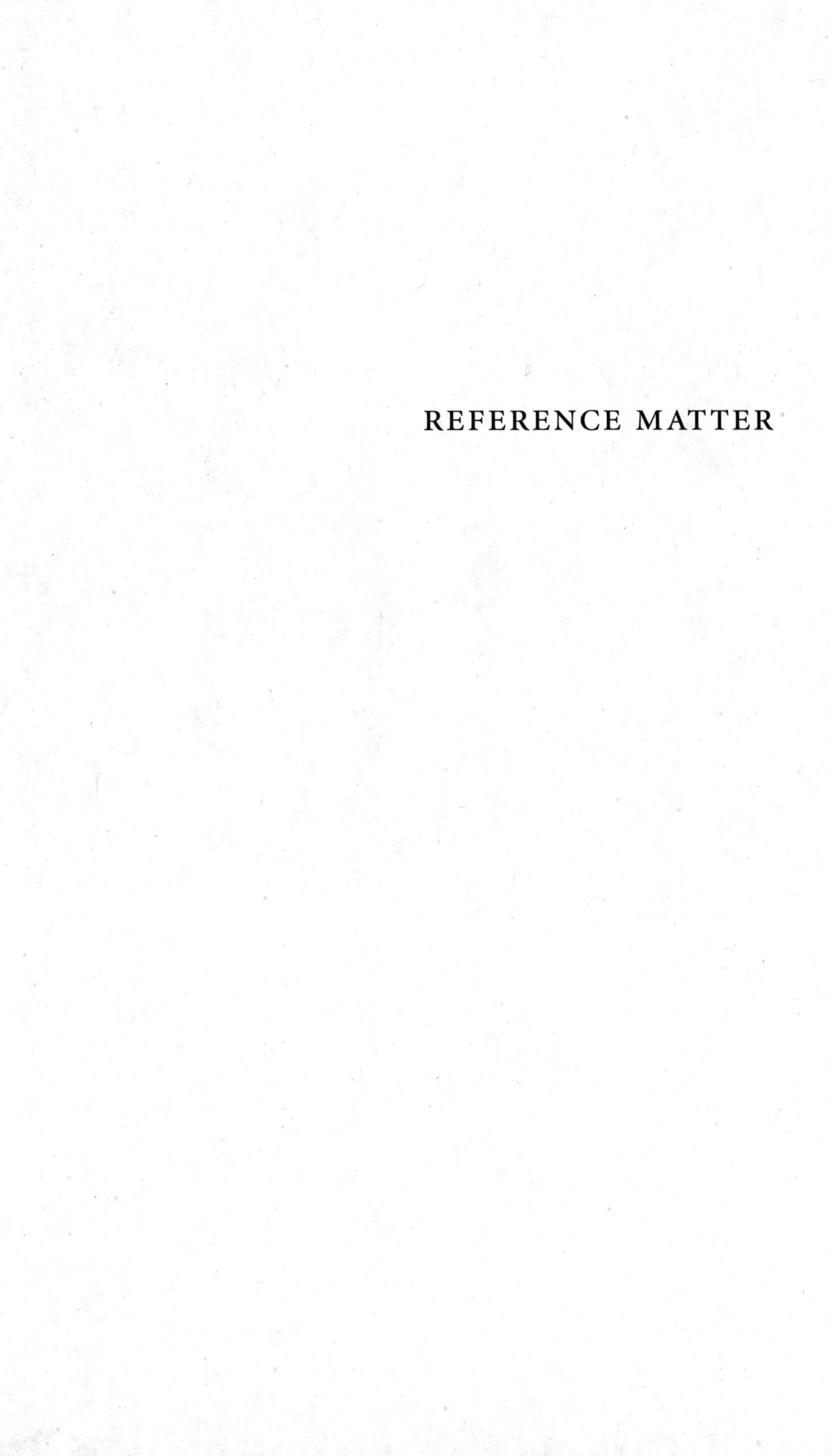

REFERENCE MATTER

Notes

Prologue

1. The memoirs of the senior Soviet officer were cited in an article by the Moscow magazine *Kommersant Vlast* on September 23, 1998. This led to the publication of other articles in the Russian press based on interviews with Petrov. A dramatized version of the incident, along with an interview with Petrov, can be seen on Flashback Television's documentary program *1983: The Brink of Apocalypse*, which was first shown in the US, on Discovery TV, on September 2, 2007, and in the U.K. on January 5, 2008.

2. Zbigniew Brzezinski, interviewed by Professor Odd Arne Westad, May 7, 1994.

3. Lord Butler (Chairman), *Review of Intelligence on Weapons of Mass Destruction* (2004), 7–16.

4. President John F. Kennedy, Commencement Address, Yale University, June 11, 1962.

Chapter 1

1. The early history of America's relations with Russia and the Soviet Union is excellently covered in John Lewis Gaddis, *Russia, the Soviet Union and the United States: An Interpretive History* (2nd ed., 1990).

2. Quoted in Ilya Zemtsov, *Encyclopaedia of Soviet Life* (1991), 48.

3. Arthur Koestler, *The Invisible Writing* (1954), 53.

4. Vladimir I. Lenin, *Collected Works*, vol. 8 (1964), 233–34.

5. *The Times*, London, July 15, 1920.

6. Alexander N. Yakovlev, *A Century of Violence in Soviet Russia* (2002), 234.

7. David Remnick, *Lenin's Tomb* (1993), 406; Simon Sebag Montifiore, *Stalin—The Court of the Red Tsar* (2003), 175–248.

8. Cited in Christopher Andrew and Vasili Mitrokhin, *The Mitrokhin Archive: The KGB in Europe and the West* (1999), 122. See also David E. Murphy, *What Stalin Knew: The Enigma of Barbarossa* (2005).

9. Joseph Stalin, broadcast to the Soviet people, July 3, 1941, *The Soviet Union Today*, Moscow, Aug. 1941.

10. Winston S. Churchill, *The Second World War,* vol. 3 (1950), 331.

11. Andrew and Mitrokin, *Mitrokhin Archive: Europe and the West,* 125–26.

12. Francis Harry Hinsley, *British Intelligence in the Second World War* (1988), 59–60; Chris Bellamy, *Absolute War: Soviet Russia and the Second World War* (2007), 570.

Chapter 2

1. Henry Kissinger, *Diplomacy* (1994), 412.

2. U.S. State Department, *Foreign Relations of the United States (FRUS): The Conferences at Cairo and Tehran (1943)* (1961), 554.

3. Lord Strang, *At Home and Abroad* (1956), 199; Philip E. Mosely, "Dismemberment of Germany—The Allied Negotiations from Yalta to Potsdam," *Foreign Affairs,* Apr. 1950, 487–99.

4. This subject is analyzed in Vladimir Pechatnov, "The Big Three After World War II," CWIHP, Working Paper no. 13, May 1995.

5. Stalin quoted in Pechatnov, *Big Three*, 21.

6. Stalin quoted in Vladislav M. Zubok, *A Failed Empire: The Soviet Union in the Cold War from Stalin to Gorbachev* (2007), 13.

7. Roosevelt quoted in FRUS, *The Conferences at Malta and Yalta, 1945* (1955), 628.

8. Tessa Stirling, Dria Nalecz and Tadeus Dubicki, Report of the Anglo-Polish Historical Committee, vol. 1, *Intelligence Co-operation between Poland and Great Britain during World War II* (2005).

9. Molotov quoted in Pechatnov, *Big Three*, 23.

10. Stalin quoted in Milovan Djilas, *Conversations with Stalin* (1962), 114.

11. "Operation Unthinkable: 'Russia: Threat to Western Civilization,'" Draft and Final Reports: May 22, June 8 and July 11, 1945, Public Record Office, London, CAB 120/691/109040/001.

12. Mikhail Milstein, a former Soviet Military Intelligence officer, quoted in Zubok, *Failed Empire*, 16.

13. Truman quoted in David McCullough, *Truman* (1992), 353.

14. Quoted in Niall Ferguson, *Colossus: The Price of America's Empire* (2004), 68.

15. Alexander N. Yakovlev, *A Century of Violence in Soviet Russia* (2002), 174–75.

16. Professor Robert Tucker, who was present in Red Square that day, quoted in Jack F. Matlock, *Reagan and Gorbachev: How the Cold War Ended* (2004), 281–82.

17. Stalin quoted in Djilas, *Conversations with Stalin*, 90.

Chapter 3

1. Stalin quoted in Geoffrey Roberts, "Stalin at the Tehran, Yalta and Potsdam Conferences," *Journal of Cold War Studies*, Fall 2007, 18. This article reviews the original Soviet transcripts of these conferences, which contain details not contained in earlier published accounts.

2. Stalin quoted in Vladislav Zubok and Constantine Pleshakov, *Inside the Kremlin's Cold War: From Stalin to Khrushchev* (1996), 48.

3. Stalin quoted in FRUS, *The Conference at Berlin (the Potsdam Conference) 1945*, vol. 2, 305.

4. Norman Davies, *God's Playground: A History of Poland*, vol. 2 (rev. ed. 2005), 380.

5. Stalin quoted in Marc Trachtenberg, *A Constructed Peace: The Making of the European Settlement, 1945–1963* (1999), 31–32.

6. Stalin quoted in Philip E. Mosely, "Across the Green Table from Stalin," in *Current History*, no. 148, vol. 15, 131.

7. David Holloway, *Stalin and the Bomb: The Soviet Union and Atomic Energy, 1939–1956* (1994), 116–17.

8. FRUS, *The Conference at Berlin (the Potsdam Conference), 1945*, vol. 1, 586.

9. Stimson quoted in James Byrnes, *All in One Lifetime* (1958), 290–91.

10. Stalin quoted in W. A. Harriman and E. Abel, *Special Envoy to Churchill and Stalin, 1941–1946* (1975), 491.

11. Stalin quoted in David Holloway, *The Soviet Union and the Origins of the Arms Race* in *Origins of the Cold War*, ed. Melvyn P. Leffler and David S. Painter (1994), 100.

12. Holloway, *Stalin and the Bomb*, 153.

13. Stalin's interview with Alexander Werth, Sept. 17, 1946, quoted in Holloway, *Stalin and the Bomb*, 171.

14. Stalin quoted in Vladimir O. Pechatnov, "The Allies are pressing on you to break your will…": "Foreign Policy Correspondence between Stalin and Molotov and other Politburo Members, Sept. 1945–Dec. 1946," CWIHP, Working Paper no. 26, Sept. 1999).

15. Stalin quoted in Pechatnov, "The Allies," 5.

16. Stalin quoted in Pechatnov, "The Allies," 6.

17. Stalin quoted in Andrzej Werblan, "The Conversation between Wladyslaw Gomulka and Josef Stalin on 14 November 1945," CWIHP, *Bulletin* issue 11, Winter 1998, 136.

18. Kennan quoted in Kenneth M. Jensen (ed.), *Origins of the Cold War: The Novikov, Kennan, and Roberts 'Long Telegrams' of 1946* (1991), 17–31.

19. At the end of 1946, American cryptographers painstakingly began decipher-

ing some of the more than one thousand Soviet Intelligence cables (the Venona transcripts) that they had collected since 1940; see Robert Louis Benson and Michael Warner (eds.), *Venona: Soviet Espionage and the American Response, 1939–1957* (1996). According to John Hayes and Harvey Kheler, *Venona: Decoding Soviet Espionage in America* (2000), 15), 349, Americans had some covert relationship with Soviet intelligence. Less than half have been identified by name; those who have, include the Rosenbergs, Alger Hiss and Harry Dexter White.

20. Winston S. Churchill, *The Sinews of Peace*, Mar. 5, 1946, Churchill Archive Centre, Cambridge, CHUR 2/226.

21. Natalia Yegorova, "The 'Iran Crisis' of 1945–1946," CWIHP, Working Paper no. 15, May 1996, 19.

22. Walter J. Boyne, "The Early Overflights," *Journal of the Air Force Association*, June 2001, 60.

23. Molotov quoted in Zubok and Pleshakov, *Kremlin's Cold War*, 93–94.

24. Clifford and Elsey, report on *America's Relations with the Soviet Union*, Sept. 24, 1946, Harry S. Truman Library, 81 pages.

25. Truman quoted in Margaret Truman, *Harry S. Truman* (1973), 374.

26. Novikov quoted in Jensen, *Novikov, Kennan and Roberts*, 3–16.

27. President Truman's address, The Truman Library; *The New York Times*, Oct. 24, 1946.

28. Natalia Yegorova, "The 'Iran Crisis' of 1945–1946," 23–24.

Chapter 4

1. Stalin quoted in Mark Kramer, "The Soviet Union and Later—A Review Article," *Europe-Asia Studies*, Sept. 1999, 1093–1106.

2. Hankey note, Oct. 25, 1946, quoted in Anne Deighton, *The Impossible Peace: Britain, the Division of Germany and the Origins of the Cold War* (1990), 108.

3. President Harry S. Truman, "Special Message to the Congress," Mar. 12 1947.

4. Stalin quoted in Walter Bedell Smith, *Moscow Mission, 1946–49* (1950), 212–13.

5. Scott D. Parrish and Mikhail M. Narinsky, "New Evidence on the Soviet Rejection of the Marshall Plan, 1947," CWIHP, Working Paper no. 9, Mar. 1994, 45.

6. Masaryk quoted *ibid.*, 51.

7. "X" (George Kennan), "The Sources of Soviet Conduct," *Foreign Affairs*, July 1947.

8. Robert A. Pollard, "The National Security State Reconsidered: Truman and Economic Containment, 1945–1950," in Michael J. Lacey (ed.), *The Truman Presidency* (1989), 213.

9. Zhdanov quoted in Parrish and Narinsky, "Soviet Rejection of the Marshall Plan," 33.

10. Walter Millis (ed.), *The Forrestal Diaries* (1951), 350–51.

11. Public Papers of President Harry S. Truman, Truman Library, Doc. 52.

12. Niall Ferguson, "Dollar Diplomacy," *The New Yorker*, Aug. 27, 2007, 82–84.

13. Stalin quoted in Leonid Gibianskii, "The Soviet Bloc and the Initial Stage of the Cold War," CWIHP, *Bulletin* issue 10, Mar. 1998, 130.

Chapter 5

1. Vladislav Zubok and Constantine Pleshakov, *Inside the Kremlin's Cold War: From Stalin to Khrushchev* (1996), 52.

2. Derek Leebaert, *The Fifty Year Wound: The True Price of America's Cold War Victory* (2002), 74.

3. John Newhouse, *The Nuclear Age: From Hiroshima to Star Wars* (1989), 67.

4. Jean Edward Smith (ed.), *The Papers of General Lucius D. Clay* (1974), 1170.

5. Stalin to Liu Shaoqi, July 27, 1949, quoted in Sergei N. Goncharov, John W. Lewis and Xue Litai, *Uncertain Partners: Stalin, Mao and the Korean War* (1994), 69.

6. Truman quoted in Robert J. Donovan, *Conflict and Crisis: The Presidency of Harry S. Truman, 1945–1948* (1996), 101.

7. Ismay quoted in Michael Mandelbaum, *The Dawn of Peace in Europe* (1996), 12.

8. Nikita Khrushchev, *Khrushchev Remembers* (1970), 280.

9. Stalin quoted in Isaac Deutscher, *Stalin: A Political Biography* (1949), 537.

10. Thomas C. Reed, *At the Abyss: An Insider's History of the Cold War* (2004), 110–11.

11. Melvyn P. Leffler, *A Preponderance of Power: National Security, the Truman Administration, and the Cold War* (1992), 355–60; Ernest R. May (ed.), *American Cold War Strategy: Interpreting NSC 68* (1993), 23–81.

Chapter 6

1. See Conversation with Zhou Enlai, Aug. 20, 1952 in "Stalin's Conversations with Chinese Leaders," CWIHP, *Bulletin* issue 6–7, Winter 1995–96, 13.

2. Derek Leebaert, *The Fifty Year Wound: The True Price of America's Cold War Victory* (2002), 68.

3. Walter J. Boyne, *The Early Overflights*, Journal of the Air Force Association, June 2001, 60–65.

4. Stalin quoted in Evgueni Bajanov, "Assessing the Politics of the Korean War, 1949–51," CWIHP, *Bulletin* issue 6–7, Winter 1995–96, 87.

5. Stalin quoted in Katheryn Weathersby, "'Why Should We Fear This?': Stalin and the Danger of War with America," CWIHP, Working Paper no. 39, July 2002, 10–11.

6. *Ibid.*

7. Chen Jian, *Mao's China and the Cold War* (2007), 53.

8. Stalin quoted in Vladislav M. Zubok, *A Failed Empire: The Soviet Union in the Cold War from Stalin to Gorbachev* (2007), 80–81.

9. Leebaert, *Fifty Year Wound*, 138.

10. "Conversation between Joseph Stalin and the SED leadership, 7 Apr. 1952," CWIHP, Virtual Archive; also in Library of Congress, Dmitri Volkogonov Collection.

11. David Holloway, *Stalin and the Bomb: The Soviet Union and Atomic Energy, 1939–1956* (1994), 240.

12. David Rosenberg, "A Smoking Radiating Ruin at the End of Two Hours," *International Security*, Winter 1981–2, 25.

13. Vojtech Mastny, *The Cold War and Soviet Insecurity: The Stalin Years* (1996), 113.

14. Jonathan Brent and Vladimir Naumov, *Stalin's Last Crime: The Plot Against Jewish Doctors, 1948–53* (2003).

15. Oleg Troyanovsky, "The Making of Soviet Foreign Policy," in William Taubman, Sergei Khrushchev and Abbott Gleason (eds.), *Nikita Khrushchev* (2000), 209.

16. Miklos Kun, *Stalin: An Unknown Portrait* (2003), 85.

17. Litvinov quoted in FRUS, vol. VI (1946), 763.

Chapter 7

1. *Pravda*, Mar. 12, 1953.

2. Sergo Beria, *Beria My Father: Inside Stalin's Kremlin* (1999), 251–67.

3. William Taubman (ed.), *Khrushchev on Khrushchev: An Inside Account of the Man and His Era by His Son, Sergei Khrushchev* (1990), 671.

4. Taubman, *Khrushchev*, second page of illustrations following page 300. The black tie and jacket probably belonged to the photographic studio.

5. Stalin quoted in Nikita Khrushchev, *Khrushchev Remembers* (1970), 392.

6. Khrushchev quoted in Melvyn B. Leffler, *For the Soul of Mankind* (2007), 158.

7. Eisenhower quoted in Vojtech Mastny, *The Cold War and Soviet Insecurity: The Stalin Years* (1996), 165.

8. Vladimir Zubok, "Soviet Intelligence and the Cold War," CWIHP, Working Paper no. 4, 1992, 12.

9. Derek Leebaert, *The Fifty Year Wound: The True Price of America's Cold War Victory* (2002), 97.

10. For more details of the Solarium Project see Robert R. Bowie and Richard H. Immerman, *Waging Peace: How Eisenhower Shaped an Enduring Cold War Strategy* (1998), 122–38.

11. Eisenhower quoted in Bowie and Immerman, *Waging Peace*, 190.

12. Campbell Craig, *Destroying the Village: Eisenhower and Thermonuclear War* (1998).

13. John Foster Dulles, *Memorandum of 6 September 1953*, FRUS 1952–54, vol. 2, 457–60.

14. Khrushchev quoted in Vladislav M. Zubok, *A Failed Empire: The Soviet Union in the Cold War from Stalin to Gorbachev* (2007), 101.

15. Cited in Mark Kramer, "The Early Post-Stalin Succession Struggle and Upheavals in Eastern Europe (Part 1)," *Journal of Cold War Studies*, Winter 1999, 6–7.

16. Stalin quoted in Charles S. Maier, *Dissolution: The Crisis of Communism and the End of East Germany* (1997), 12.

17. Kramer, "Early Post-Stalin Succession Struggle," 12.

18. *Ibid.*, 28.

19. Quoted in Hope M. Harrison, "The Berlin Wall, Ostpolitik, and Détente," in the *Bulletin of the German Historical Institute,* Supplement no. 1, 2004, 9.

20. Andrei Alexandrov-Argentov quoted in Zubok, *Failed Empire*, 102.

21. Khrushchev quoted in Taubman, *Khrushchev*, 349.

22. Sergei Khrushchev (ed.), *Memoirs of Nikita Khrushchev*, vol. 3: *Statesman [1953–64]* (2007), 399–400.

23. Eisenhower quoted in Larry Tart, *The Price of Vigilance: Attacks on American Surveillance Flights* (2002), 119.

24. Thomas C. Reed, *At the Abyss: An Insider's History of the Cold War* (2004), 40–49.

25. James Bamford, *Body of Secrets: Anatomy of the Ultra-Secret National Security Agency* (2002), 36.

26. Matthew Brzezinski, *Red Moon Rising: Sputnik and the Rivalries That Ignited the Space Age* (2007), 24–25.

27. Correspondence with Cargill Hall, Emeritus Chief Historian of the National Reconnaissance Office, an intelligence arm of the Department of Defense; Cargill Hall, "Clandestine Victory: Eisenhower and the Overhead Reconnaissance in the Cold War," in Dennis E. Showalter (ed.), *Forging the Shield* (2005), 1–31; see also William E. Burrows, *By Any Means: America's Secret Air War in the Cold War* (2001).

Chapter 8

1. President Dwight D. Eisenhower, first inaugural address, Jan. 20, 1953.

2. David Holloway, *Stalin and the Bomb: The Soviet Union and Atomic Energy, 1939–1956* (1994), 339.

3. Malenkov quoted in John G. Hines, Phillip A. Petersen and Notra Trulock III, "Soviet Military Theory from 1945–2000: Implications for Nato," *The Washington Quarterly,* Fall 1986, 119.

4. Molotov quoted in Vladislav Zubok and Constantine Pleshakov, *Inside the Kremlin's Cold War: From Stalin to Khrushchev* (1996), 168.

5. President George H. W. Bush, letter to the author, Apr. 4, 2005.

6. Quoted in Fred Kaplan, *The Wizards of Armageddon* (1983), 254.

7. David Alan Rosenberg, "The Origins of Overkill: Nuclear Weapons and American Strategy, 1945–1960," *International Security*, Spring 1983, 24.

8. Based on an analysis done for the author by Matthew McKinzie of the Natural Resources Defense Council, using the U.S. Department of Defense computer code HPAC (Hazard Prediction and Assessment Capability), see www.dtra.mil/newsservices/fact_sheets/display.cfm?fs=hpac).

9. Powers quoted in Kaplan, *Wizards*, 246.

10. Anatoly Dobrynin, *In Confidence: Moscow's Ambassador to America's Six Cold War Presidents* (1995), 524–25.

11. Phillip A. Petersen and Notra Trulock, "Gleiche Sicherheit: GröBere Stabilität bei niedrigeren Stitkräftestand," in *Die sowjetsche Militärmacht und die Stabilität in Europa*, ed. Gerhard Wettig, Schriftenreiche des Bundesinstituts für ostwissenschaftliche und internationale Studien (1990), 137–68.

Chapter 9

1. Sergei Khrushchev (ed.), *Memoirs of Nikita Khrushchev*, vol. 3: *Statesman [1953–64]* (2007), 35 and 41.

2. Sergei N. Khrushchev, *Khrushchev and the Making of a Superpower* (2000), 83.

3. William Taubman (ed.), *Khrushchev on Khrushchev: An Inside Account of the Man and His Era by His Son, Sergei Khrushchev* (1990), 353.

4. David Holloway, "Soviet Nuclear History," CWIHP, *Bulletin* issue 4, Fall 1994, 16.

5. S. Khrushchev (ed.), *Memoirs*, vol. 3, 50.

6. I am grateful to Michael Ploetz for drawing my attention to this speech—Referat des Genossen Staatssekretär auf der Parteiaktivtagung am 9, Aug. 1955, BSTU, ZA, MfS-BdL, Dok. Nr. 005802.

7. Taubman, *Khrushchev*, 352.

8. Vladislav Zubok and Constantine Pleshakov, *Inside the Kremlin's Cold War: From Stalin to Khrushchev* (1996), 185.

9. Taubman, *Khrushchev*, 274.

10. Markus Wolf, *Man without a Face: The Autobiography of Communism's Greatest Spymaster* (1997), 84.

11. Gomulka quoted in Taubman, *Khrushchev*, 293–94.

12. Khrushchev quoted in Mark Kramer, "The Soviet Union and the 1956 Crises in Hungary and Poland: Reassessments and New Findings," *Journal of Contemporary History*, Apr. 1998, 172.

13. For a detailed account of the Hungarian Revolt (or as many people call it, the Hungarian Revolution), see Csaba Bekes, Malcolm Byrne, Janos Rainer (eds.), *The 1956 Hungarian Revolution: A History in Documents* (2002), and Charles Gati, *Failed Illusions: Moscow, Washington, Budapest and the 1956 Hungarian Revolt* (2006).

14. Dulles quoted in Gati, *Failed Illusions*, 136.

15. Khrushchev quoted in Mark Kramer, "New Evidence on Soviet Decision-Making and the 1956 Polish and Hungarian Crises," CWIHP, *Bulletin* issue 8–9, 1997, 358–84.

16. Gati, *Failed Illusions*, 196.

17. Alexandr Fursenko and Timothy Naftali, *Khrushchev's Cold War: The Inside Story of an American Adversary* (2006), 134.

18. Fursenko and Naftali, *Khrushchev's Cold War*, 133.

Chapter 10

1. Matthew Brzezinski, *Red Moon Rising: Sputnik and the Rivalries That Ignited the Space Age* (2007), 24–25.

2. Sergei Khrushchev (ed.), *Memoirs of Nikita Khrushchev*, vol. 2: *Reformer [1945–1964]* (2006), 456.

3. Khrushchev quoted in Vladislav Zubok and Constantine Pleshakov, *Inside the Kremlin's Cold War: From Stalin to Khrushchev* (1996), 253.

4. Thomas C. Reed, *At the Abyss: An Insider's History of the Cold War* (2004), 71.

5. Sidney Graybeal, former Chief of CIA's Missile Division, interview on Jan. 29, 1998, for CNN's *Cold War*—Spies: Episode 21; for transcript see National Security Archive.

6. Reed, *Abyss*, 71.

7. Philip Taubman, *Secret Empire: Eisenhower, the CIA, and the Hidden Story of America's Space Espionage* (2004), 177.

8. Khrushchev quoted in Taubman, *Khrushchev*, 244.

9. Derek Leebaert, *The Fifty Year Wound: The True Price of America's Cold War Victory* (2002), 152.

10. Leonid Vladimirov, *The Russian Space Bluff: The Inside Story of the Soviet Drive to the Moon and Beyond* (1971), 54–55.

11. Eisenhower quoted in James R. Killian, *Sputnik, Scientists and Eisenhower: A Memoir of the First Special Assistant to the President for Science and Technology* (1977), 10.

12. Steven T. Usdin, *Engineering Communism: How Two Americans Spied for Stalin and Founded the Soviet Silicon Valley* (2005), 197–98.

13. Vladimirov, *Space Bluff*, 73.

14. www.gwu.edu/~nsarchiv/NSAEBB/NSAEBB139/Nitze.02.pdf.

15. Walter McDougall, *The Heavens and the Earth: A Political History of the Space Age* (1985), 8.

16. Mao quoted in Sergei Khrushchev (ed.), *Memoirs of Nikita Khrushchev*, vol. 3: *Statesman [1953–64]* (2007), 436.

17. Dwight D. Eisenhower, *Waging Peace, 1956–1961: The White House* (1965), 180.

18. Alexandr Fursenko and Timothy Naftali, *Khrushchev's Cold War: The Inside Story of an American Adversary* (2006), 182–84.

19. S. Khrushchev (ed.), *Memoirs*, vol. 3, 290–91.

20. Fursenko and Naftali, *Khrushchev's Cold War*, 182–84.

Chapter 11

1. Khrushchev quoted in Dean Rusk, *As I Saw It* (1990), 227.

2. Khrushchev quoted in Hope M. Harrison, *Driving the Soviets up the Wall: Soviet-East German Relations, 1953–61* (2003), 65.

3. Sergei Khrushchev, *Nikita Khrushchev and the Creation of a Superpower* (2000), 328–29.

4. Sergei Khrushchev (ed.), *Memoirs of Nikita Khrushchev*, vol. 2: *Reformer [1945–64]* (2006), 516.

5. Steven J. Zaloga, *The Kremlin's Nuclear Sword: The Rise and Fall of Russia's Strategic Nuclear Forces, 1945–2000* (2002), 61.

6. Derek Leebaert, *The Fifty Year Wound: The True Price of America's Cold War Victory* (2002), 246.

7. See "Khrushchev's Supreme Soviet Report on a Troop Cut," *The Current Digest of the Soviet Press*, vol. 12, no. 2, 3–16.

8. Alexandr Fursenko and Timothy Naftali, *Khrushchev's Cold War: The Inside Story of an American Adversary* (2006), 255–56.

9. Matthias Uhl: "Krieg um Berlin? Die sowetische Militär- und Sicherheitspolitik," in *Der zweiten Berlin-Krise 1958 bis 1962* (2008), 234.

10. Matthew Evangelista, "'Why Keep Such an Army?': Khrushchev's Troop Reductions," CWIHP, Working Paper no. 19, Dec. 1997.

11. Robert Standish Norris, "United States Nuclear Weapons Deployments Abroad, 1950–1977," PowerPoint presentation in the History of the Nuclear Age Dinner Series, 8 (Carnegie Endowment for International Peace, Nov. 30, 1999); see also Department of Energy figures quoted in "The U.S. Nuclear Stockpile, Today and Tomorrow," *Bulletin of Atomic Scientists*, Sept.–Oct. 2007 and David A. Rosenberg, "The Origins of Overkill: Nuclear Weapons and American Strategy, 1945–60, *International Security*, Spring 1983, 3–71.

12. Department of Defense, *History of the Custody and Deployment of Nuclear Weapons, July 1945 through September 1977* (Office of the Assistant to the Secretary of Defense (Atomic Energy), Top Secret (declassified), 77.

13. Eisenhower quoted in Fursenko and Naftali, *Khrushchev's Cold War*, 226.

14. Steven T. Usdin, "Tracking Julius Rosenberg's Lesser Known Associates," *Studies in Intelligence*, vol. 49, no. 3 (2005), 13–15.

15. Stephen E. Ambrose, *Eisenhower: Soldier and President* (1990), 470.

16. Jussi M. Hankimaki and Odd Arne Westad, *The Cold War: A History in Documents and Eyewitness Accounts* (2003), 390–91.

17. William Taubman, "Nikita Khrushchev and the Shoe," *The International Herald Tribune*, July 26–27, 2003.

18. Peter Lunak, "Khrushchev and the Berlin Crisis: Soviet Brinkmanship Seen from Inside," *The Journal of Cold War History*, Jan. 2003, 69.

Chapter 12

1. The Inaugural Address of President John F. Kennedy delivered in Washington, DC on January 20, 1961, www.jfklibrary.org/Historical+Resources/Archives/.

2. McNamara quoted in Thomas C. Reed, *At the Abyss: An Insider's History of the Cold War* (2004), 94.

3. FRUS, 1961–63, vol. 14, doc. 30, 81–82.

4. Khrushchev quoted in Alexandr Fursenko and Timothy Naftali, *Khrushchev's Cold War: The Inside Story of an American Adversary* (2006), 355.

5. State Department memo quoted in David Reynolds, *Summits: Six Meetings that Shaped the Twentieth Century* (2007), 183.

6. Kennedy quoted in Richard Reeves, *President Kennedy: Profile in Power* (1993), 171.

7. Jerrold L. Schecter and Peter Deriabin, *The Spy who Saved the World: How a Soviet Colonel Changed the Course of the Cold War* (1992), 185–91.

8. Address by President Kennedy to the American people, July 25, 1961; see President Kennedy's *Public Papers 1961, Doc. 302.*

9. Quoted in Hope M. Harrison, *Driving the Soviets up the Wall: Soviet-East German Relations, 1953–61* (2003), 191.

10. Markus Wolf, *Man without a Face: The Autobiography of Communism's Greatest Spymaster* (1997), 96–97.

11. Ulbricht quoted in Harrison, *The Wall*, 185.

12. Khrushchev quoted Harrison, *The Wall*, 205.

13. Kennedy quoted in Norman Gelb, *The Berlin Wall: Kennedy, Khrushchev,and a Showdown in the Heart of Europe* (1986), 213.

14. Khrushchev quoted in Fursenko and Naftali, *Khrushchev's Cold War*, 406.

15. Khrushchev quoted in Fursenko and Naftali, *Khrushchev's Cold War*, 412–13.

16. Khrushchev quoted in Harrison, *The Wall*, 215.

17. Khrushchev quoted in Fursenko and Naftali, *Khrushchev's Cold War*, 414.

18. Air Marshal Sir John Walker, who was one of the fighter pilots; interview, London, Nov. 11, 2003.

19. Department of Defense (Office of the Assistant to the Secretary of Defense, Atomic Energy), *History of the Custody and Deployment of Nuclear Weapons, July 1945 through September 1977*, Top Secret (declassified), 77.

20. Richard Ned Lebow and Janice Gross Stein, *We All Lost the Cold War* (1994), 33.

21. Brown, Interview and transcript of Musgrove Plantation Conference, May 7, 1994, 53.

22. Moskalenko quoted in Sergei Khrushchev, *Nikita Khrushchev and the Creation of a Superpower* (2000), 474.

Chapter 13

1. Khrushchev quoted in Alexandr Fursenko and Timothy Naftali, *Khrushchev's Cold War: The Inside Story of an American Adversary* (2006), 435.

2. *Ibid.*, 441–43.

3. McCone quoted in Jerrold L. Schecter and Peter Deriabin, *The Spy who Saved the World: How a Soviet Colonel Changed the Course of the Cold War* (1992), 331.

4. Kennedy quoted in Aleksandr Fursenko and Timothy J. Naftali, *One Hell of a Gamble: Khrushchev, Castro, and Kennedy, 1958–1964: The Secret History of the Cuban Missile Crisis* (1998), ix.

5. Speeches of John F. Kennedy, John F. Kennedy Museum and Library.

6. Danilevich, Interviews, BDM, *Soviet Intentions 1965–85*, vol. 2: *Soviet Post–Cold War Testimonial Evidence* (1995), 30–31.

7. Rusk quoted in Fursenko and Naftali, *Khrushchev's Cold War*, 482.

8. Michael Dobbs, *One Minute to Midnight: Kennedy, Khrushchev and Castro on the Brink of Nuclear War* (2008), 43.

9. Khrushchev quoted in Sergei Khrushchev, *Nikita Khrushchev and the Creation of a Superpower* (2000), 584.

10. Dobbs, *One Minute to Midnight*, xiii.

11. Fursenko and Naftali, *Khrushchev's Cold War*, 487–89.

12. Kennedy quoted in Ernest May and Philip Zelikow, *Kennedy Tapes: Inside the White House during the Cuban Missile Crisis* (1997), 512.

13. The Cuban Missile Crisis, 1962: Materials from the 40th Anniversary Conference, Havana, Cuba, 10–12 Oct. 2002, National Security Archive Website.

14. Dobbs, *One Minute to Midnight*, 237.

15. *Ibid.*, 244.

16. Quoted in Vladislav Zubok and Constantine Pleshakov, *Inside the Kremlin's Cold War: From Stalin to Khrushchev* (1996), 266.

17. Nikita S. Khrushchev to John F. Kennedy, Oct. 28, 1962, *FRUS, 1961–1963*, 11: Doc 102.

18. Quoted in Svetlana Savranskaya, "Tactical Nuclear Weapons in Cuba: New Evidence," CWIHP, *Bulletin* issue 14–15, Winter 2003–2004, 386.

19. National Security Archive, Electronic Briefing Book 75, Oct. 31, 2002; see also Peter A. Huchthausen, *October Fury* (2002) and Dobbs, *One Minute to Midnight*, 303.

20. FRUS 1961–63, vol. 5, Soviet Union, Document 260.

21. Khrushchev quoted in Melvyn B. Leffler, *For the Soul of Mankind* (2007), 157.

22. Khrushchev quoted in Leffler, *For the Soul of Mankind*, 498.

23. Khrushchev quoted in Fursenko and Naftali, *Khrushchev's Cold War*, 506.

24. Kennedy quoted in Theodore C. Sorensen, *Kennedy* (1965), 732.

25. Kuznetsov quoted in Charles Bohlen, *Witness to History 1919–1969* (1973), 495.

26. Quoted in Fursenko and Naftali, *Khrushchev's Cold War*, 537.

27. Khrushchev quoted in William Taubman (ed.), *Khrushchev on Khrushchev: An Inside Account of the Man and His Era by His Son, Sergei Khrushchev* (1990), 154.

28. Khrushchev quoted in Taubman, *Khrushchev*, 242.

29. Roderick MacFarquhar, Gerry Scott's cousin; see also Larissa MacFarquhar, "The Jazz Singer," *The New Yorker*, Aug. 18, 2003.

30. Denis Healey, *Time of My Life* (1989), 243.

Chapter 14

1. PPPUS: LBJ: 1966 vol. 2, p. 1128 (7 Oct. 1966).

2. Steven J. Zaloga, *The Kremlin's Nuclear Sword: The Rise and Fall of Russia's Strategic Nuclear Forces, 1945–2000* (2002), 118.

3. William Burr and Jeffrey T. Richelson, "Whether to 'Strangle the Baby in the Cradle': The United States and the Chinese Nuclear Program 1960–64," *International Security*, vol. 25, issue 3, Winter 2000/01, 71.

4. Charles de Gaulle, *Memoirs of Hope: Renewal—1958–62* (1971), 257–58.

5. Mark Kramer, "Ideology and the Cold War," *Review of International Studies*, Oct. 1999, 545.

6. Brezhnev quoted by Jaromir Navratil (ed.), *The Prague Spring 1968* (1998), 345–56.

7. Vojtech Mastny, "Was 1968 a Strategic Watershed of the Cold War?," *Diplomatic History*, vol. 29, no. 1 (2005), 167–68.

8. Christopher Andrew and Oleg Gordievsky, *The KGB—The Inside Story of Its Operations from Lenin to Gorbachev* (1990), 406.

9. Quoted in Joan Urban (ed.), *Moscow and the Italian Communist Party* (1992), 254–56.

Chapter 15

1. Public Papers of President Nixon, vol. 1 (1969), Document 279, Informal Remarks in Guam with Newsmen, July 25, 1969.

2. Speech by Robert McNamara, San Francisco, Sept. 18, 1967.

3. Kosygin quoted in Robert S. McNamara, *Blundering into Disaster: Surving the First Century of the Nuclear Age* (1986), 57.

4. Department of Defense, *A Brief History of Minuteman and Multiple Reentry Vehicles*, www.gwu.edu.~narchiv/nsa/NC/mirv/mirv.html.

5. Danilevich, Interview, BDM, *Soviet Intentions 1965–85*, vol. 2: *Soviet Post–Cold War Testimonial Evidence* (1995), 33.

6. Alexandr G. Savelyev and Nikolai N. Detinov, *The Big Five: Arms Control Decision-Making in the Soviet Union* (1995), 3.

7. Danilevich, Interview, BDM, *Soviet Intentions,* vol. 2, 29.

8. Mozzhorin, Interview, BDM, *Soviet Intentions*, vol. 2, 123.

9. Illarionov, Interview, BDM, *Soviet Intentions,* vol. 2, 80–82.

10. See also David C. Geyer and Bernd Shaefer (eds), *American Détente and German Ostpolitik, 1969–1972, Bulletin of the German Historical Institute*, Supplement no. 1, 2004; Wjatscheslaw Keworkow, *Der geheime Kanal; Moscow, der KGB und die Bonner Ostpolitik* (1995); Willy Brandt, *My Life in Politics* (1992).

11. Author's conversation with Petrovsky, Turin, Mar. 6, 2004.

12. Markus Wolf, *Man without a Face: The Autobiography of Communism's Greatest Spymaster* (1997), 214–15.

13. Douglas Selvage, "The Treaty of Warsaw: The Warsaw Pact Context," *Bulletin of the German Historical Institute*, Supplement no. 1, 2004, 75.

14. Wolf Interviews; see also Wolf, *Man without a Face*, 156.

15. Willy Brandt, *People and Politics* (1978), 399.

16. Selvage, "Treaty of Warsaw," 73.

17. Bahr quoted in Geyer and Shaefer, *American Détente and German Ostpolitik*, 138.

18. Quoted in Geyer and Schaefer, *American Détente and German Ostpolitik*, 1.

Chapter 16

1. Gromyko quoted in Raymond L. Garthoff, *Détente and Confrontation: American-Soviet Relations from Nixon to Reagan* (rev. ed., 1994), 66.

2. Karen Brutens quoted in Vladislav M. Zubok, *A Failed Empire: The Soviet Union in the Cold War from Stalin to Gorbachev* (2007), 215.

3. Christopher Andrew and Oleg Gordievsky, *The KGB—The Inside Story of Its Operations from Lenin to Gorbachev* (1990), 435.

4. This subject is well analyzed in Chen Jian, *Mao's China and the Cold War* (2001).

5. Alexander M. Haig, Jr., *Inner Circles: How America Changed the World* (1992), 257.

6. http://www.gwu.edu/~nsarchiv/NSAEBB/NSAEBB49/—see Document 10.

7. FRUS, 1969–76, Meeting on February 23, 1972, Electronic vol. E-13, doc. 92.

8. Anatoly Dobrynin, *In Confidence: Moscow's Ambassador to America's Six Cold War Presidents* (1995), 242.

9. Dobrynin, *In Confidence*, 248.

10. Richard M. Nixon, *RN: The Memoirs of Richard Nixon* (1978), 609.

11. Public Papers of President Richard Nixon, vol. 4 (1972), Document 177.

12. Henry Trofimenko, "The Third World and the U.S.-Soviet Competition: A Soviet View," *Foreign Affairs*, no. 57 (1980), 1027.

13. Brezhnev quoted in Dobrynin, *In Confidence*, 256.

14. Grinevsky quoted in Peter Schweizer, *Reagan's War: The Epic Story of His Forty Year Struggle and Final Triumph over Communism* (2002), 75.

15. Willam Bundy, *A Tangled Web: The Making of Foreign Policy in the Nixon Presidency* (1998), 325.

16. Schlesinger, Interviews; see also Special National Intelligence Estimate 11-4-73 *Soviet Strategic Arms Programs and Détente: What Are They Up To?*

17. Alexandr G. Savelyev and Nikolai N. Detinov, *The Big Five: Arms Control Decision-Making in the Soviet Union* (1995), 7.

18. Danilevich, Interviews, BDM, *Soviet Intentions 1965–85*, vol. 2: *Soviet Post–Cold War Testimonial Evidence* (1995), vol. 2, 27.

19. *Ibid.*

20. Tsygichko, Interviews, BDM, *Soviet Intentions*, vol. 2, 145.

21. Danilevich, Interviews, BDM, *Soviet Intentions*, vol. 2, 58–62.

22. Brezhnev's handwritten diary excerpts, Volkogonov Collection, Reel 17, Container 24—on file at the National Security Archive, READDRADD Collection, Box 19.

23. Chubarian, Interview.

24. I am grateful to Professor Vojtech Mastny for providing me with this quote from the Czechoslovak Party Archives in Prague.

Chapter 17

1. Brezhnev quoted in Anatoly Dobrynin, *In Confidence: Moscow's Ambassador to America's Six Cold War Presidents* (1995), 300.

2. Raymond L. Garthoff, *Détente and Confrontation: American-Soviet Relations from Nixon to Reagan* (rev. ed., 1994), 505–8.

3. Andropov quoted in Odd Arne Westad (ed.), *The Fall of Détente: Soviet-American Relations during the Carter Years* (1997), 19.

4. Andropov quoted in Odd Arne Westad, *The Global Cold War* (2005), 215.

5. Dobrynin, *In Confidence*, 361.

6. Ponomarev quoted in Dobrynin, *In Confidence*, 362.

7. Interview transcript for CNN's *The Cold War*, television documentary, no. 28/68, Liddell Hart Centre for Military Archives, King's College, London.

8. Westad, *Fall of Détente*, 20.

9. Interview transcript for CNN's *The Cold War*, television documentary, no. 28/68, Liddell Hart Centre for Military Archives, King's College, London.

10. Nikolai Leonov, *ibid.*, no. 28/68 and 28/84.

11. Henry A. Kissinger, *Years of Renewal* (1999), 269.

12. Richard M. Nixon, *RN: The Memoirs of Richard Nixon* (1978), 1031.

13. Brezhnev quoted in Vladislav M. Zubok, *A Failed Empire: The Soviet Union in the Cold War from Stalin to Gorbachev* (2007), 244.

14. James Blight, letter to the Hon. Jimmy Carter summarizing the Musgrove Plantation Conference, May 13, 1994.

15. Kornienko interviewed by Odd Arne Westad and quoted in Westad (ed.), *The Fall of Détente*, 12.

16. Alexander Bovin, *Izvestia*, Feb. 6, 1975.

17. Quoted in Andrei Gratchev, *Gorbachev's Gamble* (2008), 18.

18. Grinevsky quoted in Peter Schweizer, *Reagan's War: The Epic Story of His Forty Year Struggle and Final Triumph over Communism* (2002), 127.

19. S. Akhromeyev and G. Kornienko, *Glazami Marshala i Diplomata* [*Through the Eyes of a Marshal and a Diplomat*] (1992), 22.

20. Henry A. Kissinger, Statement before the Senate Committee on Foreign Relations 'On US Relations with Communist Countries," GPO (1975), 260.

21. "Intelligence Community Experiment in Competitive Analysis: Soviet Strategic Objectives, An Alternative View, Report of Team 'B,'" in Donald P. Steury (ed.), *Intentions and Capabilities: Estimates on Soviet Strategic Forces, 1950–1983* (1996), 365–90; the issues are analyzed in Anne Hessing Cahn, *Killing Détente: The Right Attacks CIA* (1998), 100–184.

22. Danilevich, BDM, *Soviet Intentions 1965–85*, vol. 2: *Soviet Post–Cold War Testimonial Evidence* (1995), 23.

Chapter 18

1. Tsygichko, Interviews, BDM, Interview, *Soviet Intentions 1965–85*, vol. 2: *Soviet Post–Cold War Testimonial Evidence* (1995), 137, 139, 142.

2. *Ibid.*, 137.

3. The rapid buildup of Soviet forces in Central Europe is analyzed by Phillip A. Karber in Uwe Nerlich, *Soviet Power and Western Negotiating Policies*, vol. 1: *The Soviet Asset: Military Power in the Competition Over Europe* (1983)—"To Lose an Arms Race: The Competition in Conventional Forces Deployed in Central Europe, 1965–1980" (ch. 1) and "The Battle of Unengaged Military Strategies" (ch. 6).

4. Quoted by Phillip A. Petersen and John G. Hines, "The Conventional Offensive in Soviet Theater Strategy," *Orbis*, Fall 1983, 704.

5. Alexander M. Haig, Jr., *Inner Circles: How America Changed the World* (1992), 522.

6. The consultancy firm BDM was set up by Joe Braddock and his two partners, Bernie Dunn and Dan McDonald.

7. Andropov quoted in Michael Ploetz, "Nato and the Warsaw Treaty Organization at the Time of the Euromissile Crisis, 1975 to 1985," in Gustav Schmidt (ed.), *A History of Nato—The First 50 Years,* vol. 2 (2001), 217.

8. Michael Alexander, discussions with author, Geneva, July 1975; see also his *Managing the Cold War: A View from the Front Line* (2005), 64.

9. Viktor Sukhodrev (Gromyko's interpreter), Carter-Brezhnev Project (Records of Musgrove Plantation Conference, May 1994), 63.

10. Quoted in Odd Arne Westad, "Moscow and the Angolan Crisis, 1974–76: A New Pattern of Intervention," CWIHP, *Bulletin* issue 8–9, Winter 1996–1997, 21.

11. Michael Alexander, discussions with author, Geneva, July 1975.

12. These issues were explored in the Carter-Brezhnev Project conferences. See James Blight's letters to the Hon. Jimmy Carter of May 13, 1994, and Apr. 17, 1995.

13. Ernest Lee Tuverson, *Redeemer Nation: The Idea of America's Millennial Role* (1980).

Chapter 19

1. My apologies to the "perceptive commentator," whose name I have misplaced; if he or she would kindly let me have their name I will include it in the next edition.

2. NIE 11-4-77, *Soviet Strategic Objectives*, 12 Jan. 1977.

3. President Jimmy Carter, Inaugural Address, 20 Jan. 1977.

4. Bessmertnykh quoted in James Blight's letter to the Hon. Jimmy Carter of May 13, 1994, on the Musgrove Plantation Conference.

5. *Pravda*, Jan. 19, 1977.

6. Sukhodrev quoted in Odd Arne Westad (ed.), *The Fall of Détente: Soviet-American Relations during the Carter Years* (1997), 17.

7. This subject is well covered in Olav Njolstad, "Key of Keys? Salt II and the Breakdown of Détente," in Westad, *Fall of Détente,* 34–71.

8. Vance, transcript of the Musgrove Plantation Conference, 62.

9. The full version of what Gromyko and Vance said is recorded in Memorandum of Conversation, A. A. Gromyko and C. Vance, Moscow, Mar. 28, 1977 (Carter-Brezhnev Collection, National Security Archive).

10. Danilevich, Interview, BDM, *Soviet Intentions 1965–85*, vol. 2: *Soviet Post–Cold War Testimonial Evidence* (1995), 64.

11. Raymond L. Garthoff, *Deterence and the Revolution in Soviet Military Doctrine* (1990), 83.

12. Danilevich and Kalashnikov, Interviews, BDM, *Soviet Intentions*, vol. 2, 68 and 90.

13. Kalashnikov, Interview, BDM, *Soviet Intentions*, vol. 2, 89–90.

14. Benjamin B. Fischer, "The Soviet-American War Scare of the 1980s," *International Journal of Intelligence and Counter-Intelligence*, Volume 19, Number 3, Fall 2006, 480–518.

15. Richard Pipes, "Why the Soviet Union Thinks It Could Fight and Win a Nuclear War," *Commentary*, July 1977, 29–31.

16. Quoted in Dana H. Allin, *Cold War Illusions: America, Europe and the Soviet Union, 1969–1989* (1998), 63.

17. Brown's statement before a joint meeting of the House and Senate Budget Committees in early 1979, quoted in Suzy Platt (ed.), *Respectfully Quoted* (1989).

Chapter 20

1. Danilevich, Interviews, BDM, *Soviet Intentions Soviet 1965–85*, vol. 2: *Soviet Post–Cold War Testimonial Evidence* (1995), vol. 2, 33.

2. Batenin, Interview, BDM, *Soviet Intentions*, vol. 2, 7.

3. Benjamin Weiser, *A Secret Life: A Biography of Ryszard Kuklinski* (2004).

4. Milt Bearden and James Risen, *The Main Enemy: The Inside Story of the CIA's Final Showdown with the KGB* (2003), 195.

5. Benjamin B. Fischer, review of Weiser's biography of Kuklinski, *International Journal of Intelligence and Counter-Intelligence*, summer 2005, 364–74.

6. Petersen, Interviews; LTC John G. Hines and Dr. Phillip A. Petersen, "The Changing Soviet System of Control for Theater War," *Signal*, Dec. 1986, 97–110.

7. DIA declassified testimony by Petersen before the US Senate Committee on Armed Services, 96th Congress (1980), 1933.

8. *Ibid.*; Phillip A. Petersen and John G. Hines, "Military Power in Soviet Strategy Against NATO," *RUSI Journal*, Dec. 1983, 53.

9. Benjamin Schemmer, "US Unveils Multi-Source Evidence of New Soviet Threats in German Forum," *Armed Forces Journal International*, Aug. 1984, 51–53.

10. Quoted by Michael Ploetz in "Troy Besieged: Marxism-Leninism in the Second Cold War (1979–85)—A Reconstruction from East German Sources" (Ph.D. thesis, University of London, Sept. 1997), 65.

11. Quoted in Vojtech Mastny (ed.), *Oral History Interviews with Polish Generals*, Parallel History Project (2002), 27.

12. Helmut Schmidt, "Peace Through Strength," address to the IISS, London, Oct. 1977, *Survival*, vol. 20, issue 1, Jan. 1978, 2–10.

Chapter 21

1. This subject is well covered in Zbigniew Brzezinski, *Power and Principle: Memoirs of a National Security Adviser* (1983).

2. Peter Schweizer, *Reagan's War: The Epic Story of His Forty Year Struggle and Final Triumph over Communism* (2002), 101–2.

3. Carter quoted in Odd Arne Westad, *The Global Cold War* (2005), 283.

4. The lack of success of Soviet Intelligence in Iran before and after the fall of the Shah is described in Vladimir Kuzichkin, *Inside the KGB: My Life in Soviet Espionage* (1990).

5. Andrei Gratchev, *Gorbachev's Gamble* (2008), 23.

6. See Gaddis Smith, *The Last Years of the Monroe Doctrine, 1945–1993* (1994), 139–230.

7. Quoted in Robert M. Gates, *From the Shadows: The Ultimate Insider's Story of Five Presidents and How They Won the Cold War* (1997), 90.

8. Gates, *Shadows*, 90–92.

9. Gates, *Shadows*, 94.

10. *Ibid.*

11. Sir Curtis Keeble, who was the first British Ambassador to the GDR.

12. John O. Koehler, *Stasi: The Untold Story of the East German Secret Police* (1999), 8.

13. A CIA report quoted in Gates, *Shadows*, 88.

14. Brezhnev quoted in Hans-Hermann Hertle, "Germany in the Last Decade of the Cold War," in Olav Njolstad (ed.), *The Last Decade of the Cold War: From Conflict Escalation to Conflict Transformation* (2004), 268.

15. Gates, *Shadows*, 200; Christopher Andrew and Vasili Mitrokhin, *The Mitrokhin Archive: The KGB in Europe and the West* (1999), 511–12.

16. Douglas J. MacEachin, *Predicting the Soviet Invasion of Afghanistan: The Intelligence Community's Record* (2002); Westad, *Global Cold War*; CWIH *Bulletin*, issue 8–9, Winter 1996–1997, 133–62.

17. Andropov, Politburo meeting, Mar. 17, 1979, in Arne Westad, "Concerning the Situation in 'A': New Evidence on the Soviet Intervention in Afghanistan," CWIHP, *Bulletin* issue 8–9, Winter 1996–97, 144.

18. Gates, *Shadows,* 146.

19. Dobrynin quoted in Westad, *Global Cold War,* 318.

20. Andropov quoted in Westad, *Global Cold War,* 319.

21. Ustinov and Andropov quoted in Westad, *Global Cold War,* 320.

22. Ogarkov quoted in Vladislav M. Zubok, *A Failed Empire: The Soviet Union in the Cold War from Stalin to Gorbachev* (2007), 263–64; Odd Arne Westad, "The Road to Kabul: Soviet Policy on Afghanistan, 1978–1979," in Westad (ed.), *The Fall of Détente: Soviet-American Relations during the Carter Years* (1997), 135–36.

23. Carter quoted in Raymond L. Garthoff, *Détente and Confrontation: American-Soviet Relations from Nixon to Reagan* (rev. ed., 1994), 1054.

24. Jimmy Carter, *Keeping Faith: Memoirs of a President* (1982), 483.

25. Dobrynin quoted in Westad, *Global Cold War,* 325.

26. Pope John Paul II quoted in Timothy Garton Ash, *The Polish Revolution: Solidarity* (rev. ed., 1999), 31–32.

27. Ash, *Solidarity,* 70–72.

28. For details of Soviet plans throughout the crisis see Douglas J. MacEachin, *US Intelligence and the Polish Crisis, 1980–1981* (2000).

29. Quoted by Zbigniew Brzezinski, who drafted the letter, in "White House Diary, 1980," *Orbis,* Winter 1988, 36–37.

30. Kania by Vojtech Mastny in "The Non-Invasion of Poland in 1980/81 and the End of the Cold War," CWIHP, Working Paper no. 23, Sept. 1998, 15.

31. Gates, *Shadows,* 232–33.

32. Quoted in Nigel West, *The Third Secret: The CIA, Solidarity and the KGB's Plot to Kill the Pope* (2001), 84.

33. Bronislaw Dabrowski, *The Vatican Talks of Archbishop Dabrowski* (Warsaw, 2001) (in Polish).

34. Quoted in William I. Hitchcock, *The Struggle for Europe: The History of the Continent Since 1945* (2004), 308.

35. Suslov quoted in Mastny, *Non-Invasion of Poland,* 26.

36. Andropov quoted in Mark Kramer (ed.), "Declassified Soviet Documents on the Polish Crisis," CWIHP, *Bulletin* issue 5, 1995, 121–23.

37. How much Soviet pressure was put on Jaruzelski to declare martial law remains a subject of much debate, see Mark Kramer, "Jaruzelski, the Soviet Union, and the Imposition of Martial Law in Poland: New Light on the Mystery of December 1981," CWIHP, *Bulletin* issue 11, Winter 1998, 5–133.

38. This subject is analyzed in MacEachin, *Polish Crisis, 1980–1981.*

39. Nancy Mitchell, "US Foreign Policy Under Jimmy Carter," *Cambridge History of the Cold War,* vol. 3 (Cambridge: CUP, forthcoming).

40. Carter, "Address to the Nation," Apr. 25, 1980, *American Presidency Project* http://www.presidency.ucsb.edu/ws/ (APP).

41. Leslie Gelb, Carter-Brezhnev Project, Fort Lauderdale Conference, Mar. 1995, Transcript of Proceedings, 165; for details, see NIE 11-3/8-79: *Soviet Capabilities for Strategic Nuclear Conflict Through the 1980s,* issued Mar. 17, 1980, in Donald

P. Steury, *Intentions and Capabilities: Estimates on Soviet Strategic Forces, 1950–1983* (1996), 407–27.

42. Gus Weiss, *Duping the Soviets: The Farewell Dossier*, Studies in Intelligence, no. 5, 1996.

43. For further details see William Odom, "The Origins and Design of Presidential Directive 59: A Memoir" in *Getting MAD: Mutual Assured Destruction, Its Origins and Practice*, ed. Henry Sokolski (2004).

44. Gates, *Shadows*, 113–14.

45. *Ibid.*

46. Chernyaev's diary, Jan. 9 and 15, 1977, National Security Archive, Washington, D.C., quoted in Vladislav M. Zubok, *A Failed Empire: The Soviet Union in the Cold War from Stalin to Gorbachev* (2007), 255.

Chapter 22

1. Dmitri Simes, *After the Collapse: Russia Seeks Its Place as a Great Power* (1999), 29.

2. Bessmertnykh, Interview.

3. Mikhail Gorbachev, *Memoirs* (1996), 94; Zdenek Mlynar and Mikhail Gorbachev, *Conversations with Gorbachev on Perestroika, the Prague Spring, and the Crossroads of Socialism* (2002), 38, 96.

4. Georgi Arbatov, *The System: An Insider's Life in Soviet Politics* (1992), 133–34.

5. Kevorkov, Interview.

6. Andropov quoted in Oleg Kalugin, *Spymaster* (1994), 262.

7. A. A. Konovolov, the Institute of the USA and Canada, quoted in Michael Ellman and Vladimir Kontorovich, *The Destruction of the Soviet Economic System: An Insider's History* (1998), 66.

8. Bogomolov, Interviews.

9. Gorbachev, *Memoirs*, 174.

10. Starodubov quoted in Andrei Gratchev, *Gorbachev's Gamble* (2008), 16.

11. *The Soviet Bloc Financial Problem as a Source of Western Influence*, National Intelligence Council Memorandum–82-10004, Apr. 1982, 11.

12. Andropov quoted in Christopher Andrew and Vasili Mitrokhin, *The Mitrokhin Archive: The KGB and the World* (2005), 471.

13. Goodpaster quoted by Michael McCGwire, from his notes of what Goodpaster said at the Woodrow Wilson Center in Washington in May 1983.

14. Giscard d'Estaing and Schmidt quoted in Raymond L. Garthoff, *Détente and Confrontation: American-Soviet Relations from Nixon to Reagan* (rev. ed., 1994), 1089.

Chapter 23

1. Neuberger quoted in Cahn, *Killing Détente: The Right Attacks the CIA* (1998), 191.

2. I. Edwards, M. Hughes and J. Noren, "US and USSR: Comparisons of GNP," in *The Soviet Economy in a Time of Change* (US Congress Joint Economic Committee, 1979).

3. Schlesinger quoted in Peter Schweizer, "Who Broke the Evil Empire?" *National Review*, May 30, 1994.

4. Odom quoted in Olav Njolstad, "The Carter Legacy: Entering the Second Era of the Cold War," in Njolstad, *Last Decade of the Cold War*, 218.

5. Zbigniew Brzezinski, in Gerald K. Haines and Robert E. Leggett (eds.), *Watching the Bear: Essays on CIA's Analysis of the Soviet Union* (2002) 264–65.

6. James Billington, Interview; see also his paper "Soviet Attitudes and Values: Prospects for the Future," at the seminars on "The USSR and the Sources of Soviet Policy" in April–May 1978 under the joint sponsorship of the Council of Foreign Relations and the Kennan Institute for Advanced Russian Studies of the Wilson Center.

7. George P. Shultz, *Turmoil and Triumph: Diplomacy, Power and the Victory of the American Ideal* (1993), 124.

8. "Population and Manpower Trends in the USSR," a paper presented by Murray Feshbach, from the Foreign Demographic Analysis Division of the Bureau of the Census, at the seminars mentioned in note 6.

Chapter 24

1. Anatoly Chernyaev, *My Six Years with Gorbachev* (2000), 8–9.

2. Andropov quoted in Georgi Arbatov, *The System: An Insider's Life in Soviet Politics* (1992), 89.

3. Alexander Yakovlev, *A Century of Violence in Soviet Russia* (2000), 8.

4. Yakovlev quoted in Jonathan Steele, *Eternal Russia: Yeltsin, Gorbachev and the Mirage of Democracy* (1994), 175.

5. Chernyaev, *Gorbachev*, 323.

6. Sakharov quoted in Robert D. English, *Russia and the Idea of the West: Gorbachev, Intellectuals, and the End of the Cold War* (2000), 107–8.

7. Moscow News, 23 July 1989.

8. Arbatov, *The System*, 311.

9. Arbartov quoted in Matthew Evangelista, *Unarmed Forces: The Transnational Forces to End the Cold War* (1999), 249–338.

Chapter 25

1. For Reagan's thinking on how the Cold War could be ended and nuclear weapons abolished see Paul Lettow, *Ronald Reagan and His Quest to Abolish Nuclear Weapons* (2005).

2. Reagan quoted in Peter Schweizer, *Reagan's War: The Epic Story of His Forty Year Struggle and Final Triumph over Communism* (2002), 36.

3. Which is what Reagan said to Thomas Reed, one of his advisers, in March 1982; see Thomas C. Reed, *At the Abyss: An Insider's History of the Cold War* (2004), 227.

4. Brezhnev quoted by Anatoly Dobrynin, *In Confidence: Moscow's Ambassador to America's Six Cold War Presidents* (1995), 460.

5. Dobrynin, *In Confidence*, 484–85.

6. Dobrynin, *In Confidence*, 495.

7. Dobrynin, *In Confidence*, 486–88.

8. Bessmertnyk, Interview.

9. Kevorkov, Interviews.; see also Wjatscheslaw Keworkow, *Der geheime Kanal: Moskau, der KGB und die Bonner Ostpolitik* (1995), 155–56.

10. Schweizer, *Reagan's War*, 192–93.

11. Reagan quoted by Richard Allen, *1985–2005: Twenty Years that Changed the World*, Report of The World Political Forum 2005, 182.

12. Petersen, Interviews.

13. As part of a Pentagon program designed to help get the Pershing-II missile deployed, DIA analyst John Yurechko laid out the General Staff's expectations in "Command and Control for Coalitional Warfare: The Soviet Approach," *Signal*, Dec. 1985.

14. See also Ghulam Dastagir Wardak (comp.) and Graham Hall Turbiville (ed.), *The Voroshilov Lectures: Materials from the Soviet General Staff Academy*, 3 vols. (1989–92).

15. Ustinov quoted in Christian Nuenlist (ed.), *Records of the Committee of Defence Ministers, 1969–90*, Parallel History Project (2001), 12.

16. Ustinov quoted in John G. Hines, Phillip A. Petersen and Notra Trulock III, "Soviet Military Theory from 1945–2000: Implications for Nato," *The Washington Quarterly*, Fall 1986, 129.

Chapter 26

1. Andropov quoted in Christopher Andrew and Oleg Gordievsky, *Comrade Kryuchkov's Instructions: Top Secret Files on KGB Foreign Operations, 1975–1985* (1993), 67–90.

2. Markus Wolf, *Man without a Face: The Autobiography of Communism's Greatest Spymaster* (1997), 221.

3. Alexandr G. Savelyev and Nikolai N. Detinov, *The Big Five: Arms Control Decision-Making in the Soviet Union* (1995), 57.

4. Peter Schweizer, *Victory: The Reagan Administration's Secret Strategy That Hastened the Collapse of the Soviet Union* (1994), 8.

5. Kalugin interviewed on Flashback Television's *1983: The Brink of Apocalypse.*

6. General Sergei Kondrashev, KGB, Carter-Brezhnev Project, Transcript of discussions at Musgrove Plantation, May 1994, 44.

7. Wolf, *Man without a Face,* 299–301; Stuart A. Herrington, *Traitors amongst Us* (1999); Pete Early, *Family of Spies: Inside the John Walker Spy Ring* (1988); Vojtech Mastny, "Did East German Spies Prevent a Nuclear War?," Nov. 2003, 3 at the Parallel History Project/Stasi Intelligence on Nato.

8. Benjamin B. Fischer, *More Dangerous Than We Thought? Reflections on the Soviet War Scare*, Nobel Symposium, Lysebu, June 2002, 26.

9. Benjamin B. Fischer, "The Soviet-American War Scare of the 1980s," *International Journal of Intelligence and Counterintelligence,* Volume 19, Number 3, Fall 2006, pp. 480–518.

10. Ogarkov quoted in Mastny, *East German Spies*, 3.

11. Benjamin B. Fischer, *A Cold War Conundrum: The 1983 Soviet War Scare* (1997), 8.

12. Sontag and Drew, *Blind Man's Bluff: The Untold Story of American Submarine Espionage* (1998), 231–58.

13. Mastny, *East German Spies*, 3.

14. Air Chief Marshal Sir John Walker, Interview.

15. Kataev, Interview, BDM, *Soviet Intentions 1965–85*, vol. 2: *Soviet Post–Cold War Testimonial Evidence* (1995), 100.

16. Gareev, Interview, BDM *Soviet Intentions*, vol. 2, 74. General Gareev had been closely involved with nuclear weapons training from 1974 to 1984.

17. Korobushin, Interview, BDM, *Soviet Intentions*, vol. 2, 107 and 134.

18. Dr. Viktor Surikov, Deputy Director of the Central Scientific Research Institute for General Machine Building (i.e. strategic missiles) 1976–92, Interview, BDM, *Soviet Intentions,* vol. 2, 134–35.

19. Korobushin, *Soviet Intentions*, vol. 2, 107.

20. *Time Magazine*, Feb. 24, 1992, 28.

21. Ronald Reagan, *An American Life* (1990), 554.

22. Thomas C. Reed, *At the Abyss: An Insider's History of the Cold War* (2004), 235–37.

23. Gus Weiss, *Duping the Soviets: The Farewell Dossier*, Studies in Intelligence, no. 5, 1996.

24. Reed, *Abyss*, 268–69.

25. This report is also cited in Robert M. Gates, *From the Shadows: The Ultimate Insider's Story of Five Presidents and How They Won the Cold War* (1997), 188 and Richard Pipes, *Vixi: Memoirs of a Non-Belonger* (2003), 153.

Chapter 27

1. Derek Leebaert, *The Fifty Year Wound: The True Price of America's Cold War Victory* (2002), 500 and fn. 12 on 693.

2. Jones quoted in FitzGerald, *Way Out There in the Blue: Reagan, Star Wars and the End of the Cold War* (2000), 187.

3. George P. Shultz, *Turmoil and Triumph: Diplomacy, Power and the Victory of the American Ideal* (1993), 468.

4. McFarlane quoted in FitzGerald, *Way Out There*, 195.

5. Alexander M. Haig, *Caveat: Realism, Reagan, and Foreign Policy* (1984), 229.

6. National Intelligence Council Memorandum, *What Should We Do About the Russians?*, June 26, 1984, 1.

7. Ben B. Fischer, "Intelligence and Disaster Avoidance: The Soviet War Scare and US-Soviet Relations," in *Mysteries of the Cold War*, ed. Stephen J. Cimbala (1999), 96.

8. The official has declined to be named.

9. Academician Alexander Chubarian, Director of the Institute of World History, Interview, Moscow Ocober 7, 2004.

10. Interviews with Kevorkov and Churbarian; see also Georgi Arbatov, *The System: An Insider's Life in Soviet Politics* (1992), 254–86.

11. Chubarian, Interviews.

12. Yuri Andropov, *Speech to the Political Consultative Committee of the Warsaw Pact*, Jan. 4, 1983, National Security Archive Electronic Briefing Book, no. 14, Doc 19.

13. Christopher Andrew and Vasili Mitrokhin, *The Mitrokhin Archive: The KGB in Europe and the West* (1999), 512.

14. The relationship between the "peace struggle" and the "armed struggle" in the strategy of the Soviet Communist Party is examined in Michael Ploetz, "Mit RAF, Roten Brigaden und Action Directe—Terrorismus und Rechtsextremismus in der Strategie von SED und KPdSU," in *Zeitschrift des Forschungsverbundes SED-Staat*, no. 22, 2007, 117–44.

15. Anatoly Dobrynin, *In Confidence: Moscow's Ambassador to America's Six Cold War Presidents* (1995), 517–20.

16. Christopher Andrew and Oleg Gordievsky, *Comrade Kryuchkov's Instructions: Top Secret Files on KGB Foreign Operations, 1975–1985* (1993), 69–81.

17. *Newsweek*, Feb. 18, 1983, cited in Frances FitzGerald, *Way Out There*, 179.

18. Thomas C. Reed, *At the Abyss: An Insider's History of the Cold War* (2004), 239–40.

19. Kalugin interviewed in Flashback Television's *1983: The Brink of Apocalypse.*

20. Report of the President's Commission on Strategic Forces, Apr. 6, 1983.

21. "Replies of Yu. V. Andropov to questions from a *Pravda* correspondent," *Pravda*, Mar. 27, 1983.

22. Interview with a former senior Pentagon official.

23. Leslie Gelb, "Foreign Affairs: Who Won the Cold War?," *New York Times*, Aug. 20, 1992, 27.

24. Markus Wolf, *Man without a Face: The Autobiography of Communism's Greatest Spymaster* (1997), 317.

25. Andropov quoted in Michael Ploetz in "Troy Besieged: Marxism-Leninism in the Second Cold War (1979–85)—A Reconstruction from East German Sources" (Ph.D. thesis, University of London, Sept. 1997), 230.

26. Andropov quoted in Benjamin B. Fischer, *More Dangerous Than We Thought? Reflections on the Soviet War Scare*, Nobel Symposium, Lysebu, June 2002, 3–4.

27. Andropov quoted in Vojtech Mastny, *Did East German Spies Prevent a Nuclear War?*, Parallel History Project on Nato and the Warsaw Pact, Stasi Intelligence on Nato, Nov. 2003, 4.

28. Shultz quoted in Jack F. Matlock, *Reagan and Gorbachev: How the Cold War Ended* (2004), 61.

29. Benjamin B. Fischer, *A Cold War Conundrum: The 1983 Soviet War Scare* (1997), 8.

30. Robert M. Gates, *From the Shadows: The Ultimate Insider's Story of Five Presidents and How They Won the Cold War* (1997), 267.

31. General Ivan Tretyak (Soviet Air Force, Far East) and Gennadi Osipovich (Soviet fighter pilot), Interviews in Flashback Television's *1983: The Brink of Apocalypse.*

32. Andropov quoted in Dobrynin, *In Confidence,* 537.

33. Dobrynin, *In Confidence*, 540.

34. Andropov quoted in Michael MccGwire, *Perestroika and Soviet National Security* (1991), 392 and note 28.

35. I am grateful to Mark Kramer for sharing with me his discussions with General Yarynych.

Chapter 28

1. Gelii Batenin, Interview, BDM, *Soviet Intentions 1965–85*, vol. 2: *Soviet Post–Cold War Testimonial Evidence* (1995), 10.

2. Sergei Tarasenko quoted in William C. Wohlforth (ed.), *Witnesses to the End of the Cold War* (1996), 71.

3. General Ivan Yesin, background interview for Flashback Television's *1983: The Brink of Apocalypse.*

4. Pavel Palazhchenko, *My Years with Gorbachev and Shevardnadze: Memoirs of a Soviet Interpreter* (1997), 20.

5. George P. Shultz, *Turmoil and Triumph: Diplomacy, Power and the Victory of the American Ideal* (1993), 372–73.

6. General Bernard Rogers quoted in Bob Furlong and Macha Levinson, *International Defense Review*, 2, 1986, 151.

7. Many new insights into how the two sides viewed these events are contained in Flashback Television's documentary *1983: The Brink of Apocalyse.*

8. Oleg Gordievsky, *Next Stop Execution* (1995); Margaret Thatcher, *The Downing Street Years* (1993), 463.

9. Christopher Andrew and Oleg Gordievsky, *Comrade Kryuchkov's Instructions: Top Secret Files on KGB Foreign Operations, 1975–1985* (1993), 87–88.

10. Yesin quoted in Flashback Television's *1983: The Brink of Apocalypse.*

11. General Ivan Yesin, transcript of background interview for *1983: The Brink of Apocalypse.*

12. Yesin quoted in *1983: The Brink of Apocalypse.*

13. Yesin, transcript of background interview for *1983: The Brink of Apocalypse.*

14. Danilevich, Interviews, BDM, *Soviet Intentions,* vol. 2, 26 and 42.

15. Rainer Rupp quoted on Flashback Television's *1983: The Brink of Apocalypse.*

16. General Werner Grossman, Deputy Head of East German Intelligence, quoted on Flashback Television's *1983: The Brink of Apocalypse.*

17. Batenin, Interview, BDM, *Soviet Intentions*, vol. 2, 8.

18. Ronald Reagan, *The Reagan Diaries* (2007), 199; Ronald Reagan, *An American Life* (1990), 585–86.

19. "Statement by . . . Yuri Andropov," *Pravda*, Nov. 25, 1983.

20. Grinevsky quoted in Peter Schweizer, *Reagan's War: The Epic Story of His Forty Year Struggle and Final Triumph over Communism* (2002), 230.

21. Ustinov quoted in Don Oberdorfer, *From the Cold War to a New Era: The United States and the Soviet Union, 1983–1991* (1998), 69.

22. Robert M. Gates, *From the Shadows: The Ultimate Insider's Story of Five Presidents and How They Won the Cold War* (1997), 271.

23. *Congressional Quarterly Texts*, Oct. 27, 1984, 2828–38.

24. Anatoly Dobrynin, *In Confidence: Moscow's Ambassador to America's Six Cold War Presidents* (1995), 545.

25. See Gates, *Shadows*, 272; SNIE 11-10—84/JX, 18 May 1984.

26. A former senior CIA officer I interviewed who has declined to be named.

27. SNIE 11-10—84/JX, *Implications of Recent Soviet Military-Political Activities*, May 18, 1984.

28. Gates, Interviewed on Flashback Television's *1983: The Brink of Apocalypse.*

29. Flashback Television, *Brink of Apocalypse.*

30. Shultz, *Turmoil and Triumph*, 539.

31. Wolf, Interview; see also *Man without a Face: The Autobiography of Communism's Greatest Spymaster* (1997), 318.

32. Chernyenko quoted in Michael Ploetz, "Nato and the Warsaw Treaty Organization at the Time of the Euromissile Crisis, 1975 to 1985," in Gustav Schmidt (ed.), *A History of Nato—The First 50 Years*, vol. 2 (2001), 216.

33. Casey quoted in George Crile, *Charlie Wilson's War* (2004), 121.

34. Dobrynin, *In Confidence*, 555.

35. Dobrynin, *In Confidence*, 557; Mikhail Gorbachev, *On My Country and the World* (2000), 66.

36. Lavrenti Beria quoted in Sergo Beria, *Beria: Inside Stalin's Kremlin* (2001), 286.

Chapter 29

1. Zdenek Mlynar and Mikhail Gorbachev, *Conversations with Gorbachev on Perestroika, the Prague Spring, and the Crossroads of Socialism* (2002), 22.

2. Mlynar and Gorbachev, *Conversations*, 48.

3. Mlynar and Gorbachev, *Conversations*, 6, 42–43; Mikhail Gorbachev, *Memoirs* (1996), 127–29.

4. Anatoly Chernyaev, *My Six Years with Gorbachev* (2000), 4.

5. Andrei Gratchev, Interview; see also Gratchev, *Gorbachev's Gamble* (2008), 50–51.

6. Mikhail Gorbachev, *Memoirs*, 207.

7. Oleg Gordievsky, *Next Stop Execution* (1995), 310–11 and interview with him, Sept. 12, 2005.

8. Margaret Thatcher, *The Downing Street Years* (1993), 463.

9. George P. Shultz, *Turmoil and Triumph: Diplomacy, Power and the Victory of the American Ideal* (1993), 507.

10. Gorbachev, *Memoirs*, 212.

11. Gorbachev quoted in Dusko Doder and Louise Branson, *Gorbachev: Heretic in the Kremlin* (1990), 207.

12. Joseph S. Nye, "Gorbachev and the End of the Cold War," *New Straits Times* (April 5, 2006); Seymour Goodman, "Information Technologies and the Citizen: Toward a 'Soviet-Style Information Society'?" in *Science and the Soviet Social Order*, ed. Loren R. Graham (1990), 373; see also Slava Gerovitch, *From Newspeak to Cyberspeak: A History of Soviet Cybernetics* (2002).

13. Chernyaev and Gorbachev quoted in Gratchev, *Gorbachev's Gamble*, 55.

14. Mikhail Gorbachev, *On My Country and the World* (1999), 180–86.

15. Chernyaev quoted in William C. Wohlforth (ed.), *Witnesses to the End of the Cold War* (1996), 15.

16. S. Akhromeyev and G. Kornienko, *Glazami Marshala i Diplomata* (*Through the Eyes of a Marshal and a Diplomat*) (1992), 315–16.

17. Chernyaev, *Gorbachev*, 40.

18. Bessmertnykh quoted in Wohlforth, *Witnesses*, 35.

19. Chernyaev quoted in Wohlforth, *Witnesses*, 15.

20. Gorbachev quoted in Vladislav M. Zubok, *A Failed Empire: The Soviet Union in the Cold War from Stalin to Gorbachev* (2007), 284.

21. Gordievsky, *Next Stop Execution*, 354.

22. A former senior CIA officer I interviewed who declined to be named.

23. Robert M. Gates, *From the Shadows: The Ultimate Insider's Story of Five Presidents and How They Won the Cold War* (1997), 342.

24. Shultz, *Turmoil and Triumph*, 586–94; Palazhchenko, Interviews, Moscow, Feb., 2005.

Chapter 30

1. Tarasenko quoted in Peter Schweizer, *Reagan's War: The Epic Story of His Forty Year Struggle and Final Triumph over Communism* (2002), 249.

2. George Shultz, in the foreword to *Stories in His Own Hand: The Everyday Wisdom of Ronald Reagan*, ed. Kiron Skinner, Annelise Anderson and Martin Anderson (2001), xi–xii.

3. Mikhail Gorbachev, *Memoirs* (1996), 523.

4. Pavel Palazhchenko, one of Gorbachev's interpreters, quoting a conversation with Michael Reagan, the president's son.

5. For the official US record see National Security Archive, Electronic Briefing Book 172, Documents 15–24; see also Reagan quoted in Schweizer, *Reagan's War*, 251.

6. Bessmertnykh quoted in William C. Wohlforth (ed.), *Witnesses to the End of the Cold War* (1996), 11.

7. Pavel Palazhchenko, *My Years with Gorbachev and Shevardnadze: Memoirs of a Soviet Interpreter* (1997), 44.

8. Mikhail Gorbachev, *On My Country and the World* (1999), 187.

9. Gratchev Interview, Paris.

10. Chernyaev quoted in William C. Wohlforth (ed.), *Cold War Endgame: Oral History, Analysis, Debates* (2003), 36–37.

11. Anatoly Chernyaev, *My Six Years with Gorbachev* (2000), 83.

12. Vladislav M. Zubok, *A Failed Empire: The Soviet Union in the Cold War from Stalin to Gorbachev* (2007), 292.

13. Velikov, Interview with Robert D. English, quoted "The Road(s) Not Taken . . ." in Wohlforth, *Endgame*, 261.

14. Chernyaev, *Gorbachev*, 65.

15. See also Mikhail Gorbachev, *Panyat Perestroiku…: Pachyemu Eta Vazhno Seichas* (2006) (To understand Perestroika: Why it is important now).

16. Andrei Gratchev, *Gorbachev's Gamble* (2008), 79.

17. George P. Shultz, *Turmoil and Triumph: Diplomacy, Power and the Victory of the American Ideal* (1993), 690.

18. Robert M. Gates, *From the Shadows: The Ultimate Insider's Story of Five Presidents and How They Won the Cold War* (1997), 353.

19. Gorbachev quoted in Zubok, *Failed Empire*, 287.

20. Jack F. Matlock, *Reagan and Gorbachev: How the Cold War Ended* (2004), 191 and 195.

21. For an extensive documentary account of the summit, based on Soviet and American archives, see the National Security Archive's "The Reykjavik File," Electronic Briefing Book 203.

22. Gorbachev quoted in Zubok, *Failed Empire*, 299.

23. Chernyaev, *Gorbachev*, 83–84.

24. Matlock, *Reagan and Gorbachev*, 213.

25. Gratchev, *Gorbachev's Gamble*, 83.

26. Gorbachev quoted in Paul Lettow, *Ronald Reagan and His Quest to Abolish Nuclear Weapons* (2005), 225–26.

27. Bessmertnykh, Interview, Moscow, Feb. 28, 2006; see also Wohlforth, *Witnesses*, 168.

28. "Bud" McFarlane quoted by Jim Matlock, Wohlforth, *Witnesses*, 58.

29. Shultz, *Turmoil and Triumph*, 775.

30. Gorbachev, *Memoirs*, 541.

31. Bessmertnykh, Interview; Gorbachev, *Memoirs*, 541.

32. Margaret Thatcher, *The Downing Street Years* (1993), 471.

33. Matlock, *Reagan and Gorbachev*, 241.

34. Gorbachev quoted in National Security Archive, Electronic Briefing Book 238.

35. Gratchev, *Gorbachev's Gamble*, 96.

Chapter 31

1. Gorbachev quoted in Anatoly Chernyaev, *My Six Years with Gorbachev* (2000), 104.

2. Gorbachev quoted in Chernyaev, *Gorbachev*, 105.

3. Records of the Political Consultative Conference of the Warsaw Pact in East Berlin, in the "Collections" of the Parallel History Project.

4. Andrei Gratchev, *Gorbachev's Gamble* (2008), 104.

5. Artemy Kalinovsky, "Old Politics, New Diplomacy: The Geneva Accords and the Soviet Withdrawal from Afghanistan," *Cold War History*, vol. 8, no. 3, August 2008.

6. Ronald Reagan, *An American Life* (1990), 699.

7. For an extensive documentary account, from Soviet and American sources, see the National Security Archives' Electronic Briefing Book 238, "The INF Treaty and the Washington Summit: 20 Years Later."

8. Gorbachev quoted in Lawrence Wittner, *The Struggle against the Bomb*, vol. 3: *Toward Nuclear Abolition: A History of the World Nuclear Disarmament Movement, 1971 to the Present* (2003), 57.

9. Shultz, *Turmoil and Triumph*, 1012.

10. Gorbachev quoted in Chernyaev, *Gorbachev*, 143.

11. Chernyaev quoted in William C. Wohlforth (ed.), *Witnesses to the End of the Cold War* (1996), 95.

12. Chernyaev quoted in William C. Wohlforth (ed.), *Cold War Endgame: Oral History, Analysis, Debates* (2003), 21.

13. Chernyaev, *Gorbachev*, 108.

14. Mikhail Gorbachev, *Memoirs* (1996), 590–91; Jack F. Matlock, *Reagan and Gorbachev: How the Cold War Ended* (2004), 302.

15. Gorbachev quoted in Archie Brown, "The Soviet Union: Reform of the System or Systemic Transformation?," *Slavic Review*, vol. 63, no. 3 (Autumn, 2004), 497.

16. Nikolai Shishlin, *Le Monde*, Sept. 7, 1988.

17. Timothy Garton Ash, *In Europe's Name: Germany and the Divided Continent* (1994), 132.

19. Gorbachev quoted in Chernyaev, *Gorbachev*, 192.

19. An extensive selection of documents on German unification is contained in Anatoly Chernyaev and A. Galkin, *Mikhail Gorbachev i Germanskij Vopros: Sbornik Dokumentov, 1986–1991* (2006) (Mikhail Gorbachev and German unification: Selected documents, 1986–1991).

20. Shakhnazarov quoted in Mark Kramer, "Realism, Ideology and the End of the Cold War," *Review of International Studies*, Jan. 2001, 124.

Chapter 32

1. Gareev, Interview, BMD, *Soviet Intentions 1965–85*, vol. 2: *Soviet Post–Cold War Testimonial Evidence* (1995), 72.

2. Interview with General Klaus Naumann.

3. Batenin, Interview, BDM, *Soviet Intentions*, vol. 2, 8.

4. See also Phillip A. Karber and Diego A. Ruiz Palmer, "Coalition Strategy and

the Operational Level of Warfare," in Robert L. Pfaltzgraff, Jr. and Richard H. Schultz, Jr.(eds.), *US Defense Policy in an Era of Constrained Resources* (1989), 165–92.

5. Diego Ruiz-Palmer, "Countering Soviet Encirclement Operations: Emerging Nato Concepts," *International Defense Review*, 11, 1988, 1413–18.

6. *Ibid.*

7. Christian Nuenlist (ed.), *Records of the Committee of Ministers of Defence, 1969–1990*, Parallel History Project (2001), 13.

8. Ruiz-Palmer, "Countering."

9. Anatoly Chernyaev, *My Six Years with Gorbachev* (2000), 116.

10. Akhromeyev quoted in Raymond L. Garthoff, *Deterrence and Revolution in Soviet Military Doctrine* (1990), 182–83.

11. Gorbachev quoted in Chernyaev, *Gorbachev*, 192.

12. Chernyaev, *Gorbachev*, 194–95.

13. Mikhail Gorbachev, *Memoirs* (1996), 604.

Chapter 33

1. Shultz quoted in William C. Wohlforth (ed.), *Witnesses to the End of the Cold War* (1996), 91.

2. Anatoly Chernyaev, *My Six Years with Gorbachev* (2000), 226.

3. George H. W. Bush and Brent Scowcroft, *A World Transformed* (1999), 44.

4. Bush quoted in Raymond L. Garthoff, *The Great Transition: American-Soviet Relations and the End of the Cold War* (1994), 380.

5. Baker quoted in William C. Wohlforth (ed.), *Cold War Endgame: Oral History, Analysis, Debates* (2003), 18.

6. Bogomolov quoted in Jacques Lesveque, *Enigma of 1989: The USSR and the Liberation of Eastern Europe* (1997), 93–109.

7. Wojciech Jaruzelski, Interviews; see also Jaruzelski, *Les chaines et le refuge: Mémoires* (1992).

8. Conversation between M. S. Gorbachev and Károly Grósz, General Secretary of the Hungarian Socialist Workers Party, Moscow, Mar. 23–24, 1989, National Security Archive.

9. Bush and Scowcroft, *A World Transformed*, 39.

10. Bush quoted in Philip Zelikow and Condoleezza Rice, *Germany Unified and Europe Transformed* (1997), 31.

11. *Ibid.*

12. Gorbachev quoted in Vladislav Zubok, "New Evidence on the 'Soviet Factor' in the Peaceful Revolutions of 1989," CWIHP, *Bulletin* issue 12–13, Fall–Winter 2001 7.

13. Alexander Yakovlev quoted in Mark Kramer, "Realism, Ideology and the End of the Cold War," *Review of International Studies*, Jan. 2001, 126.

Chapter 34

1. Kohl quoted in Timothy Garton Ash, *In Europe's Name: Germany and the Divided Continent* (1994), 132.

2. Markus Wolf, *Man without a Face: The Autobiography of Communism's Greatest Spymaster* (1997), 219.

3. NIE 11-18-89, *The Soviet System in Crisis*, Nov. 1989, vi.

4. National Security Archive's Briefing Book for the conference on "The End of the Cold War in Europe, 1989," Musgove Plantation, May 1–3, 1998.

5. Vladislav M. Zubok, *A Failed Empire* (2007), 325.

6. Ivan Kuzmin, *Development of Social and Political Crisis in the GDR and Reactions of the USSR Senior Leaders*, Nobel Symposium, Oslo, June 2002, 11.

7. Mikhail Gorbachev, *Memoirs* (1996), 677.

8. Gerasimov quoted in Michael R. Beschloss and Strobe Talbot, *At the Highest Level: The Inside Story of the End of the Cold War* (1994), 134.

9. Krenz quoted in Vojtech Mastny, "Did Gorbachev Liberate Eastern Europe?" in Njolstad, *Last Decade of the Cold War* (2004), 415; for a full account of the meeting see Krenz's report to his Politburo, CWIHP, *Bulletin* issue 12–13, Fall–Winter 2001, 140–51.

10. Quoted in Charles S. Maier, *Dissolution: The Crisis of Communism and the End of East Germany* (1997), 224.

11. Talks of Chancellor Kohl with the President of the "Solidarity" Trade Union, Walesa; Warsaw, Nov. 9, 1989. www.gwu.edu/~nsarchiv/news/19991105/9nov89.htm.

12. Ivan Kuzmin, *Development of Social and Political Crisis in the GDR and Reactions of the USSR Senior Leaders*, Nobel Symposium, Oslo, June 2002, 20.

13. Chernyaev, Diary Nov. 10, 1989, CWIHP, *Bulletin* issue 12–13, Fall–Winter 2001, 20.

14. For a fairly detailed account of the main points discussed, based on Chernyaev's notes, see CWIHP, *Bulletin* issue 12–13, Fall–Winter 2001, 229–41.

15. Anatoly Chernyaev, *My Six Years with Gorbachev* (2000), 234.

16. Chernyaev, *Gorbachev,* 234–35.

17. Chernyaev quoted in William C. Wohlforth (ed.), *Cold War Endgame: Oral History, Analysis, Debates* (2003), 55.

18. Kohl's Ten-Point Program for Policy on Germany, statement to the Bundestag, Nov. 28, 1989.

29. Andrei Gratchev, *Gorbachev's Gamble* (2008), 131–62, contains some fascinating new details of the different Soviet views on handling German Unification.

20. Jacques Lévesque, *The Enigma of 1989, The USSR and the Liberation of Eastern Europe* (1997), 255.

21. Chernyaev, *Gorbachev*, 271–72.

22. George H. W. Bush and Brent Scowcroft, *A World Transformed* (1999), 252.

23. Ross interview; see also Bush and Scowcroft, *World Transformed*, 252.

24. James W. Davis and William C. Wohlforth, "German Unification," in Richard K. Herrmann and Richard Ned Lebow, *Ending the Cold War* (2004), 143.

25. George Bush, letter to the author, Apr. 4, 2005.

26. Lévesque, *Enigma of 1989*, 235.

27. Gorbachev quoted in Chernyaev, *Gorbachev*, 272.

28. Chernyaev, *Gorbachev*, 240.

Chapter 35

1. Timothy Garton Ash, cited in Benjamin B. Fischer (ed.), *At Cold War's End: US Intelligence on the Soviet Union and Eastern Europe, 1989–1991*, xi.

2. Gorbachev quoted in Anatoly Chernyaev, *My Six Years with Gorbachev* (2000), *270*.

3. Chernyaev, *Gorbachev*, 269.

4. Andrei Gratchev, *Gorbachev's Gamble* (2008), 244–55.

5. "Germany Clears Way for German Unity," *New York Times*, July 17, 1990.

6. Alexander Bessertnykh quoted in Michael R. Beschloss and Strobe Talbott, *At the Highest Levels: The Inside Story of the End of the Cold War* (1993), 240.

7. Yazov quoted in Andrei Gratchev, *Gorbachev's Gamble* (2008), 190.

8. What Soviet leaders have written in their memoirs about the collapse of the Soviet system is reviewed by Michael Ellman and Vladimir Kontorovich in "The Collapse of the Soviet System and the Memoir Literature," *EUROPE-ASIA STUDIES*, no. 2 1997, 259–79.

9. Quoted in Raymond L. Garthoff, *The Great Transition: American-Soviet Relations and the End of the Cold War* (1994), 441.

10. Gorbachev quoted in Garthoff, *Great Transition*, 443.

11. Gorbachev quote in Chernyaev, *Gorbachev*, 329.

12. Baker quoted in Benjamin B. Fischer (ed.), *At Cold War's End: US Intelligence on the Soviet Union and Eastern Europe, 1989–1991* (1999), xxiii.

13. Mark Kramer, "The Collapse of the Soviet Union (Part 2)," *Journal of Cold War Studies*, Fall 2003, 9.

14. Gratchev, *Final Days*, 190.

15. For the full text of Gorbachev final address see Andrei Gratchev, *Final Days: The Inside Story of the Collapse of the Soviet Union* (1995), 203–6.

16. Pavel Palazhchenko, *My Years with Gorbachev and Shevardnadze: Memoirs of a Soviet Interpreter* (1997), 165.

17. Beschloss and Talbot, *Highest Levels*, 464.

18. Gratchev, *Gorbachev's Gamble*, 18–19.

19. Zdenek Mlynar and Mikhail Gorbachev, *Conversations with Gorbachev on Perestroika, the Prague Spring, and the Crossroads of Socialism* (2002), 145.

20. Gratchev, *Final Days*, 192–93.

Chapter 36

1. Chernyaev, Interview, Feb. 27, 2006.

2. Danilevich, Interviews, BDM, *Soviet Intentions*, vol. 2, 62; Korobushin, Interview, BDM, *Soviet Intentions 1965–85*, vol. 2: *Soviet Post–Cold War Testimonial Evidence* (1995), 107; Viktor Surikov, Interview, vol. 2, 134–35.

3. Joseph Nye, "Lesson of the Cold War for the Contemporary World," *From Fulton to Malta: How the Cold War Began and Ended*, The Gorbachev Foundation, Moscow, Mar. 1, 2006.

4. Rodric Braithwaite, *Across the Moscow River: The World Turned Upside Down* (2002), 52.

Chapter 37

1. Gates, background interview in 2006 for Flashback Television's *1983: The Brink of Apocalypse*.

2. The most comprehensive review of the literature is by Raymond L. Garthoff, "Foreign Intelligence and the Historiography of the Cold War," *Journal of Cold War Studies*, Spring 2004, 21–56; see also interviews cited in this book.

3. Christopher Andrew and Vasili Mitrokhin, *The Mitrokhin Archive: The KGB in Europe and the West* (1999), 439–61.

4. Raymond L. Garthoff, "The KGB Reports to Gorbachev," *Intelligence and National Security*, vol. 11 (1996), no. 2, 226; "New Evidence on Soviet Intelligence: The KGB's 1967 Annual Report, with commentaries by Raymond Garthoff and Amy Knight," CWIHP, *Bulletin* issue 10, Mar. 1998, 211–19; Andrew and Mitrokhin, *The Mitrokhin Archive: The KGB in Europe and the West*, 459; Christopher Andrew, "Espionage, Covert Action, and the Cold War," *Cambridge History of the Cold War*, vol. 2 (2009).

5. Oleg Kalugin, *Spymaster* (1994), 84.

6. Documentation, CWIHP, *Bulletin* issue 4, Fall 1994, 67–70.

7. Shebarshin interviewed by John Kampfner, *The Daily Telegraph*, London Dec. 1, 1992.

8. MacEachin, Interviews; see also Robert M. Gates, *From the Shadows: The Ultimate Insider's Story of Five Presidents and How They Won the Cold War* (1997), 319, and Noel E. Firth and James H. Noren, *Soviet Defense Spending: A History of CIA Estimates, 1950–1990* (1998), 57–139.

9. Soviet National Security Policy: Responses to the Changing Military and Economic Enviroment—SOV 88-10040CX, June 1988.

10. Gates interviewed on Flashback Television's *1983: The Brink of Apocalypse*.

11. Percy Cradock, *Know Your Enemy: How the Joint Intelligence Committee Saw the World* (2002), 289.

12. Documentation, CWIHP, *Bulletin* issue 4, Fall 1994, 67–70.

13. The quality of these discussions is apparent from the interviews conducted by BDM.

14. Gates, *Shadows*, 202.

15. Gates, *Shadows*, 340.

16. V. V. Shlykov quoted in Michael Ellman and Vladimir Kontorovich, *The Destruction of the Soviet Economic System: An Insider's History* (1998), 43; Danilevich, BDM, vol. 2, 47–48.

17. For details see Firth and Noren, *Soviet Defense Spending*.

Chapter 38

1. The full importance of Korval's intelligence only came to light when President Putin honored him posthumously in Nov. 2007; see *The Independent* (London), Nov. 13, 2007, 27.

2. Molotov quoted in Vladislav Zubok and Constantine Pleshakov, *Inside the Kremlin's Cold War: From Stalin to Khrushchev* (1996), 87.

3. David E. Murphy, Sergei A. Kondrashev and George Bailey, *Battleground Berlin* (1997), 423–28; David Stafford, *Spies Beneath Berlin* (2002).

4. Howard Stoertz quoted in Jerrold L. Schecter and Peter Deriabin, *The Spy who Saved the World: How a Soviet Colonel Changed the Course of the Cold War* (1992), 279.

5. Clarence E. Smith, *CIA's Analysis of Soviet Science and Technology*, 122, in Gerald K. Haines and Robert E. Leggett, *Watching the Bear: Essays on CIA's Analysis of the Soviet Union* (2003).

6. Benjamin B. Fischer, "One of the Biggest Ears in the World: East German SIGINT Operations," *International Journal of Intelligence and Counterintelligence*, Spring 1998, 142–53.

7. John O. Koehler, *Stasi: The Untold Story of the East German Secret Police* (1999), 9.

8. General Klaus Naumann, former Chief of Staff, Armed Forces of the Federal Republic of Germany, interview.

9. Gates interviewed on Flashback Television's *1983: The Brink of Apocalypse*; Jack Anderson, "CIA Eavesdrops on Kremlin Chiefs," *The Washington Post*, Sept. 16, 1971.

10. Milt Bearden and James Risen, *The Main Enemy: The Inside Story of CIA's Final Showdown with the KGB* (2003), 11.

11. Christopher Andrew and Vasili Mitrokhin, *The Mitrokhin Archive: The KGB in Europe and the West* (1999), 451–52.

12. Arkady N. Shevchenko, *Breaking with Moscow* (1985).

13. Vladimir G. Treml, *Censorship, Access and Influence: Western Sovietology in the Soviet Union* (1999) 36–37.

14. Vojtech Mastny, "The New History of Cold War Alliances," *Journal of Cold War Studies* (Spring 2002), 81.

15. The text of the 5th (US) Corps' General Defense Plan of December 16, 1982, can be found on the PHP's website—Collections/Intelligence/Stasi Intelligence.

16. Otis quoted in Stuart A. Herrington, *Traitors Amongst Us*, 1999, 409.

17. London *Daily Telegraph*, May 23, 1968; June 12, 1968; June 16, 1968 and Jan. 10, 1969.

18. Benjamin B. Fischer, "Entangled in History: The Vilification and Vindication of Colonel Kuklinski," *Studies in Intelligence*, Summer 2000, no. 9, 19–34.

19. Benjamin Weiser, *A Secret Life: A Biography of Ryszard Kuklinski* (2004), 328.

20. Lt.-General Sir John Foley, Interview; Tony Geraghty, *BRIXMIS* (1997), gives many additional details.

21. Phillip A. Karber in Uwe Nerlich, *Soviet Power and Western Negotiating Policies*, vol. 1: *The Soviet Asset: Military Power in the Competition Over Europe* (1983)—"To Lose an Arms Race: The Competition in Conventional Forces Deployed in Central Europe, 1965–1980" (ch. 1) and "The Battle of Unengaged Military Strategies" (ch. 6), 31–88 and 207–29.

22. Rezun, Interview; this figure was confirmed by General William Odom.

23. Barry G. Royden, "An Exceptional Espionage Operation: Tolkachev, a Worthy Successor to Penkovsky," *Studies in Intelligence*, no. 3, 2003, 6–33; Thomas C. Reed, *At the Abyss: An Insider's History of the Cold War* (2004), 315.

24. Personal inscription by Mrs. Thatcher on a photo of herself and Gordievsky that she sent to him in 2007.

25. Raymond L. Garthoff, "The KGB Reports to Gorbachev," *Intelligence and National* Security, April 1996, 226–27.

26. The official concerned has declined to be named.

27. Koehler, *Stasi*, 232 and 238.

28. Cited in "Spy Credited with Improving East-West Ties," Associated Press release, *Washington Post*, June 20, 1990, and quoted in Raymond L. Garthoff, *A Journey Through the Cold War* (2001), 235.

29. Raymond L. Garthoff, "Foreign Intelligence and the Historiography of the Cold War," *Journal of Cold War Studies*, Spring 2004, 53; Ken Alibek, *Biohazard: The Chilling True Story of the Largest Covert Biological Weapons Program in the World, Told from the Inside by the Man Who Ran It* (1999).

30. Shebarshin, *Daily Telegraph*, London, Dec. 1, 1992.

31. Woolsey quoted in Elaine Shannon, "Death of a Perfect Spy," *Time Magazine*, Aug. 8, 1994.

Chapter 39

1. Gates, background interview in 2006 of Flashback Television's *1983: The Brink of Apocalypse.*

2. Raymond L. Garthoff, "Polyakov's Run," *Bulletin of Atomic Scientists,* Sept.–Oct. 2000, 37–40.

3. CIA has released 147 of these research papers, totalling some 11,000 pages, on its website.

4. V. V. Shlykov quoted in Michael Ellman and Vladimir Kontorovich, *The Destruction of the Soviet Economic System: An Insider's History* (1998), 45.

Sources

Author's Interviews

As I mentioned in the Prologue, I interviewed around one hundred people in connection with this book. Over half of them are quoted in it, and they are named below. To avoid a surfeit of footnotes in the text, I have only footnoted quotes from these people when they are taken from a published source. I am greatly indebted to all of them for being so generous with their time and for all the help they gave me.

With interviews conducted years after the event there is always the risk of lapses of memory or what might be called the improvement of memory in the light of the outcome of events or the information now available. As Douglas MacEachin, the former Deputy Director of Intelligence at the CIA, likes to point out, "A lot of Sauls became Pauls as they saw the light at the end of the Cold War road." Fortunately, the wealth of documents now available provides some valuable cross-checks.

The more positive aspect of interviews is, of course, that you can ask questions, not just take the information already available. Another advantage is that interviews often provide insights that are not to be found in documents, because within that particular circle or for a particular audience, some things did not need to be spelled out or should not be spelled out. Interviews also often convey better than documents the atmosphere of the time or how events were viewed.

Interviewees

Richard V. Allen: Reagan's chief foreign and defense policy adviser, 1977–80; National Security Adviser, 1981–82. (London, Oct. 18, 2005)

Egon Bahr: Helped Brandt develop his ideas on *Ostpolitik;* after Brandt became Chancellor in 1969 Bahr served as his chief of staff and negotiated the Moscow Treaty of 1970. (Berlin, Nov. 9, 2004)

Milt Bearden: A senior CIA officer who directed the Agency's operations against Soviet forces in Afghanistan from 1986 to 1989. He was in charge of intelligence operations against the Soviet Union and Eastern Europe during the last three years of the Cold War. (Washington, Dec. 8, 2004)

Alexander Bessmertnykh: Soviet deputy foreign minister, 1986–90; ambassador to Washington, 1990–91, after which he became Soviet Foreign Minister. (Turin, Mar. 6, 2005; Moscow, Feb. 28, 2006)

James Billington: A scholar of Russian history, who was appointed Librarian of Congress in 1987. He accompanied President Reagan to the Soviet Union in 1988. (Washington, Dec. 7, 2004—by telephone)

Oleg Bogomolov: Director of the Institute of Economics of the World Socialist System, Moscow, from 1967 to 1991. (Moscow, Oct. 7, 2004; Turin, Mar. 5, 2005)

Joseph Braddock: A founder member of BDM, a Washington-based consultancy firm that in the seventies and eighties undertook major research projects for the Pentagon to help Nato develop new strategies. (Washington, Mar. 19, 2007)

Dr. Harold Brown: A nuclear physicist who headed the Livermore Laboratory; he had worked closely with the Pentagon before serving as Secretary of Defense from 1977 to 1981. (Washington, Dec. 10, 2004)

Zbigniew Brzezinski: A scholar of communism and director of the Trilateral Commission, who advised Carter on foreign policy during his presidential campaign and then served as his National Security Adviser from 1977 to 1981. (Washington, Dec. 1, 2003)

Vladimir Bukovsky: A prominent Soviet dissident, who for a total of twelve years was in and out of the infamous psychiatric "hospitals" and prison before being expelled to Switzerland, then Britain, in 1976 (Cambridge, UK, June 14, 2005)

Anatoly Chernyaev: Sent to Prague in 1958 to edit *Problems of Peace and Socialism* and returned to Moscow in 1961 to join the International Department of the Central Committee; from 1986 to 1991 he was Gorbachev's foreign affairs adviser. (Moscow, Oct. 6, 2004 and Feb. 27, 2006)

Alexander Chubarian: A member of the Russian Academy of Sciences and Director of the Institute of World History. (Moscow, Oct. 4 and 7, 2004)

Christopher Donnelly: During the seventies he taught the British military about the Soviet armed forces, before becoming special adviser to the Secretary General of Nato in 1989. (London, Nov. 11, 2003)

Fritz Ermarth: A Soviet expert who in 1984 became the National Intelligence Officer for the Soviet Union on the National Intelligence Council, of which he served as chairman from 1988 to 1993. (Washington, Dec. 4, 2002, Dec. 12, 2004, Mar. 12, 2007)

Benjamin B. Fischer: A senior CIA officer dealing with Soviet and East European affairs. In 1995, he joined the history staff of the Agency's Center for the Study of Intelligence, retiring as chief historian in 2005. (Washington, Dec. 1, 2003, Dec. 7, 2004, Dec. 16, 2007)

Lt.-General Sir John Foley: Head of Brixmis, the British "liaison" mission to Soviet forces in East Germany, 1987–89, then Deputy Chief of Defence Intelligence, 1987–89. (Guernsey, Feb. 3–4, 2004)

Colonel Oleg Gordievsky: SIS's leading KGB source, first in Copenhagen from 1975 to 1978, then from 1982 in London, where he rose to be the acting head of the KGB in early 1985. He was smuggled out of the Soviet Union by SIS that summer; his defection was announced in September 1985. (London, May 14, 2003, Sept. 12, 2005)

Field Marshal Lord Inge: Served in Germany in the early eighties with General Sir Nigel Bagnall, later following in his footsteps to command the British Army of the Rhine, then Nato's Northern Army Group. (London, Oct. 22, 2004)

General Wojciech Jaruzelski: A professional soldier who became minister of defense in 1968, then prime minister and head of the Polish Communist Party in 1981, before declaring martial law that December. Following Poland's return to democracy in 1989, he served as president from 1989 to 1990. (Warsaw, Aug. 30–31, 2005)

Phillip Karber: Between 1974 and 1978 was at the Pentagon in charge of making the comparative assessment of Nato-Warsaw Pact general purpose forces; later worked with BDM Corporation on the development of "assault-breaker" weapons. (Washington, Mar. 19, 2007)

General Vyacheslav Kevorkov: A leading KGB expert on German affairs who served as the "back-channel" between Moscow and Bonn during the development of Soviet-German relations from 1969 into the early seventies. (Moscow, Feb. 25, 2006; London, Apr. 3, 2007)

Sergei Khrushchev: Discussed many aspects of Soviet policy with his father, Nikita Khrushchev, and accompanied him on several of his trips abroad; he has edited his father's tape-recorded memoirs and written his own accounts of his father's career. (Brown University, RI, Dec. 20, 2004)

George Kolt: An Air Force intelligence officer, Kolt became the deputy National Intelligence Officer for the Soviet Union and Eastern Europe in 1981. He became director of the CIA's Office of European Analysis in 1986 and then in 1989 director of the Office of Soviet Analysis. (London, Sept. 14, 2003; Washington, Dec. 1, 2003, Dec. 15, 2004) †July, 2005

Douglas MacEachin: One of the CIA's senior analysts on the Polish Crisis of 1980–81, then intelligence briefer to the secretary of state and vice president. In 1984 be became head the office of Soviet Analysis and four years later took over as chief of the arms control intelligence staff. In 1993 he was appointed the CIA's overall deputy director for intelligence. (Washington, Dec. 3, 2003, Mar. 10, 2007)

Andrew Marshall: Strategic analyst who became director of strategic studies at RAND in 1969, before working for Kissinger on the National Security Council in 1972. Since 1973 he has been the director of the Office of Net Assessment in the Pentagon. (Washington, Dec. 2, 2003, Dec. 9, 2004, Mar. 18, 2007; London, Apr. 16–17, 2005 and Sept. 22, 2006)

Vadim Medvedev: One of Gorbachev's close associates; responsible for relations with socialist countries (1986–88), then a member of the Politburo in charge of ideological issues; during 1990–91 he served as a member of the Presidential Council and advised Gorbachev on foreign economic relations. (Moscow, Feb. 27, 2006)

General Klaus Naumann: Joined Bundeswehr in 1958; in 1986 he became commander of the 1st German Corps. He was promoted Chief of Defense in the Federal Armed Forces in October 1991, which included dealing with the withdrawal of Soviet forces from East Germany. (London, Dec. 9, 2003)

James Noren: Spent over thirty years in the CIA conducting research on and analyzing the Soviet economy. (Washington, Dec. 13, 2004)

Lt. General William Odom: Military assistant to Brzezinski, President Carter's national security adviser (1977–81), Army's Assistant Chief of Staff for Intelligence (1981–85), then director of the National Security Agency (1985–88). (Washington, Dec. 3, 2003, Dec. 8, 2004) †May 2008

Pavel Palazhchenko: Principal English interpreter for Gorbachev and Foreign Minister Shevardnadze; took part in all the US-Soviet summits from 1985 to 1991. (Moscow, Feb. 27, 2006)

Vladimir Petrovsky: Between 1971 and 1979, he held senior positions in the Soviet Foreign Minstry dealing with Soviet-American relations, the Helsinki Final Act and disarmament issues. He became deputy foreign minister in 1986. (Turin, Mar. 6, 2005)

Dr. Phillip Petersen: Defense Intelligence Agency analyst; in the eighties headed a Pentagon team that used sensitive intelligence to inform NATO commanders on how the Soviet General Staff intended to conduct its strategic offensive operations against Western Europe. (London, Sept. 9 2004; Washington, Dec. 6, 2004)

Lord Powell: Private Secretary (foreign affairs) to Margaret Thatcher, the British Prime Minister (1983 to 1990), and then to Prime Minister John Major (1990 to 1991). (London, Feb. 17, 2005)

Sir Michael Quinlan: Britain's leading nuclear strategist. Closely involved with British and Nato nuclear force modernization as Director of Policy at the Ministry of Defence (1977–81) and later as its Permanent Under Secretary (1988–92). (London, Feb. 1, 2007)

Mieczyslaw Rakowski: Editor of *Polityka* (1958–82), deputy prime minister (1981–85), deputy speaker of Parliament (1985–88), prime minister (1988–89), and the last leader of the Polish Communist Party (1989–90). (Warsaw, Aug. 29 and 31, 2005)

Viktor Rezun: Served in Soviet Army before joining GRU; in 1974 posted to Geneva, where he worked with SIS, before defecting to Britain in 1978. (London, Sept. 12, 2005)

Dennis Ross: During the Reagan Administration was on the staff of the National

Security Council, then Deputy Director of the Office of Net Assessment at the Pentagon; from 1989 to 1992 he was head of policy planning in the State Department under James Baker. (Washington, Mar. 20, 2007)

Diego Ruiz-Palmer: From 1980 to 1991, prepared net assessments of the Nato–Warsaw Pact military balance, pursuant to National Security Study Memorandum 186, for the Office of Net Assessment at the Pentagon. (Brussels, Sept. 20–21, 2004; London, Oct. 8–9, 2005)

General Hans-Henning von Sandrart: Joined the Bundeswehr in 1956, was head of the political-military affairs office in the Ministry of Defense in Bonn (1977–79), Chief of the Army Staff (1984–87), then Commander in Chief of Nato's central front (1987–91). (London, Mar. 18, 2005)

James Schlesinger: Director of strategic studies at RAND in late sixties; Chairman of Atomic Energy Commission (1971–72); 1973 appointed Director of Central Intelligence, then after six months made Secretary of Defense (1973–75); Secretary of Energy in the Carter Administration (1977–79). (Washington, Mar. 15 and 19, 2007)

Lt. General Brent Scowcroft: Air Force general and Soviet expert. Military Assistant, then Deputy National Security Adviser to President Nixon; National Security Adviser under President Ford (1975–77) and President Bush (1989 to 1993). (Washington, Dec. 14, 2004)

Walter Slocombe: Joined staff of National Security Council in 1969; principal deputy assistant secretary for international security affairs at the Department of Defense (1977–79), then Deputy Undersecretary for Defense (Policy Planning) (1979–81). (Washington, Dec. 13, 2004)

Air Marshal Sir John Walker: Commander RAF Bruggen, a nuclear air base in Germany during the latter seventies; Deputy Chief of Staff, Allied Air Forces Central Europe, 1987–89; Deputy Chief of Defence Intelligence, Ministry of Defence, 1989–91. (London, Nov. 11, 2003)

Colonel Ghulam Dastagir Wardak (Afghanistan): Afghan army, attended Voroshilov Military Academy in Moscow (1973–75); joined Afghan resistance in 1980, later settled in US. (Washington, Dec. 7, 2004)

Edward Warner, III: A senior air force officer; joined RAND in Washington in 1982 as a senior defense analyst working on the Soviet Union and the use of precision-guided munitions in Nato's strategy. (Washington, Dec. 3 and 5, 2003)

General Markus Wolf: Educated in Moscow (1933–45); returned to Berlin in 1945 with first group of German Communists; head of the East German foreign intelligence service (1953 to 1986). (London, July 24, 2005; Berlin, Aug. 25, 2005; Prenden, Aug. 26, 2005) †Nov. 2006

James Woolsey: Undersecretary of the Navy (1977–79), Scowcroft Commission (1983), START negotiations, Geneva (1983–86), Head of US delegation to CFE negotiations, Vienna (1989–91), then Director of Central Intelligence (1993–96). (Washington, Dec. 7, 2004)

Alexander Yakovlev: Considered the leading architect of *glasnost* and *perestroika* and played a major part in shaping Gorbachev's foreign policy. He sat at Gorbachev's side during the four summit meetings with President Reagan and that with President Bush at Malta. (Moscow, Oct. 5, 2004) †Oct. 2005

Cold War Archives

The web is now a rich source of material on the Cold War. There are several important sites, including:

The Gorbachev Foundation in Moscow. Its Research and Information Center has an extensive archive on the Gorbachev era. www.gorby.ru

The Davis Center at Harvard University in Cambridge, MA. It has an important collection of Soviet documents on foreign affairs and intelligence, and publishes the *Journal of Cold War Studies.*

The Cold War Studies Centre of the London School of Economics. It publishes the journal *Cold War History* and has coordinated Cambridge University Press's three volume work *The Cambridge History of the Cold War*, which provides the most detailed account yet available of the Cold War from 1917 to 1991. The first volume is due to appear in 2009.

The American Journal of Physics. The January 2008 issue contains a resource letter on Nuclear Arms Control, which provides an extensive review of both nuclear weapons and the history of arms control and links to sites showing nuclear weapon tests.

The Cold War International History Project at the Woodrow Wilson Center, Washington, D.C. As of May 2008 it had published 16 volumes of the *Bulletin* (containing documents and analysis) and over 50 research *Working Papers;* it also provides an extensive "virtual" archive. www.wilsoncenter.org.

The National Security Archive at George Washington University, Washington, D.C. Its *Digital National Security Archive* is the most comprehensive collection available of significant primary documents central to US foreign and military policy since 1945. Over 61,000 of the most important, declassified documents, totaling more than 475,000 pages, are included in the database. It also has *Electronic Briefing Books* on a wide range of Cold War issues, including some important Soviet material. www.gwu.edu/~nsarchiv

The National Archives and Records Administration in Washington, D.C. It is the repository of U.S Federal archives. Much important material is also held by each of the Presidential Libraries. www.archives.gov

The Center for the Study of Intelligence in Washington, D.C. Provides an extensive range of material on intelligence during the Cold War and Assessments made by the CIA and the National Intelligence Council. www.cia.gov

The Parallel History Project on Cooperative Security in Zurich. It has a wide-ranging on-line archive dealing with the Warsaw Pact and Nato, as well as the texts of several books that it has published. www.php.isn.ethz.ch

German Archives. There are several important archives in Germany: Stiftung Archiv der Parteien und Massenorganisationen der DDR im Bundesarchiv (SAP-MO; Postfach 450569, 12175 Berlin) holds the party archives of the East German Communist Party and its mass organizations; Bundesarchiv-Abteilung Militärarchiv, Postfach, 79024 Freiburg, contains the documents of the East German Army and the Bundeswehr.

The Stasi-Archive is Die Bundesbeauftragte für die Unterlagen des Staatssicherheitsfdienstes der ehemaligen DDR (BStU; Zentralstelle, Berlin; Abteilung Archivbestände, Postfach 218, 10106 Berlin; Auswärtiges Amt—Politisches Archiv, Kurstraße 40, 10117 Berlin). This archive holds documents of both the East and West German foreign ministries.

Documentary Films

Documentary films can provide a valuable compliment to the printed material on the Cold War because they often capture the mood of the time so well. CNN's 24-part series on *The Cold War,* which was first shown in America in 1998, contains some exceptionally good material. The series is still available in video, which is now supplemented by an interactive website and a revised edition of the profusely illustrated book *The Cold War* (2008).

The typed transcripts of the extensive interviews made in connection with the programs, which run to thousands of pages, can be seen in the Liddell Hart Centre for Military Archives at King's College, London.

The Second Russian Revolution, comprising eight 1-hour episodes, was first shown on the BBC in 1991. A DVD is available from Brook Lapping in London. The transcripts of the full interviews are available at the Library of the London School of Economics.

Index